# HAVING YOUR SAY

## Reading and Writing
## Public Arguments

### Davida H. Charney
*University of Texas at Austin*

### Christine M. Neuwirth
*Carnegie Mellon University*

*with*
### David S. Kaufer
*Carnegie Mellon University*

### Cheryl Geisler
*Renesselaer Polytechnic Institute*

**PEARSON**
Longman

New York  San Francisco  Boston
London  Toronto  Sydney  Tokyo  Singapore  Madrid
Mexico City  Munich  Paris  Cape Town  Hong Kong  Montreal

Acquisitions Editor: Lauren Finn
Development Editor: Anne Brunell Ehrenworth
Senior Supplements Editor: Donna Campion
Media Supplements Editor: Jenna Egan
Executive Marketing Manager: Megan Galvin-Fak
Production Manager: Eric Jorgensen
Project Coordination, Text Design, and Electronic Page Makeup: Electronic Publishing
    Services Inc., New York City
Cover Design Manager: John Callahan
Cover Designer: Kay Petrino
Cover Photos: Courtesy of Getty Images, Inc.
Photo Researcher: Julie Tesser
Manufacturing Buyer: Roy L. Pickering, Jr.
Printer and Binder: Quebecor World Taunton
Cover Printer: Coral Graphic Services

**Library of Congress Cataloging-in-Publication Data**

Charney, Davida.
  Having your say : reading and writing public arguments / Davida H. Charney, Christine M. Neuwirth ; with David S. Kaufer, Cheryl Geisler.
        p. cm.
  Includes bibliographical references (p.   ) and index.
  ISBN 0-321-12230-5
  1. English language--Rhetoric.   2. Persuasion (Rhetoric)   3. Report writing.   I. Neuwirth, Christine M.   II. Kaufer, David S.   III. Geisler, Cheryl.   IV. Title.

PE1431.C47 2005
808'.042--dc22

                                                                    2005029305

Visit us at www.ablongman.com

0-321-12230-5

12345678910—QWT—08070605

# BRIEF CONTENTS

# DETAILED CONTENTS

# PREFACE
# FOR INSTRUCTORS

## Why This Book?

*Having Your Say* grows out of a pedagogy for argument writing that has been popular nationally for almost 20 years. In this approach, students learn to recognize and write definition arguments, causal arguments, value arguments, and proposals. Many best-selling textbooks have followed this tradition.

We share with this approach its grounding in rhetorical theory, its attention to both analytic reading and persuasive writing, and the importance it assigns to enabling students to participate in the discourse of public policy. *Having Your Say* extends this approach to address three goals that we think deserve additional attention:

- **Context:** Students should contextualize their positions historically, politically, or socially.
- **Conflict:** Students should address other positions seriously and fairly.
- **Ownership:** Students should develop a personal position in which they are truly engaged and about which they want to communicate.

Our approach is to treat these goals as interrelated. In order for students to engage deeply, they need the freedom to find their own angle on a timely issue. They need sufficient opportunities to explore an issue in depth, to find an array of relevant positions, and to come to insights they think are worth sharing.

We find it difficult to give students these opportunities when they choose new topics for each paper over the course of the term. For each topic, they need all the research time available just to learn enough to have an informed opinion. But when we ask students to stay with one topic for the term, we find that they delve much more deeply, take other positions more seriously, and develop more original standpoints.

When students spend more time on a topic, they realize that issues have histories against which readers will judge the ideas that they are developing. They realize that problems evolve over time and that solutions they think of as new have track records. They realize that events change the way an issue should be framed. They recognize, for example, that any argument regarding U.S. security today will be judged as antiquated if it ignores the terrorist attacks of 9/11.

Apart from setting issues in an historical context, we ask students to contextualize themselves in relation to their issue. Students look at arguments "in the wild," drawn as-is from the latest round of public debate. We want students to see themselves as potential contributors to an ongoing conversation; in short, as authors, owners of ideas. Only then will they appreciate learning to address opposing viewpoints responsibly.

The texts we chose from "the wild" have complex lines of argument that move through several of the classic types of arguments (stases): existence, definition, value, cause, and proposal. To enable students to analyze and challenge these texts, we transformed the sequence in which they learn about the stases. Many textbooks teach students about one stasis at a time, showing them readings that develop at just one stasis and asking them to write relatively pure forms of these arguments themselves. Our approach is to introduce students to a complete framework for public policy arguments at the very beginning.

With this framework in view, students can work with more complex texts, successively analyzing them at greater depth to recognize different types of arguments, to see how they work together, and to see how authors make choices of selection and emphasis to fit their purposes. Similarly, our students have the flexibility when writing to devote space to whatever types of argument turn out to be the most important, regardless of stasis.

To address these goals, *Having Your Say* introduces three major innovations: an in-depth focus on issues, a rhetorical framework, and an inquiry-based approach to the processes of reading, researching, and writing.

## The Topics

This book allows students to work within one broad topic area for the entire term. The two topic areas we explore in depth are environment and crime.

After working with one or both of these topics, instructors can easily adapt the pedagogy to topics of their choice. For those who find the choice between environment and crime restrictive, we offer guidance in developing new topics in the instructor's manual and on the Companion Website.

Students in our classes have not found the environment and crime topics to be limiting. They always raise new and interesting angles to explore. No two students have ever produced papers with an identical array of issues or positions. Of course, no student is able to "do justice" to either topic. The subject of the course is argumentation, not the topic. We make no effort to provide a comprehensive grounding in the topic; rather, we encourage students to examine an interesting slice of the current debate.

To get students started, we provide readings representing a range of positions in each topic area. Students discuss the issues and comment on each other's writing more effectively when they have read at least some texts in common.

These readings let students begin building a collection of relevant sources early in the course. Students, acting as individuals, in groups, or as a class, also seek out and select sources that they find more timely and interesting. The result is that we encourage students to adopt a new conceptualization of library research. Instead of seeing research as a way to find evidence for claims, students begin to see it as a way to find a conversation to join. Students are encouraged to seek out authors whose views will be important to take into account, whether they agree or disagree. We place no restrictions on the angles students choose to take, however controversial. However, we do expect students to treat allies and opponents fairly and responsibly.

We speak explicitly of "allies" and "opponents" with the intention of rehabilitating these terms, defusing their unfortunate connotations of hostility. Allies are not inextricably bound together on every point and every issue. Opponents are not enemies, but merely people who disagree on some substantial point.

This approach reflects our philosophy of argument: Disagreements are what make argument a productive form of inquiry, when there is a common goal of resolution. Our teacher and colleague Richard E. Young is fond of quoting Hannah Arendt's formulation of this approach, "Violence is the failure of argument." Authors who are committed to resolving problems through language can avoid violence, even when the argument is heated. Our position is also aligned with the "deliberative agonistic" approach to composition that Patricia Roberts-Miller describes in her recent book *Deliberate Argument* (Southern Illinois UP, 2004). The best way to argue constructively about heated controversies is to exorcize the demons and treat all positions in the debate as worthy of sustained consideration and response.

## Framework for Rhetorical Strategies

The second major innovation in *Having Your Say* is the framework in Part I. The framework begins with the problem–solution structure of public policy arguments and situates within it the basic rhetorical strategies: stases (existence, definition, value, cause, action) and appeals (ethos, pathos, logos). We include full treatments of two neglected aspects of argument: strategies for concession and rebuttal (Chapter 5) and strategies for a rhetorical style (Chapter 6).

This framework is novel in its attention to the hierarchical structure of arguments from large sections down to the phrasing of sentences. It follows the spirit of Stephen Toulmin's system of analyzing arguments into parts such as claim, support, warrant, backing, qualification, and so on. It differs from Toulmin, though, in offering greater specificity and deeper hierarchy. It is more specific in describing the structure of the stases, which each call for a different kind of development. Its hierarchy is deeper because we begin with far larger units. We show how claims at different stases may be combined into an argument about a problem or into an argument about a solution. At the next level, we describe how appeals to ethos, pathos, and logos can support each type of claim. Then we address matters of style.

We illustrate the framework with reference to a set of readings from each topic area. By returning to the same texts at different levels of analysis, students gain a better sense of how argumentative strategies work together and how written arguments on an issue interrelate. It will be clear from our analyses of these readings that we view the framework as a dynamic set of choices, not as a narrow prescriptive outline.

Having this material at the opening of the book enables the early introduction of timely texts that combine the strategies in novel ways to suit the author's audience and purpose. This framework also gives students initial acquaintance with concepts that they will revisit as they read and write arguments.

## Exploratory Process Approach

The pedagogy in *Having Your Say* employs a process approach to inquiry and argument as well as to reading and writing. This approach has three main components: scaffolding, thesis discovery, and reflective experimentation with process.

### Scaffolding

We adopt a Vygotskian approach to learning in which students are given an early view of a skillful performance, guided through an approximation of skilled performance, and given opportunities to practice and improve their skill on their own.

This approach is reflected in Part I in the successively deeper analyses of readings. Within each chapter, we explain the purpose of each type of argument strategy and provide explicit verbal cues to help students detect them. We model the analysis for a pair of readings. Then we invite students to practice these skills through exercises at the end of each chapter and through independent analysis of additional readings. We do not expect students to master the analysis in any chapter before continuing; rather, we expect students to return to these chapters throughout the term to refine their understanding.

### Thesis Discovery

We ask students to investigate and think through an issue at length before arriving at a position that they wish to share with others. Each inventional chapter in Part II shows students a way to find an angle of the topic that matters to them and a way to seek out other important perspectives. These include strategies for analyzing and responding to individual texts, fleshing out a rhetorical situation, using case-based reasoning, conducting targeted research, exploring problems and solutions, and synthesizing and analyzing different positions.

### Reflective Experimentation with Process

In our discussion of reading and writing processes, we emphasize their flexibility and recursiveness. We do not identify any particular path through a process as correct. We invite students to add to their repertoire of processes by trying out other approaches to reading and writing.

## How to Use This Book

This book is intended for a first-year writing course that is focused on argument, whether in the first or second term. It is structured to present a coherent approach to argument writing while providing great flexibility to instructors to set up different class environments, to choose among assignment options, and to choose among inventional processes.

In a typical term, we would expect students to complete at least three of the major writing assignments in Part III. We offer more assignments than can be accomplished in any given term to give instructors the flexibility to adapt to the interests and experience levels of their students.

- Part I. Our goal in this section is to provide the "big picture" of the argument framework. While we unpack each aspect in some detail, instructors may choose how long to dwell on the framework. It is not necessary for students to come to a level of "mastery" of each aspect before moving on. We find that students' grasp of these concepts becomes more intuitive over time; they internalize the framework as the apply it.

- Part II. This section introduces a wide array of strategies to help students find a meaningful issue and explore it from a variety of perspectives. The chapters in Part II can be assigned independently at any point in the term, such as Chapter 8 on finding and evaluating sources. However, some chapters are designed to integrate smoothly with particular writing assignments from Part III.

- Part III. This section presents a variety of writing assignments, arranged from less to more challenging: an argument analysis, a response paper, an analysis of the current state of debate on an issue, a problem analysis, and a proposal of a solution. The assignments are directed towards different audiences, similar to the goals of different published readings.

    These assignment chapters may be paired with one or more chapters from Part II, such as exploring through response (Chapter 9) and writing a response paper (Chapter 14) or drawing a map of authors' positions (Chapter 12) and writing on the state of the debate (Chapter 15).

- Part IV. This part provides strategies for expanding a student's repertoire of reading and writing strategies, from planning to peer review. It also explains both MLA and APA conventions for documentation (Chapter 22). These chapters can be assigned at any point in the term.

## Instructor's Manual

The Instructor's Manual provides detailed guidance for using *Having Your Say*, including three alternate syllabi, tips for each chapter, and detailed analyses of the lines of argument of all twelve readings. The alternate syllabi enable instructors to choose whether to emphasize critical thinking, independent research, or adaptation to various audiences. An annotated bibliography offers a wide range of choices for additional readings on the environment and crime topics. Advice for developing other topics is also provided; materials for additional topics (media, health, privacy) are available on the Companion Web site.

## Acknowledgments

The ideas in this book have been matters of discussion among the co-authors for many years. Its existence is itself evidence that allies with a common goal can work through many differences of position toward a more satisfying outcome.

Charney drafted and revised all the chapters, except for part of Chapter 9 and Chapters 12 and 15 which were drafted in their entirety by Neuwirth. Neuwirth, Kaufer, and Geisler reviewed the entire text. Charney and Neuwirth classroom-tested all parts of the book over several years.

Neuwirth developed many pedagogical techniques for scaffold-building, articulating the steps needed to apply a strategy and developing visual representations to support learning. Much of the in-depth discussion of how to support and challenge claims grows out of her philosophical approach to argument. She provided material and intellectual support throughout the drafting and revising stages.

Many strategies offered in Part II grow out of Geisler's study of first-year and graduate students coping with a writing task very similar to the "State of the Debate" assignment in Chapter 15. Her research is reported in detail in *Academic Literacy and the Nature of Expertise* (Mahwah, NJ: Lawrence Erlbaum Associates, 1994). Other strategies grew out of Kaufer's theory-building on novelty in public and academic arguments and his close study of arguments as they develop through exchanges among allies and opponents over time and distance. This work is published in *Rhetoric and the Arts of Design* with Brian Butler (Mahwah, NJ: Lawrence Erlbaum Associates, 1996). Earlier versions of these strategies were incorporated into Kaufer, Geisler, and Neuwirth's *Arguing from Sources* (Harcourt Brace Jovanovich, 1989).

We all owe a debt to our sage advisor, Eben Ludlow, who encouraged us and shaped our thinking from the first day we talked about this project. We gratefully acknowledge the painstaking work of Anne Brunell Ehrenworth who coordinated the book's development and who cajoled us to set, keep, and stay within shouting distance of all the deadlines along the way. We have been materially assisted by the comments of many colleagues who reviewed this book in its early stages.

We also wish to thank the instructors who reviewed this manuscript at various stages of development and who provided invaluable feedback: Lauren Ingraham, University of Tennessee at Chattanooga; Peggy Jolly, University of Alabama at Birmingham; Sidney I. Dobrin, University of Florida; Marie D. Goodwin, Louisiana State University; Rachel Diehl, Drexel University; Judy Donaldson, Paul Quinn College; Teriann Gaston, University of Texas at Arlington; Debra B. Black, Arizona State University; James Thomas, Mount San Antonio College; Judith G. Gardner, University of Texas at San Antonio; Carolyn Miller, North Carolina State University; Nathan K. Nelson, Ferris State University; Gardner Rogers, University of Illinois at Urbana-Champaign; Richard Fulkerson, Texas A&M Commerce; Stephen Wilhoit, University of Dayton; Joshua J. Mark, Marist College; J. Michael Mullins, University of Texas at El Paso; Peter Dorman, Central Virginia Community College; Susan Romano, University of New Mexico; Barry Mauer, University of Central Florida; Sarah Kretz McDowell, Augustana College; Lisa Loderhose, Pasadena City College; Kenneth R. Wright, James Madison University.

- I have been privileged to benefit from my co-authors' insights and scholarship, as well as their friendship, for nearly 25 years. I am most greatly indebted to the scores of undergraduates who worked with the materials in this book as they evolved over the past seven years. In the early years, it was not all that difficult to coax students toward well-developed arguments. But this book emerged through the effort to answer their challenging questions about why and how. (DHC)

- I am greatly indebted to the dedicated and talented students and instructors in Carnegie Mellon's first-year writing course, 76-101, Interpretation and Argument. I taught my first "trial version" of the curriculum in 76-101, and the responses from students helped shape each subsequent version; during my stint as director of first-year writing, I had the privilege of working with the 76-101 instructors to create versions of the curriculum that were compatible with their own teaching philosophies, and I benefited from their insights about how to teach various aspects of the curriculum more effectively. I am also indebted to Linda Flower and Richard Young for their seminars on composing processes, invention, and the pedagogy of writing, and to all those who shaped my rhetorical education. And I am most grateful for my co-authors' colleagueship and friendship over 25 years. (CMN)

- To Barb, Aaron, and Mollie, and Bev Kaufer (DK)

- To all my students for whom authorship has become the journey (CG)

We dedicate this book to Bill O'Reilly, Rush Limbaugh, Howard Stern, and James Carville for inspiring us every day to teach students to deal with dissent with substance, accuracy, and civility.

DAVIDA H. CHARNEY
CHRISTINE M. NEUWIRTH
DAVID S. KAUFER
CHERYL GEISLER

# CHAPTER 1

# What It Takes to Have Your Say

What does it take to "have your say"? You might think it is easy—you just say whatever is on your mind. Speaking your mind is enough if you are among friends, if the topic of conversation is not that serious, or if you already know a lot about the topic. In many situations, though, you won't be taken seriously if you say whatever comes into your head. To discuss a problem with others who have thought long and hard about it, you need to explore the issue first. Exploring is different from gathering information. Exploring an issue is like stepping into the unknown to find your way.

## Writing as Exploration

When venturing into the unknown, explorers rely on imperfect maps of unfamiliar territories. Lewis and Clark, for example, started their westward expedition with only sketchy maps of the Missouri River. On the way back, Native Americans showed Lewis and Clark a much better route than they had taken, a shortcut that saved them 750 miles and 50 days!

Like all true explorers, Lewis and Clark knew that their maps were flawed; they didn't know exactly where they would end up, but they went anyway. Along their journeys, explorers go through four phases:

- They analyze the maps of others.
- They compare the maps to plan a route of their own.
- They go out into the unknown and record observations.
- They return to design a new map and make it available to others.

Exploring, then, involves sketching out what a community already knows and then resketching to account for the latest reports.

Exploring a physical territory is like exploring an **issue,** an unsettled question that matters to a community. Like physical explorers, authors of an argument map

*"O.K., there's the sun, so that direction is 'up.'"*

**Some explorers use maps more skillfully than others.** © The New
Yorker Collection 2002 Pat Byrnes from cartoonbank.com. All Rights Reserved.

out an issue—not with physical maps but mental ones. Where physical maps show
well-maintained trails, maps of an issue show areas of shared knowledge or agreement. Where physical maps show rough or steep terrain, maps of an issue show
points where there is so little information or so much disagreement that it is difficult to go any further.

Just as traveling companions argue over where they are now, how they got
there, where to go next, and which route to take, so authors argue about the current state of affairs, the choice of goals, and the choice of means: What is the world
like? Why is it that way? What should it be like? How should it be changed? The
authors might be scientists and scholars, politicians, engineers, executives, artists,
members of social or religious organizations, journalists, or private citizens.

Authors share their maps by entering into public conversations, by writing
books and articles for journals, newspapers, and Web sites. As more people explore

the same issue and publish their positions, their maps change. Some points become smoother with more agreement, while others become more controversial. Authors who care about an issue pay close attention to the reports of other explorers. They keep their maps as complete and up-to-date as possible.

Your courses in college are preparing you to enter into public conversations, no matter what your academic major. You are studying issues that matter to the people in your discipline, learning about the important positions that people have taken, and gaining the appropriate techniques for exploring and describing unfamiliar terrain.

When you write argument essays for class, for the college newspaper, at work, or for a social or political group, you are also discovering where to go, choosing the best way to get there, and trying to move readers from where they are now towards your position. If you start off with a map that reflects points from other authors, you will go further yourself and convince more people to add your points to their maps. If you convince others that your maps are carefully drawn and worth following, your map can change the world.

This book will teach you how to explore an issue, drawing on the maps of others, and how to have your say about where to go and how to get there.

## The Purpose of Arguing

An old Scottish-Irish prayer wishes there were no need for argument: "O Lord, grant that I may always be right for Thou knowest how hard I am to turn." Arguing involves grappling with your own ideas as much as with those of others. If everyone agreed already, there would be no need to argue. Likewise, if no one were willing to come to an agreement, there would be no purpose to arguing.

Arguing means treating an issue as open instead of settled. If authors are fair and open-minded, arguing helps everyone understand the issue better, find weaknesses in their positions, and sometimes increase the amount of agreement.

Reaching agreement is difficult. Sometimes it requires overcoming mistrust and prejudices. Agreeing does not mean giving up important convictions without strong reason. But it does require listening carefully and responding politely to what others say, looking for shared concerns and ways to work together. The goal is to argue, not quarrel; have a civil conversation, not a fight.

## Arguing at a Distance

When you think of people arguing, you probably imagine them in the same room, talking and interrupting each other. But to reach more people over time, authors don't argue face-to-face, they argue in print. They publish their arguments in newspapers, magazines, and journals, on Web sites, and in books. These outlets reach a wider audience, including people whom the author might never imagine meeting. If even a few of these readers follow the same path or take it further, the prospects for change are better than if the author speaks to people one at a time.

Arguing in print creates a **public record** of a conversation. The conversation stretches across time and space, but it is still a conversation. Authors in far-off countries can participate. Authors who wrote long ago made points that today's authors still respond to. For example, judges and lawmakers today often refer to the arguments of America's founders and even those of judges and lawmakers from the distant past. Research studies from the past often influence ongoing work in the sciences. Sometimes a new technology or new evidence will emerge that revives interest in theories and findings published many years before. Someone remembers an earlier scientist's contribution, recognizes its new significance, and reinterprets it to make new predictions.

You will be expected to know about the public record before you speak. Imagine having a conversation with people who paid no attention to what was said before. The same point would be repeated over and over again. Or the topic would change every time another person spoke. These exchanges would not add up to a good conversation. A conversation is possible only if the speakers understand what is under discussion and what information the group considers old and new. If you try to join the conversation without paying attention to the public record, you will seem rude or out of place. Your comments might be dismissed or they might fall flat, completely ignored.

But if you try to learn the complete record before speaking, you will never have a chance to talk. So how do newcomers enter a conversation? Think of what happens when a newcomer joins a computer chat room, e-mail discussion list, or newsgroup. Most newcomers lurk in the background, reading the exchanges instead of posting messages themselves. They look back in the archives to see what others have said. Lurking and reviewing are good strategies if you want your posts to be taken seriously. These strategies give you clues about the topic of the discussion, the participants, and the ways speakers are expected to express themselves and respond to others. If you use these clues to plan your own contribution, you are more likely to communicate effectively.

You will follow the same approach to entering a public conversation in this book. In order to "have your say," to take part in a public argument yourself, you need to learn about the issue, some of the people who care about it, and what they have said. By reading a range of authors who publish on an issue, you will learn about the current state of the debate and some of the major participants. By analyzing and evaluating their methods, and by practicing these methods yourself, you will learn to use them in your own arguments.

# Exploring the Issues in This Book

The issues explored in this book come from two topic areas: environment and crime. Both topics involve public policies that relate to your everyday life. They are topics in which you may already be interested or can readily take an interest. They are also topics with wide arrays of published positions from politicians, researchers, social organizations, and ordinary citizens.

But this is *not* a book about environment or crime; it is a book about writing arguments. You will not come away knowing everything there is to know about environmental or criminal justice issues. You will get a piece of the conversation, just enough for you learn what it takes to have your say.

To get a snapshot of the ongoing conversation, you will read a series of written arguments. Why start with arguments instead of encyclopedia entries or news reports? One reason is that arguments do more than just inform people about an issue. Arguers try to engage with people who see the issue in another way.

"Issues" gives examples of crime and environment issues.

---

## ISSUES

**Environment:** *What should we do to preserve Yosemite National Park for future generations?*

How can our city get the energy and water it needs?

**Crime:** *Does the police department in our city treat minorities fairly?*

What should we do to prevent underage drinking on our campus?

---

Issues affect people with different goals or roles in society. Because they all have different perspectives, people often argue about what the issue really is.

"Perspectives on Issues" provides examples.

---

## PERSPECTIVES ON ISSUES

**Environment:** *What is the current condition of Yosemite National Park?*

1. **Families on Vacation.** My family planned a trip to Yosemite for six months. But when we got there, the park ranger told us that Half-Dome and Yosemite Falls were off-limits to tourists. He said overuse of these areas diminished their quality and they needed time to recover. We felt cheated and frustrated. (Brad, undergraduate)

2. **National Park Service.** We plan to reduce congestion at the Yosemite Falls Crosswalk by moving the road instead of building a pedestrian underpass. Moving the road would let visitors enter a

variety of paths, instead of all using the same crossing. An underpass could be expensive and unattractive and could interfere with water flows to the Merced River. (Mihalic, *Yosemite Valley Plan*)

3. **Disabled Americans.** Disabled equestrians have a variety of ailments but share a common solution: They use a horse or mule to carry their worn out bodies to the places millions of Americans enjoy. We want to watch the water soaring, feel the mist, hear the roar of Waterwheel Falls and Yosemite Falls. Recently, however, national and state parks have been closing trails to horses, and limiting places to park a horse trailer. All we wish are reasonable modifications to policies that limit our access to the parks, forests and open space our taxes pay for. (Pugh, Disabled Equestrians Organization)

4. **Sierra Club.** The plans for the Lower Yosemite Falls area are awful. The new restroom looks like it belongs in the suburbs, not a national park. The new shuttle bus stop will destroy the quiet on the eastern trail. Widening the western trail to 16' would make it a veritable road. (Whitmore, California Sierra Club)

### *Crime:* **What is the current situation on gang ordinances in Chicago?**

1. **Teenager.** Where are we supposed to go to hang out? We weren't doing anything wrong.

2. **Housing Association Manager.** After a drug dealer moved into one of our units last year, the whole complex suffered. There were people coming and going at all hours of the day and night, gangs were hanging around the entrances harassing people coming in and out. Without a reason to call the cops, there's no way to catch them.

3. **Parent.** I understand the right to privacy, but when my baby can't play outside and your baby can't go to school without being shot and killed, what about their rights? (Alverta Munlyn, resident of public housing)

4. **Advocacy Group.** It is disappointing and disheartening that a majority of the City Council today voted to reinstate the discredited gang loitering ordinance, an approach that failed both in the courts and on the streets. (ACLU)

By reading argument essays, you will learn about the issue itself. You will learn what authors are saying about it. What kinds of people care enough to write about it? What groups do they represent? Whom do they enlist as allies or treat as opponents? What event or occasion prompted them to write when they did? Whom do they choose to address and what do they want to have happen? What reasons have they given for what they believe? You will also learn about your own beliefs and attitudes. Which authors do you agree with? In what ways do you disagree? Can you give good reasons for your beliefs, reasons others will accept? Do you have anything new to say? Learning about the conversation helps you prepare to enter it yourself.

Reading argument essays will also help you write arguments. You will learn to recognize how authors construct their line of argument and to evaluate whether they have done so as responsibly and as convincingly as possible. When you see an author using a technique in a way you admire, you can start using it in your own essays, in school and outside the classroom. The techniques and strategies you will learn will be useful in many professions and disciplines, even though they differ on what kinds of claims and evidence they count as convincing.

Your task as a writer will not be to report on the issue or the controversy surrounding it. Your task will be to explore an issue and contribute to the conversation about it with your own arguments. The authors of readings in this book take a wide range of positions. Some will seem convincing and others will seem far off-base. Because it will reflect your interests and your analysis, your position need not match one taken by an author, by your instructor, or by the majority of your classmates, and it will depart in important ways from all the other positions. On the other hand, for your position to be seen as part of the ongoing conversation, it cannot be entirely new and different from anything anyone has said before. All exploration starts from what a community knows and goes on to shape what is said about the unknown. Your goal will be to create something partly new—new for your own thinking and new for the people arguing about the issue. Your exploration should go a little further and your map should be a little better than the maps already on the table.

## Having YOUR Say

To have your say as an authentic author, you have to do four things: (1) connect to an issue, (2) act like an **author** instead of an **emcee**, (3) act like an **explorer** instead of a **dogmatist** or a **demagogue**, and (4) act like a **pioneer** instead of a **tourist**.

To have YOUR say, you have to connect to an issue.

Like other authors, you have to care enough about an issue to take the time to explore and write about it. Environment and crime are broad enough topics for most students to relate to through background knowledge and personal experience. You will tune into current events that spark your motivation by focusing on one topic over time. Something will happen that suddenly makes you aware that there is a real and urgent **problem.** You might hear about a striking incident at a social gathering, religious service, or recreational event, from friends or family, or from a news report. The problem might be something new or a long-standing annoyance. It might be local to your neighborhood or workplace, or it might be a national or global topic that you are studying. Something about the situation will grab your attention and nag at you enough that you want to find out more and try to change it.

Reading argument essays about an issue can be the "something" that happens. You might disagree strongly with what you have read. Or you might read about a promising **solution** and realize it might work for a local case that you care about.

To have YOUR say, you have to act like an author instead of an emcee.

An emcee is short for "Master of Ceremonies," someone who keeps a ceremony or entertainment program moving along but is not one of the main performers. The emcee greets the audience, gets them in the mood for the event, and announces who is about to appear. He provides background information and finds a clever way to connect one performance to the next, but then he gets off the stage until the "real" performer finishes. An emcee doesn't do much of his own talking and doesn't create anything original. Instead an emcee just describes and quotes the "experts."

You are writing like an emcee if you simply collect expert sources and string bits of their positions together with an introduction and conclusion. The final result might look like an argument if you side with one author instead of another. However, acting like an emcee is not being an author and will not help you learn to become one.

Having your say means being the main performer, being the driver and not the passenger, being the author. It means figuring out claims that you think are true and important and expressing them in your own words. It means planning a path for readers to follow, making the destination seem attractive and the path to it well built.

To have YOUR say, you have to act like an explorer instead of a dogmatist or a demagogue.

A dogmatist is someone whose mind is so completely made up about the absolute truth of her position that she won't admit that it has any weaknesses and won't treat any other views as reasonable. New ideas and evidence make no difference. If astronomers had been dogmatic, we might still think that the earth is flat.

**Dogmatists lecture but don't listen.** *Courtesy of* Rubberball Productions/Getty Images.

Like dogmatists, explorers stake out a position they believe is right. In some sense, then, explorers and dogmatists are equally "biased." But unlike dogmatists, explorers are candid about their uncertainties, admitting that their maps are sketchy and incomplete. Explorers also take the views of others seriously, admitting someone else's route might be better than theirs. Instead of claiming that they already have it right, explorers keep trying to come up with the best possible route.

A demagogue is someone like Senator Joe McCarthy who will say anything to help his or her side win and make opponents look bad, someone willing to gain popularity by exaggerating, spreading false claims, or playing on popular prejudices. Like a dogmatist, a demagogue wants to do all the talking without admitting that others might legitimately see things another way.

Explorers are like demagogues in hungering for the glory that comes with going the farthest, or being the first. But unlike demagogues, explorers care more about accuracy than popularity. Explorers take responsibility for their positions;

**Demagogues use suspect claims and evidence.**
"I HAVE HERE IN MY HAND ---" *from* Herblock: A Cartoonist's Life (Time Books, 1998)

when they describe the territory and alternative routes through it, they want readers to agree that what they say corresponds to what is out there.

Writing from an exploratory outlook does not mean suppressing conflict. Without conflict over what is known and unknown, or over different ways of proceeding, there would be no reason to explore. Explorers treat conflict as part of the challenge. Reasonable people might prefer a path that departs from yours, one that leads in a direction you don't like. To argue that your path is better, you have to try to understand why that other path looks attractive and find reasons why others should choose yours instead.

To have YOUR say, you have to act like a pioneer instead of a tourist.

It doesn't count as exploring if you follow well-paved streets through a long-settled neighborhood, even if it is unfamiliar to you. Explorers add something new to our knowledge by venturing at least a little farther into the unknown or by challenging what is known.

By exploring, writers change our understanding of the significance of an issue, or the nature of the problem, or the best way to solve it. To make a **contribution,** a writer need not solve the entire problem. Problems are usually so complex that no single argument could possibly address them entirely. To count as a contribution, your argument only needs to make an advance for some conversational group. To advance, you need to learn about the current state of agreement and disagreement of that group.

**Tourists look for sights, not insights.** *Courtesy of* Corbis.

# Learning to Have YOUR Say

It takes hard work and some courage to become an author. The only way to learn the skills is to try them, find out how well they work, and then try again perhaps with a few changes.

The sequence of assignments in this book is designed to help you become an effective author. You will be following the same kinds of processes that professionals and researchers use when they inquire into an issue and formulate a contribution to the conversation in their area of expertise. Like professionals and researchers, you will think about and write about the issue in a variety of ways as you explore and develop your own position.

You will use writing to achieve several goals:

- to analyze and evaluate other authors' positions,
- to sketch out areas of agreement and disagreement among authors who write on an issue,
- to argue for what you see as the most significant aspect of the issue,
- to argue about the nature of the problem, and
- to argue about plausible solutions to the problem.

Authors with these goals write many kinds of articles, such as book reviews or response articles that comment on one author's work, review essays that interrelate many authors' positions, and essays that focus on the problem or its solution. This book starts with analyzing and evaluating the conversation about an issue, because these steps will help you prepare to enter the conversation yourself.

## EXERCISES

### Backtalk: What Do You Say?

How does the kind of writing described in this chapter compare to the writing you have done in school so far? Do you think many students write as tourists or dogmatists? If so, why do you think they write this way? What do you think is the biggest challenge for writing as an explorer?

### Recognize/Evaluate

Each of the following passages is characteristic of an emcee, a dogmatist, a demagogue, or a tourist. Which passages would you identify with each type of writer? Which passage is most persuasive? Why? Are explorers always the most persuasive?

1. My goal is to find other solutions for the access problem. Tramways would benefit the old and the handicapped, but will they actually use this form of transportation? A new solution could include better hiking trails. Better hik-

ing trails would make it easier for more people to climb and hike through the mountains and wilderness. I definitely do not agree with tramways. They should not be built in our wilderness areas. Julber's idea should not even be considered on the aspect that it deals with building and maintaining tramways in the natural beauty. I intend to research topics about access and the dangers of building in our wilderness. (Kelley, undergraduate)

2. John DiIulio, Jr., credits the problem with prison overcrowding to the lack of supervision paroled convicts receive and the lack of organization in this and other well-meaning programs. DiIulio addresses the issue of lack of funding, on top of all the other problems, in his article, "Unlock 'Em Up" printed in the *Slate Archives*. DiIulio hypothesizes that "only about one in 100 crimes actually result in ... prison time ... [and] most felony defendants are sentenced not to prison but to probation." Since this is the case, more time ought to be focused on improving this system so as to prevent another repeat offense. "Probationers who are categorized as high-risk offenders receive little direct ... oversight" because "probation officers are overworked and underpaid" (DiIulio, "Unlock"). How can a system work efficiently under these circumstances? DiIulio feels we should focus on the reinvention and reorganization of parole and probation programs. (Kari, undergraduate)

3. The so-called gang violence and juvenile crime prevention initiative derives from the great mid-nineties panic about feral youth, when crime pundits like Prof. John DiIulio were rampaging across the *Wall Street Journal*'s editorial pages, predicting a wave of youthful superpredators robbing and killing the older citizenry at will. It turned out that DiIulio and his fellows were spectacularly wrong, and in a just world would be relieved of tenure status and sentenced to 5000 hours of community service scooping up dog shit in public places. As with adult crime, the juvenile stats have been plummeting in all categories. (Alexander Cockburn, "How to Make a Criminal")

4. To me, the National Parks Foundation symbolizes everything that is wrong with the wilderness issue today. They represent the hard-core environmentalists and purists who are trying to keep the tax-paying public out of the wilderness they so deserve to visit. Without humanity to appreciate them, resourceless wilderness areas like Yosemite serve very little purpose. (Brad, undergraduate)

## Detect

Find an article on the Internet that takes a strong position on a crime or environment issue. Would you characterize the author as an explorer? A dogmatist? A demagogue? A tourist? Give reasons.

## Produce

Take one of the passages in Recognize/Evaluate and rewrite it so that it is more exploratory. Explain the changes you made and give reasons.

# PART I

## Critical Reading:
## Exploring a Point of View

### Chapters

Critical reading means more than being careful to understand everything an author is saying. Critical reading means constructing an interpretation of why the author has chosen to write, whom she expects to address, why she included the points she did and expressed them as she did, and what effect she wants to have on the reader—in short, what the author is doing with an argument. Critical reading—reading for more than just surface understanding—is crucial for exploring points of view in depth. The chapters in Part I describe what to look for in interpreting and constructing arguments.

# CHAPTER 2

# Spans: Building the Segments of an Argument

The first step in exploring an issue is learning how authors typically set up their arguments. In this chapter, you will learn to find **spans,** the biggest segments that arch across an argumentative essay or article, and consider why the author constructed them as he did. The choice of segments and their lengths are clues to what the author thinks the audience needs to know. For example, an author who thinks that readers are completely unaware of an issue might spend most of the article establishing that it exists and that it is important.

In an argument about public policy topics such as environment or crime, the three most common spans are "seeing the issue," "exploring the problem," and "selecting a solution."

In the remainder of the chapter, these spans will be described in more detail. Spans and other parts of an argument article will be illustrated throughout this text by referring to the environment and crime articles at the end of Part I. Before continuing, skim one of the following two articles:

- **Environment.** C. J. Chivers's vivid argument about the effects of mobile fishing gear on sea-life habitats in "Scraping Bottom."
- **Crime.** Michael Castleman's personal stance toward crime prevention in "Opportunity Knocks."

As you read, try to spot the places where the spans begin and end and compare your constructions with the ones presented here.

### TABLE 2.1  Spans and Their Functions

| Span | Functions | Style and Content Options |
|------|-----------|---------------------------|
| Issue | Raise awareness of the issue in concrete terms<br><br>Generate concern | Narrative with vivid detail<br>Appeal to reader to identify with those involved<br>Create a reversal |
| Problem | Analyze the nature and causes of the problem<br><br>Identify neglected or misunderstood aspect | Shift in scope: local to ge neral or general to local<br>Historical review<br>Analysis of conflicts |
| Solution | Identify and describe available solutions<br><br>Argue that a solution should or should not be adopted | Imperatives and future tense<br>Analysis of feasibility, effectiveness, costs, benefits |

# The Issue Span: Seeing the Issue

In the issue span, the author makes readers aware that something is wrong, trying to make them care enough to consider the underlying problems and solutions. If the span is effective, you will feel that you have something at **stake,** some value or goal that is at risk as long as the issue is unresolved. If the span doesn't move you, you will probably stop reading; you won't care much about whatever else the author has to say. Because it is designed to help readers see and care about the issue in general, the issue span comes at the beginning of an article.

Authors have more than one way to create interest in the issue; three common strategies are paradigmatic problem cases, ideal images, and value conflicts.

- **Paradigmatic Problem Case.** The article opens with the story of an incident in which a problem occurred. The story is told vividly with details of a provocative event or disaster in a real place, such as the giant oil spill in Alaska from the Exxon Valdeez or the shootings at Littleton High School. For the author, this incident is "paradigmatic"; it illustrates exactly what is worst about this type of situation.
- **Ideal Image.** The opening of the article conjures up an image of a world that seems normal, as expected, or even ideal. The description or narration includes vivid details that help you project yourself imaginatively into the scene. Then the author undermines that image, showing that the situation is "too good to be true," or that circumstances now threaten its existence.
- **Values Clash.** The article begins with a description of abstract principles or values (such as safety, justice, freedom) that are endangered in the current situa-

tion. Even if the language is more abstract, the author may ask you to imagine your feelings of loss or frustration if the situation stayed as it is.

Even though the language can be more dramatic and vivid than anything else in the article, the issue span does more than simply create a mood. This is where the author raises specific aspects of the issue that she will address in both the problem and solution spans. The incident described in the opening may be just one example of a larger problem that the author will analyze. Or the incident may serve as a standard, a case that any acceptable solution must address.

## Variations in the Issue Span

An issue span may be long (several paragraphs) or very short (a few sentences). If the issue is already in the public eye, an author might skip this span altogether or write only a few sentences about it. If the issue is being overlooked or underrated, the author is likely to devote much more space, or even the entire article, to inspiring readers to recognize the existence and importance of the issue.

Whatever its length, the span frequently has two parts. In one part, the reader is asked to identify with the people involved in an incident; in the other, the reader is surprised by a reversal.

In the identification move, authors often appeal to your senses or your imagination, asking you to "see" a situation as if you were an eyewitness. "Identification Moves" describes these moves in Castleman's and Chivers's issue spans.

### IDENTIFICATION MOVES

#### Environment: Chivers's Expected Image

The opening of Chivers's article is more like an adventure story than an argument. Chivers vividly describes being out in a fishing boat on a seemingly empty ocean, with all the sights, sounds, and smells. Anyone who has been on a boat can identify with the idea that the ocean looks empty.

#### Crime: Castleman's Ideal Image

Castleman describes his seemingly tranquil, idyllic neighborhood in the first two paragraphs. As a reader, you might find yourself wishing you lived in a neighborhood just like his. He makes it easy to see why someone would assume, as a neighbor does, that the neighborhood is a great place to live and safe from crime.

The second part of the issue span, the reversal, conveys a sense of conflict or uneasiness or puzzlement, a sense that things are not as they should be: everything is not what it seems; the ideal is an illusion; expectations are confounded; tragedy strikes; goals are at risk. "Reversal Moves" discusses these moves in Castleman's and Chivers's articles.

## REVERSAL MOVES

### Environment: Chivers, "All is Not as it Seems"

Chivers trumps the reader's image of an empty ocean with the expertise of the boat's captain, Peter Taylor (par. 3), who knows it is full of life and structure. Chivers wants readers to see the ocean floor as lively and valuable. Then, in par. 4–5, Chivers describes a conflict between traditional hook-and-line fishermen, like Captain Taylor, and people who fish "aggressively" with mobile gear that destroys the valuable parts of the ocean floor. As a result of dredging and trawling, many of Captain Taylor's fishing spots are gone; the ocean floor is becoming as empty as it originally seemed. At this point, you might feel that you "see" the ocean differently, as a place where hidden treasures are in danger.

### Crime: Castleman, "It's Too Good to Be True"

In par. 3, Castleman undermines the "naive" assumption that his town is idyllic. He introduces evidence that a startling number of crimes occur, reported to the police and recorded each month in the local newspaper. In par. 4, he vividly describes some close encounters he himself has had with crime near home. Then in par. 5, he argues that his neighborhood is not unique by describing crimes in nearby neighborhoods that also seem beautiful and safe. At this point, you might feel that you "see" Castleman's neighborhood differently—and other neighborhoods like it, too.

## Recognizing the Boundaries of the Issue Span

To recognize the issue span, be alert for vivid details, the use of narrative, reversals of expectations, and appeals for a new "view" of an issue. "Words to Watch For" presents some typical phrases found in issue spans:

## WORDS TO WATCH FOR: ISSUE SPANS

"This is really happening every day . . . "

"Imagine/picture this happening to you . . . "

"How would it feel . . . ?"

"This is not the only case . . . "

"One aspect has been overlooked . . . "

"Things are not what they seem . . . "

# The Problem Span: Understanding the Problem

Any issue spawns many kinds of problems. For public policy topics such as crime and environment, a problem can be thought of as a collection of similar incidents with bad outcomes. In the problem span, the author focuses on one key element that is shared by all the incidents that the author sees as problematic. The author develops an argument about what this element is, why it is significant, and how it contributes to the bad outcomes. "Problems Arising from an Issue" illustrates how different problems can emerge from the same issue.

## PROBLEMS ARISING FROM AN ISSUE

### Environment: What Is the Problem with Diminishing Fish Stocks?

The issue of diminishing fish populations is illustrated by Chivers with the image of a teeming ocean floor being swept bare. John Robinson, the author of another reading, is also concerned about people reducing wildlife populations. However, Chivers and Robinson diverge on what kind of problem this issue poses. Chivers focuses on the economic problem faced by fishermen who will be driven out of business if all the fish disappear. Robinson focuses on the ethical problem of whether humans have the right to change the environment in ways that affect the survival of other species.

### Crime: What Is the Problem with Street Crime?

The issue surrounding street crime can be vividly illustrated by the story of a violent assault; this approach is used in two of the readings, Castleman's "Opportunity Knocks" and Bruce Shapiro's "One Violent Crime." However, even though Castleman and Shapiro are exploring the same issue, they diverge on the nature of the underlying problem. For Castleman, the problem is that residents who think they are safe fail to take steps to reduce opportunities for crime in the neighborhood. He doesn't think the problem is poverty and social conditions. For Shapiro, the problem is that the story of his violent assault is being used to promote crime legislation that is counterproductive. He does think steps should be taken to strengthen the social safety net.

The issue span and problem span have similar functions. An author argues about the existence and significance of the issue in the issue span. The issue span often includes one incident or case that illustrates the way he or she sees the issue. In the problem span, the author chooses a problem related to the issue and argues in depth the existence, significance, causes, and other aspects of this problem.

The author's main concern in the problem span may be to convince you that the problem he or she is focusing on is real and important, perhaps comparing it to other problems involved with the issue. If the problem is well known, the author can devote most of the problem span to the causes of the problem. Because most public policy problems are complicated, the author has to convince you that his or her way of analyzing the problem picks out the most important aspects. The author directs your attention to aspects that might be changed to reduce or eliminate the problem. If the author is successful, at the end of this span you will want to consider solutions to the problem.

## Explaining the Tension

Authors use the problem span to identify and explain the **tension,** which is what makes the problem a problem. The tension is what bugs you about the situation, what nags at you to investigate and write about the problem. A simple cause of tension is having a goal (e.g., a well-paying job) but not achieving it because of some sort of gap (e.g., lack of experience) or obstacle (e.g., unfair treatment). Another cause of tension is having to choose between two desirable objects or goals when you can't have both (e.g., clean air and unlimited energy, secure borders and personal privacy).

Public policies affect large numbers of people in a society who may not see the same incidents as problematic; what is a major problem to you (e.g., a new ban on horses in national parks or a new system of handgun registration) may seem to be a minor inconvenience to someone else. For this reason, authors have to spell out the social values or goals that the problem jeopardizes.

## WORDS TO WATCH FOR: PROBLEM SPANS

| | |
|---|---|
| **Values** | Efficiency, fairness, good health, justice, knowledge, morality, profits, reputation, safety, civil rights |
| **Problem** | Problem, difficulty, harm, challenge |
| **Tension** | But, however, unfortunately, frustrated, blocked, at risk, at stake, in jeopardy, tragic, inexplicable, intolerable |

## Change in Scope: Separating the Issue and Problem Spans

Because the issue span and problem span are so closely related, it can be difficult to decide where one ends and the other begins. One clue is a change in the author's scope of attention, widening it to address a large number of similar incidents or narrowing it to address what to do about a particular local incident.

If an author begins the article by describing a specific local incident in vivid detail, she may widen the scope in the problem span to address the general problem that affects a larger area or a larger group of people. If the author opened with a more abstract discussion of the values at stake, she may narrow the scope to a specific instance of the problem that she wants readers to act on.

"Problems Spans" discusses these sections in Castleman's and Chivers's articles: how they change scope and how they argue for the existence and significance of the problem and its causes.

## PROBLEM SPANS

### *Environment: Chivers, "What's the Harm?"*

Chivers's focus changes in par. 6–7 from Captain Taylor to dredging and trawl fishing in general. He describes the equipment in great detail, giving graphic details of its size, shape, and operation. In par. 8–9, Chivers reviews how these methods, which have been around for a long time, turned into such a big problem. Changes in technology made mobile gear safer, stronger, and less expensive. In par. 9–11, Chivers argues that dredging and trawling are now the most common method for catching fish worldwide, with lists of fish caught in different regions and statistics for how much of the ocean floor is dredged each year.

In par. 12–15, Chivers describes the growing significance of the problem as scientists and the public came to take it more seriously. The news media began reporting on drops in fish populations. Chivers also describes scientific studies that investigated the effects of dredging and trawling and their conclusions that dredging and trawling disrupt the habitats of underwater creatures.

### *Crime: Castleman, "Why Does it Happen?"*

Castleman's focus changes in par. 6 from his neighborhood to the United States as a whole. He addresses any Americans who think they can avoid crime in a "safe neighborhood." The tension is that the illusion of safety keeps people from taking steps to prevent street crime. However, there are no safe neighborhoods (par. 7–8).

Castleman argues significance by citing the bad consequences of ignoring the problem. Ignoring street crime increases the danger of being a victim. Castleman also disputes the assumption that crime is going or has gone away. In par. 9–18, he gives two reasons why crime remains significant. In par. 11–12, he argues that crime will increase because the population of teenaged men is increasing. Men commit street crimes as teens because they haven't learned how risky and unprofitable it is. Castleman also argues that crime is significant because people feel unsafe even when the crime rate is low (par. 15–16).

Castleman spends the most space (par. 17–32) arguing about the causes of street crime. He criticizes both liberals and conservatives who think that crime is caused by large social forces (par. 17–24). Starting in par. 25, he discusses three more immediate causes: impulse, alienation, and opportunity, supporting his reasoning with personal experience. Of these three causes, he ends up deciding that opportunity is the factor that people can do most about.

The problem span can take up a small or a very large proportion of the whole. Castleman spends two-thirds of his total space on the problem span (26 out of 39 paragraphs). For Chivers, the problem span represents less than half of the article (10 out of 23 paragraphs). The length of the span reflects the author's decision about where the real change needs to come, whether in the understanding of the problem or in the steps needed to solve it. Some problems have been around such a long time that the author can move quickly to talking about competing solutions. Other problems are so unfamiliar that it is a real contribution to bring readers to understand their nature. In some cases, clarifying the problem makes the solutions seem obvious. At other times, clarifying the problem is the first step toward a search for solutions that no one is ready to talk about yet.

# The Solution Span:
# Finding and Evaluating Options

At the solution span, the author turns to the question of whether a change in beliefs or action can make the situation get better. If nothing can be done, then everyone might just have to learn to live with the problem. But if an aspect of the situation can be changed, then the problem might be made less severe or eliminated altogether. Starting with the solution span, the author tries to convince readers to make a change in attitudes, beliefs, or actions. The solution may be an approach that has worked elsewhere or it might be something totally new. If more than one solution is possible, the author might argue that one solution is better than the others.

The solution span is easy to recognize because the language changes in predictable ways. Instead of talking about the past or present, the author shifts to talking about the future and what would, should, or must happen. Instead of talking about who caused the problem or who suffers from it, the author starts talking directly to the readers about what "we" must do.

## WORDS TO WATCH FOR: SOLUTION SPANS

| | |
|---|---|
| **Solution** | Solve, approach, plan, steps, phase, action, remedy, reform |
| **1st or 2nd Person** | We, us, our, you, your |
| **Imperatives** | We must (not) . . . , we have to . . . , it's time to . . . , this will lead to . . . , we will not see results immediately |
| **Sequence** | First, second, before, next, then, after |
| **Values** | Costs, benefits, feasibility, effectiveness, advantages, side effects, proven, untested, successful, risky |

"Solution Spans" describes these sections for Castleman and Chivers.

## SOLUTION SPANS

### Environment: *Chivers's Solution Span*

Chivers describes several proposals for reducing the harm to the ocean floor (par. 16–23), including regulating the size of catches, barring dredges and trawlers from specific places, regulating the size and power of dredging equipment, and setting aside fish sanctuaries. Chivers identifies the environmental and fishermen's groups that back each proposal, but he does not come out and state his own preference. In the last four paragraphs, Chivers again portrays Captain Taylor using traditional fishing methods on his boat. Chivers ends with a call to action, quoting Captain Taylor's question, "At what point do these people stop talking and start doing what needs to be done?"

### Crime: *Castleman's Solution Span*

Castleman shifts to the solution span in par. 32, where he promotes neighborhood action as a successful way to reduce opportunities for crime. His solutions include getting to know your neighbors, developing "street smarts," and using good locks. He argues that these elements are part of all proven crime prevention programs. Instead of telling people what they should do directly, Castleman simply describes his own practices and implies that others should adopt them.

## Is There Any Solution?

Not all authors offer solutions to the problems they raise. You may feel disappointed if an author convinces you that a problem is urgent and then stops short of telling you what to do about it. However, sometimes this is the best the author can do at the time. In the lifetime of an issue, solutions are rarely quick, obvious, or long-lasting. Important issues in the areas of environment and crime never go away. People will always argue about what should count as a crime, how to prevent it, and how to punish it. People will always argue about how to use and preserve our natural resources. Because issues last a long time and change over time, authors might enter the discussion at a point when the problem seems well understood or when it is a complete mystery. If authors had to wait until they had solutions completely worked out, they might never be able to speak.

## Drawing Lines Between the Spans

To understand a new author's argument, your first step should be to try to divide the entire article into three sections, one for each span. This is not as easy a task as it might seem. An author is not required to include all three spans. The spans may differ drastically in length. Understanding an author's argument is a matter of interpretation and judgment; there are no "answers in the back of the book" that tell you where the spans "really" are. However, because policy articles so frequently include these spans, looking for all three spans is a useful starting assumption.

The best way to identify the spans in an article is to create a visual sketch, following these steps:

1. On a copy of the article, number all the paragraphs.

2. On a separate sheet, write a list of all the paragraph numbers. Beside each number write one word or phrase that captures the point of the paragraph.

3. Looking closely at the article, look for a place to draw one line between the final paragraph of the issue span and the first paragraph of the problem span. Draw another line between the final paragraph of the problem span and the first paragraph of the solution span.

There may be several plausible places to draw these two lines. The border between two spans is like the border between two states or countries. Sometimes it is easy to find because there is a geographic landmark, like the river between Ohio and Kentucky. But sometimes there is nothing on the ground at all and it is hard to tell when you have crossed over from one state to the next, from Colorado to New Mexico. Borders are matters of discussion and agreement. Likewise, some authors provide headings and subheadings that give you clues to where spans may begin and end. But even without headings, you can make educated guesses and draw lines where you think the spans begin and end.

It is usually easiest to spot where the solution span starts, so it is a good idea to draw that line first, after consulting the descriptions and "Words to Watch For." Then highlight phrases within the span that describe what aspects of the situation the solution would change.

To find the problem span, look for the highlighted phrases earlier in the article. The problem span often discusses what those aspects are like now, without the solution. So then, working backwards, look for a place to draw the line between the problem span and the issue span.

Because the issue span is so changeable in size, the border between the issue and problem spans can be hardest to pin down. In one paragraph, you may see points that seem to be about both the issue and the problem. Identify any shifts in topic or specificity and decide which one works best as the boundary. Look for a shift in scope, from one case in one city to many cases across the country (or vice versa). Look for a shift in specificity from abstract, general language to concrete, detailed language. Look for a shift in tone from personal and descriptive to impersonal and formal. Or look for a shift in audience from people with a personal stake in the problem to a more general readership. Draw the line where the most significant shift takes place.

# Inferring the Author's Starting Point

Once you have divided up the article into the spans, you will be able to step back and look at the overall shape of the argument. Which span takes the most space? Why did the author devote so much space there?

Part of your job in analyzing an author's argument to interpret why he or she made these choices. Some choices tell you about the community or group that the author is addressing. Eventually, you will have to identify communities that are potential audiences for your own arguments. To make a convincing argument to an audience, you have to make hunches about what that group will agree with and what they will consider controversial.

Identifying how an author allocates space among the spans provides important clues to the points they think readers will accept. Other important clues come from learning more about the author and the publication where the argument appeared. Figure 2.1 shows how Castleman and Chivers divided their articles into spans and "Allocation of Spans" interprets their reasons for doing so.

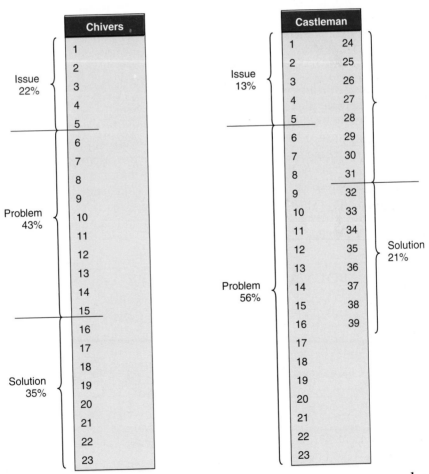

**FIGURE 2.1  How Chivers and Castleman allocated space among spans by paragraphs.**

# ALLOCATION OF SPANS

### Environment

Chivers devotes the most space to the problem but the spans are relatively close in size, suggesting that he believes his audience will need convincing on all aspects of the argument.

### Crime

Castleman devotes two-thirds of his space to the problem. The solution span is twice the size of the issue span. This distribution suggests that Castleman believes that his readers will agree quickly that street crime is an important issue but will resist his idea that opportunity is the key cause of the problem. Once he makes the case for opportunity, he can easily describe suggestions for reducing opportunity.

To test your hunches about the author's choices, you have to find out more about the author and the readership of the journal where the article appears. Most journals and many Web sites provide information about the author, either in a note attached to the article or in a listing of authors. You can also find information about the author by searching on the Web or in reference books. Many journals and their sponsoring organizations have Web sites that provide information about their goals and readership. Reference books and sites like *Ulrich's International* can also tell you about journals. Tips on using these sources are provided in Chapter 7. "Clues about Authors, Journals, and Readers" provides information from these sources about Castleman and Chivers.

# CLUES ABOUT AUTHORS, JOURNALS, AND READERS

### Environment: Chivers and Wildlife Conservation

#### Author

Chivers is a reporter who covers national and international topics for the *New York Times*. In this article, he is an active spectator because he is on the boat. He remains silent about any personal stake in the issue and which solution he prefers. But his sympathy for Captain Taylor and the traditional hook-and-line fishermen comes across clearly. He offers no arguments in favor of trawling and dredging, even to refute them. He assumes his readers are ordinary Americans who don't think much about where the fish they are eating comes from or how it was caught.

### Journal

*Wildlife Conservation* is published by the Wildlife Conservation Society (WCS), based at the Bronx Zoo in New York City since 1895. The WCS's goal, stated on its Web site wildlifeconservation.org, is saving "wildlife and wild lands throughout the world" by combining the "resources of wildlife parks in New York with field projects around the globe to inspire care for nature, provide leadership in environmental education, and help sustain our planet's biological diversity."

### Readers

*Wildlife Conservation* readers are probably ordinary people who enjoy the outdoors, go to zoos, and watch wildlife programs on TV. They are not experts, so they probably need the description of the mobile gear and how it works. If the WCS's goal is to "save" wildlife, then these readers already support environmentalist positions. So Chivers may be safe to assume that they will reject dredging and trawling if he compares their effect to clear-cutting a forest. Since the WCS is based in New York, Chivers is wise to focus on a New England fisherman before widening to the global problem. To appeal to readers who are not committed environmentalists, Chivers would have to respond more to opponents. But focusing on the fishermen instead of the fish allows him to widen his appeal to people who value the economy more than the environment.

### Crime: *Castleman* and *Mother Jones*

### Author

Castleman is identified as an author of books about healthcare. He cares about crime because it affects his daily life. He uses personal experiences to support claims about the myths surrounding safety, the causes of the street crime, and the advantages of his solution. He identifies himself as on the left politically, but he criticizes both liberals and conservatives. He probably assumes his readers are on the political left, because he spends extra time on points that liberals might dispute.

### Journal

On its Web site motherjones.com/mother_jones, *Mother Jones* identifies itself as "a magazine of investigation and ideas for independent thinkers. Provocative and unexpected articles inform readers and inspire action toward positive social change. Colorful and personal, *Mother Jones* challenges conventional wisdom, exposes abuses of power, helps redefine stubborn problems and offers fresh solutions." *Mother Jones* was named after a labor organizer, so it may attract readers who identify with the political left. An orientation toward the political left is also associated with the goal of social change and the assumption that power is often abused.

### Readers

If *Mother Jones* really does publish arguments that are "fresh" and "provocative," then readers of this magazine will probably accept Castleman's casual, personal style. If they associate themselves with the political left, they will see Castleman as an insider when he also identifies himself as "a person of the left." But if these readers really do pride themselves as being "independent thinkers," they should tolerate Castleman's criticisms of the left and occasional praise of the right. People on the political left are known for sympathizing with the problems of the disadvantaged, so they should not be repelled when Castleman admits that he has a "criminal past." Castleman's article seems appropriate for this magazine but it would have to be changed quite a lot if he wanted to publish it in a more mainstream outlet.

As you find out about authors and journals, you will find that both reflect political or social leanings. For example, *Mother Jones* is published and read by people with leftist politics; *Wildlife Conservation* is published and read by wildlife advocates. Other readings included in this book also have leanings: *National Review,* where Dave Shiflett's "Parks and Wreck" appears, has a conservative outlook; *U.S. Catholic,* where George Brooks's "Let's Not Gang Up on Our Kids," is read by Catholics. All these sources are "biased" in some way; so are their authors. This does not mean that you should dismiss these authors or these journals. Every argument is biased in some way or it wouldn't be an argument. The central question is whether people with biases are still able to be fair to opponents and accurate on the facts.

## Using Spans to Analyze, to Explore, and to Guide

In this chapter, you learned about the major segments of a line of argument about public policy, the spans for seeing the issue, defining the problem and choosing a solution. In the next few chapters, you will learn about smaller segments of arguments that build up into the spans.

Thinking about different kinds of segments will help you write by reminding you of aspects you might need to investigate. The segments will also help you transform your experience of exploring your issue into a line of argument that readers will find convincing. Readers do not need or enjoy an exact play-by-play of your sequence of thoughts in exploring an issue. Instead, they expect you to make your argument in a sequence they can understand. For similar reasons, Lewis and Clark did not publish an exact tracing of their journey across the American frontier with all of its stops, starts, blind alleys, and wrong turns—instead their map was a much neater symbolic representation of the terrain, presented using conventions that mapmakers had been developing over time.

Similarly when writing to a specific audience, an author ends up leaving out points that she considered during the exploration. She may have started exploring by thinking about solutions, but decided to spend the whole article on the problem.

Learning to recognize and construct these segments will not give you a fool-proof formula for writing a convincing article. Even though you will learn about the segments in an order that makes sense (e.g., starting with seeing an issue and ending with choosing a solution), there are no rules requiring a specific sequence. Arguing is not like filling in a form. Authors are free to leave some segments out, repeat them, or rearrange them. Your own choices about what claims to make, how much to support them, and how to arrange and express them all have to be judged with a specific audience in mind. Learning to recognize the segments can be help-ful both for exploring the issue and eventually writing your argument article.

---

## EXERCISES

### Backtalk: What Do You Say?

What is your reaction to Castleman? Chivers? Do you agree about the serious-ness of the problem? Why? Has the author offered a good enough solution? Why or why not? Provide examples of the language the author uses that show that there is a serious problem. If you agree that the author has offered a good solu-tion, what do you find most convincing about his solution? If you disagree with his solution, where do you find gaps?

### Recognize/Evaluate

The following passages include phrases that typically signal the issue, problem, or solution span. For each one, identify which span it comes from.

1. As the first step to getting things right for the future, I urge all of us to reflect hard on what tough gang laws can mean to tomorrow's children.

2. On a recent hike into the high country, a friend of mine pulled out his cell phone at 13,000 feet, sat on the edge of a stunningly beautiful rock precipice and dialed his wife two states away. I didn't know that he had taken the phone, and was immediately torn by strong, opposing opinions. On one hand, the romance of it all. I mean, what woman wouldn't love to hear her lover's voice from a mountaintop? To know that amid such beauty he was thinking of her? But the pit in my stomach told me that deeper feelings prevailed; feel-ings that had to do with the cell phone's immediate transformation of the wilderness. (Christina Nealson, "In Wilderness, Don't Phone Home")

3. But, unlike the dozens of management trends—from teams to Total Quality Management—that come and go each year, successories have ignited a firestorm in the otherwise dreary field of human resources. In one camp is a group of academics and irritated employees called "The Hards," in light

of their endless demands for hard data to prove that successories work. In the other camp are corporate executives and a few business school professors called "The Sensors," who maintain that not all information can be quantified and that people like Galloway prove successories work. (Stephen Glass, "The Writing on the Wall")

4. Now, many of us would not approve of killing jet skiers, at least without a prior legal proceeding. We will also agree with manufacturers that snowmobiles and ATV's allow handicapped Americans access to the outdoors they would not otherwise enjoy. We agree that some waivers should be granted, though recipients should have no more than one leg at most. But we remain adamant that these people are national pests and should be kept out of national parks. (Dave Shiflett, "Parks and Wreck")

5. A national poll done by the research group Public Agenda in 1997 found that a solid majority of American adults—two-thirds—spontaneously describe adolescents in starkly negative terms: wild, rude, irresponsible. Half give those descriptions even to younger children. Granting that some young people deserve those descriptions, it also is demonstrably true that most do not. (Peter Scales, "The Public Image of Adolescents")

## Detect

Read another essay and identify and write a description of the spans. Your instructor may assign you one or allow you to choose one yourself.

## Produce

Write a paragraph or so that imitates a passage from the Chivers or Castleman essay on a different issue. For example, write a Chivers-like passage with computer technology taking the place of trawling and dredging. Or write a Castleman-like passage about gossip instead of neighborhood crime. Choose a specific passage from the problem or solution span. Try to imitate the author's reasoning, examples, and style.

# CHAPTER 3

# Stases: Taking Standpoints Along a Path

In Chapter 2, you learned about three spans that authors often use as the main segments of a public policy argument: seeing the issue, defining the problem, and choosing a solution. This chapter looks at a sequence of claims that authors use to construct a path across each span.

Each span is constructed out of five types of claims, referred to as five **stases**. The word "stasis" (pl. "stases") comes from the Greek word for standing or stopping at some point. The five stases are kinds of points that may be controversial, depending on the audience. People who are having an argument pause, or take a stand, at the most controversial point, the point where they have to work hardest to convince their audience. It is helpful to think of the stases in the form of questions that an author and an opponent may answer differently. Table 3.1 depicts the five stases in the form of questions.

A span (Chapter 2) is made up of arguments that give the author's answers to these questions. The answers may be short or long depending on whether opponents are likely to agree. As rhetoricians in ancient Athens and Rome recognized, people on opposing sides do not necessarily contest every single point. Even today, lawyers on opposing sides may start off a trial by listing out a set of points that they agree on (or "**stipulate** to") and then dig in their heels on other points. If opponents are likely to agree on a point, the author may make few, if any, claims at that stasis and move on to the next one. Moving readers toward action depends on gaining their agreement at all the stases along the way.

Within each span, the stases often follow a sequence: existence, definition, value, cause, and action. This sequence makes sense. It is a waste of time to argue about what punishment to impose if no one agrees that a crime occurred. Likewise, if minerals in a wilderness area are not worth extracting, why argue about the effects of a mine on the environment? This sequence is frequent but it is not obligatory. There is no rule that authors have to include claims at every stasis; they can leave out any they like, arrange them in different orders, or use one stasis over and over. These choices depend on the author's sense of what points in the argument

| TABLE 3.1 **The Stases in the Form of Questions** | |
|---|---|
| *Stasis* | *Typical Questions* |
| Existence | Does something exist? Did an event really happen? Could an object or event be brought into existence? |
| Definition | Does an object or event belong to any known category? Which one? Can it be treated like other members of that category? |
| Value | How good or bad is it compared to other objects or events? Is it unendurable or irritating? Is it expensive? Is it ethical? |
| Cause | How did the object or event come about? What makes it happen or prevents it from happening? What effects does it produce? |
| Action | What should be done about it? Who has the right or responsibility to take action? |

are under dispute, what points are worth arguing, and what points will seem obvious to readers. For example, an author arguing about national security knows that the events of 9/11 and their significance are well understood, so she can spend very little time on the existence and value stases and focus on her view of what caused the attack and how to prevent similar ones.

# The Stasis Sequence in Different Spans

While claims at each stasis can occur in any span, the questions that the stases pose are phrased slightly differently at each one.

## Issue Span
*Existence:* Has something happened? What is the current situation? Are there cases of a problem? *Definition:* Has the issue been mischaracterized? *Value:* Why is the issue worth attention? So what? Why should we care? *Action:* What do we need to know about it? What new angle or approach do we need to take?

## Problem Span
*Existence:* Is there a problem? *Definition:* What kind of event is it? Have cases of the problem been misclassified? *Cause:* What causes it? How did it get this way? *Value:* How serious is it? *Action:* Should we try to solve it?

## Solution Span
*Existence:* Is a solution possible? Have any solutions been tried or proposed already? *Definition:* What kinds of solutions are they? *Cause:* Will the solution cause the problem to go away? Will it at least cause the problem to diminish? *Value:* What are the

advantages and disadvantages of the solution? Which solution will cost the least and produce the most benefits? *Action:* Who should act on the solution and how?

# Dividing a Span into Stasis Passages

Just as an entire article can be divided into three spans, each span can be divided up into passages focusing on the stases. The remainder of this chapter will help you identify passages that focus on a single stasis by describing the purpose of each stasis and providing textual cues. A passage can be as short as a sentence or as long as several paragraphs or several pages. Identifying the main claims being developed and supported in each passage will help you learn important aspects of the issue, understand the author's article fully, and find ways to challenge it. Analyzing an author's sequence of claims will also give you ideas for how to construct your own article.

Figure 3.3 at the end of this chapter shows the Castleman and Chivers articles divided into spans, with passages focusing on different stases.

# Existence Claims

Existence claims answer questions about a particular situation in a particular time and place. Authors can make a positive claim that something does exist or a negative claim that it doesn't.

Positive existence claims are used in two ways: to describe the details of a situation or to change beliefs about the reality of a phenomenon. Many questions arise about the details of a situation: Was there a gun at the scene of the crime? Are there minerals in an undeveloped tract of public land? Some questions arise about reality itself, about things that might be imaginary (such as hearing voices), undetermined (such as global warming), fabrications (such as a false accusation), or unrealized potentialities (such as a power plant based on nuclear fusion).

Negative existence claims are used in the same ways. An author may argue that an event never happened or that what did happen was different from an opponent's description. For example, a lawyer might argue that a defendant was not in a certain place at a certain time. Authors can also challenge beliefs about reality because things are not always what they seem: a $20 bill turns out to be counterfeit, a twisty object on the ground turns out to be a tree branch and not a snake, or the earth turns out to be round instead of flat. Authors can also argue that objects are impossible in principle (such as a perpetual motion machine).

## The Purpose of an Existence Claim

Talking about what exists might seem unnecessary or obvious. In policy debates, however, authors use existence claims to set the stage and to call attention to situations or details that are new, ignored, or misunderstood. Readers may not know about the leatherback turtle, for example, or might not have it foremost in their

# DEBATE THE ISSUES

"... AND TONIGHT OUR PUNDITS WILL BE DEBATING THE ISSUE, 'DO EXTRA TERRESTRIALS EXIST?' "

**Some existence issues are easy to settle.** *Courtesy of* Dave Carpenter.

minds. A claim that something exists in the world makes it exist in the reader's conscious attention. Existence claims make a phenomenon seem **present** or **salient** so that readers will be prepared to understand other claims about it.

People often disagree about the facts. We are all more confident about some facts than others. In the natural sciences, researchers may never be absolutely certain that a fact has been established. However, to make decisions and take action on public policy issues, we need ways to decide on the facts. In public, governmental, or legal disputes, parties argue before someone with the authority to decide what will be reported as fact. For example, in courtrooms, lawyers argue about the facts but the jury decides what happened. The parties accept the jury's decisions, except when appeals are granted.

## Developing Existence Passages

Existence claims can be about **objects** (Bill Gates, democracy, a bright object in the sky), **events** (a hit-and-run accident, the 2000 Presidential election in Florida), or **categories** (millionaires, executives of high tech companies, mayoral elections, forms of government, UFOs). For each kind of phenomenon, an author elaborates on existence in somewhat different ways.

## Objects

In this book, the term **object** refers to everyday material things like books, animals, and weapons. Existence claims convey details about an object: how it looks, sounds, tastes or smells; what it is made of; when it came into being, developed, or disappeared; where it is found; how many exist; and what it does. Each of these aspects of an object can be described at length, so a passage describing an object may consist of a large number of existence claims.

Abstract concepts, such as countries, theories, beauty, and injustice, have qualities too. The state of Hawaii has a location, a geographic shape, and a history. Geologists can tell when the islands came into being. Historians can tell when Hawaii became a state. Politicians can tell whether it is mostly Democratic or Republican. Even a concept like democracy has a history and features such as elections, majority and minority parties, and representative legislatures.

## Events

An **event** involves changes to objects over time. Event claims are about whether specific changes really happened or could happen. Umpires hear arguments about whether the ball went foul or whether a player touched a base. Lawyers argue about whether someone committed a crime or entered into a contract. Meteorologists discuss whether a hurricane will hit a coastline or not.

Events involve the elements of a story. Who did something or took action? What did the agents/participants do? Where and when did it happen? What were the agents' reasons for acting? What consequences did the action have on other objects or other events? Each of these aspects of an event can be described at length, usually with a series of existence claims.

## Categories

A **category** exists if many similar objects or events can be treated alike as **cases** of the same phenomenon. The category of thefts, for example, includes many past cases and possible cases in which a crime occurred. Every case of theft is unique, but all involve owners, objects in their possession, and criminals who take the objects without right or permission. These elements of a category can be described briefly or at length.

Categories group a set of objects or events together and separate them from similar kinds of objects or events. Besides theft, the legal system has categories for other transfer events, such as rentals, gifts, purchases, and finds. Rentals and purchases with receipts create legal contracts that can be disputed in court. Some gifts, such as inheritances, and finds, such as shipwrecks, can also be subject to legal oversight.

A claim that a category exists can be a matter for debate because it may have just emerged or gone unnoticed. To establish that a category exists, an author has to argue that the pattern of cases is not merely a coincidence or an accident by showing what features they share, and what features or criteria distinguish them from cases in other categories. For example, AIDS became a new category of disease when doctors realized that there were many cases and all patients had a similar virus in their bloodstreams. "Existence Claims" gives examples of these claims for environment and crime.

---

# EXISTENCE CLAIMS

## *Environment*

### Object

Imagine an enormous plastic net, roughly the shape of a Santa Claus cap turned on its side. The opening is about 200 feet across. The lower edge of the opening, touching the sea floor, is a steel hawser, adorned with chains and rubber rollers. . . . This is an otter trawl. (Chivers)

### Event

Tempers have run so high in some states that people on opposing sides have nearly turned violent. "One of our board members had a gun pulled on him by a guy because the A.T.V. users were going anywhere they wanted, and he went out and dragged some debris against the trail," said Brent Martin, director of Georgia Forestwatch. (Canedy)

### Category

Two different philosophies have lately emerged to compete for strategic and intellectual dominance of the conservation movement as the world enters the make-or-break decades of the struggle. The two views appear to be taking firm root, and it remains to be seen whether they will reinforce or work against each other. (Stevens)

## *Crime*

### Object

I live in a sunny, picturesque neighborhood of San Francisco called Noe (Noh-ee) Valley. It has quiet streets, magnificent views, four coffee bars, three bookstores, two bakeries, two parks, a half-dozen fine restaurants, the church featured in the Whoopi Goldberg movie *Sister Act*, and lovingly restored Victorian and Edwardian homes. (Castleman)

### Event

Last spring, a man in his teens armed with a handgun held up another man in mid-afternoon in front of the corner store within spitting distance of my front door. The gunman fled on foot right past my house.

Every time a grisly horror unfolds in some far-off corner of the country, the papers always quote the locals as saying, "Things like that just don't happen here." But "crime can happen anywhere," says Wilbur Rykert, Ph.D. . . . (Castleman)

### Category

> In the early 1990s, a new kind of crime emerged when police in New York noticed a rash of car thefts that involved drivers being forced from their cars. They called these incidents "car jackings."

## Clues to Spotting Existence Passages

A passage that develops points at the stasis of existence will include phrases about things and phrases that refer to an observable state of being.

### WORDS TO WATCH FOR: EXISTENCE CLAIMS

- **Existence**     Something strange happened last night. The mugging took place outside the bank. There were twelve eagles living in the canyon last year. Frodo lives. Stuff happens. Anything is possible.

- **Nonexistence**  It was nothing. No one has ever seen a mountain lion in this area. The source of the noise cannot be verified. It wasn't really that big. It didn't happen that way. That's impossible. The noise went away.

# Definition Claims

Whereas existence claims are about the reality of objects, events, and categories, definition claims are about whether a **case** (a specific object, event, or subcategory) belongs in a category. Definition claims are used when readers agree that the case and the category exist, but disagree over classifying the case. Adding a case to a category is controversial when the consequences are high, such as when claiming that a particular U.S. citizen is a traitor. Ejecting a member from a category can be controversial for the same reason, such as when claiming that a captured enemy combatant is not a prisoner of war.

Definition passages develop and support claims for why a case belongs in a category and how it is like or unlike other members. These claims involve references to basic features of the cases and categories. A case can only be included in a category if it shares features with other cases.

The most interesting definitional arguments are those that concern the most specific category that the case can fit into. It is more interesting to argue over whether a teenager is an adult than whether she is a living being.

## The Purpose of a Definition Claim

Definition claims are important because we usually treat cases in a category alike. Assigning a case to a different category changes how we treat it.

*"What you hate is walking. This is hiking——hiking is different from walking."*

**Recategorizing an activity changes how it is treated.** © The New Yorker Collection 2004 David
Sipress from cartoonbank.com. All Rights Reserved.

An argument of definition can be a crucial step in an argument about what we
should do about a problem. The categories in which we put things have subtle consequences. Suppose, for example, that the city council is debating what to do about
a neighborhood with many run-down houses. The houses could equally well be
categorized as "run-down old Victorians" or as "slum housing." But the council is
likely to propose very different action for the first category (restoration) than the
second (demolition).

In the crime topic, the abortion issue involves a series of definition claims,
including what counts as a human life and what counts as a medical procedure.
Our justice system already has a category, murder, that sets punishments for taking a human life with criminal intent. Pro-life advocates argue that an abortion is
a case of murder because it is a violent act intended to deprive a human being of
life. Pro-choice advocates argue that a fetus is not a case of the category of human
beings until it is viable independently and that an abortion is a case of a medical
procedure intended to benefit a patient, the mother.

In the environment topic, definitional arguments affect how a piece of territory
or a species of animal is treated. Regulations restrict people's actions in very different ways depending on whether they are in a place categorized as a national
park, a wilderness area, a historic district, or a migration route.

Definition arguments are also important because adding a controversial item can change our understanding of the nature of the category and everything else in it. Consider the problem of defining what counts as a religion.

**Defining Religion** In 1997, a group called the "Ethical Cultural Fellowship" (or ECF) applied to the state of Texas for tax-exempt status as a religious group. The ECF argued that it was a religious group because it conducted regular spiritual services, set ethical principles, instructed children, and had leaders to officiate at ceremonies such as marriages. However, the Texas comptroller argued that the ECF was not a religious group because they do not worship a supreme being.

A minister of the Unitarian Universalist Church, a recognized religion in Texas, supported the ECF because belief in a supreme being is not a required tenet of his own faith. A Baptist pastor in Texas opposed the ECF application because his definition of religion was "faith in Christ."

Counting the ECF as a religion is controversial because the decision seems to call the membership of other cases into question. If the ECF is admitted, the state may find it harder to distinguish religions from service organizations, such as the Boy Scouts. Admitting the ECF might lead people in religions that worship a deity to question its tenets. But excluding the ECF also has consequences. It might raise doubts about the eligibility of currently recognized religions that don't have a deity (such as Unitarianism or Buddhism) or ones that are non-Christian (such as Islam, Judaism, or Hinduism).

## Developing Definition Passages

Depending on the author's sense of agreement with his readers, passages that focus on definition may take a few sentences or several pages; they may even be completely absent. "Definition Claims" gives examples of these claims for environment and crime.

### DEFINITION CLAIMS

#### Environment

Chivers does not have definition claims in his argument. He describes trawls and dredges in detail but is not arguing that any particular boat belongs in one of these categories.

#### Crime

Castleman devotes par. 9–12 to developing the definition of a category of street criminals who have these features: young, male, risk-taking, satisfied with low payoff, uneducated, and often intoxicated. He assumes that these features are somewhat unfamiliar to his readers. Later, he also includes himself in this category.

A lengthy definitional passage can be developed in two ways: by analyzing the characteristics of a case to see whether it meets the **criteria** for membership and by comparing a candidate case to accepted members of the category.

## Membership Criteria

A definitional argument often spells out a set of criteria or features that members of a category usually share. In some cases, the criteria are so familiar that we can't imagine questioning them. For example, an animal meets the criteria for mammals if it is warm-blooded, bears its children alive, and suckles its young. In other cases, the criteria are matters of custom or choice. For example, high schools can set different criteria for naming a student to an Honor Roll, including standards for grades, attendance, and demerits.

For this reason, a definitional passage often includes claims at the stasis of existence about the characteristics of a case. For example, an author who argues for removing an animal from the endangered species list is likely to include claims about occasions when the animals were observed in an area, the number of babies they have, and the patterns of migration they follow year after year.

## Comparisons

If a case is similar to an accepted member of a category, then an argument for inclusion is easier for readers to accept. But the members of a category are never completely alike. Any category involves three kinds of cases:

- **typical cases** that just about everyone agrees do belong,
- **borderline cases** that most people include but admit are atypical, and
- **outsiders,** cases that most people exclude that are similar to members in several important ways.

Among birds, a robin is typical and an ostrich is atypical, but a bat is an outsider. A bat is similar to birds because it has wings, flies, and eats insects, but it is not a bird because it bears its young live, not in eggs. Among mammals, a bat is a borderline case of the subcategory of rodents, a mouse with wings.

Because cases differ so much, an author often has to argue that some criteria are more important than others. For animals, reproductive processes count more than physical features. For U.S. citizenship, birthplace is more important than religion, ethnicity, physical appearance, preferences in sports or food, native language, or length of residence.

Issues of defining U.S. citizenship and prisoner-of-war status emerged in the war against terrorism. Does someone who was born in the United States still count as an American citizen if he fought against U.S. soldiers or joined a terrorist organization? Even if a prisoner is a borderline case, he has all the rights of an American as long as he is a citizen. If he is not a citizen, then membership in other categories can be considered. He might be categorized with foreign combatants who have other rights, such as prisoners of war to whom the Geneva Conventions apply. If prosecutors do not want to treat him like the members of any available category of prisoners, they might propose a new category (e.g., enemy combatant) and argue that he belongs in that. This move allows prosecutors to create a new set of rules for how some prisoners are to be treated.

"Criteria and Comparisons" provides examples of definitional passages for environment and crime.

## CRITERIA AND COMPARISONS

### Environment

**Criteria**

[The list of species at risk in Canada includes some items that don't belong.] The Queen Charlotte Islands population of the Woodland Caribou *(Rangifer tarandus dawsoni)*, listed as one of two mammal extinctions in Canada, is not a species by the standard biological definition but a subspecies *(dawsoni)* of the plentiful species *Rangifer tarandus.* (Jones and Fredericksen)

**Comparisons**

. . . [I]n this case what the ESA [Endangered Species Act] is protecting is not exactly a species, in the normal sense of the term. A "species" usually means all animals that can interbreed. By this definition there are only six species of Pacific salmon—Chinook, sockeye, coho, chum, pink, and cherry (the Atlantic salmon is a separate species)—none of which is threatened with extinction. . . . But for salmon the ESA has been applied not to entire species but to "distinct population segments" or "evolutionarily significant units." These are, essentially, populations of Chinook, sockeye, coho, or other salmon that spawn in particular geographic areas—streams, lakes, and watersheds. If the salmon runs returning to a specific stream diminish, then that "unit" is listed and must be protected. (Jones and Fredericksen)

### Crime

**Criteria**

Given their youth and lack of education, street criminals are typically people with little competence in the adult world. In addition, says Marc Mauer, assistant director of The Sentencing Project, a Washington, D.C., organization specializing in criminal justice policy, "Half of all violent offenses are committed by people intoxicated on alcohol and/or other drugs." (Castleman)

**Comparisons**

[Noe Valley is not a safe neighborhood. Are the suburbs safe places to move to?] You might try Petaluma . . . where Polly Klaas was murdered. Or Grass Valley . . . where two 16-year-old girls were murdered. Or Concord . . . where my cousin was knifed to death. (Castleman)

## Clues to Spotting Definition Claims

Definition claims include phrases referring to a case, phrases referring to a category, and a phrase denoting inclusion or exclusion.

- **Inclusion:** A bat is a rodent, a mammal, an animal, and a living thing that flies. My little brother belongs right in there with the monkeys. Any 15-year-old who is taking care of a younger sister is an adult. Making Bart listen to Mozart was cruel and unusual punishment.

- **Exclusion:** A bat does not count as a bird. A plastic bag is not a toy. A 15-year-old cannot be considered an adult. The Founding Fathers left out classical music when they banned cruel and unusual punishment. A 21-year-old is not qualified to be a Cub Scout.

## WORDS TO WATCH FOR: DEFINITION CLAIMS

| | |
|---|---|
| **Inclusion** | Is, counts as, meets the qualifications, can be considered, belongs in, typifies, is defined as |
| **Exclusion** | Is not, falls outside, is distinct from, lacks the necessary features of, is a separate case, differs from |
| **Categories** | Class, kind, family, type, group, cluster, camp |
| **Cases** | Instance, case, member, item, candidate, representative, individual |
| **Criteria** | Qualifications, standards, parameters, yardstick, grade, rules, test, earmarks |
| **Typicality** | Classic, typical, central, atypical, unrepresentative, borderline, fringe |

## Distinguishing Between Definition and Existence Claims

You may have trouble deciding whether a claim is an existence claim or a definition claim because both involve the characteristics of objects, events, and categories. Instead of trying to classify individual sentences into the existence or definition categories, look for the longest passage that stays on the same topic. Then classify the entire passage by looking at how it is developed.

Definition arguments are rarely about what an item is really like. The members of the Ethical Cultural Fellowship acknowledged that they did not worship a supreme being; what they disputed was whether that feature was necessary for ECF to be classified as a religion. A definition argument about whether a government is a democracy is not likely to be about the existence of elections, but about whether the existing elections count as free.

Treat a passage as an existence argument if several claims refer to what is real or what is possible, if several connected claims describe a vivid or unusual occurrence and what it was really like, or if the passage occurs very early in an article or section.

Treat a passage as a definition argument if several choices of categories are presented, if features are treated as criteria, if the case's features are compared to those of other cases, or if the passage has references to inclusion or exclusion.

A public policy argument does not always include claims at the definition stasis. In many texts, you will not find any definition claims at all. Some issues raise questions of definition more than others. If you cannot easily identify a category and a case whose membership is being disputed, you probably do not have a definition claim.

## Value Claims

Value claims are about the relative worth of cases in a category. They are built on agreement at the stases of existence and definition; the dispute is not over whether an object or event exists, or in which category it belongs, but how that case ranks among other members.

In value arguments, cases in a category are arranged along a scale, such as popularity, monetary worth, importance, or morality. Scales can be constructed for any feature that varies in quantity or quality. We can arrange tomatoes by ripeness; basketball players by shot percentage; champagne by dryness; theories by consistency; and potential jurors by impartiality. A value claim establishes the author's ranking of one case among the rest.

Value claims are controversial. Assessments of a case can vary widely from person to person because of differences in circumstance or perspective. "Worst Cases" illustrates how difficult it is to decide which case deserves the most immediate attention. People can have good reasons for rating these cases differently.

## WORST CASES

### Environment

Students may disagree on which case of campus problems is the worst:

- Graffiti is scribbled all over the dorms on campus.
- Detergent poured into a fountain kills the fish and plants.
- The university creates parking by paving over student garden plots.
- The university buys food from a company that uses harmful pesticides in South America.

### Crime

Students may disagree on which case of campus problems is the worst:

- A male African-American student walking in the Student Union after hours is singled out by a campus cop and asked for ID.
- Your roommate gets flashed.

- A sophomore is injured in a fight at frat house.
- A faculty member walking to the parking lot is mugged.
- A student walking across campus at night is run over by a bike.

In policy articles, an author wants readers to address a case that the readers are neglecting. Readers are more willing to act to save things they cherish and to remove things they dislike. Therefore, the author must persuade readers that they are underestimating a case that they should cherish or overestimating a competing case. If the author fails to raise the readers' estimate of the case, the audience will stop reading and do nothing.

## The Purpose of a Value Claim

Value claims are similar to opinions. An opinion, "Stubbs is the best live music venue in Austin," has few important consequences; if friends disagree, they can go to Stubbs one night and La Zona Rosa the next. But value arguments matter. Consider, for example, this question: Which National Park deserves more maintenance money in next year's budget? You might think that the biggest parks deserve the most money. Someone else might say the parks that have the most visitors. But the parks come out in different orders when ranked by size than by visits, as shown in Table 3.2 which lists public use statistics.

Great Smokey is smaller than Yosemite but gets almost three times as many visitors, the most of any park listed. So is Great Smokey more in need of funds than Yosemite? Park rangers from Yosemite could argue for adding criteria to the evaluation, especially quality or length of stay. Most of Great Smokey's visitors drive straight across the mountain ridge with few stops, but Yosemite's visitors camp,

**TABLE 3.2** **National Parks Arranged by Different Scales**

| National Parks | Recreational Visits 2002 | Acres of Federal Land |
|---|---|---|
| Big Bend | 329,000 | 775,300 |
| Bryce | 1,070,000 | 35,830 |
| Grand Canyon | 4,105,000 | 1,180,900 |
| Great Smokey | 9,198,000 | 521,200 |
| Yellowstone | 2,759,000 | 2,219,300 |
| Yosemite | 3,369,000 | 759,530 |

hike, and congregate at particular vistas. So rangers at Yosemite could argue that they need more funds because visitors put greater wear and tear on Yosemite's trails and sights than Great Smokey's. In this kind of situation, a value argument leads to decisions and actions that affect many people.

Value claims are about changing attitudes. Our knowledge about the world and our actions in it are closely connected to our feelings. We seek things that interest us and protect things we care about. We wish for things that don't exist and work to bring them into reality. Authors seek to make readers more concerned about a problem or readier to act on it.

Our attitudes toward an object or event are more changeable than our belief in its existence or category membership. Our desires change with our circumstances. A student who is torn between buying a winter coat and a stack of new DVDs chooses differently in August than in November. We judge which values are most important at the current moment. People who cherish freedom, justice, and human life may change their rankings when considering issues of war, capital punishment, abortion, or healthcare for an injured relative.

Within the topic of environment, many values are in play. Is use of a mineral today more important than saving it for the future? Are the environmental effects of one extraction method easier to clean up than another method? Is the beauty of the scenery important enough to block the construction of wind-powered turbines?

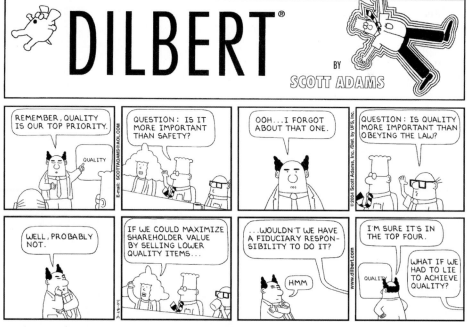

**Rankings of competing values change with the circumstances.** © Scott Adams/Dist. by United Features Syndicate, Inc.

Within the crime topic, values may seem less relevant at first. Everyone agrees that crime is bad. So what is there to argue about? Value issues arise in deciding what to do about crime. Is it fair to apply the death penalty to people who are incapable of distinguishing right from wrong? Are certain kinds of criminals getting unfair special treatment? Is increasing enforcement of "quality of life" crimes the best, quickest, most effective, or least expensive way to reduce urban crime?

## Developing Value Passages

While all value arguments involve the ranking of cases in a category, some also involve the scales along which the cases are evaluated. There are several ways a value passage can develop:

- Comparing cases to convince readers to change their rankings relative to each other.
- Moving a case higher or lower along a scale to convince readers to see a case differently.
- Challenging the weight given to different scales in a value judgment, to convince car buyers, for example, to focus more on fuel efficiency than on cost.

"Value Claims" illustrates types of claims for environment and crime.

---

### VALUE CLAIMS

#### *Environment*

**Comparing Cases**

In terms of raw fishing power, these devices, known as mobile fishing gear, are a huge leap from the stationary nets and traps set by many vessels, and a further leap still from hand-set hooks and jigs. (Chivers)

**Moving a Case on a Scale**

Does the number of endangered species in Canada represent a problem serious enough to warrant the consideration of federal legislation? (Jones and Fredericksen)

**Challenging the Scales**

[Many Westerners see rural land as something to be] conquered, colonized, [or] grazed. The forests contain hardwoods valuable on the international market. The cleared forest then provides land for the landless and pastures for the cattle industry. Traditional [Western] conservationists, on the other hand, see the aesthetic, biological, and ecological value of the same land but do not necessarily see the people. They often fail to see the effects of past or current human actions, to differentiate among types of human use, or to recognize the economic value of sustainable use. (Gómez-Pompa and Kaus)

# Crime

### Comparing Cases

Just as few homicides involve large numbers of victims, very few occur in schools. Schools continue to be the safe havens that they were traditionally perceived to be, however much media coverage of these killings has eroded that perception. While there is serious violence in a few schools, and considerable gun violence outside of schools, gun violence in schools is extremely rare. (Kleck)

### Moving a Case on a Scale

Laws based on stereotyping and guilt by association are being passed in the name of crime prevention. Laws that seemed impossible after the McCarthy era now encourage discriminatory and arbitrary law enforcement. Many of these laws are being found unconstitutional. All these laws are morally reprehensible. (Brooks)

### Challenging the Scales

According to the police, Service Area 109, which includes my house, has had thirty murders since 1992—an average of 3.8 homicides a year, or about one every three months. Additionally, police officers have shot and killed three alleged assailants in this area. These numbers can seem modest or horrifying, depending on what one considers 'normal' or expects from a neighborhood like mine. (Myers)

## Comparisons

Value arguments often involve a comparison of cases against each other. For example: "Wetlands are more fragile than tundra"; "Stopping terrorism is more difficult than winning a conventional war"; and "dredging the ocean floor is equivalent to clear-cutting a forest."

In developing this kind of value passage, authors describe the characteristics of each case and compare them to each other. Because this type of argument looks only at isolated cases, not at their position within the category as a whole, authors often must explain their choice of cases. If the cases aren't compatible in some sense, the author would be "comparing apples and oranges."

## Rating along a Scale

Instead of raising or lowering one case in comparison to another, some value arguments seek to place a case along a familiar scale. The author's goal is to raise or lower a reader's current estimation of the case in relation to the category as a whole. Raising the estimation of a case can make a problem seem more urgent or a solution seem more advantageous. Lowering the estimation makes a case seem ordinary rather than exceptional.

- **Environment.** Chivers raises readers' estimates of the amount of fish caught by trawling and dredging.
- **Crime.** Castleman raises readers' estimates of the numbers of crimes that take place in a nice neighborhood.

Ratings along a scale involves an implied comparison of one case against all the others in the same category. For example, when we say that an $8 magazine is expensive, we mean that it is expensive as compared to other magazines; as compared to a textbook, an $8 magazine would be considered cheap.

So in developing this type of value passage, an author talks about moving the case higher or lower than the point where most people position it ("Noe Valley is more dangerous than you think"), relates the position of the case to the extreme ends of the scale ("mobile gear fishing is the biggest source of seafood in the world"), such as the "best," "worst," or "average" case.

Our judgment of a case is often a composite of ratings along several dimensions. A value argument can be used to adjust the rating of a case on one or more of these scales. Figure 3.1 illustrates how Chivers might rate the qualities of mobile gear on fishing boats improved between the 1970s and now.

Value arguments involving scales also involve standards. A standard is a dividing line or cutoff point on a scale. Everything above the cutoff point is given one value and everything below it is given another value. For example, in a numerical grading system, there are points used as cutoffs between an A and a B and between a B and a C.

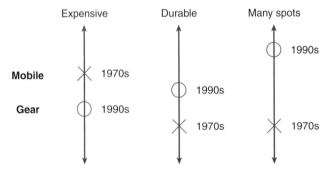

**FIGURE 3.1** How Mobile Gear Improved, 1970s–1990s. Compared to the 1970s, the cost has dropped, the durability has increased, and more spots are accessible.

A standard can be a matter of taste, a matter of policy, or matter for negotiation. You and your roommate, for example, may agree that your dorm room is cluttered but disagree on whether it crosses the line between "lived-in" and "pigsty."

Authors often use labels for the points on a scale to reinforce their views of a case. An author who views a case positively will use a positive label to describe its ranking on the scale, while an opponent would use a negative label for the same position on the scale. For example, an environmental activist and a rancher might agree on the number of wolves inhabiting a grazing area, but the activist might describe the wolves as "plentiful" while the rancher describes them as "rampant." Here are positive and negative labels for the endpoints of a few scales.

**Cost**        Positive: valuable/inexpensive; Negative: over-priced/cheap

**Judgment**    Positive: bold/careful; Negative: reckless/timid

**Morality**    Positive: scrupulous/tolerant; Negative: puritanical/slack

## Challenging the Criteria
When people disagree on complicated public policy issues, it is often about which problem is the most urgent or which solution is most effective. These disagreements concern the value of scales themselves, rather than cases along a scale. Figure 3.2 illustrates how Kleck might argue that violence in schools is less urgent than street crime.

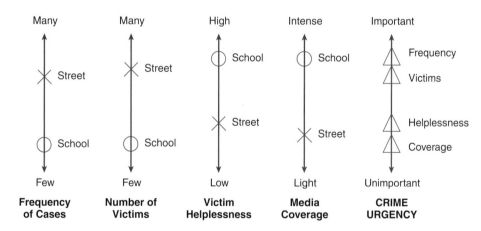

**FIGURE 3.2  How scales are rated.** Kleck argues that in rating the urgency of a crime, frequency and number of victims are more important than victim helplessness or media coverage.

Kleck would not dispute the relative rankings of these two types of crimes on the Frequency of Cases, Number of Victims, Victim Helplessness, and Media Coverage scales. Instead, he would rank frequency and number of victims higher than helplessness and media coverage on a composite Crime Urgency scale.

Thus, the development of a value argument can include a series of points, with claims and evidence about cases and their relation to a standard, about how cases compare to each other, and about scales and how they compare.

## Clues to Spotting Value Claims

You can recognize value claims by the presence of terms that describe qualities and amounts, especially adjectives and adverbs, as well as terms describing likes and dislikes.

### WORDS TO WATCH FOR: VALUE CLAIMS

| | |
|---|---|
| Quality | Good, healthy, fair, worthwhile, important, trivial, useless, unjust, dangerous, bad, excellence, safety |
| Quantity | All, every, some, 10 percent, few, none, huge, amount, size, weight, number, price, temperature |
| Comparison | Best, better, most, more, greater, heavier, the same, equal, fair, lighter, less, fewer, least, comparison, above, below |
| Scales | Tops, average, bottom of the heap, measure, yardstick, standard, criterion, balance, estimate |
| Preference | Like, love, prefer, choose, favor, pick, select, reject, dislike |

## Distinguishing Between Value and Definition Claims

Value claims and definition claims are sometimes hard to distinguish because both refer to items in a category, to criteria for membership, and even to values on a scale.

You will sometimes see value claims used in the development of a definition claim because setting a standard or cutoff in effect creates separate subcategories. For example, within the category of people who drink alcohol, subcategories like alcoholics, social drinkers, and binge drinkers are defined by setting standards on three scales:

| | |
|---|---|
| Number of drinks | Social drinker, one or two drinks in a row; binge drinker, five or more drinks in a row; alcoholic, various amounts |
| Work impairment | Social drinker, minimal; binge drinker, high; alcoholic, various levels |

**Craving for more**　　Social drinker: low; binge drinker, various degrees; alcoholic, high

To distinguish whether a passage is a definition argument or a value argument, examine the main point under dispute in the entire passage. If it is a controversy over the membership of a case in a category, then this is a definition argument. If the main point is a controversy over what case to select or single out, then this is a value argument. Here are two similar claims that illustrate the difference:

**Definition claim**　　Brad is a social drinker but he is not an alcoholic.

**Value claim**　　Helen goes on binges even more often than Peter.

Because people consider alcoholism a bad condition, you might think that the claim "Brad is an alcoholic" is a value claim. After all, isn't that claim about the same as saying "Brad is engaging in harmful, unhealthy behaviors"? But "Brad is an alcoholic" only claims that Brad belongs in the category. The related value claims might compare Brad to other alcoholics, or compare alcoholism to smoking.

## Cause Claims

Cause claims attempt to explain why things change over time. A causal argument involves an event, with a before and after. An object starts off one way, then a **factor** sets off changes, after which the object is different. For example, changes in paper color can tell detectives where a gun was fired. They pat objects in a suspected location with photographic paper and then spray the paper with a special solution. If the paper changes color, then barium, antimony, and lead (chemicals used in priming a gun) are present. These chemicals are factors that change the color of the paper. If the paper stays the same color, then these chemicals are not present and it is unlikely that a gun was fired in that spot.

When making cause claims, authors assume that readers agree on the nature of a situation but not on how it became that way, why it stays that way, or how it could be changed. Cause claims are controversial because, in complicated situations, many elements are plausible as causal factors. It is difficult to pick out the elements that lead to changes from the ones that don't.

Cause is tied directly to the other stases because the way in which something changes may involve its existence, classification, or ranking within a category. A solution to a problem can make a harmful object go away (existence), transform it into a different class of object (definition), or change it in severity or scope (value). For example, efforts to reduce pollution can seek to eliminate contaminants from the air or water, transform waste products into useful commodities through recycling, or reduce the danger by bringing the amount of a contaminant to safe levels. A solution that fails is one that doesn't have the intended effect.

## The Purpose of a Cause Claim

Cause claims are used to analyze what happened in the past. For example, a doctor can diagnose what virus caused a person's illness and what **factors,** such as diet or exercise, prevented the illness from being worse. Cause arguments also predict the future **effect** of some action. In the 1990s, computer systems analysts predicted that the old way of encoding dates would cause computers programs worldwide to malfunction on January 1, 2000; billions of dollars were spent all over the world to prevent the Y2K bug from doing damage.

Cause arguments are crucial to authors who seek to persuade others to take action to change a problematic situation. First, cause claims are important for establishing why the problem persists. Without understanding the cause of a problem, it is hard to figure out how to affect it. Second, cause claims are used to predict the effects of different solutions on the problem.

Cause claims arise in almost any argument about crime. Police identify the motive behind a crime in order to narrow down the suspects; forensic scientists trace the cause of death to determine what weapon was used; police study ways to reduce or prevent crime; and legislators argue over the effect of long prison sentences on the amount of crime.

**Cause and effect can be difficult to tell apart.** © Scott Adams/Dist. by United Feature Syndicate, Inc.

In the environment topic area, cause claims are very frequent. Before allowing landowners to build, the government requires them to submit a report, an Environmental Impact Statement, that predicts how the development will affect the environment. Activists seeking to preserve rare species identify factors that prevent reproduction and increase survival.

## Developing Cause Passages

The way a cause argument develops is somewhat like a story. The characters are agents who take steps that start or prevent changes; the setting or environment contains factors that affect what happens. The plot is the sequence of changes in objects and phenomena over time. The outcome may be the one desired (for a happy ending) or there may be unexpected complications, as when the wrong people are held responsible or when a plan goes wrong. "Cause Claims" illustrates this type of claim for environment and crime.

---

### CAUSE CLAIMS

#### *Environment*

... [A]ggressive methods of modern fishing, known as trawling and dredging, rearrange the seabed, uprooting plants, destroying protective structures, crushing animals and even removing terrain features. (Chivers)

The leading culprits in the decline of birds are a familiar set of interrelated factors: habitat alteration, overhunting, exotic species invasions, and chemical pollution of the environment. (Tuxhill)

#### *Crime*

As Robert Frost wrote: "Good fences make good neighbors." Good dead bolts help too. (Castleman)

... [G]ood lighting deters criminal activity and increases the public's perception that the facility is safe (which may increase patronage). Installing a parking-lot lighting system reduces the need for active security and reduces or eliminates car break-ins. (Abbott and Fried)

---

A cause passage develops with elaborations on any or all of these three key elements: agent or instigator, factors or actions that produce the changes in objects, and before-and-after outcomes.

## Agent

The agent can be a person who takes steps intentionally: "Complaints about harassment gradually decreased after the mayor introduced community policing." Or the agent may be a force of nature: "Hurricane Katrina destroyed large sections of the Gulf Coast levees." The objects that change can be abstract (feelings of harassment) or concrete (coral reefs).

## Changes in Objects

Objects can change in existence, definition, or value. A change in existence means that an object disappears or comes into being. For example, we use chemicals to wipe out insects and we combine chemicals to create plastics. A change in definition occurs when an object is affected so dramatically that it can no longer be considered the same kind of thing. For example, a long drought could change a prairie into a desert. A change in value means that some aspect of the object increases or decreases in quality or quantity. For example, target hardening decreases the chances of theft, but does not eliminate them entirely.

## Outcomes

In addition to describing a process of change, causal passages also describe the final state of an object and consequences of the change. The final state may be described in concrete terms: "What was a complex of sponges, shells, and other organisms was smoothed to a cobblestone street." Or the final state may be an abstract account: "The result of all the protest was a five-year delay in the building of the dam at an extra cost of $5 million."

## Factors

The heart of a cause claim is the identification of factors and an analysis of how their presence set off changes that led to the outcome. In everyday conversation, we can speculate on the factors (or causes) and argue for one or another without much evidence. But many important decisions in public policy, such as the licensing of medications or the determination of guilt, require a high degree of confidence that the factors behind a change are identified accurately. In an effort to reduce the chances of errors, philosophers such as John Stuart Mill developed strategies for ruling out unrelated factors by comparing and even experimenting with cases. Mill proposed five major strategies: comparison, correlation, analysis of sufficiency, analysis of necessity, and experimentation.

**Comparison**  The basic strategy for identifying a causal factor is to collect and compare information about similar cases in which a phenomenon was likely to happen, like schools where violent incidents occurred and those where it was prevented. Any feature shared by all the cases where violence occurred is a potential factor. See "Comparison Method" for examples.

# TESTING FACTORS

## Environment

### Comparison Method

Intensive trawling in the Gulf of Mexico was followed by drops in the shrimp population. Similarly dolphins died out after fisherman were once again allowed to use nets to capture tuna.

### Correlation Method

The more times the ocean bottom was scoured per year, the faster the marine life disappeared.

### Necessity and Sufficiency Method

Federal ownership of significant amounts of western land is . . . the only way to ensure that the interests of nonwesterners are considered when land use decisions are being made. (Nie)

### Experimental Method

Activists who clean up polluted streams need simple chemical tests for detecting the presence of toxins. Scientists inserted genes from fireflies into minnows called zebrafish. They conducted experiments with the fish in aquariums. When the fish are put into tanks with clean water, nothing happens. But when they are in tanks with dangerous chemicals such as PCBs and dioxin, the fish begin glimmering with a green light.

## Crime

### Comparison Method

I committed my crimes driven by a momentary impulse I can't really explain. I consider myself a thoughtful person but I don't recall thinking much about my criminal escapades. I just did them. I believe everyone experiences criminal impulsiveness. How else can you explain affluent executives padding their expense account or cheating on their taxes? What else explains a priest embezzling? (Castleman)

### Correlation Method

There is no consistent correlation between poverty and crime. The studies go back 100 years, and they show only a weak correlation at best. Most poor people are law abiding, and many rich people break the law. (Wolfgang)

### Necessity and Sufficiency Method

An offense-specific approach [to crime prevention] requires analysis of acts to determine the conditions necessary for them to occur. For example, graffiti requires an instrument capable of spreading paint over large surfaces quickly and reasonably accurately and a paintable surface that is accessible to the offender and unobserved for some period during which offenders are active but otherwise generally observable. Graffiti also requires an unrestrained offender. (Gottfredson and Hirschi)

### Experimental Method

Many people believe that violent movies and computer games cause young children to become more violent. Researchers have conducted many experiments to investigate this claim. They show violent media to one group of children and non-violent media to a second group. Then they watch the children as they interact freely. The children who watch the violent media act more aggressively, such as hitting, yelling, throwing toys, twice as often as the others.

Full-length comparison passages involve detailed descriptions of what happened in each case, what potential factors were present in all cases, and what factors were present in some and absent in others. Thus many causal passages are filled out with existence claims.

This information is sufficient for ruling out some potential factors. A factor cannot be a true cause if it is present both when the effect occurs and when it doesn't. For example, students and teachers are present at virtually all incidents of school violence but also at all cases where no violence occurs. So the presence of students and teachers cannot be a cause of violence.

While comparison is useful for ruling out elements, it cannot positively identify the factors that lead to change. So additional strategies are used to narrow down the possibilities further.

*Correlation*  Identifying a correlation is used in situations where more than one factor may be involved. Finding a correlation (sometimes called a **relationship** or **association**) involves comparing changes in value over time for two or more potential factors. In a simple correlation, the value for one factor increases whenever the other factor increases. For example, if playing video games is related to violence in kids, then the number of violent incidents at a school should increase on days when more students play for more hours and decrease on days when the time for gaming is limited. In an inverse correlation, the value for one factor only goes up when the value of the other goes down. For example, because fire uses up oxygen, the longer a fire burns in a closed room, the less oxygen will remain. See "Correlation Method" for examples.

Because correlations involve comparing values on scales for different cases, causal passages can also be built up out of value claims.

Like comparisons, identifying a correlation is a useful pointer to likely factors, but finding a correlation is not enough evidence that a factor caused an outcome. For example, in young children, height increases with weight but one does not cause the other; instead, height and weight are themselves related to factors like diet and age.

*Sufficiency* A strong strategy for causal argument involves eliminating all possible factors until only one is left that still produces the change. A sufficient factor is enough to produce the effect all by itself, whenever it is present. If a school has a zero-tolerance policy for drugs, for example, then the presence of any single instance of a drug is sufficient to trigger the penalty, no matter what the drug is or how much of it is present. Zero-tolerance means that any is enough. So if playing video games is a sufficient factor for violence, then violence should occur whenever students play. Many changes can be set off by any of several alternative factors. For example, any one of the following behaviors could be sufficient for a student to be expelled from high school: possessing drugs, possessing a weapon, disrupting a class, or skipping school.

*Necessity* Sometimes a change occurs only if a certain set of factors is present; these are known as necessary factors. For starting a fire, three factors are necessary: fuel, oxygen, and a source of ignition. If any one of these is missing, no fire can break out. A necessary factor is one that must be present every time the change occurs. For example, if Goth music is necessary for school violence, then violence occurs in every school where Goth music is played, but never at schools where no Goth music is allowed. If a set of infractions were necessary for expulsion, then only students who had brought a weapon AND possessed drugs AND disrupted class AND skipped school could be expelled.

*Experimentation* Figuring out whether a factor is necessary or sufficient often requires experimentation. An experiment is an active way to test the factors, instead of simply comparing cases that have already happened. Researchers start by creating cases that are virtually identical. Next, they introduce a candidate factor to just one of the cases and observe what happens in both cases. If the outcome routinely happens when the factor is present but rarely when the factor is absent, then the factor probably causes the effect. See "Experimental Method" for examples.

Experiments are good evidence for cause claims, especially if many researchers are able to reproduce the results. For this reason, you will often see references to experimental studies in policy arguments. The authors usually do not conduct the experiments themselves; instead they cite studies conducted by biologists, ecologists, sociologists, psychologists, criminologists, and other researchers.

## Clues to Spotting Cause Claims

You can recognize cause arguments by looking for a story of changes over time, one that focuses on who did what to produce change in something and what happened.

### WORDS TO WATCH FOR: CAUSE CLAIMS

*Agents*

| | |
|---|---|
| **Specific people** | Names of individuals, groups, institutions |
| **General** | Instigator, prime mover, culprit, guilty party, catalyst, source |

*Types of Changes*

| | |
|---|---|
| **Existence** | Create, invent, produce, bring forth, introduce, arise, appear, disappear, vanish, prevent, remove, destroy, wipe out, obliterate |
| **Definition** | Change, convert, transform, reclassify, turn into |
| **Value** | Increase, promote, improve, impair, leave the same, lower, worsen, decline |

*Timing*

| | |
|---|---|
| **Sequence** | Before, after, then, first, second, third, next |
| **Speed** | Slowly, gradually, quickly, suddenly |

*Factors*

| | |
|---|---|
| | Proper conditions, cause, factor, is associated with, is correlated with, is unrelated to, is necessary for, is sufficient for |

*Outcomes*

| | |
|---|---|
| **Final state** | Result, consequence, outcome, ending |

# Action Claims

Action claims are about what needs to happen to lessen or eliminate a problem or keep it from becoming worse.

Action claims build on cause claims; even if people agree on the cause of a problem, they often disagree on what to do, who should do it, and how. For example, there is general agreement that smoking increases the risk of lung cancer. But there are strong disagreements over what approach to take: Is it more important to persuade people to stop smoking, to prevent kids from taking up smoking, or to make smoking less dangerous? Who is responsible for taking action: individual smokers, parents, employers, schools, the government? Action claims provide the author's position on questions such as these.

Not surprisingly, action claims appear most often in the solution span of a policy argument when the author proposes specific steps: We must act immediately; you should vote for this piece of legislation; the following steps should be taken. Action claims also appear in problem spans, in this case to persuade readers that solutions should be considered, that readers should keep reading.

Action claims are controversial because everyone has an idea about what to do but few are in contact with the authorities who have the power and resources to take action. For example, visitors to national parks are in contact with park rangers, but park rangers do not control policies about the use of snowmobiles; victims upset about a criminal case are in contact with police officers, but police officers have no control over plea bargains between prosecutors and suspects. The authorities who do have control often focus on concerns and procedures that activists know little about. So, for action claims to be persuasive, authors must know whom to address and how to address their concerns.

## The Purpose of an Action Claim

You might think that once people agree about the existence of a significant problem and its cause that it would be obvious to everyone what needs to be done. But in fact, persuading people to act can be the hardest step of all. By proposing and supporting actions, authors anticipate their readers' concerns and address them in ways that make action seem easier or more attractive.

People are often reluctant to act because they have gotten used to the way things are. Or they think it is someone else's responsibility to act. Or they feel unsure that their action can improve a situation. Or they are doubtful about which action to take. People may be especially reluctant to act when a great deal is at stake: a jury's action to convict a defendant could deprive that person of freedom or of life; an employer's action to hire or fire a job applicant could affect the company's profits and the applicant's ability to support a family.

Authors can argue for actions that they have planned out themselves or they can endorse a plan that someone else has proposed. Actions can include calling or writing the authorities, attending a rally, signing a petition, donating money, and so on. Authors can also argue against taking action.

Authors may reject steps that someone has proposed, arguing that they are not needed, that they would worsen the situation, that they would have such bad consequences that doing nothing would be better.

## Developing Action Passages

Action passages, like cause passages, include descriptions of agents, participants, setting, occasion, and sequence of actions. However, action passages are aimed directly at the people who can take action so that authors can address their concerns and persuade them to get started. To understand the development of an action passage, you have to figure out whom the author is addressing.

The format of the text and the place of publication are key for recognizing the audience, such as a letter to an individual or a group, an opinion column in a daily newspaper, an article in an outdoors magazine, a corporation's Web site, the newsletter of an activist group, or an article in public policy journal.

In "Action Claims," Chivers invites readers of *Wildlife Conservation* to volunteer their support to an organization of fishermen like Captain Taylor. This excerpt comes from a sidebar to the article. John J. DiIulio, Jr., a political science professor, discusses what state governments should and should not do about the drinking age. DiIulio does not address readers directly as "you," because he is not trying to persuade officials in a specific state. Because his article appeared in *Brookings Review,* a public policy journal read by elected officials at the local, state, and federal levels, he can reach officials in many states.

---

## ACTION CLAIMS

### Environment

Advocates for primitive fishing styles say they must force a return to low-impact fishing methods: harpooning, trapping, jigging, potting, trolling, and handlining. The easiest way to do this is to zone the sea bottom according to its vulnerability, and to forbid modern harvesting from sensitive areas. To support this effort, contact the Cape Cod Commercial Hook Fisherman's Association. Address: North Chatham, MA 02650; phone: 555-555-2432. (Chivers)

### Crime

States should refuse to enact any measure that would increase alcohol consumption and particularly consumption among young people. Unless one simply refuses to accept the overwhelming weight of evidence on the relationship between drinking, disorder and crime, one must believe that reducing the minimum drinking age or any other measure that would increase, rather than further limit, the availability of alcohol would have socially undesirable, even disastrous, consequences—most especially in America's inner-city neighborhoods. (DiIulio)

---

## Clues to Spotting Action Claims

Action claims are relative easy to recognize. The agent or authority is often named directly. The verbs are in future tense or combined with imperatives. The descriptions of specific actions are often arranged in a sequence, using terms like first, second, third.

## ⊘WORDS TO WATCH FOR: ACTION CLAIMS

| | |
|---|---|
| **Agent phrases** | We, you, authorities, your organization |
| **Action verbs** | Start, enact, approve, stop, refuse, delay, consider, speak out |
| **Future tense and imperatives** | We must (not) . . . , we have to . . . , it's time to . . . , don't do it . . . , just say yes |
| **Invitation phrases** | I urge you to . . . , we discourage your workers from . . . , we recommend. . . |
| **Sequence phrases** | First, next, finally, after that |

For example:

"We must act quickly to stop the situation from getting worse."

"The first step is for you and other concerned citizens to contact your representatives in Congress. Then organize a meeting in your neighborhood."

"It's time for Calumet to follow the panel's recommendation to hire four more detectives and give officers bigger raises over the next three years."

# Treating the Stases as a Flexible Sequence

The stasis sequence is a set of options, not a rigid formula. Authors develop passages at the stases that are useful for whatever they are doing at the moment. When they are exploring the issue for themselves, they ask themselves *all* the stasis questions. They take their time, backtrack, and explore many distant corners of an issue. But when constructing an argument to present to readers, they don't use everything they discovered in the same order that they discovered it. Instead they guide readers along the smoothest and most attractive path they can construct. Their choices depend on the current state of the issue: Is it well known or completely unfamiliar to the public? How far can readers be persuaded to go in one trip?

It is impossible to predict how much space an author will need to accomplish any one of these goals. Some authors direct their arguments at readers who already agree about the problem, so they need to spend very little space there. For other authors, the whole challenge is to convince people that the problem really does exist.

Therefore, different authors spend different amounts of space on the stases within a span and may skip one or more entirely.

Figure 3.3 illustrates how Chivers and Castleman allocated space for the stases within their spans.

## CHIVERS—SPANS & STASES

| | | ISSUE SPAN |
|---|---|---|
| 1<br>2<br>3 | Existence: | Taylor's boat is at sea. Nothing seems to exist in ocean wilderness. But various creatures and formations do exist on ocean floor. |
| 4<br>5 | Existence:<br>Cause: | Traditional fishing and mobile gear clash.<br>Mobile gear destroys habitat; some fishing spots still exist but others are gone. |

| | | PROBLEM SPAN |
|---|---|---|
| 6<br>7 | Existence: | What trawls look like and how they work. What dredges look like and how they work. |
| 8 | Value: | Mobile gear is more powerful than traditional fishing. It used to be expensive and less durable and therefore less practical. |
| 9 | Cause:<br><br>Value: | New technology increased sturdiness of mobile gear, which enables gear to go to more areas, which increases<br>Mobile gear now catches more fish than traditional fish harvests. fishing. |
| 10<br>11 | Existence: | Mobile gear is in use world-wide. It scours large areas of ocean floor, some areas very often. |
| 12<br>13<br><br>14<br>15 | Value:<br><br>Cause:<br><br>Cause: | Mobile gear problem was urgent only to traditional fishermen & scientists in 1970s-80s.<br>Collapse of fish populations increased urgency for public, leading to more research.<br>Showed mobile gear<br>Research destroys habitat. |

| | | SOLUTION SPAN |
|---|---|---|
| 16<br>17<br>18<br>19 | Existence: | Possible solutions have been proposed that change New England regulations to create ocean zoning, limit gear, create undersea sanctuaries. |
| 20<br>21<br>22<br>23 | Value: | Captain Taylor believes that traditional fishing has least impact and is most sustainable. He prefers solution of barring mobile gear from hard ocean bottom (zoning?). He approves of other solutions. He wants action. |

FIGURE 3.3  Chivers's and Castleman's spans and stases.

## CASTLEMAN SPANS AND STASES

| | | *ISSUE SPAN* |
|---|---|---|
| 1 | *Existence:* | Noe Valley seems nice, prosperous, safe. |
| 2 | *Value:* | NV is not as safe as it seems because of crime. |
| 3, 4, 5 | | Nearby towns are no safer than NV. |

| | | *PROBLEM SPAN* |
|---|---|---|
| 6 | *Existence:* | Americans think safe places exist but they don't. |
| 7 | *Value:* | No place is safe enough. |
| 8 | *Cause:* | Ignoring local crime increases the danger. |
| 9 | | Street criminals are young men who accept |
| 10 | | low payback, take risks, are uneducated, and |
| 11 | *Definition:* | intoxicated. They choose easy targets, |
| 12, 13 | | like young Castleman. |
| 14 | *Cause:* | Age makes Castleman wiser and a harder target but |
| 15 | | not less fearful. |
| 16 | *Value:* | Fear outweighs facts about declining crime rate. Crime is worth addressing. |
| 17 | | Liberals blame crime on antisocial rage caused by |
| | *Cause:* | poverty, racism, lack of opportunity. Conservatives |
| 18 | | blame crime on liberals preventing police and courts from locking up criminals. Both blame weak families. |
| 19 | | Rebuttal to conservatives. More prisons has not |
| 20 | *Cause:* | increased safety. Punishment stops crime if it is |
| 21 | | immediate, certain, severe. It is not immediate or |
| 22 | | certain. |
| 23 | | Rebuttal to liberals. Poverty and crime are not |
| | *Cause:* | correlated. Fighting racism does not reduce crime but |
| 24 | | fighting crime may reduce racism. |
| 25 | | Castleman committed crimes because of impulse, |
| 26 | *Cause:* | alienation, opportunity. Nothing can eliminate impulse |
| 27 | | or alienation. Opportunity can be reduced. |
| 28, 29, 30, 31 | | Neighborliness reduces alienation. |

| | | *SOLUTION SPAN* |
|---|---|---|
| 32 | *Cause:* | Castleman reduces risk by making kids feel neighborly, |
| 33 | | reducing alienation. When turnover reduces |
| 34 | *Value:* | neighborliness, he holds parties. He recommends |
| 35 | | target hardening over car alarms that alienate neighbors. |
| 36, 37, 38, 39 | | He recommends vigilance even among friends. |

# EXERCISES

## Backtalk: What Do You Say?

Find a claim where you disagree with Chivers or Castleman, or doubt that he is right. What is the stasis of the claim? Give your reasons. Write a response to the author describing why you disagree on that claim.

## Recognize/Evaluate

Identify the stasis at which each of the following claims is addressed.

### A. Environment

1. Agricultural and industrial pollution of waterways further reduce habitat for fish and other aquatic life. (Tuxhill)

2. An equally disturbing trend is population declines in more widespread species. (Tuxhill)

3. Roads are human creations and are understood relative to human purposes. In environmental documents, roads appear as access in descriptions of development projects. . . . In this domain, roads provide access to project sites as well as a means to transport resources over land. Roads appear as impacts when they are connected to wilderness values. (Ginger)

4. In the face of current and expected declines, the world's governments have clear moral and practical reasons to act. (Robinson)

5. Like many mountain bikers, I'm happiest when I'm charging up and down hills through the West's spectacular public lands. (Carroll)

### B. Crime

1. Are [the prisoners] soldiers taken on the field of battle, and therefore prisoners of war entitled not just to humane treatment, but also to all the protections enshrined in the Geneva Conventions? Are they the modern equivalent of Barbary pirates, international criminals outside the rules of law who can be tried by whatever country seizes them, and questioned like any criminal? Or are international terrorists a new category, for which the rules are evolving only now? (Schememann)

2. Spotting a criminal without such help is usually difficult; experts generally start with a few rules of thumb. . . . Look for suspicious spending like Gebauer's and Miano's. Gebauer's lifestyle screamed trouble. He made only $150,000 a year at Morgan yet lived like an emperor, throwing outrageous parties at his lavish Park Avenue apartment. . . . Such a gap between salary and conduct usually suggests chicanery. (Dumaine)

3. Now: Repeal mandatory-minimum drug laws in New York and elsewhere. Find the fugitives. Serve the unserved warrants. Incarcerate the really bad guys. Mandate drug treatment for the drug-only addicts and abusers. (DiIulio)

4. Street criminals are not masterminds. (Castleman)

5. We need to confine fewer young people and do more freeing of spirits and souls. (Brooks)

6. A number of studies have reported an association between the homicide rate and alcohol consumption rate. For example, a study of homicide rates in the United States in the early 1980s found that states with higher rates of alcohol consumption had higher rates of several types of homicide. (DiIulio)

## Detect

On your own or in a group, work on the same articles you chose before and assign paragraphs to stases within the problem span and within the solution span.

## Produce

### A. Definition.

Choose from the cases below (created by George Hillocks) the ones that you would categorize as courageous. Using your list of cases, write a definition of courage that explains the criteria clearly enough that a partner will be able to predict which cases you chose and which you rejected.

1. A student jaywalks across the Northside Highway.

2. A bystander crawls out onto a roof to bring a child to safety.

3. To impress friends, a teenager jumps onto the top of a moving train.

4. A driver successfully stops a truck after the brakes fail.

5. A firefighter crawls out onto a roof to bring a child to safety.

6. To gain membership, a gang initiate confronts and taunts a member of a rival gang.

7. A person walks out of a room just before the ceiling collapses.

### B. Claim Formation.

Think of an issue from the crime or environment topic. Write at least one claim at each stasis (existence, definition, value, cause, and action) using the "Words to Watch For" from each section.

# CHAPTER 4

# Supporting Claims: Appealing to Logos, Ethos, and Pathos

The issue, problem, and solution spans described in Chapter 2 are the main segments in a line of argument that an author wants you to follow. As described in Chapter 3, each span is made up of passages that focus on existence, definition, value, cause, and action claims. Each type of claim, or stasis, develops in its own way with its own distinctive language. This chapter discusses how claims of all kinds are supported with reasons and evidence.

A claim by itself can be shaky and weak. Readers can reasonably ask, "How do you know?" or "Why do you think so?" Supporting claims strengthen the point by addressing the questions readers may raise. Support is like the beams and girders under a highway overpass. If there were not enough beams at the point where the highway leaves solid ground, the overpass would be shaky and no one would want to drive on it. The higher the bridge and the more traffic, the more support is needed. Similarly, the more controversial the claim and the wider the audience, the more support is needed.

The forms of support reflect the three ways we learn: from observing the world and reasoning about it (appealing to **logos** or our logical capacity), from listening to other people (**ethos** or our capacity for trust), and from consulting our senses and emotions (**pathos** or our capacity to feel). "Appeals" illustrates a few of the many ways these appeals can be made.

---

### APPEALS

#### Environment

Chivers makes a cause claim that dredging and trawling destroy sea-life habitats. What reasons does he give you for believing his claim? Chivers appeals to logos, or observations of the world, by giving a history of drops in fish populations and by describing the appearance of the sea floor before and after a trawler passes through. He appeals to credibility, or ethos, by citing the observations of people with direct knowledge of the issue: veteran fishermen, marine biologists, state wildlife managers. Finally, he appeals to pathos, emotion and imagination, by describing Captain Taylor's feelings and by comparing the ocean floor to a clear-cut forest.

### Crime

Castleman claims that crime in his neighborhood is more serious than it seems. He supports this value claim with appeals to logos, such as statistics in the weekly newspaper and his experiences with neighbors who hear intruders. He appeals to ethos by citing credible sources for these observations, such as police officers and neighbors that readers can identify with. Finally, he appeals to pathos by describing the fears that these crimes evoke.

Unlike the spans and stases, appeals do not appear in any particular order and do not create delimited sections of the text. Appeals to logos, ethos, and pathos can come separately in one or several sentences each or they can be intertwined in a single sentence. The examples in this chapter will not be pure representations of a single type of appeal, but one appeal will be primary.

In public policy arguments, some varieties of appeals carry more weight than others. For example, your professors probably prefer appeals to logos over appeals to pathos, while the general public responds more to arguments with many pathos appeals. Identifying how an author supports claims is important for judging the quality of the argument: Is there enough support? Does the author rely too much on one kind of support? Is the support appropriate for the audience?

The appeals that support a claim look just like the claims that present the main points of a passage. The difference is the role of these statements in constructing the author's path. Major claims move the discussion further along the author's line of argument, moving to the next stasis or the next span. Supporting claims deepen a point instead of moving forward to a new point. Because claims and support look very similar, telling them apart is important for understanding the author's line of argument, dividing the article into its main spans, and the spans into passages at different stases.

## Appeals to Logos

As the name implies, logos appeals involve logical reasoning, what philosophers call rationality. Logos also involves observations of the world, what philosophers call empirical evidence. There are three main kinds of logos appeals: physical evidence and records; observations, testimony, and statistics; and logic, common sense, and probability.

## Physical Evidence and Records

You are more likely to believe a person claiming to have found a gold mine if she can produce a chunk of gold. In situations where people are arguing face to face, such as in a courtroom, actual physical objects can be produced for people to examine. For example, if a student is accused of stealing a bicycle, the bicycle can be produced in court. In both oral and written arguments, physical evidence can also be represented in graphic form, with photographs or drawings.

A **record** is a symbolic form of physical evidence. A fax machine creates a record by stamping the current date, time, and phone number on each page it sends; a cell phone records the number of every call. Everyone creates and keeps records for day-to-day activities, such as calendar entries, receipts, diaries, bills, ticket stubs, report cards, souvenirs, and paychecks. A student accused of stealing a bicycle who produces a receipt showing he or she bought it has strong support for a claim to innocence.

The **public record** is information that citizens are free to consult, such as accounts of daily events in a newspaper, official reports to a public agency, or logbooks like a police department's record of complaints.

## Observations, Testimony, and Statistics

Many of our beliefs are based on our experiences, on seeing things for ourselves. We observe what is going on around us every day, we try new sports to see what they are like, and we travel to places we want to observe firsthand. In a more formal way, scientists design experiments to observe phenomena more systematically than nature allows. In public policy arguments, authors often describe what they observed as they investigated an issue or how they were personally involved in a problem. Personal experiences are an important source of evidence for Chivers, Kristof, and Shiflett in the environment topic and Brooks, Castleman, and Shapiro in the crime topic.

Most of what we know, though, concerns objects and events that we haven't actually observed. For example, you know about your neighborhood from being there and watching what happens, but you can't see everything. You learn of many events, such as break-ins or deer-sightings, by talking to neighbors or reading the newspaper. Textbooks, news reports, road maps, and Web sites are built up out of records and reports from countless individuals over years of time.

A public record of a person's direct observations is known as **testimony.** In a courtroom setting, testimony is given under oath and recorded verbatim. In public policy arguments, testimony appears in narratives and descriptions attributed to the author or another observer. The content of the testimony is an appeal to logos; the credibility of the observer is a matter of ethos, discussed in the next section.

In general, the more details in the testimony, the more convincing it is; a crime victim who is unable to provide details of an alleged attack is less likely to be believed. The more witnesses, the stronger the support; if ten people identify a suspect, the testimony is stronger than if there is only one witness.

Statistics are a form of observation because they summarize large numbers of individual reports and records. A Webmaster, for example, identifies the most popular Web sites by adding up and comparing their total hits. Simple totals can also be transformed by calculations, such as computing the average score, miles per gallon, or five-year trends in campus crimes.

While testimony and statistics seem convincing, they are surprisingly easy to challenge: Witnesses can disagree; physical evidence can be overlooked or contaminated; documents can be lost, altered or forged; data can be hard to interpret. For controversial claims, authors include even more supporting information about the procedure for collecting and analyzing the evidence. For example, in a murder investigation, the prosecutors have to trace the handling of every piece of physical evidence and the recording of every word of testimony. "Observational Logos" illustrates passages with this type of appeal.

---

# OBSERVATIONAL LOGOS

## *Environment*

### *Direct Observation*

"During one experiment, I sat on the sea floor and watched a scallop dredge rumble by, and then swam into the path where the dredge had just passed to see much of the complexity of the sea floor removed," [Peter Auster] says. (Chivers)

### *Records*

Over the 15 years I was captain, I managed to fish virtually every part of Georges Bank. . . . During all this time I kept written records of each and every tow that I made. I would mark down my position from the beginning of my tow to the point where I turned around or, if it was a straight tow, to the end of the tow. I kept the bearings of each tow and the results of each, along with notes to describe the catch, the bycatch, the bottom characteristics, and the weather and sea state. (Kendall)

### *Statistics*

. . . [T]he presence of protected wildlands played a significant role in the location decisions of 60% of those newcomers [who moved to counties with wilderness areas]. Moreover, 45% of existing residents indicated that the proximity of those wildlands was an important reason for their staying in the area." (Power)

---

## *Crime*

### *Direct Observation*

. . . [T]he other night, a neighbor called to say she'd seen a creepy guy lurking around her front door, and would I please come out and make some noise to send him on his way, if he was not already gone? He was. (Castleman)

*Records*

> I'm a devoted reader of the police column in our monthly neighborhood news-paper, the *Noe Valley Voice*. In a typical month, our 100-block neighborhood expe-riences a few burglaries and car thefts, one or two muggings or sexual assaults, and a half-dozen acts of vandalism. (Castleman)

*Statistics*

> In 1992, the average mugging netted $672 in cash and property (watches, jew-elry, etc.), the average burglary $1,278, according to victims' reports to police. (Castleman)

## Logic, Common Sense, and Probability

Another kind of logos is an appeal to logical reasoning, to what makes sense, to "what any rational adult would believe." Logical appeals grow out of physical or mathematical laws, logical principles, common sense, and probability.

### Physical and Mathematical Laws

Physical laws involve concepts like gravity, velocity, and distance. Mathematical laws involve concepts like prime numbers, geometric shapes, or equations. A lawyer can appeal to physical laws to support a cause claim that a car traveling at a certain speed on a wet road could not have stopped within a certain distance. A civil engineer can appeal to principles from math and physics to estimate how much water could be stored in a reservoir or how much energy would be produced by a hydroelectric dam.

### Logical Principles

Logical principles (or propositions) look like the definition claims described in Chapter 3 because they describe objects, features, and categories. Unlike definition claims that focus on individual cases, however, logical propositions deal with uni-versals. They include combination terms (or Boolean operators), such as AND, OR, NOT, ALL, NONE, and IF . . . THEN, that you have probably seen in computer pro-gramming classes or Internet search engines.

    A logical principle called on in public policy arguments is the law of noncon-tradiction, stating that a fact can be true or false but not both at the same time. For example either a suspect had a gun or he didn't. Another common logical princi-ple in courtroom cases is the law of identity, stating that a person or object cannot be in two places at the same time. An alibi is a claim that a suspect was observed away from the crime scene at the moment the crime occurred. If the alibi is true, then the claim that the suspect committed the crime must be false. Similarly, an environmental advocate might argue that resources that are used up today will not be around in the future.

At first glance, appealing to logical principles seems to be a clincher, the kind of support that every reader must agree with. The drawback of logical propositions is that real-world situations never involve only logic. If problems could be solved with logic, we wouldn't need juries or elections and we wouldn't need to argue about public policy. Most authors, therefore, combine logical reasoning with other kinds of support.

## Common Sense

In most situations, we rely on common sense, intuitions about what is normal or what works best, to decide what claims to believe. A lawyer is appealing to common sense if she argues that a blind client had no motive to steal binoculars. However, common sense is not necessarily true. Nothing prevents a blind person from wanting binoculars. Similarly, it seems absurd at first to claim that setting fires can prevent forest fires, but many forest managers have evidence to support this claim.

## Probability

Appealing to a mathematical probability is similar to an appeal to logical principles. For example, the statistical methods that compute the odds of buying a winning lottery ticket are based on a mathematical formula relating the number of tickets printed, the number of tickets sold, and the number of possible combinations of "lucky numbers." In most public policy arguments, however, appeals to probability are not based on formulas, they are more like appeals to common sense. For example, Castleman relies on probability to predict that an increase in the teen population will increase crime; Chivers predicts that if you have eaten fish in a restaurant, it was caught by dredging or trawling. "Common Sense Logos" illustrates this kind of support.

---

## COMMON SENSE LOGOS

### Environment

It makes no sense to list a species on the Canadian [endangered] list when only the very northernmost part of its range crosses into southern Canada. Sage Thrashers are plentiful in the United States. But, at most, there have only ever been 30 pairs of Sage Thrashers in Canada and today there are between 5 and 10 pairs. The Sage Thrasher is naturally rare in Canada, so why is it included on the "at risk" list? (Jones and Fredericksen)

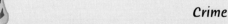

### Crime

[Criminals] don't have much interest in our cars, a 10-year-old Ford and an 8-year-old Plymouth. In fact, my neighbors' cars protect mine, because any thief with half a brain would choose theirs. (Castleman)

> If crime result[s] from social conditions, then governments [are] obliged to intervene to correct them. If it result[s] from individual malfeasance, the logical response [is] simply to punish and deter. (Naylor)

## Certainty and Accuracy

A common but misleading appeal to logos is a claim to absolute certainty. Beware of authors who use phrases like: "no sane person could disagree that . . . ," "you must be nuts if you think that . . . ," or "anyone who had given this a moment's thought would have to agree. . . ." An appeal to certainty often comes in place of evidence for the validity of a claim; instead of providing support, the appeal belittles the intelligence of anyone who disagrees with the author (and thus includes an emotional appeal designed to intimidate anyone who disagrees).

Authors who act as though they have "The Truth" come across as arrogant and closed-minded; they seem convincing only to readers who already agree with them and they repel those with other positions. Ironically, admitting uncertainty can strengthen an author's case, making the argument more accurate, practical, and realistic and appealing to a wider audience. In fact, in academic writing, acknowledging uncertainty is strongly preferred over claiming certainty.

How could it be a good idea to admit doubts and expose the weaknesses of an argument? Aren't authors who make such concessions admitting that they are wrong? Concessions are important because certainty is rare and temporary. Many facts that now seem obvious were once controversial and even violently suppressed. Five hundred years ago, for example, when observations about the nature of the earth and heavens contradicted religious claims based on Biblical texts and authority, scientists could be punished as heretics for claiming that the earth revolves around the sun and denying that the sun rises in the east. Even today, you may feel social pressure not to question claims that others "take for granted," for example, that poor people are lazy or that criminals come from bad homes. In the readings, Meares and Kahan challenge the assumption that black inner-city residents can't protect their own civil rights; Gómez-Pompa and Kaus challenge the assumption that Western agricultural methods are better for the environment than traditional practices in underdeveloped nations.

Facts have a history; they do not exist "out there," waiting to be discovered. They are established or discredited by people using evidentiary procedures of logos, ethos, and pathos. The word "fact" itself is derived from the Latin roots *facere* and *factum,* which mean "to make" or "to do."

Certainty in a fact grows as people keep challenging its validity, testing it in different situations, in different places and times, and using different technologies. A few claims that now seem hotly contested will "stand the test of time" and start being treated as well known, unremarkable, and obvious facts. Just as important, some claims that were once considered certainties will eventually be reexamined and rejected as mistakes. This is why authors who treat all of their claims as completely certain come across as dogmatic or closed-minded.

*"In theory, yes, Mrs. Wilkins. But also in theory, no."*

**Scientists like to admit uncertainty.** © The New Yorker
Collection 1976 Stan Hunt from cartoonbank.com. All Rights Reserved.

Authors who limit the support for their claims upfront should get credit for honesty and accuracy. They are inviting you to assign the claim an appropriate degree of belief and they are arguing that even a limited degree of belief should be enough to persuade you to move forward with the line of argument.

Authors have four ways to signal their degree of certainty in a claim, presented here in order from greatest certainty to least.

## Leaving a Claim Unstated vs. Asserting a Claim
A claim that is obviously true doesn't even need to be stated. Americans don't go around repeating obvious truths, such as "We are living in the United States." So when an author makes that claim explicitly, he is raising the idea that something is happening that does not fit with our knowledge of the United States. Stating a claim as a flat assertion without support signals that the author considers it to be uncontroversial general knowledge.

## Identifying the Source of the Information
An author who tells you how she knows that a claim is true is admitting that the claim is not common knowledge. Even prefacing a claim with "I think" makes it seem more like an opinion than a generally held fact. So when an author appeals to ethos, citing the credibility of the witnesses or authorities, she is raising doubts.

For example, Castleman supports his claim that crime is common in his neighborhood this way: "I know because I'm a devoted reader of the police column in our monthly neighborhood newspaper, the *Noe Valley Voice.*" Chivers supports his claim about the heavy use of dredging and trawling this way: "So extensive is this fishing method that it is equivalent to scouring half of the seabed between beaches and the continental shelves around the world each year, according to Elliott A. Norse, president of the Marine Conservation Biology Institute."

### Limiting the Claim Through Qualifications

The author includes explicit limits on when or how often the claim will be true, such as exceptional circumstances. When Chivers says: "With a few exceptions, if you've eaten a wild oceanic product, it was probably caught by mobile gear," he admits that his claim is limited to seafood caught in the ocean and does not cover all kinds of seafood. When Castleman says: "With the exception of murder (which usually involves family or acquaintances), the vast majority of crimes are opportunistic in nature," he excludes from his claim about opportunism a large set of crimes, both murders and a few other unspecified crimes.

### Using Guess Words

The author uses words that express uncertainty, labeling the claim as a "guess," "speculation," or "possibility." Chivers uses guess words here: "[T]his idea [essentially a form of ocean zoning] has gained considerable support among scientists and habitat protection advocates. . . . It also appears to meet the standards of the latest amendment to federal fishery law. . . ." Castleman supports his claim that it is normal to assume that black men are dangerous by saying, "I doubt there's an honest white liberal who acts differently."

*"A possible eureka."*

**Scientists like to signal uncertainty.** © The New Yorker Collection 1988
James Stevenson from cartoonbank.com. All Rights Reserved.

# Appeals to Ethos

As you listen or read, you are constantly making decisions about whose information to trust and how much to trust it. Partly, you are judging the information based
on its contents, using logos. But a big part of your decision is also based on your
judgment of the person who is providing the information. Is this the kind of person whose claims you are likely to believe? Ethos appeals give you reasons for
believing a claim based on the trustworthiness and experiences of the person who
is making it. Ethos appeals are about speakers and writers.

Authors appeal to ethos when they ask you to accept a claim just because of
who is saying it. For example, your parents have probably asked you many times
to accept their decision "because I said so." Besides parents, other people in our
society who are usually trusted to speak truth are teachers, ministers, the President,
and a few geniuses like Albert Einstein. At one time, a television newscaster, Wal-
ter Cronkite, was considered "the most trusted man in America." When people like
these support a claim, that in itself may make it convincing to many readers, even
if the content is counterintuitive.

## Credentials

The most common way an author appeals to ethos is providing information about
the person whose testimony or judgment is being cited: the person's credentials

"1964, reaching into the cookie jar, your
mother confronts you. You lie. Tell us,
sir, why the jury should believe you now."

**Challenging the credibility of a witness.** *Courtesy of*
www.cartoonsStock.com

(from the Latin word for belief, *credere*). Credentials usually include the person's full name, job title, or experience.

Authors cite the views of many different kinds of people, such as independent experts, eyewitnesses, stakeholders, and themselves. As a reader, you must decide what kind of person is the most credible. In order to judge credibility, consider experience closely.

## Independent Experts

You are probably most willing to believe testimony from an independent expert, someone who is trained to judge situations fairly and accurately and who has a great deal of experience. But how do you know that the person really is an expert? What if authors on opposing sides both appeal to experts? Which one do you believe? The more disagreement about a claim, the more credential information the author should provide about the expert, including job title, place of work, training, awards, and previous positions held.

## Eyewitnesses

In some situations, the most believable person is not an expert but someone you can identify with yourself, someone you expect to react in the same way you would have if you had been there. News reporters and police investigators often seek the observations of eyewitnesses who just happened to be on the scene. To increase the credibility of the eyewitnesses, authors often describe their appearance and give some biographical information; this information makes it easier for you to identify with the witness.

Witnesses can mislead you accidentally if they don't know enough about what they are talking about. A witness may also mislead you intentionally, acting on self-interested motives. For example, a witness endorsing the effectiveness of a hair treatment may secretly be employed by the company that makes the product.

## Stakeholders

The people who know most about a situation are usually the people who are directly involved. For public policy issues, the stakeholders are the officials involved in setting the policies, all the people who the policies affect, and other parties who have a special interest in the issue. For example, if a ban on fishing is proposed, the stakeholders include the hook-and-tackle fishermen, fishermen who use dredging and trawling, towns on the shore that depend on fishing and tourism, restaurants and supermarkets that want fresh fish, environmental activists, and fisheries and wildlife managers. If a neighborhood curfew is proposed, the stakeholders are local teens and their parents, other neighbors, businesses in the area, the police, and local social service agencies.

Stakeholders have personal or professional reasons for taking one side of an issue rather than the other. Having a role or interest does not make what a person says untrue. If you know what each person has at stake and if they provide other kinds of support for their claims, you can decide how much to believe each one. "Credentials" illustrates uses of these appeals.

## CREDENTIALS

### Environment

**Stakeholder**

. . . Captain Peter Taylor leans over the starboard gunnel of his 40-foot hook-and-line vessel, the *Sea Hound,* and grabs a bright orange buoy. . . . [The ocean] has the feel of an empty wilderness, a place punctuated by only by weather and birds. Taylor knows otherwise. (Chivers)

**Scientific Expert**

. . . [T]he journal *Conservation Biology* published papers documenting mobile gear's adverse impacts. At a press conference, Peter Auster, author of one of the papers and science director of the National Undersea Research Center at the University of Connecticut, described watching mobile gear. "During one experiment, I sat on the sea floor. . . ." (Chivers)

### Crime

**Stakeholder**

"I never will forget the words of Janice Hunter, whose 27-year-old daughter, Adrien, was stabbed 47 times by serial killer Nathaniel White in 1992. Mrs. Hunter spoke for every family member when she said, 'It's a heartache that all parents suffer. I have to go to the cemetery to see my daughter. Nathaniel White's mother goes to jail to see him and I don't think it's fair.'" (Pataki)

**Scientific Expert**

. . . [T]wo economists developed a complex economic model demonstrating that neighborhood action is a crucial factor in controlling crime. George Akerlof and Janet Yellin, a husband-and-wife team from the University of California at Berkeley, showed that community action. . . ." (Castleman)

## Personal Impressions

By publishing an argument, an author is inviting you and other readers to engage in a conversation. Your willingness to join in depends on your personal impressions of the author. These impressions are influenced by the author's credentials and experiences, but are probably influenced more by subtle aspects of the writing.

You already know how to judge character by the way people behave. The same qualities come across in writing. Some authors talk down to readers or ignore other people's opinions; they seem arrogant and unapproachable. Some are careful not to exaggerate and to "do their homework" by digging into the evidence; they come across as fair. Some squander their credibility by making careless mistakes or seeming disorganized. Just about every aspect of the writing contributes to an author's ethos.

"Personal Impressions" presents examples of how authors describe themselves and their experiences. On the environment topic, Edward Abbey says explicitly why his local experiences make him qualified to speak about the dam at Glen Canyon. Yet, his use of the term "damnation" instead of "damming" indicates his strong feelings. On the crime topic, Castleman appeals to his own law-breaking experience as a bid for credibility. Although people usually distrust what confessed criminals say, Castleman might earn points from readers for his candor and his ability to identify with young street criminals.

## PERSONAL IMPRESSIONS

### *Environment*

In the summer and fall of 1967 I worked as a seasonal park ranger at the new Glen Canyon National Recreation Area. . . . Having thus seen Glen Canyon both before and after what we may fairly call its damnation, I feel that I am in a position to evaluate the transformation of the region caused by construction of the dam. . . . (Abbey)

### *Crime*

A confession: Your author has a criminal past. I never did anything truly awful, but if I'd been caught and convicted every time, I might be serving a life sentence today under California's three-strikes-and-you're-out law. I don't know what causes Crime with a capital "C." But I know what caused my own crimes—a strange combination of impulse, alienation, and opportunity. (Castleman)

Authors also build credibility by their style of arguing and writing. An author who cites experts and eyewitnesses as allies comes across as responsible, giving credit to those who did the direct observational work. The more credible and well known the allies, the more "glow of association" rubs off on the author. Similarly, citing strong opponents makes an author seem ready to face any challenge.

## Appeals to Pathos

It is impossible to argue without appealing in some way to emotions; we wouldn't act on a problem if we didn't care about it. Pathos appeals concern emotions, sensations, and images. The most familiar form of pathos is sympathy, derived from the Greek words for suffering and togetherness. However, authors appealing to pathos can invoke positive as well as negative emotions.

Authors writing about crime may appeal to outrage over a terrible injustice or to sympathy toward a victim; authors writing about the environment may appeal to worries about the world our children will live in or invoke the feelings of awe aroused by entering a wilderness area.

Appeals to pathos can be more powerful than appeals to logos or ethos because they add bodily reactions to abstract mental ones. The most effective pathos appeals move the reader to identify with a situation so strongly that they feel as if they are there, imagining sights, sounds, smells, textures, and tastes. The main ways to employ pathos are naming emotions, evoking physical sensations, and using visuals.

## Naming Emotions

One way authors appeal to pathos is to talk directly about how to react to a claim, naming the emotions that readers should experience, such as anger, delight, horror, pity, pride, relief, shame, and wonder. Sometimes authors ask rhetorical questions, such as, "How could any patriotic American not feel a swell of pride?" or "How would you feel if this happened to you?" A less direct appeal is for the authors to describe their own feelings or those of people involved in the situation. "Emotion Names" illustrates passages with this form of appeal.

---

### EMOTION NAMES

#### *Environment*

From an esthetic standpoint, some of us do regret the disappearance of dinosaurs. What a thrill it would be if in national parks people could see great lumbering brontosauruses weighing forty or fifty tons grazing across the landscape, or herds of ceratopsian dinosaurs roaming like rhinoceri with three gigantic horns! (Ehrlich and Ehrlich)

#### *Crime*

According to the police, Service Area 109, which includes my house, has had thirty murders since 1992—an average of 3.8 homicides a year, or about one every three months. Additionally, police officers have shot and killed three alleged assailants in this area. These numbers can seem modest or horrifying, depending on what one considers "normal" or expects from a neighborhood like mine. (Myers)

# Evoking Sensations

Apart from naming specific emotions, another way to appeal to pathos is to evoke physical sensations of seeing, hearing, touching, tasting, and smelling.

When you read vivid, detailed descriptions of specific real-world events—descriptions of the people, the colors, smells, and noises in the background, the unfolding of the event over time—you imaginatively experience sensations. Your mental image of the event can seem like a memory of an actual experience. Once you imagine an event happening, you are more willing to believe that it did or could take place. If the description evokes unpleasant or painful sensations, you may attribute all kinds of negative values to the object or event, even if the author doesn't criticize it explicitly.

A subtle way of evoking physical sensations is to use writing techniques that are more commonly thought of as belonging in poetry or literature, such as rhythm and rhyme ("Don't do the crime if you can't do the time"), repetition of word patterns ("We had drive-by killings, run-by killings, sneak-up killings, gun-fights and battles, car chases"), alliteration ("Ahh, the sweet smell of skunk"), metaphor ("What was a complex of sponges, shells, and other organisms was smoothed to a cobblestone street"), and colorful word choice ("Slothful vandals who are unable to haul their thick butts around without the help of an internal-combustion engine"). Language patterns can make you feel emotions, from sad to excited, just as music can. "Evoking Sensations" illustrates passages with this form of appeal.

## EVOKING SENSATIONS

### *Environment*

Imagine diving to the bottom of the ocean at Georges Bank. . . . Now envision, as it churns into these same waters, a hundred-foot-long, steel-hulled trawling vessel powered by a 1,000-horsepower diesel engine the size of a bulldozer. The combined stench of fuel and dried fish is overpowering. (Russell)

### *Crime*

At the scene of another shooting, near Fifteenth and C, a pair of athletic shoes lay by themselves in the middle of the intersection, one upright and the other lying on its side. The laces were still tied. The victim had literally run out of his shoes trying to escape. At another shooting the gunman was on a bicycle—a pedal-by shooting! Our shootings seemed to be developing a pathetic ordinariness, involving bicycles or worn tennis shoes. (Myers)

## Using Graphics

Another common appeal to pathos is the inclusion of photographs, drawings, and other graphic media. Photographs appeal more strongly to emotions than drawings because they convey more realism and specificity. A photograph appeals both to logos and to pathos—logos, because the photograph is physical evidence of an observation; pathos, because the details in a photograph emphasize the uniqueness of the image and heighten its realism.

The visuals in "Photographs" convey the immediacy of a particular event. Both seal photos appeal to our human interest in furry, attractive animals with big eyes, but the photo of the trapped seal evokes feelings of pity for attractive creatures injured for no apparent purpose, while the photo of the happy seal conveys positive feelings of wonder for nature. The photos of the police present two very different perspectives. In one, the officers look menacing. In the other photo, the police officers seem protective.

## PHOTOGRAPHS

### *Environment*

**Photo evoking sympathy.**    *Courtesy of* Ron Sunford/Photo Researchers, Inc.

**Photo evoking enjoyment.** *Courtesy of* Stephen Frink/Corbis.

*Crime*

**Photo evoking fear.** *Courtesy of* AP/Wide World Photos.

**Photo evoking security.**    *Courtesy of* Chuck Savage/Corbis.

## Uses and Misuses of Pathos

Appeals to pathos can be dangerous. At one time or another, you have probably acted impulsively in a way you later regretted. Maybe you said something rash when you were angry or excited. Maybe you believed a rumor or took a dare that you would have rejected if you were calm. Most people want to base important decisions on evidence that will seem reasonable under all conditions, not only when they are in a certain mood.

People who believe emotion is more powerful than reason are suspicious of an author who uses emotional appeals, afraid that he or she is trying to "pump up" a case that can't be supported with logos. There is reason for concern if an author appeals more to pathos than to logos. As a reader, you should pay attention to the types of appeals in an argument and their relative importance.

## Clues to Spotting Appeals

Distinguishing the types of appeals is important for judging how well an author has supported the claims and for imagining ways in which the claims might have been better supported.

When identifying an appeal, base your judgment directly on the words on the page; if you have to draw extended inferences about how a passage might be appealing to pathos or ethos, then your choice of appeal is probably off-base.

Appeals are often intertwined in the same phrases or passages. To choose the primary appeal, ask yourself, "Why should I believe this claim?" If it is mainly because of who is making the claim, the appeal is to ethos. If it is mainly because of how the passage makes you feel, it is a pathos appeal. If it is mainly because of common sense or real-world observation, it is a logos appeal.

## WORDS TO WATCH FOR: APPEALS

*Logos*

| | |
|---|---|
| **Physical Evidence** | Detailed descriptions of objects |
| **Records** | Newspapers, records, logs, journals, entries |
| **Observations** | Detailed descriptions of objects or events; noticed, saw, observed, overlooked |
| **Testimony** | Said, told, described, related, attest, vouch |
| **Statistics** | Data, numbers, percentages, amounts, trends; tables, graphs |
| **Logic** | Logic, illogic, if . . . then, either . . . or, implies, entails, valid, draw a conclusion, axiom, proposition, premise, fallacy, impossible, flawed, inconsistent |
| **Common Sense** | Sensible, reasonable, reliable, prudent, plausible, sane, intuitive, off-base, delusion, unorthodox |
| **Probability** | chance, possibility, odds, likely, long shot, toss up, expect, predict |

*Ethos*

| | |
|---|---|
| **Credentials** | Expert, authority, official; professor, doctor, officer, Senator, manager, researcher; eyewitness, by-stander, on the scene, onlooker; credentials, experience, training |
| **Personal Impressions** | Aspects of writing or references to author's life |

*Pathos*

| | |
|---|---|
| **Naming Emotions** | Love, hate, enjoy, suffer, excite, interest, cherish, anger, outrage, disgust, passion; felt, sympathized, identified with |
| **Evoking Sensations** | saw, looked, viewed; listened, heard, sounds, ring, buzz, noise, silence; touched, felt, rough, smooth, palpable; taste, delicious, savor, bitter, sour; smell, odor, stench, whiff, aroma |
| **Graphics** | Pictures, drawings, colors |

# EXERCISES

## Backtalk: What Do You Say?

What's the point of learning the names of all these types of claims and appeals? If two people are really experts, how could they disagree? Would you feel comfortable admitting uncertainty in a paper? Why?

## Recognize/Evaluate

Read the passages below concerning the crime or environment topic. Identify which appeals are used (logos, pathos, ethos). Identify the subtypes of each appeal (such as naming emotions or invoking sensations for pathos). Then choose one a passage that stands out as particularly unconvincing. In one or two sentences, explain your reasons.

### A. Environment

1. Dr. John Terborgh of Duke University, an expert on tropical conservation, says efforts to save nature in some parts of the world "are just doomed to fail." In his 1999 book, *Requiem for Nature* (Island Press/Shearwater), Dr. Terborgh wrote that nature "cannot long survive" a combination of inadequate nature parks, unstable societies, and faltering institutions that plagues many developing countries. "We have a long way to go before anyone can feel comfortable about the future of nature," he wrote.

2. In other instances, though, nature tends to spring back once the cause of disturbance is removed. Depleted fish populations recover once fishing stops. Forests and grasslands retake abandoned farmland, especially when given a helping hand by restorationists. . . . Rivers tend to cleanse themselves once pollutants are no longer dumped in. That is what keeps conservationists from total despair; if people can be persuaded to stop interfering with natural processes, the situation will eventually correct itself to some degree. (Stevens)

3. It may be hard to get excited about vanished sponges and overturned rocks. But for the fishing industry—like that in New England, which has lost thousands of jobs and hundreds of millions of dollars in recent years and is suffering the resultant social consequences—habitat changes caused by fishing gear are significant. (Safina)

### B. Crime

1. [Marvin] Wolfgang, a liberal who has worked as a consultant to many anti-poverty programs, says: "There is no consistent correlation between poverty and crime. The studies go back 100 years, and they show only a weak correlation at best. Most poor people are law-abiding, and many rich people break the law." (Castleman)

2. As a chaplain, I visit 72 inmates in 12 cellblocks every week as they wait for trial anywhere from a year to three years. The majority of the detainees are

gang members and most are black or Latino. Almost all of them live in poor neighborhoods. This experience has made me more aware that the criminal-justice system works differently for them. My white, middle-class background did not prepare me for the systematic abuses that are routine for certain members of our society. (Brooks)

3. Okay, now imagine taking a gun and pointing it at your loved one and pulling the trigger. You couldn't do it, could you? It wouldn't make any sense. It would be illogical. It would be impossible. And that's why Jeff Henry could not have intended to kill his brother—that's why the killing had to have been an accident and the shotgun in his hands had to have just gone off. There is no other way for it to have happened, and anyone who thinks that he just murdered his brother—the prosecutor in Douglas County, Georgia, for instance—just doesn't know what it's like to be a twin and doesn't know how much Jeff and Greg Henry loved each other, how much they still love each other, how perfect that love is, and how much Jeff Henry believes in it. (Junod)

## Detect

1. In an article of your choice, find a long paragraph that is interesting and persuasive. Analyze its claims and support.

2. What kind of appeals does Castleman use? Which does he rely on most? What kind of appeals does Chivers use? Which does he rely on most?

## Produce

Choose one of the claims below from your topic area.

### A. Environment

- All-terrain vehicles (ATVs) should be banned from state and national parks.
- Logging reduces the risk of serious forest fires.

### B. Crime

- Watching violent video games does not lead to real-life violence.
- Binge drinking of alcohol is a greater danger than drug use on college campuses.

Use key words in the claim to search on the Internet for articles and sites related to this claim. Compose 3–5 statements, each of which supports the claim using a different appeal or a different subtype. Be sure to provide names and background in your statements for anyone you cite. Keep a list of any Web sites from which you quote or paraphrase.

# CHAPTER 5

# Junctions: Responding to Alternative Paths

He who knows only his own side of the case, knows little of that. His reasons may be good, and no one may have been able to refute them. But if he is equally unable to refute the reasons on the opposite side, if he does not so much as know what they are, he has no ground for preferring either opinion. (John Stuart Mill, *On Liberty*)

So far, you have learned how authors set out a line of argument from seeing the issue to defining the problem to choosing a solution (Chapter 2); how they make claims about the existence, nature, cause, and value of the problem; how they make claims about the existence, nature, effects, value, and implementation of solutions (Chapter 3); and how authors support these claims with appeals to logic and observation (logos), authority (ethos), and emotion (pathos) (Chapter 4).

But it is not enough for authors to set out their own line of argument and support it. It is not a conversation if one person does all the talking. To have a say in an ongoing conversation, an author has to respond to earlier turns and think ahead to future responses. In this way, an author's line of argument crosses, joins, and parts from other lines of arguments.

An author expects people to raise objections, to see problems in a different way, and to propose different solutions. Exchanging views in a group produces more and better ideas. But exchanges would take forever if authors had to wait for an opponent's response to be published before writing the next article. Instead, authors search out published arguments, predict what objections the authors would have, and build responses into their line of argument.

In this chapter, you will learn some strategies for considering opponents' arguments, making concessions, and disagreeing.

**No disagreement, no argument.** CALVIN AND HOBBES © 1993 Watterson Dies. By UNIVERSAL PRESS Syndicate. Reprinted with permission. All rights reserved.

# The Purpose of Disagreeing

In academic writing and in the best public arguments, authors treat disagreement as an opportunity for further inquiry rather than as a personal attack. An opponent is not an enemy to be vanquished, but a fellow explorer whose trip into the same terrain led to a very different map.

When an explorer realizes that her map conflicts with those of other explorers, she tries to find out why. She identifies the places where the divergences really matter. She may decide that her own map needs to be adjusted, or she may try to persuade others that their route goes in the wrong direction.

To describe constructive ways of disagreeing, we will refer to people with different views as **opponents.** By opponent, we simply mean someone whose position offers an alternative to the author's. An opponent is different from a rival, a competitor whose victory means another's defeat. An opponent is also different from an enemy or adversary, someone who seeks to injure or overthrow another. Opponents are capable of responding to a convincing argument; they can have good intentions toward each other and form alliances.

For an argument to take place, areas of agreement and dispute are both needed. You can agree with an opponent about the existence of a problem, but disagree about its cause or its severity. You can agree at the problem span, but diverge on the effectiveness or costs of a proposed solution.

The amount of space devoted to alternative paths varies quite a bit. Some authors, such as Shapiro and Robinson, say little about alternative positions, even though they risk seeming uninformed or closed-minded. For other authors, such as Kleck and Easterbrook, the entire purpose of writing is to bring up someone else's line of argument and refute it in whole or in part.

Seeing how an author treats opponents is one of the best ways to judge the quality of the argument. If authors ignore opponents or treat them with contempt, they come across as closed-minded and even untrustworthy.

**Adversaries do not consider others' views seriously.** *Courtesy of* Copley News Service.

# The Main Path and Alternative Paths

Imagine driving on a highway and seeing signs that you are approaching a junction with another road. The road toward the junction is marked by signs, telling you the distance to the exit, some destinations you could reach, and some local attractions or services. The signs make you alert in plenty of time so that you can decide whether to exit or not. The signs give you a glimpse of a different path, a path that might seem attractive. If there is more than one way to get to the same destination, you may even see signs telling you which path to follow.

The spans and stases can be thought of as the **main path** that the author wants you to follow; opposing claims are sidetracks or crossroads that invite you to turn in a different direction, onto a path that, according to the author, might lead you astray.

It is dangerous for an author to ignore sidetracks and crossroads because good readers are active and curious explorers. Active readers notice alternative paths and wonder whether they can get to the same destination along a better route or whether they should go to a different destination altogether. If the author does not give you reasons for rejecting these claims, you might take off in another direction. So like a highway crew, authors label the alternative routes clearly and describe them accurately. They also provide reasons for staying on the main path, just as a friend might say, "You might think that taking I-29 would be just as fast, but the traffic is bad there, so wait and turn at 32nd instead."

# Developing a Disagreement

Developing a fair and effective disagreement takes several steps. An author has to identify the opponents, summarize the alternative path, make concessions, state the rebuttal, and return to the main path. These steps will be illustrated with articles that challenge opponents with varying degrees of effectiveness.

Before reading on, read one of these articles:

- **Environment.** Gregg Easterbrook's critique of environmental advocates in "They Kept the Sky from Falling."
- **Crime.** Gary Kleck's critique of responses to the shootings in Columbine, "There Are No Lessons to be Learned from Littleton."

"Spans and Stases" provides an overview of how to divide these articles into spans (Chapter 2) and the spans into stasis passages (Chapter 3).

---

## SPANS AND STASES

### Environment: Easterbrook

Easterbrook approves of dams that produce energy and protect the environment as much as possible. The issue for him is that environmentalists don't see these dams the same way he does; they protest against the dams and try to stop their construction. At his **issue** span (par. 1–6), Easterbrook appeals to general readers to see one particular dam at James Bay in the same way he does and to feel as surprised as he is that environmentalists disapprove.

The James Bay dam is the **paradigm case** (or **epitome**) of the larger **problem** (par. 7–34). For Easterbrook, environmentalists are addicted to doomsaying, painting all problems as crises with horrifying outcomes. Doomsaying was needed when environmental problems were ignored, but Easterbrook believes that environmentalists no longer need such tactics. He argues that doomsaying is hurting the environmentalist cause.

His solution (par. 35–38) is ecorealism, a willingness to use environmental resources when technology is designed to minimize harms.

### Crime: Kleck

Kleck opens by describing a set of murderous school shootings. For Kleck, the **issue** (par. 1–4) is how the cases have been analyzed in the media, especially theories about why they happened. By offering a very long list of very diverse causes, all lumped together, he wants readers to view them all as somewhat ridiculous. He states his purpose as challenging the idea that lessons can be drawn from cases like Littleton.

In his **problem** section (par. 5–23), Kleck criticizes how opponents treat school shootings at several stases. He challenges the way opponents describe the set of school shootings as a phenomenon, using statistics to argue against the **existence** of a trend. Then he challenges his opponents' analysis of the **causes** of the shootings, describing most of them as unrelated to the actual events. He devotes the most space to challenging the opponents' proposed **actions** for preventing future shootings.

In his own very brief **solution** (par. 24), Kleck names a few factors that he does consider relevant to mass-murders at schools, issues that he says the media should focus on. He also recommends closer analysis of the **causes** of "ordinary" crime.

## Identifying Opponents

Opponents care about the same issue as the author but make claims or take actions that the author disagrees with, such as experts and eyewitnesses whose testimony weakens the author's point. The first step to a fair response is for the author to acknowledge that there are opponents and identify them.

### Naming Opponents

Authors treat opponents fairly by calling them by name or at least by giving the name of an agency, a company, or activist group that opponents belong to. Naming names shows that the author has paid attention to what the opponent said, takes it seriously enough to respond, and is treating the opponent as a real person. When naming opponents, an author usually includes brief phrases about their credentials to establish the opponents' ethos. Just as authors benefit from calling on important, well-trained allies to support their points, so they gain credit for responding to powerful opponents rather than weak ones. "Naming Real Opponents" illustrates how Easterbrook and Kleck name their opponents.

---

### NAMING REAL OPPONENTS

#### Environment: How Easterbrook Names Opponents

Easterbrook's named opponents include the National Audubon Society, Greenpeace, activist Jeremy Rifkin, Al Gore, and novelist and environmentalist activist Wallace Stegner. He also names opponents in the anti-environment camp, Rush Limbaugh, Newt

Gingrich, and Bob Dole. In most cases, he assumes these people are so well known to readers of *Washington Monthly* that he need not give their job titles.

### Crime: How Kleck Names Opponents

Kleck names few specific opponents, apart from Congress and the Mississippi legislature. By naming so few opponents and giving so few specific examples, Kleck risks coming across as too distant and abstract in his argument.

## Inventing a Group

Authors often speak of groups of opponents using a common descriptive term ("singles" or "college students") or making up a new term ("Baby Boomers" or "Generation X"). The act of inventing a group is like making a claim that a category exists and has a specific set of members.

By inventing group names, authors can talk about hypothetical opponents as well as real ones. For example, Castleman might anticipate objections from car alarm manufacturers; Chivers might prepare responses to dredge operators. Responding to hypothetical opponents can be persuasive, but only if the arguments attributed to them are powerful and worth refuting. Creating a weak hypothetical opponent is called "setting up a **strawman**." Knocking down a strawman is not an impressive feat, so refuting a strawman's argument does not help an author come across as fair and open to challenge.

"Inventing Groups" illustrates how Easterbrook and Kleck invent groups.

## INVENTING GROUPS

### Environment: Easterbrook

Easterbrook often describes opponents with the term "environmentalists" or "the green movement." Later, he begins calling them "enviros" and ends up calling them "doomsayers." He invents the term "unviros" for anti-environmentalists, whom he also calls "naysayers." These more casual and colorful terms convey some disrespect for extreme members of both sides. Readers may react by questioning Easterbrook's fairness. But in many cases, Easterbrook quotes specific individuals in these groups to provide evidence that at least some of these opponents really do take the positions he ascribes to the whole group. Finally, he invents a name, "ecorealists," for a group that he would like readers to join.

### Crime: Kleck

Kleck often names opponents with general group terms such as "news media," "analysts," "journalists and other writers of every ideological stripe," "pro-gun people," "pro-control people," and "those who propose preventive measures." He does not quote specific opponents in these groups; instead, he sets up hypothetical arguments. In par. 21, he writes: "One might justify drawing lessons from high-profile tragedies by arguing that . . . ." He uses "One" for an unnamed hypothetical opponent. The hypothetical opponent makes a strong point, however, so Kleck is not setting up a strawman. Heavy use of hypotheticals creates a detached and philosophical tone that is acceptable for the journal *Criminal Justice Ethics*, but would not work well in a popular magazine.

## Summarizing the Alternative Path

After naming opponents, authors summarize the claim that they want to challenge. Whether the summary is brief or lengthy, a fair author states it in a way that the opponent would agree captures the essence of his or her position.

An author who wants to solve a problem, rather than make opponents look bad, has to win over neutral readers and even those who agree with the opponent. Ridiculing or exaggerating an opponent's position might make an author and his allies feel triumphant, but it is ultimately self-defeating; it will not widen the author's base of supporters. Any fair-minded reader will see that the author has succeeded only at the easy task of wrestling a strawman to the ground and has failed to touch the real opponent.

"Summarizing Opponents' Positions" illustrates how Easterbrook and Kleck sum up opposing views.

---

### SUMMARIZING OPPONENTS' POSITIONS

#### Environment: Easterbrook

Yet many environmentalists think that in order to be pro-conservation, they must be anti-production. Orthodoxy has grown so conflicted on the subject of energy production that a few greens have pronounced that, even if an entirely benign energy source is invented, it should be withheld, since people would use that energy to commit the primal sin of altering the ecology. During the period when it briefly seemed "cold fusion" might offer zero-pollution energy from seawater, activist Jeremy Rifkin declared that clean, unlimited energy would be "the worst thing that could happen to our planet.

Easterbrook claims in par. 9 that many environmentalists think they must oppose energy production. For support, he quotes Jeremy Rifkin rejecting a promising form of energy production. Easterbrook uses the phrase "a few greens" to avoid claiming that all environmentalists are as extreme as Rifkin. However Rifkin's position is key to Easterbrook's argument; he is similar to the environmentalists who protested against the hydroelectric dam in James Bay. Is Easterbrook fair? How many environmentalists actually hold that view? To challenge Easterbrook, a reader could find articles by environmentalists who support clean energy production.

### Crime: Kleck

A partial list of the problems that have been blamed for the recent mass killings in schools would include: guns, "assault weapons," large-capacity ammunition magazines, lax regulation of gun shows; . . . excessively large high schools; inadequate monitoring of potentially violent students by schools; lazy, uninvolved Baby Boomer parents and correspondingly inadequate supervision of their children; . . . "Goth" culture among adolescents; and Southern culture.

Kleck argues that policies should not be based on improbable causes for unusual events like mass killings in schools. His very long, but still "partial," list of causes in par. 3 represents the positions of his opponents in the media and elsewhere who believe that such diagnoses are plausible. He does not quote any individuals making these diagnoses, but he seems to describe each individual case fairly. To check on Kleck, a reader would have to look up articles about individual school shootings to see if all of these diagnoses were actually proposed.

As a reader, you deserve some sign that authors you disagree with have paid attention to alternative positions. If you see your position stated fairly, you should credit the author for taking the trouble to understand your viewpoint and treat it seriously. This in turn may inspire you to consider the author's point of view more seriously, even if you remain skeptical.

## Making Concessions

A concession describes a point where an author and an opponent agree. If the opponent has already made an effective argument for a claim that the author agrees with, it makes sense for the author to point it out rather than repeating it. A concession of this kind saves time, space, and energy.

Concessions are important for several other reasons as well. They establish shared ground from which opponents can negotiate. They allow authors to narrow in on the important areas of disagreement. They also appeal to truly undecided readers, who agree with some points on each side of a debate. These readers may be turned off by authors who claim exclusive access to the truth.

Authors may go further and praise opponents, crediting them with good intentions. But beware of authors who praise opponents merely as a show of their fairness and open-mindedness. Praise is insincere and even hypocritical if it is a mere formality.

"Conceding to an Opponent" illustrates Easterbrook's and Meares and Kahan's passages with these moves.

---

## CONCEDING TO AN OPPONENT

### *Environment*: Easterbrook

"Institutional environmentalism is correct about the need to propel society beyond its fixation on fossil fuels."

"Environmentalists are well ahead of the historical curve in sensing that materialist culture has lost its way."

"This portion of [Gore's] *Earth in the Balance* is measured, thoughtful and possessed of enduring significance."

### *Crime*: Meares and Kahan

"Given its historical context . . . , the 1960s conception of rights deserves admiration."

---

## Stating the Rebuttal

For a few authors, the best part of arguing is telling people that they are wrong. But for most people, that is the hardest part. They would rather avoid conflict; they don't want to make anyone feel bad, even people they disagree with.

Seeing argument as exploration can make it easier to disagree. The goal of participants in the best scholarly and public debates is not to be right all the time; it is to find the most accurate, useful, and enlightening views of the world. So if an opponent is heading for a ditch that you tripped over a while back, she won't feel bad if you point it out.

### *Signaling Disagreement*

Authors have to signal their disagreement clearly to make sure readers can distinguish between the main path and the summary of an opponent's alternative path. Some authors are very direct in saying that they disagree with an opponent.

**Pundits are paid to point out flaws in one anothers' arguments.** © Harley Schwadron.

They describe opponents in negative terms, but the summary of the opponent's position is fair. "Signaling Disagreement Fairly" illustrates passages in which authors disagree.

## SIGNALING DISAGREEMENT FAIRLY

### *Environment: Easterbrook*

Yet many environmentalists think that in order to be pro-conservation, they must be anti-production. Orthodoxy has grown so conflicted on the subject of energy production that a few greens have pronounced that, even if an entirely benign energy source is invented, it should be withheld, since people would use that energy to commit the primal sin of altering the ecology . . . . The notion of energy production as antithetical to nature evinces a myopic view of natural history.

In par. 9, Easterbrook uses the connective "yet" to signal disagreement. He also uses parody, using religious terms like "sin" and "orthodoxy" to make environmentalism seem like a self-righteous dogma. In par. 10, he uses the faultfinding adjective "myopic," to signal that this view is defective and shortsighted.

### Crime: Kleck and Castleman

... Rather, my main point is that it is generally a mistake to diagnose the causes of violence and crime, or to identify effective ways to reduce violence and crime, via a focus on unusual, heavily publicized violent events .... (Kleck)
... [A]nyone who calls Noe Valley "safe" is living in a daydream .... Many leftists I know pooh-pooh neighborhood watch programs because they smack of Big Brother, involve cooperation with the police and don't do anything about poverty and racism. (Castleman)

Kleck is very direct in calling the opponents' view a "mistake." Castleman uses fault-finding language, "living in a daydream," and scare quotes around "safe" to dispute the apparent tranquility of his neighborhood. Later, he uses parody terms "pooh-pooh" and "smack" to make the objections seem less serious.

Sometimes authors signal disagreement using language that is so negative that it becomes unfair or pejorative, language that insults the opponent. Using pejorative language for disagreement is just as unfair as an inaccurate or exaggerated summary of an opponent's position. "Using Unfair or Pejorative Language" illustrates these forms of disagreement.

## USING UNFAIR OR PEJORATIVE LANGUAGE

### Environment: Easterbrook

Damophobia reflects the fallacy of Stop-in-Place. (Easterbrook)

In this sentence from par. 14, two terms, "damophobia" and "Stop-in-Place," are Easterbrook's inventions. "Damophobia" implies that environmentalists have irrational fears. Easterbrook describes "Stop-in-Place" as a naive philosophy. The third main term, "fallacy," is a position so logically flawed that no reasonable person could hold it. Easterbrook is leaving himself open to charges that he is being insulting and distorting the opposing position. No environmentalist would consider this a fair description of their philosophy.

### Crime: DiIulio

When it comes to the search for rational, workable crime policies, it's time to admit that the brain-dead law-and-order right is no better than the soft-in-the-head anti-incarceration left. (DiIulio)

John J. DiIulio, Jr., a professor of politics and public affairs at Princeton, wrote this in the online journal *Slate*. The terms "brain-dead" and "soft-in-the head" are equal and opposite insults being applied without qualification. DiIulio may assume that insulting both sides equally makes him seem fair and independent or that it allies him with the broad middle between these extremes. However, this pejorative language could simply turn off readers across the entire political spectrum.

## Challenging the Claim

It is not enough for an author simply to disagree with an opponent. She must specify what is wrong with the opposing position. As a reader, when you are confronted with two conflicting claims, you need reasons for accepting one and rejecting the other. This section will describe how authors challenge an opponent's claim; the next section will describe challenging the support for the claim.

The first step in challenging an opponent's claim is to recognize its stasis, whether it is a claim of existence, definition, value, cause, or action (Chapter 2). Then the author can provide counterclaims at the same stasis. For example, if an opponent claims that a solution will **cause** undesirable side effects, then the author can argue that it does not always produce those effects. Or the author can modify the solution to prevent the side effects. An author can also shift to a different stasis, for example, conceding that undesirable side effects will occur, but arguing (at the stasis of **value**) that they are mild and outweighed by the solution's other benefits. "Challenging the Claim" illustrates passages with such challenges.

## CHALLENGING THE CLAIM

### Environment: Easterbrook

Hydropower requires flooding lands from reservoirs, a practice environmentalists speak of in tones of deep horror, as though it wipes out life. Plants and animals do die when the reservoir water rises, and some wild-river ecology is lost. But what then exists? A lake ecology, brimming with living things . . . . Why such change should dismay humans would be difficult for nature to fathom . . . . Through glacial advances and retreats, nature has made and unmade uncountable rivers, lakes, and dams in what people now call Quebec. Why is it strange for women and men to do the same, especially if they can learn to do it in ways calculated to minimize harm?

Easterbrook is not challenging the causal argument that dams destroy habitat in par. 11–13. He concedes "plants and animals do die." Instead Easterbrook responds at the stasis of value: the destruction is not as bad as it seems. First, a lake ecology is equal in value to a wild-river ecology. Second, changes by humans are equal in harm to those made by natural forces. Easterbrook's use of questions rather than assertions makes this response appealing to general readers.

### Crime: Kleck

After it was found that such transfers were involved in the Littleton case, some analysts proposed restricting sales at gun shows. Gun show sales, however, had nothing at all to do with any of the other high-profile school shootings. The most common modes of acquisition of guns by shooters were theft . . . , while the Springfield shooter was given his guns by his father. Further, even in the Littleton case the three longguns . . . were purchased on the killers' behalf by [an] eighteen-year-old . . . [who was] eligible to purchase the same guns from any gun store. Further, one of the two killers turned eighteen before the shootings and was likewise eligible to buy longguns from any gun store.

In par. 15, Kleck summarizes the opponents' causal claim that regulating sales at gun shows would prevent school killings. Kleck makes two causal counterclaims. First, gun shows were not a causal factor in other cases, so restricting them will not prevent all school shootings. Second, regulations would not have prevented Littleton because the killers obtained the guns legally from a store.

## Challenging the Support

Authors can challenge the way an opponent has supported a claim, rather than the claim itself. If the opponent lacks evidence, it is fair to ask readers to give the claim less credence or reject it. Authors can challenge all three types of support: logos, ethos, and pathos (Chapter 4).

Using logos, an author can challenge observational evidence, questioning whether the data are up-to-date and whether the observations were carefully made. An author can supply good evidence that contradicts the opponent's claim or point out inconsistencies in the opponent's reasoning to show that it is illogical or conflicts with common sense.

Using ethos, an author can bring in experts and witnesses who testify against the opponent's claim. Or an author can challenge the credibility of the opponent's authorities.

Using pathos, an author can challenge the appropriateness of the opponent's emotional appeals or appeal to different emotions. For example, if the opponent appeals to fear, the author can appeal to pride; if the opponent evokes rage, the author can appeal for calmness.

Authors can also challenge the certainty level of an opponent's claims. If an opponent claims that some principle is always true, an author can supply counterexamples; if an opponent admits exceptions to the rule, an author can ask whether the exceptional cases are more representative than the other cases. "Challenging the Support" illustrates these strategies.

# CHALLENGING THE SUPPORT

### *Environment: Easterbrook*

. . . Enviro lobbyists understood about compliance cushions. They simply declined to mention this factor in congressional testimony and media interviews, sensing a chance to create a jolt of bad news. "The advocacy campaign against the provision was illogical unless the motive was to take a positive development and make it seem depressing," says [EPA Administrator William] Reilly, himself once an environmental lobbyist as head of the World Wildlife Fund.

In par. 29, Easterbrook challenges the logic of environmentalists in opposing new standards for car emissions in 1990. After conceding that the standards appeared lax, he argues that they would still lead to cleaner cars, so it would be logical for environmentalists to support them. But they didn't. Easterbrook then accuses environmentalists of omitting evidence that undermined their position. He supports this charge through ethos, by enlisting William Reilly as an ally. If readers doubt that Easterbrook's interpretation of the events is fair, they may be impressed that it is shared by Reilly, who was directly involved in the case and who has environmentalist credentials.

In response, environmentalists could challenge Easterbrook's version of this incident. Maybe they believed the new standard would not lower emissions at all or not enough to matter. Or they might concede a mistake in this case but deny that such mistakes occur in all their public positions.

### *Crime: Kleck*

Those who propose preventative measures . . . can plausibly assert that the irrelevance of their proposals to these incidents does not matter because the proposals are meritorious with respect to more common sorts of violence. If that is the case, however, honest advocates should . . . not coast dishonestly on the emotional momentum created by extraordinary violent events that their policies could not prevent. It would, however, be naive to expect those playing hardball politics to follow the intellectually honest path since they will be loathe to forego exploiting the emotional power that comes from tying their recommendations to the most horrific and frightening crimes.

In par. 20, Kleck challenges the character (ethos) of his opponents; he accuses them of dishonesty in claiming that their solution would have prevented a high-profile shooting case, when they are really hoping to prevent everyday violence. Kleck also criticizes them for appealing to emotion (pathos) about Littleton in order to prevent cases that the public would not care about as much.

Is Kleck's accusation of dishonesty fair? Dishonesty is such a harsh accusation that he should have strong evidence that it happened. But Kleck only describes general groups of opponents and hypothetical positions that they might take. Kleck's opponents could reasonably challenge him to cite specific cases of dishonesty and to show that dishonesty is typical of proposals concerning school shootings.

## Returning to the Main Path

After a lengthy challenge to an opponent, an author often restates his or her point on the main path, so that readers can tell that the detour is finished and remember where the author is heading. "Reinstating the Main Path Claim" illustrates passages with these moves.

### REINSTATING THE MAIN PATH CLAIM

#### Environment: Easterbrook

Current ecological law is hardly perfect, but by any reasoned judgment it is far stronger than in the seventies.

After conceding in par. 21 that environmental laws are still not perfect, Easterbrook restates his view that they are strong enough that the environmentalists' dire assessments are not warranted.

#### Crime: Kleck

While some of these facts were mentioned occasionally in news stories . . . , many writers nevertheless offered explanations for the non-existent "trend" in youth/school/gun violence.

Consequently, regulation of gun shows was totally irrelevant to preventing any of these massacres.

Kleck often finishes his refutation with a restatement of his main path point, as in these examples from par. 6 and par. 16.

## Clues to Spotting Disagreements

This chapter has identified five parts of a disagreement passage: identifying opponents, summarizing an alternative position, making concessions, stating the rebuttal, and returning to the main path. You can recognize the parts by looking for some key terms.

# WORDS TO WATCH FOR: DISAGREEMENT

### Identifying Opponents

Names and credentials of opponents.

### Summarizing Alternative Positions

Direct quotes or paraphrases from opponents framed with verbs of attribution (see next section).

### Making Concessions

| | |
|---|---|
| **Agreement Terms** | To my opponent's credit, he/she does admit, he/she does acknowledge, we agree, we share |
| **Truth Terms** | Granted, of course, it is true that, my opponent is right that, my opponent has a point |

### Stating the Rebuttal

| | |
|---|---|
| **Contrastives** | On the other hand, but, even though, yet, despite, though, nevertheless, however, contrary to, in contrast, while, although, unfortunately |
| **Doubt Terms** | It may appear, at first glance, allegedly, supposedly |
| **Disapproval** | We reject this notion, this is wrong, I disagree, not so |
| **Faultfinding Terms** | Wrongheaded, naive, risky, short-sighted, insufficient |

### Returning to the Main Path

| | |
|---|---|
| **Conclusion** | In short, consequently, this brings us back to, finally, therefore, as a result |
| **Replacement** | Instead, rather than, not simply, after due consideration, a careful look shows |
| **Asserting Truth** | Actually, really, ultimately, in fact, in reality, after all |

## Verbs of Attribution

An important signal of an author's degree of agreement with other authors is the use of verbs of attribution. These are the verbs that come immediately before a quote or paraphrase of another author's claim.

English has a large number of these verbs, including:

| | |
|---|---|
| accepts | hypothesizes |
| accounts | illustrates |
| adds | implies |
| addresses | indicates |
| admits | insinuates |
| affirms | insists |
| agrees | introduces |
| alleges | is silent on |
| argues | mentions |
| asks | points out |
| asserts | promotes |
| assumes | proposes |
| categorizes | questions |
| challenges | realizes |
| cites | refutes |
| claims | retorts |
| concedes | reveals |
| confesses | says |
| confirms | sees |
| decides | states |
| defines | suggests |
| denies | thinks |
| disagrees | uses |
| discovers | verifies |
| emphasizes | wants |
| exclaims | whines |
| explains | |

The simplest, most popular, and least informative verbs of attribution are "says" and "states." These convey only that language was used. But the other verbs provide clues to the beliefs of the author and of the source being quoted. Compare the versions in Table 5.1 of an outlandish claim that differ only in the verb.

## TABLE 5.1  How Verbs of Attribution Convey Attitudes and Beliefs

| Summary Sentence with Varied Verbs | Beliefs Conveyed by Verbs |
|---|---|
| Thomas said/stated that the earth is flat. | Thomas expressed a claim. |
| Thomas thought/believed that the earth is flat. | Thomas took the claim as true. |
| Thomas assumed/asserted/contended that the earth is flat. | Thomas took the claim as true but offered no reasons. |
| Thomas claimed/argued/reasoned that the earth is flat. | Thomas took the claim as true and provided reasons. |
| Thomas concluded/proved/showed that the earth is flat. | Thomas took the claim as true after some investigation. |
| Thomas agreed/admitted/realized that the earth is flat. | Thomas took the claim as true and so does the author. |
| Thomas denied/won't admit that the earth is flat. | Thomas took the claim as false but the author takes it as true. |

**Some opponents know all about your objections.**
© Dan Piraro.

Each group of verbs says something about what Thomas thinks and about how he came to his view. But some of these verbs also signal whether Thomas and the author believe the same thing. When authors cite allies, they use verbs that signal belief on both sides, such as "discovers," "agrees," "realizes," "understands." But when they want to signal disagreement with an opponent, they will use verbs such as "asserts," "insists," "contends," or "alleges."

Verbs of attribution convey attitudes of many shades. Paying close attention to what they mean and how they are used will give you important clues about the author's position.

---

# EXERCISES

## Backtalk: What Do You Say?

Some research suggests that men and women differ in how they express disagreement and how they respond to rebuttals. Do you agree? Why or why not? What do you find difficult about expressing disagreement? How do you feel when someone disagrees with you on an important point? How do you respond? How much are you willing to argue back?

## Recognize/Evaluate

### A. Environment
Following is a passage from a book by nature writer and activist Edward Abbey and three responses written by students who disagree with Abbey. Which one is fairest and most accurate in summarizing Abbey's position? Which one gives the best rebuttal? Give your reasons.

> Edward Abbey: From *Beyond the Wall* What about the "human impact" of the motorized use of [boats] of the Glen Canyon [reservoir]? We can visualize the floor of the reservoir gradually accumulating not only silt, mud, waterlogged trees and drowned cattle but also the usual debris that is left behind when the urban industrial style of recreation is carried into the open country. There is also the problem of human wastes. The waters of the wild river were good to drink but no one in his right senses would drink from Lake Powell. Eventually, as is already sometimes the case at Lake Mead, the stagnant waters will become too foul even for swimming. The trouble is that while some boats have what are called "self-contained" heads, the majority do not; most sewage is disposed of simply by pumping it into the water. It will take a while, but long before it becomes a solid mass of mud Lake Powell will enjoy a passing fame as the biggest sewage lagoon in the American Southwest. Most tourists will never be able to afford a boat trip on this reservoir, but everybody within 50 miles will be able to smell it.
>
> All the foregoing would be nothing but a futile exercise in nostalgia (so much water over the dam) if I had nothing constructive and concrete to offer. But I do. As alternate methods of power generation are developed, such as solar, and as the nation establishes a way of life adapted to actual resources and basic needs, so that

the demand for electrical power begins to diminish, we can shut down the Glen Canyon power plant, open the diversion tunnels, and drain the reservoir.

*Abbey, Edward. "The Damnation of a Canyon."* Beyond the Wall.
*Henry Holt and Company, 1984.*

*Student Responses to Abbey*

1. Abbey, an extreme environmentalist and author of "Damnation of a Canyon," describes how a lake created by a dam built on the Colorado River is killing wildlife in the area with fluctuating water levels and too many tourists. He proposes shutting down the dam and eventually destroying it. Abbey does not stop to think about the wealth that the dam provides the nearby town. It provides a power source and extra revenue because of its tourists. The nearby town will not have any source of power if the dam were to be removed. Abbey does not seem to understand this and proposes they wait for a new energy source to come along. This proposal is an extreme case of an extreme environmentalist thinking that his way of coming up with solutions is the best and refusing to listen to any other suggestions. (Keri)

2. As expected, some environmentalists out there defend the truth of their claims to the death. Edward Abbey might be one such person. In his article, "Damnation of a Canyon," Abbey rants and raves about the horrors of a dam that was built in his favorite canyon. This dam created Lake Powell. Abbey focuses almost exclusively on how the dam will cause a pile-up of mud and silt and on all of the negative effects that will come from human contact with nature in Glen Canyon. Eventually he believes, "the stagnant waters will become too foul for swimming . . . . Most tourists will never be able to afford a boat trip on this reservoir, but everyone within fifty miles will be able to smell it." Obviously, Abbey has some very strong conviction about what he thinks of Lake Powell. But the claims that he makes in his article are too extremist. They cannot be taken seriously. It appears as though Abbey has thrown his entire sense of reason out the window, and now all he can do is make emotional, nostalgic, outlandish claims. This is exactly the type of extremism that I encourage Americans to beware. There are certainly many good things about building a dam in Glen Canyon, including recreational benefits and power. But Abbey fails to inform the readers of these benefits or to acknowledge that there is any truth to them. Abbey is exactly the type of environmentalist that cannot be trusted. He wants so desperately to save his canyon that he resorts to unprofessional techniques to get his way. (Emily)

3. Edward Abbey feels that human enjoyment of nature is impaired when too much human influence is present. In his work "The Damnation of a Canyon," he describes the degradation of Glen Canyon as a result of the construction of a dam. He states that because of the varying water levels, plant life cannot sustain itself where it once could. This affects animal populations because animal life cannot be maintained where there is no plant

life. Wildlife before the dam flourished with songbirds, beavers, and sandpipers. Now the shores are silent. In this respect, Easterbrook's and Abbey's beliefs contrast with one another. While Easterbrook feels that environmental changes caused by the dam are different but not bad, Abbey believes the area is now more like a cemetery. [Instead of] a compromise, Abbey just wants the removal of the dam. Abbey wants to have his boyhood memory a reality again and so is willing to compromise the needs of others in the process. He does not take into consideration the necessity for the dam. It is probably used to supply energy to numerous houses and families. Like Easterbrook, I doubt many would be willing to give up electricity for the removal of a dam, and so, I believe Abbey's solution is unrealistic. He does not discuss the effects removing the dam would have on basic human comforts. His only concern is restoring Glen Canyon back like when he thought it was beautiful. (Steph)

## B. Crime

Following are seven responses to Castleman's article written by readers of *Mother Jones*. Which one is the fairest and most accurate in summarizing Castleman's position? Which one gives the best rebuttal? Give your reasons.

1. Anyone seeking evidence of the collapse of liberalism need look no further than Michael Castleman's essay ("Opportunity Knocks," May/June). Castleman, along with a large proportion of "liberals," have barricaded themselves into their comfortable homes with their Macintoshes and televisions only to come out warily in search of a decaf latté at Starbucks. Castleman premises the essay with a self-congratulatory note about his refusal to join the exodus of families from cities into the suburbs. His neighborhood, writes Castleman, is an urban oasis in which a diverse group of people live in harmony. What follows, though, is an ode to a suburban mindset in which everyone is seen as a potential thief, and the only reason to interact with neighbors is to form a group which agrees to keep its eyes peeled for outsiders. Even these neighborhood watch meetings are not truly safe, as Castleman suspects his fellow crime warriors to be criminals themselves. I would much rather live in the suburbs than have some paranoid guy hitch up his pants and try to get "neighborly" with me or my family in order to form an alliance against people who don't (nudge, nudge) "belong."

   The article was clearly written for a white, middle-class audience and assumes a shared paranoia about crime, specifically at the hands of nonwhite, non-middle-class people. Castleman writes that he avoids young black men because he believes that they are more likely to attack him. He is unapologetic about his blatant stereotypical and racist attitude towards African-Americans, instead complimenting himself for the logic of his actions.

   It is clear that crime is on the minds of most Americans, but the fears of an upper-middle-class white guy do not belong on the pages of *Mother Jones*. (Edward Smock)

2. On the face of it, one might want to be neighbors with Castleman. He's straightforward, speaks his mind, believes in and acts for neighborly sociableness, and speaks honestly about the effects of violence in his life and upon his family. These are serious things and command respect. As a householder in Noe Valley, he is all for watchful neighborliness with bona fide members of what he calls the "astonishingly diverse" neighborhood. And in general, he seems to prefer to engage people directly rather than calling for outside help on matters that pertain to the block. Only when he begins to speculate about crime's causes does the not-in-my-parking-space indignation begin to leak.

Noe Valley is an on-the-hill neighborhood where, Castleman notes, houses sell for half a million dollars. Its serious problems are not street crime, but the declining budgets, shortened hours, and withdrawal of white students from the wonderful local middle school; the lack of safe, funded activities and places in the community where actual young people can gather; and the real estate and banking practices which drive up the price of housing.

If Castleman is serious about organizing against crime, what about putting support into the school and other youth services? What about addressing the real estate practices and bank funding policies that make home ownership so exclusive? How about building alliances with community groups and activists to acknowledge the much larger common community interests? And how about taking a good hard look at your attitudes?

You can't have a real neighborhood party based on fear. Nor one where the host checks the silver and the window latches after you leave. This article is not about hardening the target, but hardening the heart. (Allan Creighton)

## Detect

In an article of your choice, find a long passage in which the author disagrees with an opponent. Identify whether the passage uses all of these techniques: identifying the opponent, summarizing the opponent's position fairly, making concessions, signaling disagreement, refuting the opponent's claims or support, and restating the main line of argument. How fair and accurate is this passage? Give reasons.

## Produce

From an article of your choice, select a passage that you disagree with. Write a fair and accurate paragraph of response to this passage, using as many of these techniques as possible: identifying the opponent, summarizing the opponent's position fairly, making concessions, signaling disagreement, refuting the opponent's claims or support, stating your main position.

# CHAPTER 6

# Style: Appealing Through Language

You learned, in Chapter 4, how authors support their claims to make them more persuasive to readers. In Chapter 5, you learned how authors use concession and refutation to address people who disagree with specific claims. In this chapter, you will learn to detect and evaluate stylistic choices that reflect the author's stance toward you and other readers. Looking at an author's style (including tone, voice, word choice, sentence structure, and elaborations) is a good way to find techniques that you can try in your own writing. But even more important, you need to be aware of the effects of style in order to understand and evaluate the argument fairly.

You may be used to thinking of style as a sentence-level quality that is judged in the final draft of a paper, just as you might edit for grammar and spelling. But for the Greeks and Romans who formulated many rhetorical strategies, style was just as important to the construction of the overall argument as the stases or appeals. Even today, experienced writers start planning the style of an argument as soon as they decide to write.

Stylistic choices affect far more than the clarity or elegance of individual sentences. These choices reflect the entire interaction an author establishes with a reader. Authors adopt a style to attract certain kinds of readers and to put off others. An author can use style to come across as an authority, a coach, a smart aleck, or a buddy. As a reader, you respond to these cues almost instinctively. You are probably bored by authors who seem distant, formal, and superior. You probably like writers who seem like people you know and feel repelled by those who seem hostile to people with your views.

In this chapter, you will learn to distinguish the styles of popular opinion from journalism and academic writing. You will also learn to evaluate styles that are quite provocative. Finally, you will analyze how stylistic elements can blend into a personal persuasive style that is appropriate for college writing.

*"Mr. Kellwood is looking for someone to assist him in recasting his journals into a form suitable for a wider audience. The tone should be urbane, warm, and scholarly—somewhat in the manner of Lewis Thomas, but, of course, about plywood."*

**Style is important, no matter what the topic.** © The New Yorker Collection

# Identifying Public Policy Styles

The style of an argument is created by aspects of language that cannot be neatly separated from the claims and support. The author's choice of a style for a text influences many other choices: patterning of sentences; use of "I," "we," "one," or "you"; use of headings and lists; use of slang and humor; selection of evidence; treatment of allies and opponents; themes in the introduction and conclusion; and even the title.

Three styles are discussed in this section: popular opinion, journalistic, and academic. For each one, you will consider the same elements: the author's occasion for writing, verb choices, use of outside sources, voice, degree of certainty, and connectives.

Of these characteristics, the least familiar is the occasion for writing, which is very different from what you may be used to. Writers of public policy arguments do not write in response to a teacher's assignment or on a schedule dictated by a school term. Instead, they choose a topic because of a triggering event, something that has just happened or will happen within a few days. A triggering event can be anything that moves a writer to respond, such as the enactment of a new law or policy, the publication of a government report, the opening of a new prison, the changing of a wildlife designation, an important speech by a stakeholder, coverage of a courtroom trial, or the occurrence of a serious crime or natural disaster.

## Popular Opinion Styles

Many of the readings in this book are opinion articles published in popular magazines or journals. Sometimes these articles are written by community members who are moved to write by some recent news event, by something that has happened to them, or by activism in a social, political, or religious group.

However, most public opinion articles in magazines and journals are written by **pundits.** Pundits are people whose opinions are sought, sometimes because of their background knowledge of an issue and sometimes because their styles attract readers and viewers. Some pundits are employed by a journal, some are freelance writers who are paid if an article is published, and some write on a periodic basis (one or more times a week) and distribute their articles to a syndicated network of newspapers.

A popular opinion style has these main characteristics:

| | |
|---|---|
| **Occasion** | The author writes because of a recent triggering event or out of personal motives. |
| **Verbs** | Verbs are mainly present tense. |
| **Sources** | Sources are varied, including direct quotes, references to research studies, and personal testimony. |
| **Voice** | Personal. Frequent use of "I" or "we." Readers are often addressed as "you." Tone may be casual, including use of slang. |
| **Certainty** | Authors vary widely in how strongly they signal their certainty in their claims. |
| **Connectives** | Authors vary widely in the use of transitional sentences and phrases. |

"Popular Opinion Styles" illustrates different versions of this style.

---

## POPULAR OPINION STYLES

### *Environment*

- When flying over the southwest recently, I was genuinely dismayed at all of the vehicle tracks marring the landscape. These tracks don't disappear nearly as quickly as aircraft engine noise or contrails. But I guess the powers that be don't care what I see from my airplane. (Burnside)

- Last year Washington voters considered a ballot initiative that would have banned gill-netting for salmon—a destructive and undiscriminating means of fishing. In my naïveté as a newcomer to the region (I had lived there less than a year at the time), I assumed that if salmon were endangered, catching fewer of them would be helpful, so I voted for the initiative. But many environmental groups stood shoulder to shoulder with commercial fishermen in criticizing the initiative, arguing that it would divert attention and political pressure from the "real problem"—the dams. The initiative lost. Such odd alliances and "intensify the contradictions" thinking have only become more likely because of the Administration's new plan. (Fallows)

### Crime

- ... Victimization statistics clearly show that risk declines steadily with age, as we become older and, often in spite of ourselves, wiser. But ironically, while the risk of becoming a victim plummets with age, fear of crime rises. I'm more anxious about street safety now than I was 20 years ago, even though I haven't had a problem in two decades. (Castleman)
- ... Rather, my main point is that it is generally a mistake to diagnose the causes of violence and crime, or to identify effective ways to reduce violence and crime, via a focus on unusual, heavily publicized violent events. (Kleck)

A wide array of authors use the popular opinion style. It is flexible and reflects the multiple stylistic choices available to an author. It allows the author great leeway in choosing how to allocate space among the spans and develop claims within the spans.

## Journalistic Styles

When you look for sources on an issue, you are likely to come across a large number of newspaper or magazine articles that look a lot like arguments. They will very likely lay out issues, problems, and solutions. There will be claims about definition, cause, and value, and evidence in the form of quotes from experts, statistics, observation, and emotion. But even so, most authors who use a journalistic style are not trying to take a turn in the conversation. Their goal is to provide information, not to present an individual point of view. Their articles are not contributions of the kind you are expected to analyze, respond to, and write.

As a source of information on a problem, journalistic articles will be very helpful to you. But you need to tell them apart from original arguments when your goal is to find other authors engaged in arguing about your issue.

A journalistic style is similar to that of the emcee described in Chapter 1. A journalist reports on a debate that other people are involved in, interviewing the stakeholders and presenting their views in their own words. Of course journalists always have opinions that shape the stories they write. But a journalist's job is to be accurate and fair in making observations, not to get personally involved.

A journalistic style has these main characteristics:

**Occasion**    Triggered by a news story that has just happened or will happen within a few days.

| | |
|---|---|
| **Verbs** | Verbs are mainly present tense. Storytelling verbs are common, with adverbs of sequence such as "now," "then," "next," "once," "before." |
| **Sources** | Many direct quotes from stakeholders, experts, and officials. Quotes are introduced with neutral verbs of attribution, such as "says" or "said." Views from different sides are often presented. Author's personal experiences are rarely described. |
| **Voice** | Impersonal. Very little use of "I" or "we" to refer to the author (though these often show up in direct quotes from sources). Direct address of the reader ("you") is rare. |
| **Certainty** | Claims are often stated with a high degree of certainty and few qualifiers of the kind discussed in Chapter 4. |
| **Connectives** | Rarely used so that articles can be shortened easily for use in other news sources. |

**The journalistic style is very different from an academic style.** © 1996 *The Baltimore Sun.* Used by permission.

As you explore an issue, keep track of news stories on issues related to those raised in the readings. These will be valuable sources for evaluating whether the authors are accurate and up-to-date. They will also help you challenge authors, develop your own positions, and apply them to real-world situations.

The journalistic or emcee style might seem attractive as a style for your own writing. But unless you are aiming at a career in journalism, you should strive to become a more engaged author, one who formulates an original position and contributes directly to the conversation on an issue.

"Journalistic Styles" provides examples of such styles.

## JOURNALISTIC STYLES

### Environment: A Meeting on Snowmobiles

It's a high-energy scene in the interior department's John Muir Room on the second Wednesday in June . . . . Most energetic of all is the event's host Derrick Crandall, the 50-year-old president of the American Recreation Coalition (ARC) . . . .

If democratic standards ruled, Silver [president of Wild Wilderness] would win and Crandall would lose. There would be more hiking trails, tent campsites and meadows for bird-watching; fewer recreational vehicle parks and snowmobile trails. For every activity except boating (slightly more people motorboat than canoe, kayak and row), substantially more Americans enjoy the outdoors without benefit of any internal-combustion engine except the one that got them to the lake or trailhead. This is according to a poll ARC's lobbying arm commissioned last year, so the industry group can't very well challenge the results. But market standards favor the internal-combustion recreators. The ATV driver, the recreational-vehicle camper, the motor boater and the snowmobiler require more expensive facilities . . . . "You may well see theme parks, malls and other 'amenities' on our public lands, all planned and built to wring more dollars out of you," says Lehman Holder, of the Sierra Club's southwestern Washington state chapter. (Margolis)

### Crime: Los Angeles Gangs Policy

Los Angeles Mayor James K. Hahn and Police Chief William J. Bratton were in Washington, D.C., this week to lobby for more federal assistance to fight gangs after the city finished 2002 with the most homicides in the nation . . . .

Father Greg Boyle, a Jesuit priest who has worked with gang members on Los Angeles' Eastside for nearly 20 years, say[s] police should differentiate between hard-core members and young men on a gang's periphery . . . . Gang-banging, Boyle said, falls along a continuum, "from writing on the wall, to shooting people up, to getting in their faces." Simply belonging to a gang, Boyle said, is no crime. Hahn rejects that argument. "I have a real hard time with folks who somehow try to say that just because folks are in a gang you shouldn't assume they are involved with crime. Hello? They are in a gang," Hahn said. "They are part of a group dedicated to breaking the law." (Garvey and Winton)

## Academic Styles

Compared to the style of public opinion essays, an academic style might not even seem like a style because it is much less personal and colorful. But compared to journalistic styles, an academic style is more engaged, original, and persuasive.

The hallmark of an academic style is a commitment to free inquiry and fairness. A commitment to inquiry means remaining open-minded and a bit skeptical, even toward allies. Fairness does not mean neutrality; it means trying to find and weigh the best available evidence. Academic writers have strong beliefs but they remain willing to change their minds if new or better evidence becomes available. An academic style is also known for using specialized language that conveys much more meaning to academics than to the general public.

An academic style has these main characteristics:

| | |
|---|---|
| **Occasion** | No triggering event is needed. The author joins an ongoing conversation on an issue. |
| **Verbs** | Different tenses can be used in different parts of the argument. |
| **Sources** | Most references are to other authors and few are to stakeholders; many to formal observations and few to personal experiences. Many paraphrases and few long direct quotes. Frequent use of verbs of attribution (Chapter 5), such as "denies," "confirms," "speculates," or "concludes." |
| **Voice** | Use of a personal style with "I" or "we" is appropriate in many disciplines, but an impersonal style is usual. Direct address ("you") is rarely used. Tone is formal with complex sentences and specialized vocabulary. |
| **Certainty** | Few claims are stated with a high degree of certainty. Qualifiers are frequent: "to some extent," "possibly," "approximately." |
| **Connectives** | There is frequent use of reasoning terms: "therefore," "as a result," "so," "consequently," "in contrast," "for example," "rather." |

"Academic Styles" provides examples of this style.

**An academic style can seem confusing to the public.** CALVIN AND HOBBES © 1993 Watterson

## ACADEMIC STYLES

### Environment

In many estuaries, commercial fishermen are already reporting decreases in catch because of the physical disturbance caused by personal watercraft, while other users report a serious reduction in aesthetic values such as "peace and quiet." This problem is not limited to coastal environments but threatens inland waterways as well. At issue is the freedom of personal watercraft users to take over aquatic environments where their open access subtracts ecological, aesthetic, and commercial benefits long sought by others. (Burger, 1998) Regulation of their use is in its infancy. Ultimately it may be the fatalities they cause, rather than aesthetic or economic impacts on the commons, that leads to further regulation and exclusion. (Burger and Gochfeld)

### Crime

Punishment [from the juvenile justice system] may satisfy the public need for retribution. It may also have negative side effects. For example, punishment often undermines self-restraint (e.g., Lepper 1983), stigmatizes lawbreakers and creates problems of adjustment that encourage further delinquency (Link 1987), weakens conventional community bonds by affecting job prospects and family relations (Sampson and Laub 1993), and damages conventional peer and adult relations (Zhang and Messner 1994). Ironically, punishment may also encourage lawbreakers to focus on themselves rather than their victims. Lawbreakers learn to take the punishment without taking responsibility for the offense. (Wright 1991)

An academic style highlights the reasoning behind the line of argument more than the other styles. You can detect this focus in the verbs of attribution and the qualifiers, as well as in the connective terms that link claims together. In some disciplines, the line of argument is also signaled by headings, subheadings, bulleted lists, and tables and figures.

# Dealing with Provocative Styles: Hectorers, Preachers, and Smart-Alecks

When you come across an article written in a provocative style, using false or exaggerated claims, excessive appeals to pathos, and perhaps even sarcasm or putdowns, your impulse might be to duck out. Conflict can be disturbing, so you might avoid authors who write passionately against your position.

If you do read such a text, you might be tempted to skim it with a skeptical eye, dismissing the argument without looking very closely at the claims. Provocative authors may seem like the demagogues or dogmatists described in Chapter 1, not like explorers. They seem to be writing to vent their feelings, to charge up their supporters, or to mislead unwary readers. These kinds of writing are farthest away from the academic style that colleges and universities want students to use. Why take seriously an author who resorts to such tactics?

These impulses are understandable but not very productive. Provocative arguments are everywhere: in magazines, on television and radio, and on the Web. They are easy to find because the people who feel strongest are the most likely to write. They contain the boldest version of beliefs and attitudes that many people might share in more moderate form. For these reasons, provocative arguments cannot be ignored. If you are unwilling to consider any provocative arguments, you will not learn enough about the concerns of opponents, even ones who are close to your position.

Therefore you should not simply dismiss a provocative opponent as a demagogue or as a dogmatist. In fact, most provocative texts that you find published in magazines or journals are not written by demagogues or dogmatists. Anyone who engages in a worthwhile argument will provoke dissent. Legitimate conflict or opposition occurs whenever an author takes on an important issue or addresses an audience with something at stake.

Even more important than learning to deal with provocative opponents is the skill of detecting provocative arguments that you agree with. This is an even harder skill because you may enjoy the style and find the arguments reasonable. To evaluate an argument fairly, however, you have to learn to read it from the perspective of an opponent.

By looking at a range of provocative styles, you will learn to distinguish authors who are being provocative, seeking to elicit a response from readers and other authors, and those who are being confrontational, seeking to intimidate or silence opposition.

To explore provocative styles, read one of the following arguments. Each one appeals to a very specific audience with a style that outsiders may find provocative.

- **Environment.** Journalist Dave Shiflett's "Parks and Wreck: Against Jet Skiers, Snowmobilers, and Other Louts."

- **Crime.** Chaplain George Brooks's argument against gang laws in "Let's Not Gang Up on Our Kids."

## Provocative Insiders

Some authors who seem provocative to you are trying to research a particular audience whose beliefs and attitudes they understand quite well. Remarks that you see as careless or unfeeling, such as sarcasm and put-downs, seem harmless or humorous to insiders and the authors seem justifiably strong-minded.

Three common provocative roles are the smart-aleck, the preacher, and the hectorer.

- **Smart-Aleck.** This approach appeals to a group's core values through exaggeration and sarcasm. To insiders, author comes across as a peer with the good of the group at heart. To outsiders or members of groups with opposing values, author seems irresponsible.

- **Preacher.** This approach appeals to ethical and moral values that are presented either as universal or as core values of a specific group. Author comes across either as a benevolent guide or as an angry reformer. Author seems provocative to those who follow different ethical philosophies or to those from different cultural and religious traditions.

- **Hectorer.** Author comes across as superior, as having all the answers, as appealing to rational values. Claims are stated in absolute form, as simply true or false, with few concessions or rebuttals. Opponents are treated as ignorant, irrational, or hypocritical. Provocative to those who have rational grounds for disagreeing, based on logic or observational evidence. Provocative in situations where appeals to ethos and pathos have great importance.

"Provocative Roles" illustrates the smart-aleck and preacher styles.

## PROVOCATIVE ROLES

### Environment: Dave Shiflett—A Smart-Aleck

Shiflett establishes himself as an insider in the group of conservative Republicans by *ridiculing* "bad guy" Bill Clinton for giving pardons and for having an extramarital affair. He appeals to the *good of the group* by finding one action of Clinton's that Republicans should reconsider, his opposition to snowmobiles (par. 2). He appeals to *core values*, defining true right-wingers as opposed to rude pests who don't respect Mother Nature (par. 3, par. 9). He comes across as a *peer* by using personal testimony (par. 10–13), casual language ("there is only one legitimate dog in this fight," "yeah, yeah"), exaggeration ("many of us would not approve of killing jet skiers, at least without a prior legal proceeding"), and sarcasm ("At this point, let me abandon the neutral, fair-minded tone that has marred this essay thus far").

### Crime: George Brooks—A Preacher

Brooks, who actually is a chaplain, establishes himself as an insider for the readers of *U.S. Catholic* by referring to "our Christian responsibility" to help the powerless, and by calling attention to his "white, middle-class background." His appeals for support include quotes from U.S. Catholic bishops. Brooks appeals to ethical and moral core values by saying that antigang laws "offend and outrage" him, by referring to them as "morally reprehensible" and "oppressive," and by appealing to fairness, asking middle-class readers to imagine how they would feel if the laws applied to their own children. He comes across as a *benevolent guide* by using "we" to describe things that readers should understand or do, that he already understands himself; giving personal testimony from his work as a chaplain (par. 7, par. 11, par. 18–19); and using parallel sentence structures commonly found in sermons: "We need to confine fewer young people and do more freeing of spirits and souls. We need to commit fewer people to institutions and commit to all people."

The following illustrates the hectorer style.

---

### Politics: Two Hectorers

Do not be confused by all the talk about right-wing extremists. To liberals, anybody who's not a liberal is a right-wing extremist. There is no mainstream conservatism as far as they're concerned. And it's not just those of us who host talk-radio programs and talk-TV programs who are seen as right-wing extremists. It's all who listen or watch such programs. (Rush Limbaugh)

    For many decades corporate polluters have been relentlessly using our air, water and soil as their private, toxic sewers. Their despoiling, poisoning and ruining the natural and inhabited land of our country has made large swaths of America uninhabitable due to deeply toxic territory. Year after year, lobbyists with campaign cash, oppose or undermine the laws, regulations and enforcement to reduce the sources of cancer, respiratory ailments, genetic damage and other diseases and property damage on innocent Americans. (Ralph Nader)

---

Creating one of these provocative styles involves choosing the riskiest options for all the rhetorical strategies. For example, rather than enlisting experts as allies (to appeal to ethos), a provocative author will choose someone the group idolizes. The author will also try to associate the opponents with people or events that the group considers contemptible. In discussing opponents' positions, a provocative author will invent unattractive group names, make few concessions, and use many faultfinding terms. The author may also use overly colorful verbs of attribution, such as "insinuates," or "insists." The more risky choices that are made, the less reasonable the author will seem, even to insiders. Chapter 14 discusses ways to experiment with a provocative style in your own writing.

## Putting a Provocative Style in Perspective

Style is just one aspect of an argument. It does not outweigh all other aspects combined. So in order to learn from an opponent, you must not allow the provocative elements to distract you from the basic line of argument. The argument itself may have points that you can recognize as legitimate even if you don't agree. This section describes three strategies for detaching from the effects of a provocative style in order to focus on the author's line of argument.

### Isolate the Provocative Parts

One strategy for putting style into perspective is to separate out the most provocative sections or claims. Some authors use preachy language in the issue span and the closing paragraph but nowhere else. Sometimes a value passage is phrased more provocatively than anything else. Once you have identified provocative parts, you can decide whether they outweigh the more reasonable ones in the overall argument.

## Practice Dissociation

A second strategy is to dissociate a provocative claim from its negative references. In other words, try to relate the provocative claim to something positive from your own knowledge or experience. When an author cites as an ally a person whom you dislike, try to think of a person you do respect who might say something similar.

## Read Charitably

A third strategy is to practice the virtue of charity as you read. When you read an exaggerated claim, imagine that the author said it in a passing fit of anger. Write a paraphrase of the claim in terms that you think the author might have used after he was calmer. Often a claim can be made much less provocative just by introducing terms that signal uncertainty (like those in Chapter 4). Paraphrasing provocative passages in more neutral language makes it easier to identify the stases of the claims, such as definition, value, and cause. Once you recognize the stasis of the main claim, it is easier to decide whether the supporting claims and appeals are appropriate.

"Dissociation and Charity" illustrates how to use these strategies to deal with provocative claims. Each original passage is followed by a dissociating response and a charitable paraphrase.

---

## DISSOCIATION AND CHARITY

### Environment: Shiflett

**Claim**

At this point, let me abandon the neutral, fair-minded tone that has marred this essay thus far. The fact is, if you love the majesty of nature, and recognize that it speaks to us in the most profound of all languages—silence—then you have to see these people for what they are: slothful vandals who are unable to haul their thick butts around without the help of an internal-combustion engine. One can no more enjoy a walk in the forest with one of them around than one can enjoy an opera while sitting beside a barking dog.

**Dissociation**

When my family was at the lake last year, some guys in a jet ski scared away some deer before my brother could take a picture.

**Charity**

Shiflett defines true conservatives as lovers of nature, who can only revere it in silence. Conservatives should lower their assessment of snowmobile and jet-ski users because they ruin the natural experience for no good reason, just out of rudeness and laziness.

### Crime: Brooks

**Claim**

Keith is an example of why we need to build fewer prisons and rebuild more lives. We need to confine fewer young people and do more freeing of spirits and souls. We need to commit fewer people to institutions and commit to all people.

It will only be when each member of our faith community takes responsibility to live the gospel that our society will refocus its priorities for the dignity and respect of each person.

### Dissociation

On TV, the mother of a drive-by shooting victim said she would pray for the killer.

My roommate worked at an adult literacy program in her service-learning course last year. Some of the clients were on probation.

### Charity

Brooks urges Christians to become personally involved in changing the lives of gang members. Based on his experiences as a chaplain, Brooks argues that caring interactions are better than building prisons and arresting gang members. Taking on this responsibility will help Christians improve society as a whole.

These strategies will not make you like the author or the author's position any better, but they will help you describe the author's points in the fairest possible way. And they will help you find claims that have some validity, claims that could become points for negotiation or persuasion.

When you are reading arguments from your allies, you must not allow your basic agreement to blind you to elements of the argument that outsiders will find provocative. If anything, finding exaggerations in the claims of your allies is even harder than being charitable to your opponents. Finally, it is important to remember that you can analyze these provocative styles without taking them as models for your own writing. While you should not avoid making provocative claims, you should not come across as overly preachy, smart-alecky, or hectoring.

*"It's a brilliant piece of writing, Ted, but we feel that it might prove offensive to those who've been convicted of violent crimes."*
**Sometimes writers are asked to be less provocative.**

# Combining Styles in College Writing

When you analyze papers from student authors, whether from your classmates or those reprinted here, you will see that the style most appropriate for college writing combines elements of the popular and academic styles.

The elements of inquiry and fairness from the academic style are always appropriate. The personal elements of the popular style are usually appropriate when you are writing about public issues. A style closer to the formal academic style is usually more appropriate for in-depth research using the methods of your discipline. "College Student Styles" provides examples of this style.

## COLLEGE STUDENT STYLES

### Environment

Although degradation of state and national parks and degradation of the ocean floor are different issues, they have quite a bit in common. Both deal with overuse, indifference, or unawareness towards the problem and a value claim—right of access vs. responsibility to conserve. Chivers sees several possible solutions. The first is no-fishing zones, areas where use is simply not allowed. Applied to the wilderness, there would be areas that are off-limits to people altogether. This is necessary to some extent in order to preserve a shred of truly wild earth, and to guarantee wildlife refuges completely isolated from human interference. However, as one who loves to be in nature, it is hard for me to support extensive use of an off-limits conservation solution. After all, a large amount of my sentiment concerning conservation comes from my selfish desire to enjoy it as it is. (Katie)

### Crime

Some scholars speculate that alcohol has a forbidden fruit effect, meaning that young adults drink more simply because they are forbidden to do so. Professor Ruth Clifford Engs of Indiana University argues that allowing young adults to drink in public environments such as restaurants and bars would allow adults to model responsible drinking practices and take away the forbidden fruit appeal of alcohol. While these arguments may sound appealing, especially to college students, I am not convinced. As a college student under the age of twenty-one, I try to imagine what would happen if the drinking age were lowered. Will all of these students rush out to bars to have a few beers and drink responsibly? Will the fraternity parties (infamous for their abundant supply of free alcohol) end? Or possibly start encouraging responsible drinking? No, I would have to say that these suggestions sound crazy to me. Increasing the availability of alcohol will not decrease drinking among young adults. (Lisa)

# EXERCISES

## Backtalk: What Do You Say?

Which of the authors you have read have a style that you admire? That you find boring? That you find provocative? What characteristics of the style do you think are responsible for this effect on you?

How would you describe your own writing style in terms of occasion, verbs, sources, voice, and so on? How easy would it be to learn to write in a different style? Give reasons.

## Recognize/Evaluate

### A. Environment

1. For each claim below, decide if the author is using a public opinion, journalistic, or academic style. Decide whether the opinion passages are provocative. If so, is the author acting as a preacher, hectorer, or smart-aleck? Give reasons.

2. Read the corresponding summary of each claim. Is it a charitable reading? Is it fair and accurate? Give reasons.

*Claims*

a. Foolish, outrageous claims against the necessity or even usefulness of animal-based research are common in "animal-rights" literature. These claims are as irresponsible as they are silly, because they can lead the unwary with a natural, compassionate concern for animals to contribute money to causes that actually work against the contributor's best interests. Although I believe various political leaders probably know better and lie deliberately, they are not the most culpable in my mind. Rather, I place the blame squarely on the backs of some medical professionals who speak for the animal-rights movement. They "fudge" data by misrepresenting the words of scientists and distorting the nature of scientific discovery. (Morrison)

b. Today, in my eightieth year and the Sierra Club's hundredth, I find myself once again thinking about the Sierra Nevada, the Sierra Club, and what they have done for and to each other . . . . I suspect that Muir, were he alive to consider the Club's centennial, would want to know what happened to the vigor he brought to the founding of the Club. I made this point publicly not long ago when I reprimanded the Club's leaders for too often compromising on important issues. If the Club had stood firm in 1941, there would not now be a highway to Copper Creek in Kings Canyon National Park, a park the Club worked hard to establish in the 1930s. Because the Club temporized on the routing of an "improved" Tioga Road, massive vandalism perpetrated by the National Park Service in the early 1950s now scars the polished-granite apron around Lake Tenaya in Yosemite National Park. (Brower)

*Summaries*

a. **Morrison:** Morrison basically goes on a rant against everyone, animal-rights supporters, politicians, doctors. He accuses them of lying and trying to bilk money out of the gullible public who will give anything to help some cute helpless critter.

b. **Brower:** Brower accuses the current leaders of the Sierra Club of abandoning the ideals of their founder, John Muir. According to Brower, Muir would have considered any developments in national parks unacceptable. Brower cites two cases in which roads were built in Kings Canyon and Yosemite National Parks as a result of the Sierra Club weakening its opposition. Brower considers these roads harmful and ugly.

## B. Crime

1. For each claim below, decide if the author is using a public opinion, journalistic, or academic style. Decide whether the opinion passages are provocative. If so, is the author acting as a preacher, hectorer, or smart-aleck? Give reasons.

2. Read the corresponding summary of each claim. Is it a charitable reading? Is it fair and accurate? Give reasons.

*Claims*

a. Prop 21 is a typically Californian effort to address the crisis in education. The present system is insufficiently rigorous in the overall mission of insuring that errant youth will mature into hardened criminals. As matters stand, a young person who spray-paints a bus or a building will not necessarily face the proper sanction of being tossed into state prison as a felon, raped by older inmates, denied all possibility of education and self-improvement, and then, after a number of years, turned loose as a traumatized ex-con with no skills and a skull full of terrible anger. Now, that's no way to bring up a boy! (Cockburn)

b. No one should support the unfettered, indiscriminate use of face recognition, or any other technology, for general face matching surveillance on commercial streets or in residential neighborhoods. This type of ubiquitous and arbitrary surveillance submits ordinary citizens to an unprecedented real-time continuous stream of digital lineups—without any probable cause and without a compelling security threat. Such technological tyranny can create a siege mentality, violate our right to privacy and could impinge on our ability to travel freely. (Colatosi)

*Summaries*

a. **Cockburn:** Cockburn believes that the effect of passing Proposition 21 would be to throw more young people in prison even for minor acts of vandalism. Being in prison would traumatize and criminalize these boys instead of allowing them to improve themselves through education. Cockburn thinks California often proposes solutions that make a situation worse instead of better.

b. **Colatosi:** Colatosi thinks Big Brother is watching. He is against using cameras to spy on the public and follow where everyone is going on the streets, in houses, stores, airports, anywhere.

# Detect

In a reading of your choice, decide on the predominant style (public opinion, journalistic, academic). Identify passages that would seriously provoke readers with alternative positions. Give reasons.

# Produce

1. Find a provocative or confrontational passage in a reading from an author whose views you oppose. Write a charitable paraphrase of the passage. Revise the paraphrase until you are sure that the author would agree that it captures the gist of the passage.

2. Choose a short passage from one of the readings that has a distinctive style. Compose a similar passage for another issue of your choice that imitates the style in this passage. For example, the first paragraph below was taken from Brooks and the second paragraph is a student's imitation of it.

- **Original Passage:** We must understand that young people join gangs for the family they don't have. They join for acceptance and security. They join because they don't have an education or job skills—gangs are how they can survive. Society can urge abrogating gang members' constitutional rights and demand they need family values, but isn't our Christian responsibility to help these kids? Our responsibility when good parents and a good family do not exist is to provide early and continuing intervention in young people's lives.

- **Student Imitation:** We must come to understand that young people don't vote or even register to vote out of doubt. They don't vote because they think their votes won't matter. They don't vote because they believe that they don't know enough about politics to make a good decision. Society can condemn young people as cynical or lazy, but isn't it the nation's responsibility to raise responsible voters? Patriotic Americans are responsible for making sure that our future leaders are fully aware that their votes do count and that they have a voice in our government. Our responsibility when facing cynicism or passivity is to inspire students to stay informed and get involved.

# Part I Readings

## Environment Readings

## Crime Readings

C. J. CHIVERS

# Scraping Bottom

1    Forty-six miles south by southeast from Cape Cod's characteristic elbow, on greenish-brown waves so soupy that the late-morning sun penetrates only a few yards down, Captain Peter Taylor leans over the starboard gunnel of his 40-foot hook-and-line vessel, the *Sea Hound,* and grabs a bright orange buoy. Working a foot pedal, he coaxes to life a winch and begins hauling in a rope angling from the buoy to the sea floor 200 feet below. The air is heavy with the odors of salt and diesel. Beneath his boat, a string of hooks is ascending.

2    From Taylor's vantage, the ocean seems utterly impenetrable. Washed by the swift tides that sweep through the Great South Channel, often cloaked by fog or whipped frothy by storms, it has the feel of an empty wilderness, a place punctuated only by weather and birds.

3    Taylor knows otherwise. Beneath the fine white lines that define the security of the *Sea Hound's* hull, the Atlantic conceals a remarkably rich and diverse habitat. These waters are famed, as the cape's name implies, for their cod. Once they were famous as well for door-sized halibut, and they still yield catches of hake, haddock, flounder, pollock, and lobster. On a smaller scale, the sea floor is a patchwork of rock, mud and gravel, which provides shelter and feeding stations for a variety of life. Worms, sponges, hard and soft corals, molluscs, amphipods, and other crustaceans, sea anemones, and plants live in the cool darkness below, caressed by currents and interacting in a poorly understood web. This ecosystem also provides the network of three-dimensional structures that allow immature commercial fish—such as juvenile cod—to avoid predation and, ultimately, to form thick adult schools.

4    This unseen ocean floor, so removed from everyday American life, has become the setting of a growing habitat fight. For years, Captain Taylor and his hook-fishing peers on Cape Cod have griped that New England's offshore habitat is declining. Now, sustainable fishery advocates are echoing the hook fishermen's complaints that aggressive methods of modern fishing, known as trawling and dredging, rearrange the seabed, uprooting plants, destroying protective structures, crushing animals, and even removing terrain features. The ocean floor, to borrow the words of some scientists, is being clear-cut.

5    Captain Taylor still has places to fish. But many of the old spots are gone. His voice rises as he plumbs his memories and tries to explain what he has seen. "There were underwater bumps out here that stuck up a few fathoms off the bottom," he says. "Now you can't find them. This was not sand. This was rock. And they just plowed it all away."

*Wildlife Conservation* 103 (Feb 2000): 44–51.
C. J. Chivers is a staff writer at the *New York Times*.

6      Imagine an enormous plastic net, roughly the shape of a Santa Claus cap turned on its side. The opening is about 200 feet across. The lower edge of the opening, touching the sea floor, is a steel hawser, adorned with chains and rubber rollers. The upper edge is lined with floats, which lift the mouth vertically. Far to either side are angular steel boards, called otter doors, which are connected by cable to a fishing vessel above. As the doors are tugged along by the vessel's engine, they force the net open laterally and hold it tight to the bottom. The rig sweeps along at four knots like an exaggerated butterfly net, chains tickling the sea floor and doors kicking up silt. This is an otter trawl.

7      Now imagine a thick steel frame, roughly the shape of a very large boat trailer with its wheels removed. The frame is 15 feet wide. Its lowest point, akin to an axle and riding just above the bottom is called a cutting bar. Behind the cutting bar, a series of chains radiate in arcs, ending in a large metal bag made of interconnected rings. The frame is attached to a fishing vessel, and, as the vessel moves forward, the bag and chains drag heavily on the bottom, scouring along at about five knots. This is a mollosc dredge. Usually these dredges are deployed in pairs—one to port, one to starboard.

8      In terms of raw fishing power, these devices, known as mobile fishing gear, are a huge leap from the stationary nets and traps set by many vessels, and a further leap still from the hand-set hooks and jigs. But from a fisherman's point of view, passing a net or dredge over the seabed does have weaknesses—or at least it used to. The equipment is expensive. And until recently, mobile-gear fishermen who strayed over boulders, wrecks, or corals risked snagging their gear and perhaps losing their investment. Because of these drawbacks, many habitats had long been off-limits to these fishing styles—not as a matter of law, but as a matter of practicality.

9      During the late 1970s and '80s, however, through innovation and study, skippers augmented their nets with heavy rollers called rock-hoppers or big brushes called street sweepers. Dredgers in turn attached more and sturdier chains. The new equipment allowed fishermen to penetrate areas where once they dared not tow, opening almost all of the sea floor to mobile gear. Today otter trawls and dredges are used internationally, harvesting all manner of sea life. With a few exceptions, if you've eaten a wild oceanic product, it was probably caught by mobile gear. "This is the most predominant form of fishing in the world," says Carl Safina, director of the Audubon Society's Living Oceans Program. "More than half the world's catch comes from bottom trawling."

10      In New England, trawlers pursue flounder, butterfish, squid, herring, whiting, skates, and small sharks, as well as cod and its valuable cousins. In the North Pacific, super-trawlers from Russia, Japan, and the United States catch Pacific cod, sablefish, yellowfin sole, perch, and walleye pollock. In the Gulf of Mexico, the nets chase shrimp and snapper. Europeans deploy trawlers to harvest groundfish and herring and pay African nations for access to waters near that continent's coasts. Australian crews catch orange roughy from seamounts near their home, or they did, until orange roughy stocks collapsed (see "A Tale of Two Fishes," *Wildlife Conservation* March/April 1998).

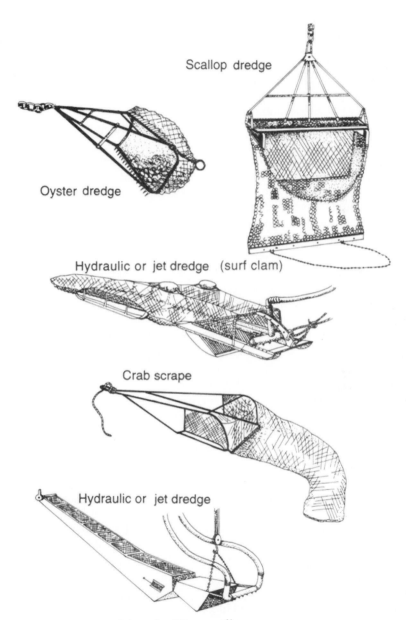

Scallop dredge

Oyster dredge

Hydraulic or jet dredge (surf clam)

Crab scrape

Hydraulic or jet dredge

**Examples of dredges used for scientific sampling.**
*These illustrations are not those originally published with this article.* Courtesy of The American Fisheries Society.

11    So extensive is this fishing method that it is equivalent to scouring half of the seabed between beaches and the continental shelves around the world each year, according to Elliott A. Norse, president of the Marine Conservation Biology Institute. Put another way, these waters equal an area twice the size of the contiguous United States. Norse's estimates factor in that the most productive waters are scoured repeatedly. On average, for example, every available inch of Georges Bank off Cape Cod, is towed over three or four times each year.

12    At various times, conservationists and some fishery managers have warned that such aggressive harvesting styles could be having adverse impacts on habitat and fish populations. But throughout the 1970s and '80s, when traditional fishermen complained that mobile fishermen were expanding their operations, the issue received little public attention. "This has been the most underappreciated of problems," Safina says. "It's the quintessential out-of-sight, out-of-mind issue."

13    Public attitudes shifted in the 1990s, when fish stocks began to crash and fishery troubles became leading media stories. As bad news and new catch regulations rippled from port to port, scientists expanded studies of the offshore floor, taking advantage of areas of the ocean that had been temporary closed to preserve remnant fish populations. These "no fishing zones," free for the moment of dredges and trawlers, provided a control for comparison. Using side-scan sonars, cameras, submersibles, and dive gear, scientists set to work. "People suddenly realized that the issue was of the magnitude that it could have an impact," says Jeremy Collie, a professor at the University of Rhode Island Graduate School of Oceanography. Collie had previously studied the ocean floor, but the fish collapses gave the work new urgency.

14    By 1998, results began reaching fishermen. That summer, the Conservation Law Foundation published a book of scientific papers and coastal anecdotes about habitat loss and damage. The studies noted that mobile fishing gear tended to "smooth out structures on the bottom" and "remove bottom fauna that contribute to sea floor complexity." They were also peppered with warnings. "If we want sustainable fisheries, we should realize that we are constrained by the ecology of the area, not by our ingenuity in catching fish," wrote Richard Langton of the Maine Department of Marine Resources. "We are effective at developing harvesting technology, but now we must begin to understand habitat relationships with the same ingenuity that we have used in the past to catch fish."

15    Later that year, the journal *Conservation Biology* published papers documenting mobile gear's adverse impacts. At a press conference, Peter Auster, author of one of the papers and science director of the National Undersea Research Center at the University of Connecticut, described watching mobile gear. "During one experiment, I sat on the sea floor and watched a scallop dredge rumble by, and then swam into the path where the dredge had just passed to see much of the complexity of the sea floor removed," he says. "What was a complex of sponges, shells, and other organisms was smoothed to a cobblestone street."

16    The press conference signaled the beginning of an organized campaign to curtail trawling. Currently, a number of movements are afoot. A federal lawsuit filed in 1996 by Captain Taylor and his peers in the Cape Cod Commercial Hook Fish-

erman's Association, seeks to have regulations governing groundfish harvests in New England declared unlawful, because they fail to account for harvesting's impact on habitat. "The New England Management Council didn't take protecting the marine environment into account," says David Farrell Jr., the association's lawyer. "They never even considered it, and they still haven't." The association hopes a judge will force the fishery council to set aside a portion of each year's catch for comparatively benign harvesting methods, such as hook fishing.

17    Another proposal would compel fishery managers to identify areas of special concern and declare them off-limits to mobile fishing gear. Essentially a form of ocean zoning, this idea has gained considerable support among scientists and habitat protection advocates, including Jeremy Collie. It also appears to meet the standards of the latest amendment to federal fishery law, which requires managers to identify essential fish habitat and take steps to protect it. "This is an option that is somewhat inevitable," Collie says.

18    Some fisherman, including William Amaru, a small boat trawler out of Chatham, Massachusetts, also propose gear limitations, such as reducing the size and weight of the rock-hopper rollers. Amaru says he trawls almost exclusively over soft bottom, which scientists say is less vulnerable to damage. He admits he is not completely comfortable with the habitat advocates' positions, and thinks they sway public opinion with language—such as clear-cutting—rather than logic. But he thinks trawlers should self-regulate. "If we are not willing to take these steps ourselves, someone else might make us."

19    The most ambitious proposals come from the nonprofit American Oceans Campaign and Marine Conservation Biology Institute, which are lobbying for large undersea sanctuaries—marine protected areas—in which mobile gear would not be allowed. "We don't want to stop people from fishing, but we need some areas that are protected to maintain habitat and other marine life," Auster says. "On land we have parks and wildlife refuges to protect areas from clear-cutting and other activities. We don't do this in the ocean."

20    Out on the Great South Channel, greater shearwaters and Wilson's petrels gather. An hour earlier, Taylor's crewman, Roscoe Chase, had set the *Sea Hound*'s hooks. Now, with Taylor at the winch, the catch rides up from the darkness: codfish, cold and plump, four- to ten-pounders with an occasional jumbo mixed in.

21    With a sweep of his right arm, Taylor gaffs the fish and sends them thumping onto the deck. The pair moves swiftly, silently, with no wasted motion. Chase lifts each brown-and-white fish by its jaw, passes a knife under the gills, pulls out the guts, and tosses the still thrashing carcasses into a rinse basin at his hip. The basin gradually turns ruby red. The shearwaters and petrels patter excitedly across the water, grabbing scraps of guts and bait.

22    Taylor is a traditional fisherman and thinks the low-tech fishing styles of yesteryear have the least impact on the bottom, and thus are the most sustainable. "It is my sincere belief that we are never going to have a good fishery recovery until the hard bottom is left alone by the mobile gear," he says.

23    But, after years of fighting, he is willing to compromise. He says he would support catch limits, ocean zoning, or perhaps gear limitations that would still

allow mobile gear to fish over soft bottom. The talk, he says, has gone on long enough. "Federal fishery people have just let this problem build and build. It makes me sick. We've been pushing this forever. At what point do these people stop talking and start doing what needs to be done.

GREGG EASTERBROOK

## They Stopped the Sky from Falling

1 . . . Hundreds of feet underground, I looked up into the shaft, wide enough for a subway train, blasted and grooved from a shield of rock millions of years old, that would join the waters of a reservoir above to power turbines below. Shining upward, a strong flashlight beam diffused into a seemingly infinite blackness. Around a corner behind me sat the nearly completed turbine intake, an arrangement of descending curvilinear shapes similar in appearance to a conch. Thousands of hours of computer simulation had gone into the design of the angles in the receiver. Once the frigid waters poised above were released by the two-foot-thick steel doors that restrained them, they would tumble through generators making about as much power as one of the units at Three Mile Island. . . . When we emerged into the daylight above it was ten o'clock on a fine sunny morning, and minus-28 degrees Fahrenheit.

2        The LaGrande Two station is part of the vast James Bay hydropower project under construction in subarctic Quebec. The James Bay project, which has hewn dozens of dams into a region rich with glacial rivers, already generates about as much power as five Three Mile Island stations. . . . If all the region's hydraulic gradients are tapped, the output of about 25 Three Mile Islands would be realized.

3        Like other hydropower enterprises, the project burns no fossil fuel and emits no greenhouse gases, smog, or toxic or solid wastes. . . . The LaGrande portion of the James Bay complex is among the first hydropower projects to have environmental protection as a formal design criterion ranked with output and cost. LaGrande Two is the first major hydroplant whose power-house— where the generators are—lies entirely underground. This means the station is a phantom on the landscape, little more than a small ridgeline with two tall red doors that appear portals into solid rock.

4        Other environmental precautions were taken. Before each sequence of blasting to form the waterfall shafts, engineers pumped high-pressure bubbles into the surrounding waters to frighten away fish. Transformers in the powerhouse use mineral oil insulation rather than poisonous polychlorinated biphenyls; the transformers sit on sloped gravel basins as a built-in containment device against

*Washington Monthly* 27.5 (May 1995): 34–42.

spills. Though many subarctic rivers have been diverted to fill the project's reservoirs, plans to tamper with one large river, the Nastapoca, were abandoned when it was suggested a species of freshwater seal that feeds at the mouth of the Nastapoca might be harmed by a reduction in water volume.

5       Caribou were expected to be devastated by reservoir flooding at James Bay. Instead, since the project began, local caribou populations have increased from about 200,000 to about 800,000. No one knows exactly why. Perhaps the roads built for construction access favor caribou migration; perhaps the population growth would have happened regardless. Transmission lines from the project across the Saint Lawrence River are among the world's first underwater power cables, so no towers spoil vistas of the Saint Lawrence. When the underwater lines were completed, piers that held towers for temporary lines were removed so as to pose no obstacle to migratory cod. In sum, it is difficult to conceptualize a large power project having less impact on the ecology.

6       What do environmentalists think of the James Bay project? Most despise it. The National Audubon Society has called the dams as bad as the burning of the Amazon rainforest, and has lobbied for laws to prohibit U.S. utilities from buying James Bay power. Greenpeace has called the project genocide and mounted a boycott of tourism to Quebec. Institutional environmentalism is correct about the need to propel society beyond its fixation on fossil fuels. . . . Yet environmental sentiment has been unable to come to terms with the need for basic energy production.

7       No matter how successful conservation initiatives may be, on the whole the globe needs a major push for new power production systems. In the Western world, new generation systems are required to replace dirty, inefficient older plants with plants having clean, lower-input designs. In the Third World, hundreds of new power facilities are needed to satisfy the basic requirements of the globe's vast underclass, only a small percentage of which today enjoys the electrification taken for granted in developed nations. Unless the world's downtrodden are to remain down and trodden, global energy must go up.

8       Beyond this there is no fundamental conflict between the production of energy and the protection of the Earth. Twenty years ago, energy was universally considered a guaranteed sure-thing, no-way-out doomsday. Today Americans steadily use less energy, spend less on energy and pollute less with energy. The clipped pace of progress in converting energy from a brute-force to a cleantech pursuit ought to provide a model for guarded optimism in other industrial arenas.

9       Yet many environmentalists think that in order to be pro-conservation, they must be anti-production. Orthodoxy has grown so conflicted on the subject of energy production that a few greens have pronounced that, even if an entirely benign energy source is invented, it should be withheld, since people would use that energy to commit the primal sin of altering the ecology. During the period when it briefly seemed "cold fusion" might offer zero-pollution energy from seawater, activist Jeremy Rifkin declared that clean, unlimited energy would be "the worst thing that could happen to our planet."

10      The notion of energy production as antithetical to nature evinces a myopic view of natural history. In a sense, the 3.8-billion-year span of the development

of life has been about finding ways to employ energy as a tool to build living complexity out of the undifferentiated blur that was the initial condition of the planet. Without controlled use of energy, complexity cannot happen. For genus Homo to pursue the production of energy is not an affront to nature. . . . [ . . . ]

11     Some ecological objections to the James Bay project are valid but some are deceptive. Hydropower requires flooding lands from reservoirs, a practice environmentalists speak of in tones of deep horror, as though it wipes out life. Plants and animals do die when the reservoir water rises, and some wild-river ecology is lost. But what then exists? A lake ecology, brimming with living things. "People think a reservoir is a liquid desert," says Gaetan Hayeur, a James Bay environmental official. "Nobody ever says that about a lake. If you propose draining a lake, environmentalists will say that would cause a shocking loss of valuable habitat. But if you propose making a reservoir, which is a lake, they say the reverse."

12     So, in a sense, when Hydro Quebec floods the frigid James Bay land, the old ecology is not wiped out. But the new ecology differs from what is already there. That is the real environmental complaint about hydropower: It causes change. Even should the entire 50,000-megawatt potential of James Bay be tapped, most of the region would remain . . . an ecology of wild rivers mixed with subarctic tundra. But there would be change. Rather than exhibit annual cycles of flood and drought, some of the rivers would flow consistently. . . . And some of James Bay would not be wild rivers but placid lakes brought about through action by design.

13     Why such change should dismay humans would be difficult for nature to fathom. Nature has rearranged the hydraulics of the James Bay region dozens of times and is certain to rearrange them again. Through glacial advances and retreats, nature has made and unmade uncountable rivers, lakes, and dams in what people now call Quebec. Why is it strange for women and men to do the same, especially if they can learn to do it in ways calculated to minimize harm? And the change brought to James Bay is reversible. Suppose someday the power from James Bay is no longer required. The project's dams can then be removed, just as nature has often removed its own dams in the region. The tundra and wild-river ecology will reassert itself [ . . . .]

## Out of Balance

14     Damophobia reflects the fallacy of Stop-in-Place. If only society would keep its hands off the land, this fallacy holds, then nothing would change. . . . Yet this desire, which environmentalists promote as honoring nature, is among the most artificial notions genus Homo has introduced on Earth.

15     That many environmentalists now oppose ecologically attractive ideas like hydropower suggests that the green movement needs to reexamine which part of its agenda is justified, what part is bluster. To be sure, environmentalism is among the most welcome social developments of the twentieth century. This phenomenal organizing success speaks both to the power of ecological concerns and to the hard labors of the people of the movement. Environmentalists began their quest for the public ear with a pittance compared to the financial reserves of the lobbies that opposed them. Through the early eighties, though outgunned

in legal talent, lobbying access, and the funds necessary to make political donations, they won victory after victory, . . . [culminating] in the 1990 Clean Air Act. On that bill environmentalists put to rout the auto lobby, the steel lobby, the utility lobby, the coal lobby, and other entrenched groups commanding trillions of dollars in economic might. . . .

16     But in the last decade environmentalists have heard more hosannas than is good for them. Commentators meet the claims of industrialists and government officials with skepticism, properly discounting for self-interests in the outcome. In contrast, the pronouncements of green figures have been treated as beyond reproach, though like everyone else they have personal and financial self-interests, too. Surely environmentalists enjoyed having their claims embraced uncritically by the opinion-making apparatus of society. But this luxury has become counterproductive, allowing the movement to avoid facing the flaws of its arguments. If you love environmentalists, as you should, today the greatest favor you can do them is to toss cold water over their heads.

17     In recent years it has become something of a pastime to make sport of failed environmental predictions from the past. . . . In 1980, a commission appointed by President Jimmy Carter issued a report, Global 2000, projecting general ecological collapse by about now. The list of null doomsday prophecies from the recent past could march onward for pages.

18     Such way-off forecasts should not be disturbing. They came when little was known about the natural resilience of the environment. . . . They came when gross pollution was widespread—bear in mind, for example, that until 1972 it was essentially legal for U.S. factories to discharge unprocessed toxics and slag directly into lakes and rivers. And the old doomsday pronouncements came when government was tucked snugly in bed with industry. . . . So, yes, the enviros made some overwrought predictions in the past. That no longer matters.

19     What does matter is that overwrought assessments continue to be generated in the present. "During the seventies we had a lot of really good environmental laws passed but most of those have been systematically subverted or undermined," the late novelist and environmental activist Wallace Stegner said in 1992. From the White House, Al Gore in 1993 declared, "human activities are needlessly causing grave and perhaps irreparable damage to the global environment." In 1994 he said, in apparent defiance of all evidence, that "the environmental crisis has grown worse" in the United States in recent decades.

20     . . . The above quotations and many more not cited show that environmentalism remains mired in instant-doomsaying thinking. Some of this fixation stems from a willful denial of progress made, an almost aching desire that news stay bad.

21     Consider Stegner's notion that the environmental laws of the seventies were good but since have been "systematically undermined or subverted." The reverse is true. Laws of the seventies were shot full of loopholes allowing acid rain, toxic air pollution, ocean dumping of sludge, and many other abuses. During the eighties, the New Right attempted to undermine environmental strictures but enjoyed little success. In that decade U.S. regulations controlling toxics, recycling, sludge, pesticide registration, waste exports, landfill safety, smog pre-

vention, acid rain, incinerators, energy conservation, nuclear wastes, and a dozen other subjects were made more strict. Current ecological law is hardly perfect, but by any reasoned judgment it is far stronger than in the seventies.

22      No one can blame Stegner or environmentalists generally for wanting to sustain the essentially youthful vision of a glorious crusade to thwart villainy. . . . Reformers privately dread the moment when the reforms they espouse come to pass and they are no longer needed. Such factors combine to make some environmentalists long for the bad old days, rather than celebrate the improving new ones. [ . . . ]

23      Consider Al Gore's *Earth in the Balance*. Seemingly on every page something is being destroyed or about to end. Gore's initial mention that environmental progress has been made in the United States does not come until page 82; the mention is perfunctory. The second half of Gore's book speculates on how modern detachment from the rhythms of Earth may help explain the dissatisfaction experienced by so many people in affluent nations, who would seem by material comfort the winners of history's lottery. This portion of *Earth in the Balance* is measured, thoughtful, and possessed of enduring significance. Yet, the quietly persuasive second half of Gore's work received no attention while the doomsday first half was widely promoted.

24      The underappreciated portion of Gore's book hints at an ecological issue that will become increasingly important in the twenty-first century, as problems like pollution control are resolved. That issue is antimaterialist sentiment. . . .

25      Environmentalists are well ahead of the historical curve in sensing that materialist culture has lost its way. . . . The problem of the soul-draining aspect of the materialist lifestyle will continue and may even worsen as clean, sustainable production extends the cycle of consumption indefinitely. Down the road, the effort to free women and men from lives of materialistic work-and-spend represents the most important contribution environmentalism will make to society. For the moment, the trouble is that hardly any environmentalist who thinks in an anti-materialist way is willing to act in an anti-materialist way.

26      Is there even one Western environmentalist who lives without electricity and heat, eats only from his or her own garden, would if ill refuse genetically engineered pharmaceuticals, never travels in any fossil-powered car, taxi, bus, train, or plane, and who declines to attend environmental conferences because it would take too long to ride there on a new bike? . . . Gore has written of watching a glade of trees removed from a housing development near his Virginia home: "As the woods fell to make way for more concrete, more buildings, more parking lots, the wild things that lived there were forced to flee." Doesn't Gore live in a house? Park his car on concrete? Why are jets and homes and driveways only objectionable when SOMEBODY ELSE desires them?

27      The idea that SOMEBODY ELSE should go without the conveniences of modern life must be eradicated if environmental thought is to proceed to the next level of usefulness to society. . . . No degree of ecological exhortation will persuade the typical citizen of America or Western Europe to abandon a heated

home, low-cost food, advanced medical care, or any similar reasonable material gain. Nor should these be abandoned. Rather they should be redesigned to
operate in conjunction with nature.

## Greenmail

28  [ . . . ] As environmentalists have become effective lobbyists they have learned the
negative tools of the trade: bluster, veiled threats, and misrepresentation. . . .
During Clean Air Act lobbying in 1990, one issue was how many grams of
unburned hydrocarbons new cars could emit. Existing regulations set the limit
at 4.1 grams per mile; EPA administrator William Reilly proposed to lower the
standards to 2.5 grams per mile. Enviro lobbyists called the deal a sellout
because 1990 cars already averaged only 2.6 grams. Their complaints about the
proposal led to denunciations of Reilly on Capitol Hill.

29      Automakers design tailpipe controls to emit less than law allows, creating
a "compliance cushion" that forestalls recalls. This is why an existing standard
of 4.1 grams led to cars emitting 2.6 grams. Reilly knew that if the limit were
lowered to 2.5 grams, the new compliance cushion would drop actual emissions
to around 1.5 grams. Automakers would be anxious for an extra reduction since
the new Clean Air Act requires them to warrant emissions systems for 75,000
miles. Enviro lobbyists understood about compliance cushions. They simply
declined to mention this factor in congressional testimony and media interviews, sensing a chance to create a jolt of bad news. "The advocacy campaign
against the provision was illogical unless the motive was to take a positive
development and make it seem depressing," says Reilly, himself once an environmental lobbyist as head of the World Wildlife Fund.

30      Once environmental lobbyists engage in tactics such as willful distortions
of the other side's positions, they place themselves on a slope that can lead
downward toward being simply another pressure group that will say or do
whatever is expedient to maintain its interests. If anything will push the enviros into that descent it is fund-raising. [ . . . ]

31      Anyone familiar with the sorts of fund-raising letters employed to frighten
the elderly about Social Security will recognize familiar themes here: claims of
plots and secret meetings; official-looking "documents"; preposterous assertions, such as that the well-entrenched environmental movement will suffer
"total and final destruction" if you don't send that check today. . . .

32      Unscrupulous fund-raisers such as Richard Viguerie showed that bogus documents, wild distortions, and the use of "devil figures" are what shake money
loose by mail. Through the eighties many enviro groups adopted these techniques
as former Interior Secretary James Watt, a raving unviro, made the ideal devil figure for direct mail. By the end of the decade Greenpeace was among the leading
direct-mailers in the U.S., often dropshipping phony-document mailings of one
million pieces. National Audubon Society mailings were emblazoned with such
banners as TEN SECONDS A MONTH CAN HELP SAVE THE PLANET! Even
the normally staid Nature Conservancy unleashed direct mail appeals containing imaginary land deeds computer-printed with the mark's name.

33      If it is dangerous to believe your own press releases, it is deadly to believe your own direct mail. . . . And direct mail dynamics compel institutional environmentalism away from the sort of ecorealism that should be the next wave of thinking.

34      As environmentalism has become entrenched, a contrapositive has sprung up, which may be called unvironmentalism. Rush Limbaugh is the leading unviro, imagining "ecofeminazis" who conspire with the EPA to control his life. William Dannemeyer, a former congressman, is another prominent unviro; in 1990 he gave a demented speech on the House floor saying the trouble with environmentalists is that they don't believe in an afterlife. (Apparently pollution is fine down below so long as skies are clear high above.) What has evolved is a strange contest between the doomsayers and the naysayers—one side asserting that life as we know it is about to end, the other that everything is peachy keen. Common sense dictates neither philosophy takes you anywhere you really want to go.

35      Ecorealism would abandon both the conventional doomsday views of the Left, and the conventional anti-regulatory views of the Right: creating, a new, ideologically neutral, middle-path philosophy for understanding environmental issues. The ecorealist would accept that society must have very strict conservation rules, but also accept that nature is resilient and around for the long haul. Ecorealism would cancel the doomsday alarm, and yet assume that further progress against pollution—including an ultimate goal of a zero-emission economy—is a desirable, sensible goal for society.

36      Consider that if an ecorealist point of view were common today, there is no way the Newt Gingrich faction in the House of Representatives, nor Bob Dole in the Senate, could be attempting to turn back the clock by undoing much of conservation law. If it were widely understood that most environmental trends in the Western world are positive, and that most American environmental programs have generated excellent results at affordable costs, there would be public outcry—even from typical middle-class voters—against the Gingrich-Dole anti-environmental assault.

37      But since the public has in recent years heard little more than doomsaying about the ecology, it is now conventionally assumed that most environmental programs aren't working. And if they're not working, why not undo them? . . . It is now widely believed that antipollution initiatives impose a burdensome drag on the economy. With a few exceptions, this is not the case: Most environmental rules are cost-effective and good for the economy. Yet Gingrich, Dole, and other anti-environmentalists are able to get away with depicting environmental rules as expensive burdens, since pessimistic environmental thinking from the Left has created a milieu in which conservation rules are spoken of only in terms of woe. . . .

38      Among the worst aspects of Washington interest groups is that at some point they begin to like negativism, as it endlessly justifies their position and funding. This descent to the lowest common denominator is often seen on the part of industrial trade associations. It would be a sad day, and a profound loss to society, if environmentalism became merely the industrial trade association of the Left.

ARTURO GÓMEZ-POMPA AND ANDREA KAUS

# Taming the Wilderness Myth

## Environmental Policy and Education Are Currently Based on Western Beliefs about Nature Rather than on Reality

1 [ . . . ] Never before has the western world been so concerned with issues relating to humankind's relationship with the environment. As concerned members of this industrialized civilization, we have recognized that humanity is an integral part of the biosphere, at once the transformer and the self-appointed protector of the world. We assume that we have the answers. We assume that our perceptions of environmental problems and their solutions are the correct ones, based as they are on Western rational thought and scientific analysis. And we often present the preservation of wilderness as part of the solution toward a better planet under the presumption that we know what is to be preserved and how it is to be managed.

2 However, we need to evaluate carefully our own views of the environment and our own self-interests for its future use. . . . Many environmental education programs are strongly biased by elitist urban perceptions of the environment and issues of the urban world. This approach . . . neglects the perceptions and experience of the rural population, the people most closely linked to the land, who have a firsthand understanding of their surrounding natural environment as a teacher and provider. It neglects those who are most directly affected by the current policy decisions that are made in urban settings regarding natural resource use. It neglects those who feed us.

3 . . . Through time and generations, certain patterns of thought and behavior have been accepted and developed into what can be termed a Western tradition of environmental thought and conservation. How accurate and sound is this vision?

## Western Concepts of Wilderness

4 [ . . . ] Wild lands are . . . seen as areas useful to modern civilization. They are presented to the public as natural-resource banks of biodiversity that merit protection from human actions and as outdoor laboratories that deserve unhindered exploration by the scientific community. And they are seen as a vital part of the environmental machinery that must be maintained to provide an acceptable quality of life in developed areas, as exemplified by current concerns about air pollution, global climate change, and deforestation. All of these concepts fall

*BioScience* 42.4 (April 1992): 271–280.

under the general term *conservation,* yet they represent mostly urban beliefs and aspirations.

5       [ . . . ] The validity of widely accepted environmental truths needs to be challenged, from our belief in the virgin nature of the tropical forests to our newly developing thoughts on global warming. . . .

6       Concepts of climax communities and ecological equilibrium, for example, have been used for most of this century as a basis for scientific research, resource management, and conservation teaching. . . . Today, few ecologists defend the equilibrium and climax concepts. Nonequilibrium models now influence ecological theory, and nature is increasingly perceived as being in a state of continuous change. . . .

7       . . . The concept of wilderness as an area without people has influenced thought and policy throughout the development of the western world (Manning 1989, Nash 1967, Stankey 1989, Whyte 1967). People see in the wilderness a window to the past, to the remote beginnings of humankind long before the comforts of modern life. . . . Yet, recent research indicates that much wilderness has long been influenced by human activities (see Gómez-Pompa and Kaus 1990).

8       The Western world has also seen the wilderness as a challenge, a frontier to be tamed and managed. Agricultural landscapes are often admired for their intrinsic beauty, as living masterpieces created by human hands from the wild. They are confirmation of an underlying belief in human technological superiority over primal forces. . . . The danger is that . . . a dichotomy of civilized and wild, . . . of human mastery over natural forces, has only too tangible consequences. . . . A belief in an untouched and untouchable wilderness has permeated global policies and politics in resource management from the tropics to the deserts, causing serious environmental problems.

9       . . . On the utilitarian side, these policies are permeated with an acceptance of destructive practices, generated from a belief that mitigating measures can halt or reverse environmental depletion and degradation. Yet, on the preservationist side, conventional resource-management policy also includes practices based on the belief that setting aside so-called pristine tracts of land will automatically preserve their biological integrity. Neither belief takes into consideration the possibilities for natural-resource management that might arise from the integration of alternative environmental perceptions and current scientific information.

## Alternative Perceptions and Conservation Practices

10      . . . The inhabitants of rural areas have different views of the areas that urbanites designate as wilderness, and they base their land-use and resource management practices on these alternative visions. Indigenous groups in the tropics, for example, do not consider the tropical forest environment to be wild; it is their home. To them, the urban setting might be perceived as a wilderness.

11          As a city dweller never looks at bricks, so the Indian never looks at a tree. There are saplings for making bows, and jatoba for making canoes, and certain branches where animals like to sit, but there are never trees noticeable for self-conscious reasons—beauty, terror, wonder (Cowell 1990, p. 25).

12      Many agriculturalists enter into a personal relationship with the environment. Nature is no longer an object, an *it,* but a world of complexity whose living components are often personified and deified in local myths. Some of these myths are based on generations of experience. . . . Conservation may not be part of their vocabulary, but it is part of their lifeway and their perceptions of the human relationship to the natural world.

13      Throughout the world, communally held resources have been managed and conserved by diverse human societies via cultural mechanisms that attach symbolic and social significance to land and resources beyond their immediate extractive value (see Feeny et al. 1990, McCay and Acheson 1990). In the Brazilian Amazon, the Kayapó belief system and ecological management, as described by Posey (1983), revolves around maintaining an energy balance between the natural and spiritual world by regulating animal and plant use via ritual and custom. Indigenous fishermen of Northern California used to place a ritual moratorium on fishing during the first few days of the salmon runs, thereby protecting the perpetuation of the salmon resource and maintaining intergroup relations along the river (Swezey and Heizer 1982).

14      External economic and political demands for natural resources have . . . led to the replacement or collapse of previous resource management systems and subsequent unrestricted or uneducated use of the region. In Chiapas, Mexico, for example, the Lacandon Maya perceived the forest as the provider of subsistence. Forests were converted temporarily to agricultural lands for corn, beans, and squash within a shifting cultivation system, or the forest fallows managed to attract wildlife (Nations and Nigh 1980). Before the entry of outsider groups with other objectives and other interests, Maya people lived within the tropical ecosystem of southern Mexico and Guatemala for centuries in ways that allowed continuous forest regeneration. Yet, the majority of Maya groups that inhabited the Lacandon forest were never consulted in the government policy decisions of land use that ultimately led to its destruction.

15      These same lands have been, and still are, viewed from the outside as lands to be conquered, colonized, grazed, or preserved. The forests contain hardwoods valuable on the international market. The cleared forest then provides land for the landless and pastures for the cattle industry. . . . Traditional conservationists, on the other hand, see the aesthetic, biological, and ecological value of the same land but do not necessarily see the people. They often fail to see the effects of past or current human actions, to differentiate among types of human use, or to recognize the economic value of sustainable use.

16      [ . . . ] . . . [E]ven with the evidence that it is our own outside interests that are ultimately responsible for the greater part of tropical deforestation, we continue to place the blame on poverty and on the land practices of the rural sector. . . . More important, our beliefs and assumptions blind us to the fact that, in many cases, the traditional land-use practices of the rural sector are responsible for maintaining and protecting the biodiversity of our wilderness and have often provided the genetic diversity that strengthens the world's major food crop varieties (Altieri and Merrick 1987, Brush 1986, Nabhan 1985, Oldfield and Alcorn 1987, Reganold et. al. 1990).

## Footprints in the Wilderness

17   Scientific findings indicate that virtually every part of the globe, from the boreal forests to the humid tropics, has been inhabited, modified, or managed throughout our human past (Gómez-Pompa 1987, Kunstadter 1978, Lundell 1937, Parsons 1975, Sauer 1958). . . . In any current dialogue regarding tropical forests, the Amazon Basin is usually mentioned as a vital area to be left untouched and protected. Yet, archaeological, historical, and ecological evidence increasingly shows not only a high density of human populations in the past and sites of continuous human occupation over many centuries but an intensively managed and constantly changing environment as well (Anderson and Posey 1989, Balée 1989, Denevan 1976, Hartshorn 1980, Hecht and Cockburn 1990, Roosevelt 1989).

18       [ . . . ] Present-day parks, reserves, and refuges in the [Maya] region are filled with archaeological sites. According to Turner (1976), the Maya population of southeastern Mexico may have ranged from 150 to 500 people per $km^2$ in the Late Classic Period, contrasting sharply with current population densities of 4.5 to 28.1 people per $km^2$ in the same region (Pick et al. 1989). These past civilizations apparently managed the forests for food, fiber, wood, fuel, resins, and medicines (Gómez-Pompa 1987). Many of the tree species now dominant in the mature vegetation of tropical areas were and still are the same species protected, spared, or planted in the land cleared for crops as part of the practice of shifting agriculture (Gómez-Pompa and Kaus 1990).

19       . . . Our late realization of this possibility stems from the long-held belief that only cleared and planted areas are managed, as in the ploughed fields of our experience, and that mature vegetation represents a climax community, a stable endpoint reflecting the order of nature given no human interference. Until we understand and teach that the tropical forests are "both artifact and habitat" (Hecht 1990), we will be advocating policies for a mythical pristine environment that exists only in our imagination.

20       . . . [We must] redefine and qualify what is meant by undisturbed habitat. The issue is not simply the presence or density of humans, but the tools, technologies, techniques, knowledge, and experience that accompany a given society's production system. The ancient societies discussed previously, for example, were more closely bound to the local environment and more dependent on regional resources for basic subsistence. Increased productivity would have come from principally internal modifications and increased human labor for more intensive ecosystem management. Production systems that were viable remained; those that failed disappeared.

21       In contrast, . . . advanced technologies, from chemical fertilizers to hydroelectric dams, that are external to the local environment . . . have the potential to impose irreversible transformations on the environment . . . at a much greater scale than ever before in human history. When we speak of protecting undisturbed habitat or wilderness, then, it is important to clarify that the word *undisturbed* refers to the absence of disturbance by modern technologies.

22       However, not all modern societies use destructive technologies, and the benefits of human interference in ecological processes are not restricted to tropical

zones or past times. . . . In the Sonoran Desert, a study of two oases on either side of the Mexico–United States border indicates that the customary land-use practices of Papago farmers on the Mexican side of the border contributed to the biodiversity of the oasis. In turn, the protection from land use of an oasis 54 km to the northwest, within the U.S. Organ Pipe Cactus National Monument, resulted in a decline in the species diversity over a 25-year period (Nabhan et al. 1982).

23     In addition, many rare varieties and species related to our major food crops can be found maintained within or bordering agricultural fields in cultivated regions. In the Sierra de Manantlan (Jalisco, Mexico), the discovery of a new perennial corn, *Zea diploperennis,* led to the establishment of a biosphere reserve to protect this species and the ecosystem in which it survives (Iltis 1988). . . . The difficulty is that *Z. diploperennis* is a secondary species that grows in abandoned cornfields. To protect the species, the slash-and-burn techniques of this form of traditional agriculture have to be continued to provide the habitat that it requires. Without all the human cultural practices that go with the habitat, the species will be lost forever. . . .

## Anthropogenic Fires in Natural-Resource Management

24     . . . The view of the white ashes of forest trees that have been felled and burned for an agricultural plot may appear to an urbanite outsider to be a desecration of the wilderness, but a farmer may see it as an essential stage of renewal. One could argue that the trees felled are the representatives of rare and endangered species, and, in selected sites, this argument might be reasonable. However, most often, many of the cut or burned trunks resprout, providing the bulk of the new forest.

25     Slash-and-burn agriculture has been an integral part of the tropical forests ecosystems for millennia. This ancient form of agriculture is not to be confused with the widespread destructive fires set by recent colonists or squatters who have little local experience or land-tenure security. Fire is today used to open new forest land, often on the edge of new timber or mining roads, or, even worse, used as a mechanism to vent anger at the impotence of poverty and inadequate government programs . . . [S]uch rapid clearing of the forest . . . is very different from the continual process of clearing, planting, and fallowing that is typical of more long-standing forms of shifting agriculture, which creates a mosaic of different ages of forest growth, including large patches of mature vegetation.

26     To give a concrete example, when a major forest fire in 1989 burned 120,000 hectares near Cancún, Mexico, the news media conveyed an image of ecocide, covering the fire's daily progress with statements about the extinction of species and the loss of invaluable forests. Environmentalists, conservationists, and most non-governmental organizations connected to environmental issues protested the lack of any fire management plan to prevent, stop, or control forest fires. Yet, no attempt was made to understand why a fire of this magnitude had occurred in the first place.

27     The Cancún fire began in several different places at the same time, and its cause remains unclear. It is unlikely that it was the result of an agricultural fire

that escaped from an area cleared for crops. . . . Agricultural fires are carefully controlled by the farmers. One of the most critical decisions they must make is when to burn the slash: when the conditions are finally dry enough, but before the first seasonal rains. The farmers know the winds, the annual climatic shifts, and past fire histories. They know how to control the size and intensity of their fires to protect the neighboring forests from burning.

28    The patchy mosaic of forests, forest fallows, and agricultural plots is an ideal landscape for controlling forest fires. The view from a helicopter flying over the burned area around Cancún revealed that the line of fire had stopped in areas of slash-and-burn agriculture. Local residents and forest authorities say that the forest burned most dramatically in areas where the valuable woods had been mined out and been subsequently devastated by Hurricane Gilberto. The actual commercial and biological value of the forest was low. Biological surveys indicate that the burned zone was in fact not rich in endemic organisms (López-Portillo et al. 1990).

29    [ . . . ] Cancún is not an isolated example. Ongoing research on the chaparral environments on both sides of the Mexico–United States California border has shown the role of fire in combatting fire (Minnich 1983, 1989). These studies indicate that the mosaic vegetation pattern in Baja California, the result of repeated small burns, has prevented the large catastrophic burns so characteristic of the equivalent ecological zone in Southern California. The composition and structure of so-called virgin forests and wilderness areas are in part artifacts of previous burns, both natural and anthropogenic (Komarek 1973, Savonen 1990, Thompson and Smith 1971). A policy of fire suppression in the United States has eliminated natural barriers to fires. . . .

30    Due to our limited knowledge of the role and experience of local human populations in managing fire, fire suppression remains the dominant policy in our management of natural resources and many national parks. We fear, and are trying to prevent, a repeat of the 1988 fire in Yellowstone National Park without fully understanding the underlying causes for its great extent, intensity, and damage. In addition, without the knowledge of the role of fire in a given ecosystem, we have developed areas so that they can no longer be subjected to prescribed burns without great risk. Yet, in so doing, these areas are also at risk from fires that cannot be controlled once they start.

## The Integration of Alternative Views of the Environment

31    . . . Research and education programs need to be redesigned to inform urban as well as rural populations (from children to adults) about appropriate and alternative resource management practices and policies. Most policy agendas and education curricula neglect rural perceptions of the environment or traditional systems of food production and resource management. They do not address the current difficulties confronted by these systems and lifeways or their contributions to conservation and our own survival. Beyond opening our eyes to the realities of the areas we call wilderness, we must learn how to listen to their

caretakers (both good and bad ones) to include local needs, experience, and aspirations within our perspectives (Gómez-Pompa and Bainbridge in press).

32 . . . The first step is to recognize that conservation traditions exist in other cultural practices and beliefs that are separate from Western traditional conservation. The rural sector is not a homogeneous group, however, and research and education efforts also need to be directed toward the social or economic constraints and incentives that lead to destructive practices or conflict with institutional conservation policies.

33 Several priorities for research and education programs can be mentioned to improve the information and alternatives available for natural-resource management programs and future resource managers:

- Research on the influence of human activities on past and present environments to understand the influence of all forms of management, whether modern or traditional, intensive or extensive, on the shape and content of the environment.

- Long-term monitoring of environmental change that includes the social and economic variables affecting such change.

- Documentation of the views and perceptions of nature and conservation found in rural populations and integration of these beliefs and corresponding empirical realities in the general pool of collective knowledge. . . .

- . . . [C]oordination of research efforts in different scientific disciplines to present conservation and management alternatives. . . .

- Collaboration with interested individuals in the rural sector to establish demonstration and experimental sites for resource management alternatives and environmental restoration techniques.

- Development of environmental education programs that integrate the knowledge and experience of scientists, educators, and local practitioners. This development should include programs that . . . take scientists and educators out to rural communities, . . . [and programs] that encourage rural residents with successful land-use techniques to teach, whether in their own communities, other rural areas, or the urban setting.

- Development of graduate programs in conservation and natural-resource management that train a new generation of professionals, scientists, and decision makers with a view of conservation issues that includes the role of humans in both environmental deterioration and enrichment. . . .

34 [ . . . ] As scientists or conservationists, we need to enter the field, literally. We speak of local participation and of developing a dialogue among the rural, research, and education communities. However, the presence of local rural residents in a classroom or conference hall does not necessarily engender participation. These locations and procedures . . . are unlikely to be familiar to the majority of indigenous or remote communities and unlikely to be conducive to an exchange of information among researchers and local people.

35      . . . One rancher from North Mexico once commented on the researchers with whom he had worked, "We tell them what it is like here, but they write about it differently."

36      We know, in fact, very little about how environmental knowledge held by farmers, ranchers, fishermen, hunters, and gatherers from the deserts to the tropics is passed from one generation or society to another. This understanding requires learning the setting and language that people use to describe their environment and their relationship with the land. . . .

37      In an informal survey, 15 people of a remote region of Durango, Mexico, were asked what the word *conservación* meant. None of them knew. "No," they replied, shaking their heads. "Qué será? (What would it mean?)" Earlier, one man from this group had pointed out ways in which he and his family were trying to protect the rangeland from the effects of drought and overgrazing and to protect the wildlife from poachers. When asked why, he turned in his saddle, viewing the range stretching away from him into the distance, and said, "Hay que cuidar, verdad? [You've got to care for it, don't you?]"

38      . . . Part of the problem in working with local people stems from our perception of wilderness as uninhabited. The attention automatically falls on the land first and the people second. We think of local people living in the buffer zone surrounding an uninhabited area and do not stop to consider that perhaps the buffer zone should be the principal area of conservation.

39      Botkin (1990) describes how resource management policies to both protect and control elephant populations in the Tsavo National Park of East Africa led to a severe deterioration of the land within the park boundaries. The inhabited area surrounding the park remained forested. The clear demarcation of the boundaries in the LANDSAT images and aerial photos appeared "as a photographic negative of one's expectation of a park. Rather than an island of green in a wasted landscape, Tsavo appeared as a wasted island amid a green land" (Botkin 1990, p. 16).

40      Perceptions of wilderness and protected areas as uninhabited means that local-level collaboration is often neglected or considered only as an afterthought and in terms of our own priorities. . . . Local cooperation, participation, or collaboration . . . deserve and require negotiation. In the Chihuahuan Desert, for example, inhabitants in the region of the Mapimí Biosphere Reserve have included a policy of wildlife conservation and an ecological research program within their own lifeway. Their willingness to stop eating the endangered Bolsón tortoise, *Gopherus flavomarginatus,* and protect it from poaching has resulted in an increase in population of this endemic species within the reserve. In turn, the researchers have opened a window to another world outside that arid basin by providing a vision of the national importance and value of local resources and efforts.

41      However, the local-level efforts up to now have not been equal. Some of the local people say they have benefitted the reserve more than the reserve has benefitted them. Why, then, did the local people accept the researchers in the first place? They say it was for *la convivencia,* the willingness of the initial researchers to live and work side by side with them, to accept their help and advice, and to include their concerns in the decision-making process. It was a matter of trust. The local people trust that their perceptions, their world, will be part of what is

taught to others who have never set foot in the Bolsón de Mapimí, part of what is taken into consideration by those who wish to alter either local land use or the reserve management.

### Environmental Conservation Responsibilities

42   Cooperative relationships with local residents in ecologically fragile areas are of utmost importance. . . . Yet, we cannot neglect our responsibilities in such relationships. . . . We need to contribute in turn and impart the information to which we have access. In this way, local people can come to understand their situation in a larger context and make informed decisions about their lives and land. But it also means orienting some of the research toward local benefits and including local-level perspectives in research design and dissemination. More important, it means including the local people in the same education process that we, ourselves, are undergoing to understand the natural environment and society's effects on it. . . .

43       The point here is not to create a new myth or fall into the trap of the "ecologically noble savage" (Redford 1990). Not all farmers or ranchers are sages, folk scientists, or unrecognized conservationists. Yet, within the rural sector can be found individuals who directly depend on the land for their physical and cultural subsistence. And within that group of individuals exists a set of knowledge about that terrain, a knowledge of successes and failures that should be taken into account in our environmental assessments. Currently, we are discussing and designing policies for something about which we still know little. And those who do know more have rarely been included in the discussion. The fundamental challenge is not to conserve the wilderness, but to tame the myth with an understanding that humans are not apart from nature.

## References Cited

Altieri, M. A., and L. C. Merrick. 1987. In situ conservation of crop genetic resources through maintenance of traditional farming systems. *Econ. Bot.* 41: 86–96.

Anderson, A. B., and D. A. Posey. 1989. Management of a tropical scrub savanna by the Gorotire Kayapó of Brazil. Pages 159–173 in D. A. Posey and W. Balée, eds. *Resource Management in Amazonia: Indigenous and Folk Strategies.* New York Botanical Garden, Bronx.

Balée, W. C. 1989. The culture of Amazon forests. Pages 1–21 in D. A. Posey and W. Balée, eds. *Resource Management in Amazonia: Indigenous and Folk Strategies.* New York Botanical Garden, Bronx.

Botkin, D. B. 1990. *Discordant Harmonies: A New Ecology for the Twenty-First Century.* Oxford University Press, New York.

Brush, S. B. 1986. Genetic diversity and conservation in traditional farming systems. *J. Ethnobiol. 6:* 151–167.

Cowell, A. 1990. *The Decade of Destruction: The Crusade to Save the Amazon Rain Forest.* Henry Holt and Co., New York.

Denevan, W. M. 1976. *The Native Population of the Americas in 1492.* University of Wisconsin Press, Madison.

Feeny, D., F. Berkes, B. J. McCay, and J. M. Acheson. 1990. The tragedy of the commons: twenty-two years later. *Human Ecol.* 18: 1–19.

Gómez-Pompa, A. 1987. On Maya silviculture. *Mexican Studies* 3: 1–17.

Gómez-Pompa, A., and D. A. Bainbridge. In press. Tropical forestry as if people mattered. In A. E. Lugo and C. Lowe, eds. *A Half Century of Tropical Forest Research.* Springer-Verlag, New York.

Gómez-Pompa, A., and A. Kaus. 1990. Traditional management of tropical forests in Mexico. Pages 45–64 in A. B. Anderson, ed. *Alternatives to Deforestation: Steps Toward Sustainable Use of the Amazon Rain Forest.* Columbia University Press, New York.

Hartshorn, G. S. 1980. Neotropical forest dynamics. *Biotropica* 12(Suppl.): 23–30.

Hecht, S. 1990. Tropical deforestation in Latin America: myths, dilemmas, and reality. Paper presented at the Systemwide Workshop on Environment and Development Issues in Latin America, University of California, Berkeley, 16 October 1990.

Hecht, S., and A. Cockburn. 1990. *The Fate of the Forest: Developers, Destroyers and Defenders of the Amazon.* Harper Perennial, New York.

Iltis, H. H. 1988. Serendipity in the exploration of biodiversity: what good are weedy tomatoes? Pages 98–105 in E. O. Wilson, ed. *Biodiversity.* National Academy Press, Washington, DC.

Komarek, E. V. 1973. Ancient fires. Pages 219–240 in *Proceedings of the Annual Tall Timbers Fire Ecology Conference No. 12.* Tall Timbers Research Station, Tallahassee, FL.

Kundstadter, P. 1978. Ecological modification and adaptation: an ethnobotanical view of Lua' swiddeners in northwestern Thailand. *Anthropological Papers* 67: 169–200.

López-Portillo, J., M. R. Keyes, A. González, E. Cabrera C., and Odilón Sánchez. 1990. Los incendios de Quintana Roo: ¿catástrofe ecólogica o evento periódico? *Ciencia y Desarrollo* 16(91): 43–57.

Lundell, C. L. 1937. *The Vegetation of Petén.* Carnegie Institute, Washington, DC.

Manning, R. E. 1989. The nature of America: visions and revisions of wilderness. *Nat. Res. J.* 29: 25–40.

McCay, B. J., and J. M. Acheson, eds. 1990. *The Question of the Commons: The Culture and Ecology of Communal Resources.* University of Arizona Press, Tucson.

Minnich, R. A. 1983. Fire mosaics in Southern California and Northern Baja California. *Science* 219: 1287–1294.

——. 1989. Chaparral fire history in San Diego County and adjacent Northern Baja California: an evaluation of natural fire regimes and the effects of suppression management. *Nat. Hist. Mus. Los Angel. Cty. Contrib. Sci.* 34: 37–47.

Nabhan, G. P. 1985. Native crop diversity in Aridoamerica: conservation of regional gene pools. *Econ. Bot.* 39: 387–399.

Nabhan, G. P., A. M. Rea, K. L. Reichhardt, E. Mellink, and C. F. Hutchinson. 1982. Papago influences on habitat and biotic diversity: Quitovac oasis ethnoecology. *J. Ethnobiol.* 2: 124–143.

Nash, R. F. 1967. *Wilderness and the American Mind.* Yale University Press, New Haven, CT.

Nations, J. D., and R. B. Nigh. 1980. The evolutionary potential of Lacandon Maya sustained-yield tropical forest agriculture. *J. Anthropol. Res.* 36: 1–30.

Oldfield, M. L., and J. B. Alcorn. 1987. Conservation of traditional agroecosystems. *BioScience* 37: 199–208.

Parsons, J. J. 1975. The changing nature of New World tropical forests since European colonization. Pages 28–38 in *Proceedings of the International Meeting on the Use of Ecological Guidelines for Development in the American Humid Tropics.* IUCN Publications New Series 31, Morges, Switzerland.

Pick, J. B., E. W. Butler, and E. L. Lanzer. 1989. *Atlas of Mexico.* Westview Press, Boulder, CO.

Pollan, M. 1990. Only man's presence can save nature. *J. For.* 88(7): 24–33.

Posey, D. A. 1983. Indigenous knowledge and development: an ideological bridge to the future. *Ciencia e Cultura* 35: 877–894.

Redford, K. H. 1990. The ecologically noble savage. *Orion* 9(3): 25–29.

Reganold, J. P., R. I. Papendick, and J. F. Parr. 1990. Sustainable agriculture. *Sci. Am.* 262(6): 112–120.

Roosevelt, A. 1989. Resource management in Amazonia before the conquest: beyond ethnographic projection. Pages 30–62 in D. A. Posey, and W. Balée, eds. *Resource Management in Amazonia: Indigenous and Folk Strategies.* New York Botanical Garden, Bronx.

Sauer, C. 1958. Man in the ecology of tropical America. *Proceedings of the Ninth Pacific Science Congress* 20: 105–110

Savonen, C. 1990. Ashes in the Amazon. *J. For.* 88(9): 20–25.

Stankey, G. H. 1989. Beyond the campfire's light: historical roots of the wilderness concept. *Natural Resources Journal* 29: 9–24.

Swezey, S. L., and R. F. Heizer. 1982. Ritual management of salmonid fish resources in California. *Journal of California Anthropology* 4: 7–29.

Thompson, D. Q., and R. H. Smith. 1971. The forest primeval in the Northeast—a great myth? Pages 255–265 in *Proceedings of the Annual Tall Timbers Fire Ecology Conference No. 10.* Tall Timbers Research Station, Tallahassee, FL.

Turner, B. L. II. 1976. Population density in the Classic Maya lowlands: new evidence for old approaches. *Geographical Review* 66: 73–82.

Whyte, L. 1967. The historical roots of our ecological crisis. *Science* 155: 1203–1207.

DAVE SHIFLETT

# *Parks and Wreck: Against Jet Skiers, Snowmobilers, and Other Louts*

1   Bill Clinton is being generously lashed for his efforts on behalf of swindlers, tax cheats, crack merchants, traitors, and other well-connected felons, to the point that it will be a long time before anyone can say "pardon me" without eliciting a smirk, just as it will be a very long time before anyone dares name a daughter Monica.

2        But in one important area, Clinton resisted the entreaties of an entire army of disreputable persons: those who ride snowmobiles and jet skis. The ex-president had the good sense to ban them from some of America's premier national parks. Unfortunately, the snowmobile industry was able to enlist another group of lowlifes (congressmen) into delaying the Clinton order. The forces of darkness will have two years to maraud while the two sides to this dispute—industry and environmentalists—battle for primacy.

3        One hates to preach heresy, but perhaps this equation could be shifted a bit. While right-wingers tend to side with industrial interests (so long as the industry is not headquartered in Hollywood), they might consider the merits of opposing the snowmobile/jet ski cartel. And this opposition can be based on truly conservative grounds. Right-wingers are by nature against loud, intrusive, arrogant, reek-

*National Review* 53.5 (19 Mar 2001): NA.

ing, self-centered pests (give or take a few radio personalities). They also believe certain places are appropriate for certain activities—no bus-station sex in the Oval Office, for example—and thus recognize that Mother Nature's bosom is no place for a bunch of motorized louts. Besides that, earning a green credential will gain wingers a measure of political respectability with their children.

4      All told, there is only one legitimate dog in this fight, and he isn't riding a jet ski.

5      It is often argued that environmentalists traffic in hysteria. There is some truth to this, as anyone who recalls warnings about the coming ice age (since changed to warnings about global roasting) knows all too well. But there is plenty of guilt to spread around. The industry is doing a lot of mouth-breathing of its own on this issue. "It's a slippery slope," the chief of the International Snowmobile Manufacturers Association told the *Los Angeles Times*. "If you took out the word 'snowmobile' and put in the word 'automobile,' you would see that they are preparing to remove automobiles in national parks." Meanwhile, jet ski interests warn that the ban on "personal watercraft" is being carried out by "extremists" with a broad agenda: "If the ban is allowed to stand, it is only a matter of time before your favorite activity becomes the target."

6      Yeah, yeah: Hysteria peddlers we will always have—and the industry's assertions should be taken for nothing more than yacking from special pleaders. Their notion that they represent the common man against elitists is especially daring. The industry's ability to enlist the efforts of two usually pro-enviro Democrats, Rep. David Obey and Sen. Tom Daschle, to overturn the national-park ban indicates a decidedly elitist ability to manipulate the political process.

7      There is also the fact that one must be something of an elitist (broadly understood) to afford these machines, a fact underscored in the industry's own literature: "The average PWC (personal watercraft) operator is not who you think he is. A study by Bowe Marketing Research revealed that the majority of personal watercraft owners are married with families (71%). The average owner is a middle-aged, highly educated, white-collar worker with extensive boating experience."

8      What this description fails to mention is that many of these people have clearly built their lives on the Jerry Springer model. They reject all sensible notions of beauty, order, and civilized behavior. A jet ski advertisement tells us all we need to know: "Scenery is for Saps." This is the mindset of the adolescent yob who gets his thrills passing gas in elevators, setting off cherry bombs in movie theaters, scaling the walls of convents, and otherwise strutting his ignorant stuff any place he can put one foot before the other.

9      At this point, let me abandon the neutral, fair-minded tone that has marred this essay thus far. The fact is, if you love the majesty of nature, and recognize that it speaks to us in the most profound of all languages—silence—then you have to see these people for what they are: slothful vandals who are unable to haul their thick butts around without the help of an internal-combustion engine.

One can no more enjoy a walk in the forest with one of them around than one can enjoy an opera while sitting beside a barking dog.

10    My first deep encounter with this subspecies took place in Colorado, specifically the Pike National Forest, an immense spread of public land where the eagles fly, the elk saunter, and the trout convert insects into entrees. It is also a place where, in some sections at least, one can be run down by dirt-bikers—many of whom no doubt have a jet ski and a snowmobile back in the garage. Thanks to their efforts, this beautiful stretch of forest sounds like downtown Los Angeles on the Fifth of May. On many days, I found myself wishing for a few long strands of piano wire to stretch between trees at roughly Adam's apple level. It is a hard thing to admit, but these intruders do turn the mind toward homicide.

11    And then there are the jet skiers. Countless times I've been driven from the riverbank by these wankers, all of whom seem equipped with a self-satisfied smirk and the belief that innocent bystanders are awestruck by their ability to make noise, create waves, and make Mennonites suddenly wish they had a Gatling gun. The standard procedure is to buzz the bank a few times until the fishing's destroyed, then move out a bit and spin the craft around and around and around until a tidal wave is created. We on the riverbank call these people "circle jerks," but that somewhat demeans the activity that initially inspired the expression.

12    I have, in fact, been present when jet skiers provoked a potentially fatal reaction among the hoi polloi. The place was a fishing pier on North Carolina's Outer Banks. The sky was blue, but the blues weren't biting. Some blamed the sun, some the tides, while others blamed a group of four or five jet skiers who periodically buzzed the pier. Finally, patience broke.

13    A few pier rats strung line through the eyes of lead weights, and when the buzzing recommenced they spun the weights above their heads and let them fly. None struck home, though it is safe to say that a three-ounce pyramid of lead upside the head can prove a fatal experience. This possibility did not restrain anyone from pressing congratulatory beers into the hands of the would-be assassins.

14    Now, many of us would not approve of killing jet skiers, at least without a prior legal proceeding. We will also agree with manufacturers that snowmobiles and ATVs allow handicapped Americans access to the outdoors they would not otherwise enjoy. We agree that some waivers should be granted, though recipients should have no more than one leg at most. But we remain adamant that these people are national pests and should be kept out of national parks. It's not as if there's a shortage of places for them to go. One study says there are 130,000 miles of designated snowmobile trails, with only 500 in national parks. But like grasping adolescents, these people must have it all.

15    True right-wingers have historically known how to handle adolescents: Be sweet, but also be firm. To this crew, let us say: "Here's some sugar, kid. Go dump it down your gas tank."

NICHOLAS D. KRISTOF

# *In Praise of Snowmobiles*

1   Environmentalists have savaged President Bush for overturning Clinton administration plans to ban snowmobiles in Yellowstone National Park. They conjure an image of rabid rednecks roaring around the geysers, terrifying the elk and leaving even the bison in need of gas masks.

2   "Yellowstone will continue to be polluted and degraded, simply to placate the snowmobile industry," the Fund for Animals declared, denouncing "the Bush administration's latest handout to industry."

3   But come to Yellowstone when it is covered in a dazzling blanket of snow, through which hot springs toil and trouble, and it looks as if President Bush did exactly the right thing. He fended off zealous environmentalists who would have closed off the park to most humans in winter, when Yellowstone's roads are closed to cars.

4   I rented snowmobiles here to see just how dreadful they are, and the bottom line is that they're the most efficient way to get around in the winter. (They're also fun, but I'm not sure I should admit that.) On one outing, while negotiating old logging roads outside West Yellowstone, I came across two bull moose. I stopped, and they were polite enough not to display any resentment at the intrusion. Should I really feel guilty that I rode a snowmobile to get to them, when otherwise I would never have seen them at all?

5   The campaign against snowmobiles in Yellowstone gathered momentum in the 1990's, when the snowmobiles were very loud and polluting. But faced with eviction from Yellowstone and perhaps other national parks, the manufacturers quickly developed something they had previously insisted was impossible: a more environmentally friendly snowmobile.

6   The new machines use smoother-running four-stroke engines like those in most cars, rather than the old two-stroke engines, and are quiet enough that you can have a conversation as several of them whiz by—and quiet enough that moose and bald eagles do not flee at the sound, as I can confirm. The four-stroke machines also do not churn out nauseating blue fumes, as two-stroke engines do.

7   So President Bush's compromise very sensibly will ban two-stroke machines in Yellowstone but will permit four-stroke snowmobiles, confined to the same roads that cars use in the summer. In the meantime, environmental groups are still trying to evict snowmobiles from Yellowstone by going to the courts.

8   But when the roads are closed in winter, the only alternative to snowmobiles is snow coaches, which are like vans on treads. Some of the snow coaches

*The New York Times,* 24 Dec 2002, A23.

are themselves very noisy (much more so than four-stroke snowmobiles), and one study found that they are also more polluting—even per passenger—than four-stroke snowmobiles.

9    I took a snow coach to Old Faithful, and it's basically a bus that stops for bison and restrooms. Taking a bus through a national park and trying to peer through fogged-up windows leaves you so removed from nature that you might as well rent a Yellowstone video instead.

10    "We're also snow coach operators, and we advertise equally, and 95 percent of our customers take snowmobiles," said Clyde Seely, a hotelier in West Yellowstone. It's pretty clear that without snowmobiles very few Americans will get the thrill of seeing Yellowstone in winter.

11    "We're outdoors people," said Heidi Keller, a nurse from Illinois who came with her husband, Jim. "We camp all summer, but we don't do anything in the winter. So we thought we'd try snowmobiling. And it's great. I enjoyed every minute of it."

12    Sure, some snowmobilers chase elk or try to catch a bison by the tail. (That's when the bison charge and send the errant snowmobiler flying through the air; more power to the bison.) But bad behavior occurs in the summer too; there was the driver who tried to push a bear into his car for a picture beside his wife.

13    Some environmentalists have forgotten, I think, that our aim should be not just to preserve nature for its own sake but to give Americans a chance to enjoy the outdoors. It's fine to emphasize preserving roadless areas and fighting development in the Arctic National Wildlife Refuge, both of which are good causes, but 99 percent of Americans will never benefit from those fights except in a psychic way.

14    And as for Yellowstone, the moose and bison should share it each winter with humans—even humans on snowmobiles.

JOHN G. ROBINSON

# The Responsibility to Conserve Wild Species

1  Until the development of urban society, the lives and deaths of wild animals and people were inextricably intertwined. People killed and consumed animals and vice-versa. This interdependence is reflected in the cultural importance given to wild animals, whose characteristics are symbolically used in a range of traditional cultures. As human beings increasingly buffered themselves, both technologically and culturally, from the actions of wild animals and concomitantly were able to control the lives of these animals, the relationship changed.

*Social Research* 62.3 (Fall 1995): 816–22.

The evolution of that relationship, as expressed in philosophy, literature, and scientific thought, has been explored in this conference. This essay addresses this same relationship but has a narrower focus: In the modern, increasingly urban society, how should we treat wild animals? Most of us personally experience wild animals only through cultural lenses, such as nature shows on television, or as interesting but vaguely threatening presences during vacation forays into the rural landscape. A more precise question is: What is the ethical justification for people living in the urban society to intervene in the lives of wild animals? This leads into a final question: What kinds of intervention are justifiable?

2          I will address these questions from the perspective of a conservationist, more precisely one who accepts Aldo Leopold's premise that "A thing's right when it tends to preserve the integrity, stability and beauty of the biotic community. It is wrong when it tends otherwise" (1949, pp. 224–25). This statement can be supported from both the utilitarian position—that to do otherwise would endanger the resource base upon which human society depends—or from a more biocentric position—that wild species, and the natural world in general, have an inherent right to exist. Conservationists have tended to synonymize integrity, stability, and beauty. A biotic community that has "integrity" has the full diversity of species, which allows the system to function ecologically in an appropriate way. The "stability" of the community, both its resilience to disturbance and its persistence through time, depends on that species diversity. And conservationists consider "beauty," while the term is not in the scientific lexicon, to be defined by that diversity and stability. For Leopold, people were an integral part of this biotic community, and anthropological research has documented the role that traditional cultures play in creating and maintaining biological diversity in many natural communities. Yet it is also clear that in our present world, the actions of both modern and traditional cultures generally tend to degrade natural systems and reduce biological diversity. The present-day rate of species extinction is perhaps higher than at any time in our planet's existence, and the actions of human beings are the single largest contributor to this global degradation.

3          The impact of humans on the rest of the biota is ubiquitous. Terms like "primeval," "virgin," "primary," "undisturbed," "pristine," even "wilderness," all of which connote biological communities uninfluenced by humans, refer to a certain ideal unattainable in the modern world. From the high deserts of Chang Tang in Tibet to the depths of the tropical forest in central Amazonia, the human presence is everywhere discernible. This is not to state that all nature is a human construct. It is not. Excepting biological communities in urban and agricultural settings, the structure and functioning of biological communities is still predominately determined by species other than humans. But humans do have a pervasive impact on wild species worldwide, and this defines how we must treat wild species. Few truly "wild" species—those uninfluenced by humans—exist today on our planet. And, thus, we cannot abnegate all responsibility for the fates of individual animals or for the continued existence of the

species—they cannot be left "to do their own thing." We must take responsibility for our influence on the lives of wild animals.

4      Our primary responsibility, if we accept Aldo Leopold's premise, is to ensure the survival of species in nature. The least intrusive action is to establish protected areas—parks and reserves for species and the biological communities on which they were a part—and then minimize human impact within these areas. Even here, human impact in and around reserves is significant, and active management is usually necessary to maintain the biological community. Population management, predator restoration, habitat modification, and landscape restoration are necessary tools for protected area managers, and all have an impact on wild species.

5      More intrusive conservation actions are frequently necessary. If the goal is the preservation of biological diversity, protected areas alone are insufficient. First, it is unlikely that we will be able to protect more than a small fraction of the planet's surface in parks and reserves, and the long-term persistence of many species and communities requires larger areas. Second, governments and regulatory agencies are unable to protect areas if local human inhabitants and other interested parties do not support the park or reserve. Park personnel tend to be inadequately funded, supported, and trained. Through political machinations or illegal actions, local peoples can undermine the best efforts of park managers—as evidenced by the recent difficulties experienced by the United States National Park Service and the Forest Service. Accordingly, conservationists frequently advocate working outside protected areas and enlisting the support of local communities in conservation efforts in and around protected areas. Local community involvement requires that local people value wildlife species, and frequently this means allowing them rights to harvest or otherwise use wild species and wild areas. This approach is considerably more intrusive because it involves treating wild animals as resources. It is also controversial because the consumptive use of wild species is seemingly in conflict with the goal of protecting them. However, it is clear that allowing local people to exploit a species in certain circumstances can vest them in the process of conserving wild species or biological communities.

6      Another potentially justifiable intrusion is to bring wild animals into captivity. When wild populations are imperiled by habitat conversion, when animals cannot be protected from hunters, or when other species endanger remnant populations, then bringing animals into captivity can be the most responsible action. The removal of the last condors from the wild in California was justified using this argument. Zoos in particular have assumed the responsibility of maintaining populations of endangered species and have become involved in reintroducing animals back into the wild when circumstances are more favorable. Successful reintroductions attest to the utility of this approach—including the efforts of my own institution, then called the New York Zoological Society, in reintroducing bison to the American west at the beginning of this century. Zoos also have brought animals into captivity with the expressed aim of introducing living animals to a generally urban public and educating them

on the need for conservation, in effect using individuals as "ambassadors" for their species. And in the United States, some 100 million people annually visit zoos, and some 14 million participate in formal zoo education programs.

7    If the goal is to preserve the biological community, then the survival of a species takes precedence over the welfare of selected individuals of the species. Human actions which promote the conservation of a species or a population at the expense of individuals are justified. The welfare of the collective as a whole is more important than the welfare of any one individual. However, even from this perspective, there are circumstances in which the individual welfare of an animal attains importance. As animals become rarer, we value individual animals more, and, thus, the mechanism to conserve species increasingly depends on protecting individuals. For instance, consider the proposed establishment of tiger farms in China to provide bones for the traditional medicine trade, or the proposed harvest of black rhinos in southern Africa for the horn trade. In both cases, arguments have been made that these actions would promote conservation of the species. Yet populations of these species are now tiny, and the risks to the population of harvesting are great. Our efforts to conserve these species depend on our success with protecting each individual, and such proposals have received little support within the conservation community.

8    I have argued that human beings are ethically justified in intervening in the lives of animals if it promotes the conservation of populations or species. Are all kinds of interventions justifiable? From a conservation perspective, the answer is yes. But this answer is incomplete. There are humane considerations that in practice are included. If wild animals are to be harvested, then the humaneness of their killing must be considered. The conservation perspective also does not consider the extent to which a wild species is sentient, yet the actions of conservationists frequently reflect a sensitivity to this issue. For instance, no proposal to bring the mountain gorillas into captivity has been advanced, not even during the recent human tragedy and political unrest in Rwanda. The agonized debates about whether to support harvests of elephants and whales within the conservation community also reflect deep concerns about animal sentience.

9    The reality that human beings significantly influence the natural world, either directly or indirectly, means that we must take responsibility for the survival of wild species. The inescapable consequence of this is the active management of individual animals, populations, and communities. The more humans intervene, the more responsibility they must assume, and as wild population dwindle, the more responsibility we must take for individual animals. And this creates the paradox. The ultimate goal is to preserve the natural world and the wildness that defines it. Yet the methods we use to conserve species, and care for individual animals, can rob animals of the wildness that we value in them. But to do otherwise is irresponsible.

## References

Leopold, Aldo, *A Sand County Almanac* (New York: Oxford University Press, 1949).

MICHAEL CASTLEMAN

# *Opportunity Knocks*

1   I live in a sunny, picturesque neighborhood of San Francisco called Noe (Noh-ee) Valley. It has quiet streets, magnificent views, four coffee bars, three bookstores, two bakeries, two parks, a half-dozen fine restaurants, the church featured in the Whoopi Goldberg movie *Sister Act,* and lovingly restored Victorian and Edwardian homes. In many ways, Noe Valley is an urban oasis where people of astonishingly diverse backgrounds live shoulder-to-shoulder in surprising harmony: owners and renters; young and old; families and childless; straight and gay/lesbian; Catholic, Protestant, and Jewish; and white, Asian, and African-American, including recent immigrants from France, Thailand, China, and the Philippines.

2       The neighborhood's popularity and tranquillity have driven housing prices sky-high, but many residents choking on rent or mortgage payments believe that they have purchased reasonable safety from crime. As I overheard one woman say to another outside our local Starbucks coffee shop recently, Noe Valley is a place where a single woman can feel safe going out alone after dark for a decaf latte. It's a good place, she added, to raise a family.

3       I agree—my little corner of the cosmos is a reasonably decent place to raise a family. But anyone who calls Noe Valley "safe" is living in a daydream. I know because I'm a devoted reader of the police column in our monthly neighborhood newspaper, the *Noe Valley Voice.* In a typical month, our 100-block neighborhood experiences a few burglaries and car thefts, one or two muggings or sexual assaults, and a half-dozen acts of vandalism. . . .

4       The *Noe Valley Voice* police column describes local crimes in considerable detail. Last spring, a man in his teens armed with a handgun held up another man in mid-afternoon in front of the corner store within spitting distance of my front door. The gunman fled on foot right past my house. More recently, three men (one with a gun) held up a corner store five blocks from my home, but only a block from the spot where my 8-year-old son catches the school bus. Within the last two years, one neighbor's new Honda Accord was stolen, and another's Mitsubishi suffered a smashed window and electrical damage resulting from a stereo/tape heist. Another neighbor lost two TVs, two VCRs, and a stereo in a home burglary. Last December, the DA's office announced that a priest at St. Paul's, the *Sister Act* church, was under investigation for allegedly embezzling tens of thousands of dol-

*Mother Jones* 20 (1995): 26+. Mother Jones Interactive. www.motherjones.com/commentary/columns/1995/05/castleman.html
Michael Castleman is the author of eight books, including *Crime Free: The Community Crime Prevention Handbook.*

lars from the parish kitty. Last year, a local realtor was shot to death in his office four blocks from my home. Finally, the other night, a neighbor called to say she'd seen a creepy guy lurking around her front door, and would I please come out and make some noise to send him on his way, if he was not already gone? He was.

5     Now what do you think of my sunny, picturesque neighborhood? Would you venture out alone at night? Would you pony up the $479,000 my neighbors four doors down are asking for their 3-BR, 2-BA Edwardian? Or would you rather take your hard-earned nest egg and move to the suburbs, where everyone knows it's safer? You might try Petaluma, the charming town an hour north of here where *American Graffiti* was filmed . . . and where Polly Klaas was abducted and murdered in October 1993. Or Grass Valley, a lovely, historic mining town in the Sierra foothills . . . where two 16-year-old girls were murdered last summer near a remote teen hangout well-known to locals but not to outsiders, strongly suggesting a resident killer. Or Concord, an upscale suburb an hour east of San Francisco, where in 1987 my beautiful, free-spirited, 21-year-old cousin, Melissa, was sexually assaulted and knifed to death shortly after stepping off a BART train.

6     . . . [M]ost Americans . . . believe that they can pull up stakes and get a new start in a better, safer place somewhere else. Many people who live outside of urban America seem to believe that God grants personal safety beyond city limits. Every time a grisly horror unfolds in some far-off corner of the country, the papers always quote the locals as saying, "Things like that just don't happen here." But "crime can happen anywhere," says Wilbur Rykert, Ph.D., a former Michigan state trooper who directs the National Crime Prevention Institute at the University of Louisville in Kentucky. . . .

7     Of course, some places have more crime than others. I live about a mile from two different hotbeds of crime—probably closer to crack-gun-gang territory than most *Mother Jones* readers, but still far enough away so that for me, and I daresay for the vast majority of you, moving somewhere else wouldn't take us much farther out of harm's way. Which means we're all too close to crime for comfort. What can we do?

8     One common response is to retreat into blissful ignorance, to turn the page quickly when the headlines refer to blood and gore. But when it comes to crime in one's own neighborhood, ignorance is not bliss. It's a significant risk factor for victimization. That's why each month, the first thing I read in the *Noe Valley Voice* is the police report. Most criminals commit their crimes within a mile or so of where they live, according to Rykert, so every crime in my neighborhood represents a potential threat to me and to my family. I'm by no means alone in my fascination with neighborhood crime. According to Tonda Rush, president of the National Newspaper Association, similar police columns are among the most avidly read sections of the 4,000 community newspapers they represent. Why? "Because," she explains, "any crime that happens next door to me is a major crime." . . .

9     [ . . . ] Overwhelmingly, street criminals are young men. More than 80 percent of those arrested are male. Men aged 15 to 24 account for 40 percent of all arrests, and men 15 to 34 account for 70 percent. Why? Because no one makes a

career out of street crime. Criminals rob and steal on and off for a few years until they grow up and make a startling discovery: Considering all the costs and benefits, the income from crime versus the risks to life, limb, and freedom, a job—any job, even one at the minimum wage—pays better.

10      For street criminals, crime is a grubby, risky existence. In 1992, the average mugging netted $672 in cash and property (watches, jewelry, etc.), the average burglary $1,278, according to victims' reports to police. . . . [T]hieves must sell stolen property at a substantial discount to unload it quickly with no questions asked. Assuming, I believe generously, that crooks net 50 percent of what statistics say they steal, a criminal from one of the crime hot spots near me would have to pull eight burglaries a month just to afford rent and groceries in San Francisco's comparatively low-rent Mission District. But my neighborhood has only two or three burglaries a month, not even enough to support one burglar at poverty level.

11      Given their youth and lack of education, street criminals are typically people with little competence in the adult world. In addition, says Marc Mauer, assistant director of The Sentencing Project, a Washington, D.C., organization specializing in criminal justice policy, "Half of all violent offenses are committed by people intoxicated on alcohol and/or other drugs."

12      Street criminals are not masterminds. They go for the easiest available targets. That's why people aged 15 to 34 account for the majority of crime victims—in about two-thirds of all violent (non-murder) crimes and three-fifths of homicides.

13      I was mugged at age 24, a demographic cliché. Though a Phi Beta Kappa college grad, I was still basically a stupid kid. As I skirted a park while walking home alone from a friend's house around midnight, two black teenagers suddenly appeared, stuck a gun in my back, and snatched my wallet. I lost $80.

14      My home was burglarized the following year. (My wife and I left a window unlocked, and I believe a smarmy neighbor hit us.) But I haven't been victimized since. That's another demographic cliché: Victimization statistics clearly show that risk declines steadily with age, as we become older and, often in spite of ourselves, wiser.

15      But ironically, while the risk of becoming a victim plummets with age, fear of crime rises. I'm more anxious about street safety now than I was 20 years ago, even though I haven't had a problem in two decades. And I'm very nervous about my children's safety. I'm not alone. A recent Gallup Poll commissioned by *Parenting* magazine showed that 54 percent of parents feared their children might be kidnapped. A child's actual kidnapping risk is one in 300,000, about the odds of being hit by a pop-up at a major league baseball game.

16      Because fear grows with age, a declining crime rate offers cold comfort. As we grow older and more cautious, we feel the streets are meaner than ever—even when it's clear that they're not.

17      Liberals blame crime on poverty, racism, and lack of educational and job opportunities, which leave people so bereft of hope that they fall victim to antisocial rage. The conservative line is that the ACLU has hog-tied the police and forced the courts to coddle criminals when we ought to lock them up and throw away the key.

18      Both sides also blame crime on the breakdown of the family, but for different reasons. Liberals maintain that a lack of childcare, social services, and affordable health care turns the disadvantaged into vengeful victims. Conservatives insist that liberal secularism—sex education and opposition to school prayer—has rent the nation's moral fabric.

19      Political progressives dismiss the pro-prison argument with one quick statistic: In 1980, there were 139 prisoners per 100,000 Americans; this figure had doubled to 373 per 100,000 as of last June, when the number of state and federal prisoners topped 1 million for the first time. "More than ever," says sociologist Marvin Wolfgang, a professor of criminology and law at the Wharton School of the University of Pennsylvania, "we are locking 'em up and throwing away the key. Does anyone feel safer? I don't think so."

20      But conservatives have a point: Punishment can be an effective deterrent when it is immediate, certain, and severe. Touch a hot stove once or twice, and you stop doing it because the punishment meets these criteria. But the criminal justice system does not. Prison sentences are neither immediate nor certain, thanks to the little detail of innocent until proven guilty.

21      So conservatives dump their karmic eggs into the severity basket. Crime, they argue, is a rational choice, and criminals will stop choosing it when the potential cost (decades in prison) outweighs the potential gain ($402 from the average convenience-store robbery in 1992). Hence their "three strikes and you're out" initiatives.

22      Surprisingly, however, some thoughtful conservatives disagree. "Swift and certain punishment," says noted conservative criminologist James Q. Wilson, a professor of management at the John E. Anderson Graduate School of Management at UCLA, "is more effective than severe penalties." And long-term incarceration is incredibly expensive, about $20,000 a year per prisoner, estimates Marc Mauer of The Sentencing Project. Keeping prisoners locked up costs $30 billion a year. "We could send them all to college for less," he says.

23      What about the liberal view? Being a person of the left, I've tried to make myself believe that poverty and racism cause crime. I'll venture that they contribute to some people's crimes, but guess what? Leading liberal criminologists remain unconvinced. Wolfgang, a liberal who has worked as a consultant to many anti-poverty programs, says: "There is no consistent correlation between poverty and crime. The studies go back 100 years, and they show only a weak correlation at best. Most poor people are law-abiding, and many rich people break the law."

24      [ . . . ] As for racism, the left's other hallowed cause of crime, I confess to considerable confusion. . . . On the street, to avoid assault, I do my best to avoid knots of young men. But most of all, I avoid young black men. I doubt there's an honest white liberal who acts differently. Does that make me—us—racist? Or prudent? Or both? I honestly don't know. But, statistically speaking, to behave otherwise tempts fate. Some African-American leaders seem to be coming to a similar conclusion. With black-on-black crime decimating their communities, a few are beginning to suggest that instead of fighting racism to

reduce crime, perhaps black people should fight crime to reduce racism and, at the same time, to secure their own safety.

25      A confession: Your author has a criminal past. I never did anything truly awful, but if I'd been caught and convicted every time, I might be serving a life sentence today under California's three-strikes-and-you're-out law. I don't know what causes Crime with a capital "C." But I know what caused my own crimes— a strange combination of impulse, alienation, and opportunity. I committed my crimes driven by a momentary impulse I can't really explain. I consider myself a thoughtful person, but I don't recall thinking much about my criminal escapades. I just did them. I believe everyone experiences criminal impulsiveness. How else do you explain affluent executives padding their expense accounts or cheating on their taxes? What else explains a priest embezzling?

26      I committed all of my crimes, predictably, from age 15 to 25. I wasn't a bad kid, but I felt disconnected from the adult world. There were too many damn rules, too many restrictions. Then Vietnam came along, revealing what I considered egregious hypocrisy on the part of the elders who could send me off to die. When Henry Kissinger, the strategist behind the bombing in Southeast Asia, won the Nobel Peace Prize, I felt alienated. Of course, poverty and racism are also alienating, and I believe they play a role in some people's crimes, but not in mine.

27      Personally, I think opportunity is the key to crime. What poor black kid in his right mind would keep mugging people if he could pad an expense account, or bilk savings and loan investors, or embezzle from a church? The poor schmuck mugs because he has no opportunity to commit more lucrative, less grubby crimes. With the exception of murder (which usually involves family or acquaintances), the vast majority of crimes are opportunistic in nature.

28      Impulse, alienation, and opportunity. I seriously doubt that the left or right, the church or state, the family or schools will ever rid us imperfect human beings of our criminal impulsiveness. I see it already in my son. Not long ago, he swiped some money off our kitchen counter that had been left for a babysitter. Why? "I don't know," he said. "It was there."

29      I also seriously doubt that the alienation engendered by youth, poverty, racism, or Bill making the basketball team over Jim can ever be eliminated. As a person of the left, I abhor all the nefarious "isms," and want to see liberty, justice, and single-payer health care for all. But I'm not holding my breath. And I confess considerable discomfort with letting people off the hook simply because they've been victimized in one way or another. Who hasn't?

30      That leaves reducing criminal opportunity as our best bet for controlling crime. As Robert Frost wrote: "Good fences make good neighbors." Good dead bolts help, too. That's why all successful crime prevention programs focus on opportunity control—street smarts to prevent assault, and "target-hardening" to prevent burglary.

31      Successful crime prevention programs also work hard to foster neighbor-to-neighbor communication, which helps minimize alienation. Many leftists I know pooh-pooh neighborhood watch programs because they smack of Big Brother, involve cooperation with the police, and don't do anything about

poverty and racism. But the fact is, they work, which is more than I can say for the political rhetoric of either the left or the right. Personally, I can take or leave neighborhood watch signs. They've proliferated to the point that they've become meaningless. But neighborliness helps minimize the alienation that nudges some people down the wrong road.

32    On my block, most of us know each other by name. We know (more or less) who belongs and who doesn't, who's home and who's away. A few months ago, an old friend came to visit whom I hadn't seen in years. Standing on my front deck, he asked about the neighborhood. I quickly sketched miniprofiles of most of the neighbors in the immediate vicinity. He was astonished that I knew so many of them. I replied that I make it my business to know all the young boys on my block, and I make damn sure that they know me. I want them to feel some neighborliness toward me and mine when they enter their crime-prone years.

33    My belief in neighbor-based crime prevention received a major boost recently when, for the first time, two economists developed a complex economic model demonstrating that neighborhood action is a crucial factor in controlling crime. George Akerlof and Janet Yellen, a husband-and-wife team from the University of California at Berkeley, showed that community action—specifically block groups in close contact with the police—raised the "cost" of crime to the criminals by increasing the certainty of punishment.

34    In the last year or so, we've had a fair amount of turnover on our block, with several homes and rental units changing hands. According to a recent census analysis, my block's transience is by no means unusual—20 percent of the nation's households moved during the 15 months before the 1990 census. For renters, the figure was 40 percent. That kind of turnover ratchets up the general level of alienation and is a big reason why picking up stakes and moving elsewhere doesn't buy safety. New arrivals disrupt the area's sense of community, and they bring the very crime-breeding alienation they left their former communities to escape.

35    I've now lived on my block eight years, and I'm enough of an old-timer to feel concerned about the recent turnover. So recently my wife and I organized a little potluck dessert party in honor of the new arrivals. Most of our immediate neighbors came. There were no formal crime prevention speeches. There didn't have to be. Everyone was an urban survivor (knock on wood), in love with San Francisco and Noe Valley, but also perpetually, realistically nervous about crime. The neighbors knew exactly why we'd invited them, and thanked us for taking the initiative. They dutifully signed in with address, phone number, and the names of everyone in their household. (A few days later, I distributed copies up and down the block.)

36    At the potluck, two neighbors with new cars were concerned about auto theft. One had bought The Club, the bar that locks across the steering wheel, interfering with a thief's ability to steer. The other had installed a car alarm. We teased the alarm owner because it had blared a few false alarms. The teasing was good-natured, but its message was clear: Those false alarms annoyed the hell out of us.

37    I have nothing against silent alarms that ring at private security companies, but for home and car security, on-site siren alarms are fundamentally wrong-

headed. False alarms alienate the very neighbors alarm owners depend upon to call the police. Safety springs not from obnoxious sirens that indicate entry, but from shrewd target-hardening that prevents entry in the first place. I have neither a home alarm system nor metal grilles on my street-accessible windows, but I've taken the safety precautions police recommend. The typical burglar is willing to work for only a few minutes to break into a home or car. Any more, and the target loses its appeal. It would take a concerted effort for a burglar to break into my home, more time and trouble than the intoxicated young turkeys who commit breaking-and-entering crimes are willing to invest.

38　　[ . . . ] Our new-neighbors party was an enjoyable low-key affair. After the car security discussion, the conversation turned to gardening, skiing, and the sale of our corner store, a key meeting place on our block. Kids ran around, people laughed, and all enjoyed chatting with the neighbors they knew and meeting the new arrivals. We all knew that any of us could be caught in the wrong place at the wrong time at the wrong end of some nut's automatic weapon. But we also knew that a great deal of our crime risk was centered right here—in our neighborhood, on our block. If nothing else, I believe that concern about crime is a good excuse to party.

39　　But I party with both eyes open. I like my neighbors, but you can't be too careful. After everyone departed, I checked all our door and window locks–just to be sure.

### Gary Kleck

## *There Are No Lessons to Be Learned from Littleton*

1　On April 21, 1999, two young men armed with guns and explosives murdered 13 people, wounded 31 others, and then committed suicide in a high school in Littleton, Colorado. This mass shooting had been preceded by three other highly publicized mass shootings in schools involving adolescent boys in the preceding year-and-a-half in Pearl, Mississippi; West Paducah, Kentucky; and Jonesboro, Arkansas (and there had been at least seven other multi-victim school shootings in the six years before that), and was followed by two more occurring within a month in Springfield, Oregon, and Conyers, Georgia.

2　 . . . A wave of commentary followed, in which journalists and other writers of every ideological stripe explained to their readers what lessons were to

*Criminal Justice Ethics* 18 (Wntr–Spring 1999): 2+.
Gary Kleck, author of *Targeting Guns: Firearms and Their Control,* is Professor, School of Criminology and Criminal Justice, Florida State University, Tallahassee.

be learned from Littleton or, more broadly, from this cluster of massacres. In a typical commentary, a writer would diagnose one or more key problems that supposedly contributed to the killings, and then prescribe one or more solutions. The diagnoses and solutions generally fitted remarkably well with pre-existing news media themes, reflecting either an impressive ability of news providers to identify causes and solutions in advance or a tendency to exclude the solutions that do not easily fit the themes.

3    A partial list of the problems that have been blamed for the recent mass killings in schools would include: guns, "assault weapons," large-capacity ammunition magazines, lax regulation of gun shows; the failure of parents to secure guns, school cliques, and the exclusion of "outsiders"; bullying and taunting in schools, especially by high school athletes; inadequate school security, especially a lack of metal detectors, armed guards, locker searches, and so forth; excessively large high schools; inadequate monitoring of potentially violent students by schools; lazy, uninvolved Baby Boomer parents and correspondingly inadequate supervision of their children; young killers not being eligible for the death penalty; a lack of religion, especially in schools; violent movies and television; violent video games; violent material and communications on the World Wide Web/Internet (including bomb-making instructions); anti-Semitism, neo-Nazi sentiments, and Hitler worship; "Industrial" music, Marilyn Manson's music, and other "dark" variants of rock music; Satanism; "Goth" culture among adolescents; and Southern culture.

4    The purpose of this essay is not to sort out which diagnoses are correct. Many of them are plausible, and some are probably even accurate. Likewise, some of the proposed preventive measures may well be effective. Rather, my main point is that it is generally a mistake to diagnose the causes of violence and crime, or to identify effective ways to reduce violence and crime, via a focus on unusual, heavily publicized violent events, because diagnoses and prescriptions developed or promoted in the immediate aftermath of such events are especially likely to be irrelevant or even counterproductive.

5    A casual consumer of the flood of news coverage of these shootings could easily draw the conclusion that violence in schools is a growing problem or that youth violence, gun violence, or violence in general has been increasing. In fact, these are the recent trends in violence:

- the homicide rate dropped by a third from 1991 to 1998,

- the juvenile share of arrests for violent crime has been declining since 1992,

- gun violence, and the gun share of violent crimes, has been declining since 1993,

- the lethality of gun crime (the share ending in death) has been declining since the mid-1970s,

- mass murder has been declining for decades (the share of homicide victims killed in incidents with four or more victims dropped in half between 1976 and 1994), and

■ school gun violence has generally declined since national statistics were first gathered for the 1992–1993 school year.

6    In sum, the cluster of mass shootings in schools that occurred in the late 1990s may well be one of the few forms of violence that have been increasing in recent years. Even gun homicides in schools have generally been declining in recent years, despite the massacres. Indeed, excluding the Littleton killings, U.S. schools experienced just two gun homicides during the 1998–1999 school year, which would have been the lowest total since national statistics were first compiled. While some of these facts were mentioned occasionally in news stories about these events, many writers nevertheless offered explanations for the nonexistent "trend" in youth/school/gun violence.

7    Misdescription of the phenomenon to be explained leads to misdiagnosis of its causes. If there is no increase in youth/school/gun violence, it is fruitless to search for contributing factors. . . . Thus, long-term or significant social trends may be irrelevant to these murders. . . . Rather, this short-term clustering may . . . [be a] process by which each new act is triggered by news media accounts of the previous ones. Adolescent boys, faced with powerlessness and anonymity, and otherwise unhappy for a multitude of diverse reasons, recognize that fame, importance, and a sort of immortality have been the rewards for previous mass killers and realistically anticipate the same rewards for themselves if they copy their actions. This process can perpetuate itself until the news media loses interest or competing stories push schoolyard massacres off the front pages.

8    . . . [A]ctions will prevent harm only to the extent that the events they can effectively head off are likely to be repeated in the future. Yet, the more bizarre an event, the less likely it is to be repeated. Thus, . . . the more narrowly a preventive measure is tailored to the specifics of such events, the less likely it is to save lives.

9    One might argue that while commentary on these media-heavy tragedies might not successfully identify measures that could prevent such events in the future, analysis of the extraordinary events might identify measures that could prevent more commonplace kinds of violence. This might make sense if the heavily publicized events closely resembled more ordinary acts of violence, but in many important ways they do not.

10    Particular violent events are heavily covered by the news media precisely because they are unusual and thus unrepresentative of broader categories of crime and violence. For example, violent incidents with many victims are the ones most likely to be covered heavily. Yet less than one percent of Americans who are murdered are killed in incidents with four or more dead victims (often regarded by experts as the admittedly arbitrary cutoff between mass killings and "ordinary" homicides). Only two percent are killed in incidents with more than two victims, and these are most commonly killings within families. Their high body count itself makes mass killings unusual and unrepresentative of murder or violence in general.

11    This would not be problematic if the causes of, and likely solutions to, mass killings matched closely with likely causes and solutions to "ordinary" violence,

but mass killings differ from ordinary violence in crucial ways. For example, mass killings are almost invariably planned, while other homicides and assaults are rarely planned. Likewise, firearms are virtually a necessity to killing large numbers of people in a single incident, but far less essential for killing a single person. Further, mass killers often come from middle-class backgrounds and have little prior record of criminal behavior, while these things are rarely true of "ordinary" killers.

12      [ . . . ] Just as few homicides involve large numbers of victims, very few occur in schools. Schools continue to be the safe havens that they were traditionally perceived to be, however much media coverage of these killings has eroded that perception. While there is serious violence in a few schools, and considerable gun violence outside of schools, gun violence in schools is extremely rare. In the 1996–97 school year, 90 percent of public schools did not experience a single serious violent crime (murder, rape, sexual battery, robbery, or attack with a weapon) regardless of gun involvement, and over 99.99 percent have never had a homicide. The violence that does occur in schools is mostly unarmed fighting (including a good deal of bullying), while gun violence, even among adolescents, is almost entirely confined to places other than schools. Less than one in 400 adolescent gun homicides in 1994 occurred in a school or on school grounds.

13      The school shootings triggered a barrage of transparently irrelevant proposed solutions, tossed out without regard to their relevance to the events that supposedly occasioned the proposals. Mississippi responded to the Pearl shootings by making murder on school property a capital offense, even though premeditated murder, regardless of location, was already a capital offense in Mississippi. The killers in this incident, moreover, were ineligible for the death penalty because of their ages, eleven and thirteen; the minimum age for the death penalty was left unchanged.

14      Following the first four of these shootings, members of Congress were pushing a bill that would "crack down" on dealers who sell firearms to children even though none of these cases involved a dealer selling a gun to a child. After the shooting in West Paducah, in which the killer was armed with five firearms and shot eight different people in the school lobby, newspapers reported that the school system was considering installing metal detectors. The stories did not explain how metal detectors could prevent attacks by those willing to shoot their way into a school.

15      After it was found that such transfers were involved in the Littleton case, some analysts proposed restricting sales at gun shows. Gun show sales, however, had nothing at all to do with any of the other high-profile school shootings. The most common modes of acquisition of guns by shooters were theft (the West Paducah, Jonesboro, and Conyers shootings, as well as a somewhat less prominent case in Edinboro, Pennsylvania), while the Springfield shooter was given his guns by his father. Further, even in the Littleton case the three longguns that accounted for all of the deaths were purchased on the killers' behalf by the eighteen-year old girl-friend of one of the shooters. Under both Colorado and federal law, she would have been eligible to purchase the same guns from any gun store. Further, one of the two killers turned eighteen before the shootings and was likewise eligible to buy longguns from any gun store.

16        Consequently, regulation of gun shows was totally irrelevant to preventing any of these massacres. One irony of addressing such proposals is that some of them make sense, but not in connection with mass killings. As a result, some people will reject a measure with regard to ordinary violence because it is irrelevant to the unusual events at hand. A prime example is extending background checks to private gun transfers at gun shows. The Littleton and other mass shootings are the worst possible examples of cases in which the background checks could succeed since determined killers who plan their murders over a long period of time are the people least likely to be blocked from getting a gun by background checks. As a long-time advocate of extending background checks to all private transfers of guns, not just the few that take place at gun shows, I worry that the real merits of such a step will be obscured by the inane debate over the nonexistent link between gun shows and the Littleton massacre. More broadly, mass killings and other premeditated murders are the very worst examples for buttressing a case in favor of gun control because they involve the perpetrators most strongly motivated and able to evade the controls.

17        Even under the best of circumstances, the lessons one could derive from the examination of individual violent events are inherently ambiguous. The fact that violence did occur necessarily means that all existing preventive measures failed. This can lead to any of a number of very different conclusions: (1) we need different preventive measures, (2) we need more of the existing measures, or (3) nothing can be done. The ongoing issue most frequently linked to the school shootings was gun control, and reactions by those on both sides of that issue were predictable. Pro-gun people concluded that despite the existence of laws completely prohibiting the purchase and carrying of guns by minors, youthful killers got guns anyway; therefore gun control is ineffective. Meanwhile, pro-control people concluded that if existing gun controls failed, it showed that stronger measures were called for–anything from tougher controls over gun shows and laws requiring guns to be kept locked to lawsuits against gun companies supposedly marketing guns to juveniles.

18        Assessments of preventive measures based on a narrow focus on violent events . . . , however, are inherently misleading because they necessarily focus only on the failures. . . . One cannot infer how much success a policy has had by counting its failures. Successes of preventive measures, unlike failures, usually cannot be observed directly. Instead, they can be detected only indirectly through careful comparison of persons, places, and times subject to the preventive measures with those not subject to them.

19        Diagnosis of the causes of violence is similarly distorted by a narrow focus on the attributes of a few violent actors, distracting attention from violent actors who lacked the attributes, and from the even larger number of people who had the attributes but were not violent.

20        Those who propose preventive measures . . . can plausibly assert that the irrelevance of their proposals to these incidents does not matter because the proposals are meritorious with respect to more common sorts of violence. If that is the case, however, honest advocates should show why their proposals are relevant to more ordinary violence and not coast dishonestly on the emotional

momentum created by extraordinary violent events that their policies could not prevent. It would, however, be naive to expect those playing hard-ball politics to follow the intellectually honest path since they will be loathe to forego exploiting the emotional power that comes from tying their recommendations to the most horrific and frightening crimes.

21       One might justify drawing lessons from high-profile tragedies by arguing that one should make use of the temporarily elevated level of concern about violence to advance worthy solutions that might not prevent unusual events, . . . but would be effective in the long run with more mundane crimes.

22       This argument, however, [assumes] . . . that people make wise choices in times of fear and hysteria. . . . Unfortunately, frightened people often favor actions that make them feel better over those that would actually make them safer, if the actions can be implemented quickly and easily and are touted as producing results immediately.

23       People are less likely to be in a logical or critical frame of mind in the aftermath of the most ghastly crimes, a situation that smart advocates exploit. In such a context, people are more willing to believe that "something must be done," and not look too closely at the details and full set of consequences of proposed solutions. Decisions about serious matters should not be made in the sort of overheated aftermath in which demagoguery flourishes. Such an atmosphere is more conducive to lynch mob justice and empty, politically easy gestures than to wise public policy.

24       Littleton and the other school shootings do raise serious issues, some largely ignored by the news media, and others only briefly mentioned and obscured by the noisy debates over the irrelevancies. These issues might include school bullying and taunting, male-on-female teen dating violence, and violence-saturated entertainment disseminated by profit-hungry corporations. But we will be best able to separate the issues that matter from the ones that do not if we learn our lessons from careful analysis of "ordinary" crime and violence rather than from the freakish events chosen for our attention by the news media.

TRACEY L. MEARES AND DAN M. KAHAN

## *When Rights Are Wrong: Chicago's Paradox of Unwanted Rights*

"Many tenants within CHA housing, apparently convinced by sad experience that the larger community will not provide normal law enforcement services to them, are prepared to forgo their own constitutional rights. They apparently want this court to suspend their neighbors' rights as well. . . . This Court has faith that par-

*Boston Review* 24.2 (Apr–May, 1999): NA.

ents and grandparents living in and around CHA housing will reclaim their families and restore to their children self respect and respect for other human beings. If they do, government efforts will succeed; if they do not, all efforts of government, whether within or without constitutional restraints, will fail."—*Judge Wayne Anderson, granting motion to enjoin mass searches of public housing*

"I understand the right to privacy, but when my baby can't play outside and your baby can't go to school without being shot and killed, what about their rights?"—*Alverta Munlyn, resident of public housing*

1    Thanks to the American Civil Liberties Union and a federal district court judge, residents of Chicago's low-income housing projects currently have the right to be free from mass building searches. The ACLU challenged the legality of such searches in a class action lawsuit filed on the residents' behalf. Judge Wayne Anderson agreed that the building searches violated the residents' constitutional rights.

2    The decision sounds like the rare case of a judge protecting a vulnerable population from police coercion, but for one important detail: an overwhelming majority of the residents *opposed* the ACLU's effort to block the building searches. The Chicago Housing Authority (CHA) adopted its building-search policy as an emergency response to the deadly outbursts of gun fire associated with incessant gang warfare; in one four-day period near this time, the police recorded more than 300 gun-fire incidents in the Robert Taylor Homes and Stateway Gardens projects. When the ACLU filed suit, the elected representatives of 18 of CHA's 19 projects intervened to support the CHA. But Judge Anderson dismissed the residents' willingness to consent to building searches as evidence of the corrosive effect of poverty and crime on their own "self-respect."

3    Judge Anderson's ruling was certainly paradoxical. We ordinarily think of rights as belonging to individuals. Rights express the respect owed to each of us as autonomous actors whose choices about how to secure our own well-being shouldn't be second-guessed by political officials. Yet in the CHA case, Judge Anderson invoked the residents' rights to *overrule* their choices on the ground that he knew better than they what policies treated them with respect.

4    As strange as this story seems, it is no aberration. The CHA building searches are only one of many law-enforcement policies attacked by civil libertarians and invalidated by courts on the ground that they violate the rights of the very individuals who support them. Before it derailed the CHA's building searches, for example, the ACLU sued to block the installation of metal detectors requested by project residents. It has also attacked youth curfews and gang-loitering provisions on the ground that these policies promote harassment of inner-city residents—even though residents of the inner-city have in fact been the driving political force behind many of these measures.

5    [ . . . ] Why do some civil libertarians and courts feel constrained to override these persons' freedom in the name of respecting their rights? The answer is that they subscribe to an anachronistic and unduly abstract understanding of individual rights—one fashioned to address political conditions that, by and

large, no longer characterize American society. Contemporary political conditions require a *new* conception of rights—one that assures that the difficult choices surrounding building searches, curfews, anti-loitering provisions, and the like are made by the individuals with the biggest stake in them.

## Rights 1960s Style

6   . . . The prevailing understanding of rights in American criminal law was fashioned in the 1960s, as a response to the problem of institutionalized racism.

7   As is well known, in the decades between the post-Reconstruction years and the civil rights movement, African-Americans were excluded from meaningful participation in American political life. The South used a host of techniques—poll taxes, literacy tests, malapportionment, and outright physical intimidation—to deny African-Americans a voice in electoral politics. Things were little better in the North, where machine politics of the kind made famous by the elder Richard Daley in Chicago effectively excluded legally enfranchised African-Americans and other minorities from meaningful influence on the political process in America's inner-cities.

8   Law-enforcement institutions . . . [reinforced] American apartheid. The horrific television images of blacks in Birmingham, including children, being attacked by police dogs and police officers wielding high pressure water hoses and clubs are indelible and poignant reminders of the South's violent resistance to civil rights progress. But Northern urban minorities were also frequently subject to violent abuse. In the late 1960s, for example, Chicago police led the nation in the slaying of private citizens, who were euphemistically characterized as "fleeing felons" to mask the routine use of excessive force by police against racial minorities. The police also exploited seemingly benign offense categories, such as disorderly conduct, vagrancy, and loitering to bully minority youths and adults who had the audacity to challenge police authority.

9   . . . African-Americans were also denied adequate police protection. In the mid-1960s, African-Americans were an especially vulnerable population: they comprised more than half of the known homicide victims, and were nearly twice as likely as whites to be the victims of robbery, rape, aggravated assault, burglary, and auto theft.

10   How did police respond to these problems? They didn't. Throughout the country, the criminal justice system paid much less attention to violent crimes committed against minorities than to those committed against whites. In addition, the police systematically disregarded more common "disorder" offenses in minority communities, dismissing prostitution, public drinking, gambling, and even simple assaults as "typically Negro." This toleration of crime and disorder helped to accelerate urban decay, driving critical commercial establishments, as well as working-class residents with the resources to leave, out of poor inner-city neighborhoods.

11   Against this background, the Warren Court fashioned its well-known array of procedural rights in criminal law . . . that together can be characterized as the *1960s conception of rights.* . . . [T]he 1960s conception is best understood contextually, as a program to counteract the distorting influence of institutionalized

racism on America's criminal justice system and, more generally, on American democracy.

12      The 1960s conception of rights showed distrust for communities. . . . Of course, all rights reflect some degree of community distrust because they protect the interests of vulnerable minorities from majority overreaching. What made the 1960s conception of rights uniquely distrustful was its extension of searching judicial scrutiny to basic neighborhood policing techniques that historically had been viewed as important to promoting the welfare of the community at large.

13      Institutionalized racism fully justified this wariness of familiar techniques and of the capacity of normal democratic politics to protect citizens from police abuse. . . . [S]earching judicial review was meant to correct for the failure of the democratic process to take into account the views and interests of African-Americans.

14      In a famous 1960 *Yale Law Journal* article, Justice William O. Douglas leveled exactly this critique against anti-loitering laws . . . because those arrested under such laws typically came "from minority groups" with insufficient political clout "to protect themselves," and without "the prestige to prevent an easy laying-on of hands by the police." Douglas later authored the Court's opinion in *Papachristou v. Jacksonville,* which invalidated anti-loitering laws as unconstitutionally "vague."

15      . . . In this decision, and others like it, the Supreme Court insisted that the authority of law enforcement officials to arrest and search be defined with exacting precision.

16      . . .The primary check against . . . abuse is the accountability of law enforcers to the community's political representatives. In the political context of the 1960s, however, law enforcement officials were accountable only to representatives of the white majority. For precisely this reason, the police predictably used their discretion to harass and repress minorities.

17      Insisting that law-enforcement authority be exercised according to hyper-precise rules . . . made it much easier for courts to detect and punish racially motivated abuses of authority. . . .

### The 1990s World

18   Given its historical context, . . . the 1960s conception of rights deserves admiration. . . . [However] the 1990s present a dramatically different set of social and political conditions.

19      To begin, African-Americans are no longer excluded from the nation's democratic political life. Voter registration levels among African-Americans skyrocketed almost immediately after the enactment of the Voting Rights Act. And in all regions of the country, African-Americans have translated voting power into political representation. Never higher than three percent before 1970, the size of the African-American contingent in Congress grew to nine percent by the mid 1990s—close to the proportion of African-Americans in the population. Between 1970 and 1983 the number of black representatives to state governments doubled. The number of African-American mayors increased more than

five-fold during the same period, and the number of city council members quadrupled. During the 1980s and 1990s, many of America's largest cities—including New York, Los Angeles, Chicago, and San Francisco—have been run by African-American mayors.

20          Growth in African-American political strength has also changed the faces of urban police forces. In Chicago, 25 percent of police officers are African-American; in Washington D.C. a majority are. New York, Washington, and Los Angeles have all employed African-American police chiefs. . . .

21          Crime in minority communities has also changed dramatically . . . : it has grown substantially worse. While national crime rates have been steadily declining during the past decade, they have been increasing in the predominantly minority neighborhoods of America's inner cities. Because most crime is intraracial, disproportionate victimization of minorities goes hand in hand with involvement of minorities in the criminal justice system. Fully one-third of African-American men between 20 and 29 are currently incarcerated, on probation, or on parole.

22          The high proportion of African-American men who have been convicted of a crime, moreover, is a cause, as well as a consequence, of the inner-city crime problem. As more persons are convicted of crime, less stigma is attached to law-breaking. The higher the number of men incarcerated, the greater the number of single mothers, whose own economic struggles deprive them of the time needed to shield their children from the pressures that draw them into crime. The perception that African-American men are disproportionately involved in crime breeds distrust and suspicion of all African-American men, putting even law-abiders at a disadvantage in the employment market and eroding the neighborly bonds essential to community self-policing.

23          In short, crime enfeebles social structures, enfeebled social structures produce more crime, and crime destroys African-Americans' wealth and security. This self-reinforcing dynamic constitutes one of the largest impediments to improving the economic and social standing of African-Americans today.

24          How well does the 1960s conception of rights fit the political reality of the 1990s? In a word, horribly.

25          . . . Only someone who fails to read the newspapers could think that racially motivated police brutality is a thing of the past. But only someone who reads the papers with astonishing selectivity could believe that the problem of police racism today is indistinguishable from what it was thirty years ago. . . . By 1998, ambitious urban mayors like New York's Rudolph Giuliani were making a public point of energetically disciplining racist cops. Meanwhile, police chiefs overseeing racist forces, such as Daryl Gates in Los Angeles, were finding themselves unceremoniously forced out of their jobs.

26          [ . . . ] These procedures do not completely eliminate the risk of harassment associated with aggressive order-maintenance policing. But given the opportunities that African-Americans now have to protect themselves from state abuse through politics, it's perfectly reasonable for them to believe, as Harvard's Randall Kennedy has written, that "the principal injury suffered by

African-Americans in relation to criminal matters is not over-enforcement but under-enforcement of the laws."

27     Ironically, the 1960s conception of rights now poses a significant impediment to vanquishing this particular legacy of racism. Reduction of crime is one of the primary purposes to which minority communities are putting their new-found political power. Instead of shunning the police, inner-city residents are demanding that police give them the protection they have historically been denied. Yet professed civil libertarians—including the ACLU—have repeatedly invoked the 1960s conception of rights to block efforts by inner-city residents to liberate themselves from the destructive effects of crime.

28     . . . [O]ne striking example of the mismatch between the 1960s conception of rights and the political reality of the 1990s . . . is the invalidation of Chicago's "gang-loitering" ordinance. Enacted in 1992, this law was designed to restrict known gang members from congregating on street corners and other public ways. The ACLU attacked the ordinance as a throwback to the pre-*Papachristou* era, when police officers used vague loitering ordinances to intimidate and harass racial minorities. A state court (in a case now on appeal to the Illinois Supreme Court) agreed, describing the ordinance as an exercise of power reminiscent of a police state.

29     The picture of Chicago's gang-loitering ordinance that the ACLU and the court painted is simply false. The law was enacted not to oppress the City's minority residents; rather, it sprang from the grievances of these very citizens, who demanded effective action to rid their neighborhoods of drive-by shootings, fighting, and open-air drug dealing. The ordinance was passed by an overwhelming margin in the Chicago City Council, with key support from Aldermen representing the city's most impoverished, crime-ridden districts, whose residents are predominantly racial and ethnic minorities.

30     The claim that the ordinance invited arbitrary or discriminatory enforcement was also unfounded. In fact, the ordinance was accompanied by a carefully considered set of guidelines. For example, only a small number of officers . . . were permitted to enforce the ordinance . . . in specified areas of a district with demonstrated gang activity. Before specifying enforcement "hot spots" district commanders were to consult with community residents.

31     What's more, it appears that the ordinance succeeded in decreasing crime before the courts intervened. Police data indicate that aggressive enforcement of the ordinance had led to substantial decreases in gang- and narcotics-related homicides and aggravated batteries in the districts with the most serious problems. Blocking the policies makes law-enforcement protection less effective while adding no new political checks against law-enforcement abuses.

32     Another effective law-enforcement policy that has fallen victim to the 1960s conception of rights is the youth curfew. More than half of major cities in the United States have enacted curfew legislation since 1990. They have been fought every step of the way by civil libertarians who argue that curfews interfere with the choices of individual teens and their parents, and invite racially motivated harassment by the police. Some (though not all) courts agree.

33      But again, the civil libertarian critique defies political reality. African-Americans, far from opposing curfews, have supplied much of the political energy behind their resurgence. Edna Pemberton—an African-American mother of 10 who spearheaded the campaign for a Dallas curfew—described the charge that curfews fuel racial harassment as "an ACLU scare tactic that polarized the community." Even inner-city teens generally favor curfews. One poll showed that 70 percent of African-American teens in Washington, D.C., supported that city's curfew.

34      The claim that curfews interfere with individual choice is naive. . . . Willingness to venture into the dangerous after-hours world can be seen as a sign of toughness among inner-city teens, and the reluctance to do so as a sign of weakness. Even youths who prefer not to participate in such behavior—and whose parents desperately prefer the same—can thus find themselves pressured to join in. Curfews help to extricate juveniles from these pressures.

35      [ . . . ] Civil libertarians and courts offer several justifications for overriding the decisions of inner-city residents, none of them satisfying. One is that individuals choose building searches, curfews, gang-loitering ordinances and the like only because society at large refuses to address the social inequities at the root of inner-city crime. It is true that society at large now refuses to address social inequities—and true, too, that residents of the inner-city face unfairly truncated options. But what follows? That those residents should live with gangs, murder, and drugs until justice rolls down like the waters? That they should be made to accept the one option—rampant crime—that they prefer least, and about which they might try to do something?

36      . . . The only thing that can force . . . change is sustained community-level political organizing. That organizing is going on, and it is often just these organizers who argue in support of curfews, building searches, and gang-loitering ordinances.

37      . . . [The] question for civil libertarians is this: Why can't we trust residents of the inner-city to decide for themselves whether the strategic objection makes sense? Shouldn't these individuals be allowed to determine whether this is the most sensible way to improve *their* lives?

38      Civil libertarians . . . [answer no]. The judgment and "self-respect" of inner-city residents, they sometimes maintain, have been deformed by social deprivation. Consequently, they lack the capacity to make critical assessments of curfews, gang-loitering ordinances, building searches, and other similar policies.

39      This contention is rife with self-contradiction. Civil libertarians usually take immense pride in their resistance to paternalism. Respecting individual dignity, they maintain, requires society to refrain from forcing an idealized set of values and preferences on its citizens. Yet upon the discovery that inner-city residents favor policies that the ACLU believes violates rights, too many civil libertarians resort to the very kind of paternalism they ought to abhor. . . . The appropriate way to show respect for *these* individuals is to enforce the rights they would value had they formed their preferences in a better environment. To treat

*them* with dignity society must—in the words of the notorious anti-liberal Jean-Jacques Rousseau—"force them to be free"!

40      . . . [T]he civil-libertarian claim that inner-city residents lack critical judgment is . . . manifestly false. When the ACLU filed suit in the building-search case, CHA residents were vigorously debating the appropriateness of the policy. Although many residents supported the existing CHA policy on searches, many others advocated guidelines to restrict the searches to the hours immediately following a report of gun fire. The heated debate concerning the CHA building searches among CHA residents demonstrates that these individuals do not just accept rules uncritically. Rather, like other self-respecting persons in a tough situation, they reflect, they complain, they demand, they argue, they fight, and they ultimately *decide* what the best course of action is—unless, of course, the power of self-government is taken away from them.

41      Indeed, the worst consequence of the ongoing commitment to the 1960s conception of rights may be its *disempowering* effect on inner-city communities. Criminologists have long recognized that inner-city crime both creates and is sustained by atomization and distrust, which in turn make it harder for individuals to engage in the cooperative self-policing characteristic of crime-free communities. A healthy democratic political life can help to repair these conditions. That is precisely what residents of the inner city enjoy when they are free to decide for themselves whether to adopt building searches, gang-loitering ordinances, curfews and the like. . . .

## Rights 1990s Style

42  What is to be done? . . . [I]t would be silly to argue that the legacy and teachings of the 1960s conception of individual rights have no relevance today. At the same time, it is equally clear that a rigid application of those views is no longer appropriate. We need a new conception of rights . . . [that fits] the unique political conditions of the 1990s, including the emergent political power of African-Americans in the inner-cities, and the devastating effects of inner-city crime on the social and economic prospects of African-Americans today.

43      A 1990s conception of rights should be informed by two principles: *community burden-sharing* and *guided discretion*. The first determines when courts should relax their individualist distrust of community judgments, while the second assures that the trust extended to exercises of community power is not abused.

44      . . . "Burden sharing," a principle associated primarily with the constitutional theory of John Hart Ely, helps courts to determine whether the balance struck by any particular policy is reasonable. If the coercive incidence of a particular policy is being visited on a powerless minority, courts make an independent assessment of whether the benefits in terms of order outweigh the costs in terms of liberty. . . .

45      But when a community can be seen as sharing in the coercive burden of a particular policy, courts are much less likely to second-guess political institu-

tions on whether the tradeoff between liberty and order is worthwhile. . . . When courts defer to the political process . . . , they are not saying that the majority gets to decide what rights minorities have, but rather that the willingness of the majority to bear a particular burden suggests that the policy in question doesn't embody the political undervaluation of liberty that "rights" are meant to prevent.

46     [ . . . ] . . . So instead of viewing all law-enforcement techniques with suspicion, . . . courts should ask whether the community in question is participating in the burden that a particular law imposes on individual freedom. If it is, the courts should presume . . . that the law does not violate individual rights.

47     Building searches easily pass the burden-sharing test. The burden of unannounced mass searches falls on everyone who lives in the projects, not just on persons suspected of wrongdoing. The political representatives of these individuals, moreover, have unambiguously expressed their support for the searches. . . . Because the dissenting individuals have every chance to voice their opposition in the political process, and because there is every reason to believe that the majority—whose members were affected in exactly the same way—give due weight to the dissenters' interests, there is no good reason for courts to second-guess the community's determination that building searches strike a fair balance between liberty and order. . . . Unless the process itself is deficient, the courts should defer to those settlements.

48     Gang-loitering ordinances and curfews likewise pass the burden-sharing test. . . . These laws do indeed burden the liberty of only a minority—gang members in the one case, and juveniles in the other—many of whom might be disenfranchised. . . . [But] inner-city teens and even gang members are linked to the majority by strong social and familial ties. . . . The pervasive sense of linked fate . . . furnishes a compelling reason *not* to second-guess the community's determination that such measures enhance rather than detract from liberty in their communities.

49     Indeed, there is a profound tension between individual liberty and judicial decisions striking down such laws. Many inner-city residents view gang-loitering ordinances and curfews as tolerably *moderate* ways to steer youths away from criminality. They realize that when courts prohibit such crime-preventive measures, legislatures compensate with longer prison terms for lawbreaking. If the police cannot order kids off the streets today, they will end up taking them to jail tomorrow. The self-defeating result is a society that shows its respect for individual liberty by destroying ever greater amounts of it.

50     Now consider the principle of guided discretion. . . . Unbounded discretion creates a risk that individual law enforcers will be able to disregard the will of the community without detection. It also creates the risk that officials will concentrate burdens on a powerless or despised segment of the community, thereby undermining the principle of community burden-sharing. . . . The principle of "guided discretion" . . . require[s] communities to allocate authority in a manner that minimizes these risks.

51    Chicago's anti-gang loitering ordinance is a good example of a law-enforcement policy that satisfies the guided-discretion principle. That law was implemented through regulations that clearly specified who counted as a "gang member," what kinds of behavior counted, which officers could enforce the law, and in what neighborhood areas it could be enforced. . . . [M]isuse of the ordinance would have been easy to spot. Given these safeguards, courts should have upheld the gang-loitering ordinance. . . .

52    The CHA building searches . . . involved little risk of selective enforcement precisely because it consisted of indiscriminate, mass searches. Nevertheless, the policy placed no limits on when such searches could be conducted. Indeed, officials sometimes failed to carry one out until several days after gun fire had been reported. As a result, nothing prevented use of the sweeps as a prophylactic, rather than as an emergency measure. Thus, the principle of guided discretion might have supported requiring the CHA to develop guidelines on the timing of building searches—a result that would have tightened the fit between this law-enforcement technique and the desires of the residents. Judge Anderson, in contrast, ruled that even such guidelines wouldn't have solved the conflict between building searches and the residents' "rights."

## The Tyranny of Legal Abstraction

53   In his 1960 *Yale Law Journal* article, Justice Douglas complained that "a disproportionate part of the energies of [the legal] profession is devoted to the semantics of the law." He continued, "[T]he discourse with which we tend to preoccupy ourselves," he continued, "is pretty much in the pattern of theological discourse. The priests of the profession argue and debate about nice points of law that may seem important to those who lead smug lives in ivory towers but quite unimportant in the life of the nation." The specific targets of Douglas' fire were courts that had invoked colonial precedents to uphold anti-vagrancy laws.

54    Though civil libertarians view themselves as Douglas' heirs, they misperceive the forest of his critique for the trees. Douglas criticized vagrancy laws on the ground that the legal abstractions used to defend them were out of keeping with contemporary circumstances—namely, the discriminatory enforcement of vagrancy laws against effectively disenfranchised minorities. But circumstances have changed since 1960. Today African-Americans exercise considerable political clout in our nation's inner-cities; and far from being terrorized by anti-loitering laws, curfews and building searches, many inner-city residents support these measures as potent weapons against the crime that drastically diminishes their economic and social prospects.

55    The courts and civil libertarians who invoke the outmoded 1960s conception of rights are now the ones guilty of reducing law to a "theological discourse" divorced from "the life of the nation." Such scholasticism, moreover, has very real and painful consequences. Defenders of liberty can do much better.

GEORGE BROOKS

# Let's Not Gang Up on Our Kids

1    Laws based on stereotyping and guilt by association are being passed in the name of crime prevention. Laws that seemed impossible after the McCarthy era now encourage discriminatory and arbitrary law enforcement. Many of these laws are being found unconstitutional. All these laws are morally reprehensible.

2    In 1992, a Chicago ordinance provided that "whenever a police officer observes a person whom he reasonably believes to be a criminal street-gang member loitering in any public place with one or more other persons, he shall order such persons to disperse from the area." Failure of the suspect to not promptly obey would authorize his or her arrest.

3    When the Illinois Appellate Court declared the law unconstitutional in 1995, many who saw the ordinance as a valid way to curb gang activity protested loudly. The court's decision was based on the ordinance's failure to include some type of illegal conduct besides loitering. In 1989 an ordinance was upheld in Milwaukee that prohibits "loitering in a place, at a time, or in a manner not used for law-abiding individuals."

4    And in Tacoma, Washington in 1992, an ordinance was upheld that prohibits loitering "in a manner and under circumstances manifesting the purpose to engage in drug-related activities."

5    Having my own law firm for 25 years, I find these ordinances legally objectionable. Yet these laws offend and outrage me even more because of my experiences over the past six years as a chaplain at Cook County Jail in Chicago. There I see young people confined for committing no crime other than being in a group. Many are guilty only by association or guilty because they adorned gang colors or gang insignias. Often the gang-loitering ordinance permits young people to be arrested for not doing anything illegal.

6    There are significant moral problems raised by gang-loitering ordinances. It is troubling when anyone can be singled out because of who they are with or the colors or symbols they are wearing rather than for what they are doing. If the ordinance were applied equally in all communities, regardless of race, ethnicity or social status, the country on the whole would be outraged. Rather than having oppressive ordinances, it would be more productive to discuss the factors that result in young people joining gangs and those conditions that can prevent them from becoming lawbreakers.

7    As a chaplain, I visit 72 inmates in 12 cellblocks every week as they wait for trial anywhere from a year to three years. The majority of the detainees are gang

*U.S. Catholic* 62.3 (Mar 1997): 18–20.

George Brooks is director of advocacy at Kolbe House in Chicago and a chaplain at Chicago's Cook County Jail.

members, and most are black or Latino. Almost all of them live in poor neighborhoods.

8    This experience has made me more aware that the criminal-justice system works differently for them. My white, middle-class background did not prepare me for the systemic abuses that are routine for certain members of our society. The abuses start at the time of arrest, continue through bail setting, include plea bargaining, and end up in the sentencing. I hear story after story of young blacks and Latinos being stopped by the police, hassled, verbally abused, and searched.

9    They are stopped because of their race or ethnicity—not because of doing anything illegal. The presumption of innocence is virtually nonexistent. The poor are unable to post bond, so they remain incarcerated until their overworked public defender can get to their case. This only increases their antagonism for the police and reinforces the belief that it is "us" against the system. The arrest of innocent people can lead to their erroneous convictions. In the past year, six minorities in Illinois alone have being released from death row in two separate cases because of evidence that absolved them from committing any crime.

10    Frequently I hear, "Well, if they're not doing anything wrong, why should they care if they get stopped and searched." That's a nice sound bite, but I don't think many middle-class parents would tolerate their kids being stopped, insulted, and searched on a regular basis.

11    Recently three Latino young men came out to my home in the suburbs to pick up a couch and some clothes. Their van broke down on the expressway. Rather than getting assistance from the police, the young men and all the contents of the van were searched. They had to walk a mile to call for help. While I was angry about what happened, they were not upset. They expected blatant discriminatory practices; they didn't look at the police as those who would help them but as those who would hassle them.

12    In February 1995, The Chicago Crime Commission issued a report saying there were 100,000 gang members in the city. These figures indicate that 10 percent of Chicagoans between the ages of 9 and 40 are gang members. Although I question the methodology for arriving at these figures, the real question is: Are we just going to condemn gang members and lock them up as soon as possible or do we want to do something about the conditions that foster gang membership?

13    We must understand that young people join gangs for the family they don't have. They join for acceptance and security. They join because they don't have an education or job skills—gangs are how they can survive. Society can urge abrogating gang members' constitutional rights and demand they need family values, but isn't our Christian responsibility to help these kids? Our responsibility when good parents and a good family do not exist is to provide early and continuing intervention in young people's lives.

14    Last year Chicago went through a tragic trial of a juvenile. An 11-year-old male, with 28 prior arrests, was suspected of killing an innocent, talented 14-year-old girl. His gang then ordered his murder, which was carried out by 14- and 16-year-olds. Having been sexually abused as a youth and born to a teenage mother and a father who is now in prison, the 11-year-old was a felon at age 9. Early and continuing intervention may have made a difference.

15    We need to be serious about youth crime. But we can't be serious when each kid does not have a decent and competitive education, a decent place to live, and decent health care. Each Christian has to be involved in changing detrimental conditions. Basic education, job training, conflict resolution, child-care skills, emotional support, substance abuse counseling, and meaningful jobs are all necessary. We can't ignore and lock up a child when those things do not exist.

16    Why not just immediately lock up the 100,000 gang members? Maybe because from a practical standpoint there aren't enough jail facilities. Or could it be that confining our youth is a violent solution?

17    In a 1995 letter "Confronting the Culture of Violence," the U.S. Catholic bishops wrote: "We are tragically turning to violence in search of the quick and easy answers to complex human problems. . . . How do we teach the young to curb their violence when we embrace it as the solution to social problems?" The bishops added that our criminal-justice system "does not offer security to society, just penalties and rehabilitation to offenders, or respect and restitution to victims." And they are right.

18    I first met Keith when he was 20 years old, a ten-year gang member. He dropped out of school when he was in fifth grade. He was arrested on a regular basis, frequently for just hanging out. He saw the police and courts as the enemy. He was usually released within a day or so with nothing being done to change his behavior or improve his life. But in jail, he responded to the influence of chaplains and quit the gang.

19    In court, Keith was found not guilty by a jury, not on any technicality, but because he hadn't committed any crime. (Keith and two other former gang members were arrested without any evidence of their involvement in a crime.) Today Keith has a job as a mentor for a social service agency and is going to school.

20    Keith is an example of why we need to build fewer prisons and rebuild more lives. We need to confine fewer young people and do more freeing of spirits and souls. We need to commit fewer people to institutions and commit to all people. It will only be when each member of our faith community takes responsibility to live the gospel that our society will refocus its priorities for the dignity and respect of each person.

JOE KOLLIN

## Why Don't We Name Juveniles?

1 Journalists should reconsider policies against identifying children.

2    Now is the time for the news media to face the fact that kids really do kill people and that we have the power to something about it.

*Quill* 91.3 (Apr 2003): 12–14.
Joe Kollin is a reporter at the *Sun-Sentinel* in Fort Lauderdale, Fla.

3    After the high school massacre in Littleton, Colo., every editorial writer, columnist and pundit had a solution. Put pressure on parents to keep their kids on the straight and narrow, many said. To pressure parents, they offered a number of suggestions ranging from tossing parents into jail to dunning them for damage caused by their kids.

4    Those solutions won't work. Parents don't fear jail or restitution. They know a judge won't put them in jail if it would mean the state taking custody of their other children. And they know a judge won't force them to pay for damage caused by Junior, or even make them pay for the kid's attorney because you can't get blood from a turnip.

5    No, the only way to get the attention of parents is to put the fear of God into them.

6    Which puts the ball into our court. We can do what juvenile justice systems can't: We can embarrass the hell out of parents. The threat of embarrassment and humiliation can have more impact on how parents raise their children than anything a judge could do.

7    When a child gets caught for snatching a purse or stealing a candy bar, we should include his or her name in our newspaper's daily lists of arrests. If the child is picked up for beating up or slashing a schoolmate, we must say so.

8    Just consider how parents react when their kids are picked up. They run into our studios and newsrooms begging and bribing us not to use Junior's name.

9    Their fear, of course, is that neighbors will wonder what kind of parents they are. They fear the whispers, gossip and stares in the supermarket, on the golf course, at work, at the beauty shop. What parent wants that?

10    It was back in the mid-1970s, as a newspaper reporter in Florida, that I learned how some parents care more about their own reputations than they do about their kids. State law prevented the police from giving us the names of most juvenile suspects, but nothing prevented us from printing names that we could get.

11    I learned the name of a teen picked up for setting a woods fire. The smoke had darkened the skies for days and sent people to the hospital with breathing problems. We printed the teenager's name. Within hours, Papa stormed into the sheriff's office demanding to know which deputy released his little boy's name.

12    The father threatened to get the deputy fired, told the sheriff that he would never hold any office again, promised to have the governor call a grand jury investigation. You get the idea.

13    Had his father been as concerned with his son as he was with his own reputation, would his kid have set the fire?

14    At about the same time, the editor of a Tennessee newspaper ended a nine-month experiment. At the request of juvenile authorities, the editor printed in his police log the names of all juveniles detained by officers.

15    Juvenile cases dropped 4 percent in the county during that time. Although not a huge number, juvenile officials said it was the first time the rate had gone down instead of up.

16    What's unusual about the situation with juveniles is that cops and authorities on juvenile crime often want us to use names. News executives, often the

same ones who challenge government officials who don't believe in freedom of information and accuse them of censorship, are the ones who refuse. Why? Some, perhaps, are afraid of embarrassing themselves or their friends. Others were taught that you can't use the names of juveniles and don't give it another thought. Others, in some states, don't know they can use names.

17      In 1978, when Florida rewrote its juvenile code, some state lawmakers and experts in the field of juvenile law tried to encourage newspaper editors to publish names as a way of reducing juvenile crime. Editors, they said, didn't even know that the existing law let them use names. The editors said they couldn't use names unless a juvenile was bound over to adult court.

18      Even when told the law, editors continued to censor juvenile names.

19      News leaders argue that using juveniles' names will brand kids as criminals for life, diminishing the chance they will ever go straight. After all, they say, the crime was just a youthful indiscretion, and I was a kid once, too.

20      Back in the 1970s, in a Florida city, two boys set off a bomb in their high school during a weekend. The explosion knocked a large hole in a wall but didn't hurt anyone.

21      The newspaper where I worked used the boys' names after they were sent to adult court. One boy pleaded guilty and was sentenced to jail. The other went to trial, was found not guilty, graduated from the same high school and, believe it or not, went on to become a sheriff's deputy in the same community.

22      And he turned out to be an exceptional deputy, especially the way he worked with kids and helped steer them onto the right path.

23      Everyone knew he had been charged with the bombing, but that didn't keep the sheriff from hiring him or the public from respecting him.

24      So the arguments against using juvenile names don't always hold up.

25      There are other arguments against publishing the names of kids, of course. Kids will consider it a mark of honor to see their names in the paper and on TV. Parents of the kids who get in trouble don't read papers or watch the news, so it won't embarrass them. The really bad kids don't have parents to be embarrassed.

26      Would the Colorado massacre have occurred if the parents of the shooters more closely supervised their children? Would they have supervised them if they knew their local media used the names of juveniles? Would it have made a difference if the kids' names had been published for previous offenses? We'll never know, obviously. But consider the lives the media might have saved.

27      Why gamble with more lives? In states where we can use names, we shouldn't hesitate to use them. In states that prohibit publication, we should challenge the laws.

28      Now is the time to rethink our policies, just as we are doing with rape (see "Rethinking Rape Coverage" *Quill*, October/November 2002). Who would have thought that one day we would use the names of rape victims?

29      The time for change is now. Just because something is taboo now doesn't mean it must remain a taboo.

BRUCE SHAPIRO

# *One Violent Crime*

1   Alone in my home I am staring at the television screen and shouting. On the evening local news I have unexpectedly encountered video footage, several months old, of myself writhing on an ambulance gurney, bright green shirt open and drenched with blood, skin pale, knee raised, trying desperately and with utter futility to find relief from pain.

2   On the evening of August 7, 1994, I was among seven people stabbed and seriously wounded in a coffee bar a few blocks from my house. Any televised recollection of this incident would be upsetting. But the anger that has me shouting tonight is quite specific, and political, in origin: My picture is being shown on the news to illustrate why Connecticut's legislature plans to lock up more criminals for a longer time. A picture of my body, contorted and bleeding, has become a propaganda image in the crime war.

3   I had not planned to write about this assault. But for months now the politics of the nation have in large part been the politics of crime, from last year's federal crime bill through the fall elections through the Contract With America proposals currently awaiting action by the Senate. Among a welter of reactions to the attack, one feeling is clear: I am unwilling to be a silent poster child in this debate.

4   The physical and political truth about violence and crime lie in their specificity, so here is what happened: I had gone out for after-dinner coffee that evening with two friends and New Haven neighbors, Martin and Anna Broell Bresnick. At 9:45 we arrived at a recently opened coffeehouse on Audubon Street, a block occupied by an arts high school where Anna teaches, other community arts institutions, a few pleasant shops and upscale condos. Entering, we said hello to another friend, a former student of Anna's named Cristina Koning, who the day before had started working behind the counter. We sat at a small table near the front of the cafe; about fifteen people were scattered around the room. Just before 10, the owner announced closing time. Martin stood up and walked a few yards to the counter for a final refill.

5   Suddenly there was chaos—as if a mortar shell had landed. I looked up, heard Martin call Anna's name, saw his arm raised and a flash of metal and people leaping away from a thin bearded man with a ponytail. Tables and chairs toppled. Without thinking I shouted to Anna, "Get down!" and pulled her to the floor, between our table and the cafe's outer wall. She clung to my shirt, I to her shoulders, and, crouching, we pulled each other toward the door.

*The Nation* 260.13 (3 Apr 1995): 437(8).

6     What actually happened I was only able to tentatively reconstruct many weeks later. Apparently, as Martin headed toward the counter the thin bearded man, whose name we later learned was Daniel Silva, asked the time from a young man named Richard Colberg, who answered and turned to leave.

7     Without any warning, Silva pulled out a hunting knife with a six-inch blade and stabbed in the lower back a woman leaving with Colberg, a medical technician named Kerstin Braig. Then he stabbed Colberg, severing an artery in his thigh. Silva was a slight man but he moved with demonic speed and force around the cafe's counter. He struck Martin in the thigh and in the arm he raised to protect his face. Our friend Cris Koning had in a moment's time pushed out the screen in a window and helped the wounded Kerstin Braig through it to safety. Cris was talking on the phone with the police when Silva lunged over the counter and stabbed her in the chest and abdomen. He stabbed Anna in the side as she and I pulled each other along the wall. He stabbed Emily Bernard, a graduate student who had been sitting quietly reading a book, in the abdomen as she tried to flee through the cafe's back door. All of this happened in about the time it has taken you to read this paragraph.

8     Meanwhile, I had made it out the cafe's front door onto the brick sidewalk with Anna, neither of us realizing yet that she was wounded. Seeing Martin through the window, I returned inside and we came out together. Somehow we separated, fleeing opposite ways down the street. I had gone no more than a few steps when I felt a hard punch in my back followed instantly by the unforgettable sensation of skin and muscle tissue parting. Silva had stabbed me about six inches above my waist, just beneath my rib cage. (That single deep stroke cut my diaphragm and sliced my spleen in half.) Without thinking, I clapped my left hand over the wound even before the knife was out and its blade caught my hand, leaving a slice across my palm and two fingers.

9     "Why are you doing this?" I cried out to Silva in the moment after feeling his knife punch in and yank out. As I fell to the street he leaned over my face; I vividly remember the knife's immense and glittering blade. He directed the point through my shirt into the flesh of my chest, beneath my left shoulder. I remember his brown beard, his clear blue-gray eyes looking directly into mine, the round globe of a street lamp like a halo above his head. Although I was just a few feet from a cafe full of people and although Martin and Anna were only yards away, the street, the city, the world felt utterly empty except for me and this thin bearded stranger with clear eyes and a bowie knife. The space around us—well-lit, familiar Audubon Street, where for six years I had taken a child to music lessons—seemed literally to have expanded into a vast and dark canyon.

10    "You killed my mother," he answered. My own desperate response: "Please don't." Silva pulled the knifepoint out of my chest and disappeared. A moment later I saw him flying down the street on a battered, ungainly bicycle, back straight, vest flapping and ponytail flying.

11    After my assailant had gone I lay on the sidewalk, hand still over the wound on my back, screaming. Pain ran over me like an express train; it felt as though every muscle in my back was locked and contorted; breathing was excruciat-

ing. A security guard appeared across the street from me; I called out to him but he stood there frozen, or so it seemed. (A few minutes later, he would help police chase Silva down.) I shouted to Anna, who was hiding behind a car down the street. Still in shock and unaware of her own injury, she ran for help, eventually collapsing on the stairs of a nearby brownstone where a prayer group that was meeting upstairs answered her desperate ringing of the doorbell. From where I was lying, I saw a second-floor light in the condo complex across the way. A woman's head appeared in the window. "Please help me," I implored. "He's gone. Please help me." She shouted back that she had called the police, but she did not come to the street. I was suddenly aware of a blond woman— Kerstin Braig, though I did not know her name then—in a white-and-gray plaid dress, sitting on the curb. I asked her for help. "I'm sorry, I've done all I can," she muttered. She raised her hand, like a medieval icon; it was covered with blood. So was her dress. She sank into a kind of stupor. Up the street I saw a police car's flashing blue lights, then another's, then I saw an officer with a concerned face and a crackling radio crouched beside me. I stayed conscious as the medics arrived and I was loaded into an ambulance—being filmed for television, as it turns out, though I have no memory of the crew's presence.

12      Being a victim is a hard idea to accept, even while lying in a hospital bed with tubes in veins, chest, penis, and abdomen. The spirit rebels against the idea of oneself as fundamentally powerless. So I didn't think much for the first 10 days about the meaning of being a victim; I saw no political dimension to my experience.

13      As I learned in more detail what had happened I thought, in my jumbled-up, anesthetized state, about my injured friends—although everyone survived, their wounds ranged from quite serious to critical—and about my wounds and surgery. I also thought about my assailant. A few facts about him are worth repeating. Until August 7 Daniel Silva was a self-employed junk dealer and a homeowner. He was white. He lived with his mother and several dogs. He had no arrest record. A New Haven police detective who was hospitalized across the hall from me recalled Silva as a socially marginal neighborhood character. He was not, apparently, a drug user. He had told neighbors about much violence in his family—indeed not long before August 7 he showed one neighbor a scar on his thigh he said was from a stab wound.

14      A week earlier, Silva's 79-year-old mother had been hospitalized for diabetes. After a few days the hospital moved her to a new room; when Silva saw his mother's empty bed he panicked, but nurses swiftly took him to her new location. Still, something seemed to have snapped. Earlier on the day of the stabbings, police say, Silva released his beloved dogs, set fire to his house, and rode away on his bicycle as it burned. He arrived on Audubon Street with a single dog on a leash, evidently convinced his mother was dead. (She actually did die a few weeks after Silva was jailed.)

15      While I lay in the hospital, the big story on CNN was the federal crime bill then being debated in Congress. Even fogged by morphine I was aware of the irony. I was flat on my back, the result of a particularly violent assault, while

Congress eventually passed the anti-crime package I had editorialized against in *The Nation* just a few weeks earlier. Night after night in the hospital, unable to sleep, I watched the crime bill debate replayed and heard Republicans and Democrats (who had sponsored the bill in the first place) fall over each other to prove who could be the toughest on crime.

16      The bill passed on August 21, a few days after I returned home. In early autumn I actually read the entire text of the crime bill—all 412 pages. What I found was perhaps obvious, yet under the circumstances compelling: Not a single one of those 412 pages would have protected me or Anna or Martin or any of the others from our assailant. Not the enhanced prison terms, not the forty-four new death penalty offenses, not the three-strikes-you're-out requirements, not the summary deportations of criminal aliens. And the new tougher-than-tough anti-crime provisions of the Contract With America, like the proposed abolition of the Fourth Amendment's search and seizure protections, offer no more practical protection.

17      On the other hand, the mental-health and social-welfare safety net shredded by Reaganomics and conservatives of both parties might have made a difference in the life of someone like my assailant—and thus in the life of someone like me. My assailant's growing distress in the days before August 7 was obvious to his neighbors. He had muttered darkly about relatives planning to burn down his house. A better-funded, more comprehensive safety net might just have saved me and six others from untold pain and trouble.

18      From my perspective—the perspective of a crime victim—the Contract With America and its conservative Democratic analogs are really blueprints for making the streets even less safe. Want to take away that socialistic income subsidy called welfare? Fine. Connecticut Governor John Rowland proposes cutting off all benefits after eighteen months. So more people in New Haven and other cities will turn to the violence-breeding economy of crack, or emotionally implode from sheer desperation. Cut funding for those soft-headed social workers? Fine; let more children be beaten without the prospect of outside intervention, more Daniel Silvas carrying their own traumatic scars into violent adulthood. Get rid of the few amenities prisoners enjoy, like sports equipment, musical instruments and the right to get college degrees, as proposed by the Congressional right? Fine; we'll make sure that those inmates are released to their own neighborhoods tormented with unchanneled rage.

19      One thing I could not properly appreciate in the hospital was how deeply many friends, neighbors and acquaintances were shaken by the coffeehouse stabbings, let alone strangers who took the time to write. The reaction of most was a combination of decent horrified empathy and a clear sense that their own presumption of safety was undermined.

20      But some people who didn't bother to acquaint themselves with the facts used the stabbings as a sort of Rorschach test on which they projected their own preconceptions about crime, violence and New Haven. Some present and former Yale students, for instance, were desperate to see in my stabbing evidence of the great dangers of New Haven's inner city. One student newspaper wrote

about "New Haven's image as a dangerous town fraught with violence." A student reporter from another Yale paper asked if I didn't think the attack proved New Haven needs better police protection. Given the random nature of this assault—it could as easily have happened in wealthy, suburban Greenwich, where a friend of mine was held up at an ATM at the point of an assault rifle—it's tempting to dismiss such sentiments as typical products of an insular urban campus. But city-hating is central to today's political culture. Newt Gingrich excoriates cities as hopelessly pestilential, crime-ridden and corrupt. Fear of urban crime and of the dark-skinned people who live in cities is the right's basic text, and defunding cities a central agenda item for the new Congressional majority.

21    Yet in no small measure it was the institutions of an urban community that saved my life last August 7. That concerned police officer who found me and Kerstin Braig on the street was joined in a moment by enough emergency workers to handle the carnage in and around the coffeehouse, and his backups arrived quickly enough to chase down my assailant three blocks away. In minutes I was taken to Yale–New Haven hospital less than a mile away—built in part with the kind of public funding so hated by the right. As I was wheeled into the E.R., several dozen doctors and nurses descended to handle all the wounded.

22    By then my abdomen had swelled from internal bleeding. Dr. Gerard Burns, a trauma surgeon, told me a few weeks later that I arrived on his operating table white as a ghost; my prospects, he said, would have been poor had I not been delivered so quickly, and to an E.R. with the kind of trauma team available only at a large metropolitan hospital. In other words, if my stabbing had taken place in the suburbs I would have bled to death.

23    "Why didn't anyone try to stop him?" That question was even more common than the reflexive citybashing. I can't even begin to guess the number of times I had to answer it. Each time, I repeated that Silva moved too fast, that it was simply too confusing. And each time, I found the question not just foolish but offensive.

24    "Why didn't anyone stop him?" To understand that question is to understand, in some measure, why crime is such a potent political issue. To begin with, the question carries not empathy but an implicit burden of blame; it really asks "Why didn't you stop him? " It is asked because no one likes to imagine oneself a victim. It's far easier to graft onto oneself the aggressive power of the attacker, to embrace the delusion of oneself as Arnold Schwarzenegger defeating a multitude single-handedly. *If I am tough enough and strong enough I can take out the bad guys.*

25    The country is at present suffering from a huge version of this same delusion. This myth is buried deep in the political culture, nurtured in the historical tales of frontier violence and vigilantism and by the action-hero fantasies of film and television. Now, bolstered by the social Darwinists of the right, who see society as an unfettered marketplace in which the strongest individuals flourish, this delusion frames the crime debate.

26      I also felt that the question "Why didn't anybody stop him?" implied only two choices: Rambo-like heroism or abject victimhood. To put it another way, it suggests that the only possible responses to danger are the individual biological imperatives of fight or flight. And people don't want to think of themselves as on the side of flight. This is a notion whose political moment has arrived. In last year's debate over the crime bill, conservatives successfully portrayed themselves as those who would stand and fight; liberals were portrayed as ineffectual cowards.

27      "Why didn't anyone stop him?" That question and its underlying implications see both heroes and victims as lone individuals. But on the receiving end of a violent attack, the fight-or-flight dichotomy didn't apply. Nor did that radically individualized notion of survival. At the coffeehouse that night, at the moments of greatest threat, there were no Schwarzeneggers, no stand-alone heroes. (In fact I doubt anyone could have "taken out" Silva; as with most crimes, his attack came too suddenly.) But neither were there abject victims. Instead, in the confusion and panic of life-threatening attack, *people reached out to one another*. This sounds simple; yet it suggests there is an instinct for mutual aid that poses a profound challenge to the atomized individualism of the right. Cristina Koning helped the wounded Kerstin Braig to escape, and Kerstin in turn tried to bring Cristina along. Anna and I, and then Martin and I, clung to each other, pulling one another toward the door. And just as Kerstin found me on the sidewalk rather than wait for help alone, so Richard and Emily, who had never met before, together sought a hiding place around the corner. Three of us even spoke with Silva either the moment before or the instant after being stabbed. My plea to Silva may or may not have been what kept him from pushing his knife all the way through my chest and into my heart; it's impossible to know what was going through his mind. But this impulse to communicate, to establish human contact across a gulf of terror and insanity, is deeper and more subtle than the simple formulation of fight or flight, courage or cowardice, would allow.

28      I have never been in a war, but I now think I understand a little the intense bond among war veterans who have survived awful carnage. It is not simply the common fact of survival but the way in which the presence of these others seemed to make survival itself possible. There's evidence, too, that those who try to go it alone suffer more. In her insightful study *Trauma and Recovery,* Judith Herman, a psychiatrist, writes about rape victims, Vietnam War veterans, political prisoners and other survivors of extreme violence. "The capacity to preserve social connection . . . " she concludes, "even in the face of extremity, seems to protect people to some degree against the later development of post-traumatic syndromes. For example, among survivors of a disaster at sea, the men who had managed to escape by cooperating with others showed relatively little evidence of post-traumatic stress afterward." On the other hand, she reports that the "highly symptomatic" ones among those survivors were "'Rambos': men who had plunged into impulsive, isolated action and not affiliated with others."

29      The political point here is that the Rambo justice system proposed by the right is rooted in that dangerous myth of the individual fighting against a hos-

tile world. Recently that myth got another boost from several Republican-controlled state legislatures, which have made it much easier to carry concealed handguns. But the myth has nothing to do with the reality of violent crime, the ways to prevent it or the needs of survivors. Had Silva been carrying a handgun instead of a knife on August 7, there would have been a massacre.

30     I do understand the rage and frustration behind the crime-victim movement, and I can see how the right has harnessed it. For weeks I thought obsessively and angrily of those minutes on Audubon Street, when first the nameless woman in the window and then the security guard refused to approach me—as if I, wounded and helpless, were the dangerous one. There was also a subtle shift in my consciousness a few days after the stabbing. Up until that point, the legal process and press attention seemed clearly centered on my injuries and experience, and those of my fellow victims. But once Silva was arraigned and the formal process of prosecution began, it became his case, not mine. I experienced an overnight sense of marginalization, a feeling of helplessness bordering on irrelevance.

31     Sometimes that got channeled into outrage, fear and panic. After arraignment, Silva's half was set at $700,000. That sounds high, but just 10 percent of that amount in cash, perhaps obtained through some relative with home equity, would have bought his pretrial release. I was frantic at even this remote prospect of Silva walking the streets. So were the six other victims and our families. We called the prosecutor virtually hourly to request higher bail. It was eventually raised to $800,000, partly because of our complaints and partly because an arson charge was added. Silva remains in the Hartford Community Correctional Center awaiting trial.

32     Near the six-month anniversary of the stabbings I called the prosecutor and learned that in December Silva's lawyer filed papers indicating he intends to claim a "mental disease or defect" defense. If successful it would send him to a maximum-security hospital for the criminally insane for the equivalent of the maximum criminal penalty. In February the court was still awaiting a report from Silva's psychiatrist. Then the prosecution will have him examined by its own psychiatrist. "There's a backlog," I was told; the case is not likely to come to trial until the end of 1995 at the earliest. Intellectually, I understand that Silva is securely behind bars, that the court system is overburdened, that the delay makes no difference in the long-term outcome. But emotionally, viscerally, the delay is devastating.

33     Another of my bursts of victim-consciousness involved the press. Objectively, I know that many people who took the trouble to express their sympathy to me found out only through news stories. And sensitive reporting can for the crime victim be a kind of ratification of the seriousness of an assault, a reflection of the community's concern. One reporter for the daily *New Haven Register*, Josh Kovner, did produce level-headed and insightful stories about the Audubon Street attack. But most other reporting was exploitative, intrusive and inaccurate. I was only a few hours out of surgery, barely able to speak, when the calls from television stations and papers started coming to my hospital room.

Anna and Martin, sent home to recover, were ambushed by a Hartford TV crew as they emerged from their physician's office, and later rousted from their beds by reporters from another TV station ringing their doorbell. *The Register*'s editors enraged all seven victims by printing our home addresses (a company policy, for some reason) and running spectacularly distressing full-color photos of the crime scene complete with the coffee bar's bloody windowsill.

34      Such press coverage inspired in all of us a rage it is impossible to convey. In a study commissioned by the British Broadcasting Standards Council, survivors of violent crimes and disasters "told story after story of the hurt they suffered through the timing of media attention, intrusion into their privacy and harassment, through inaccuracy, distortion and distasteful detail in what was reported." This suffering is not superficial. To the victim of violent crime the press may reinforce the perception that the world is an uncomprehending and dangerous place.

35      The very same flawed judgments about "news value" contribute significantly to a public conception of crime that is as completely divorced from the facts as a Schwarzenegger movie. One study a few years ago found that reports on crime and justice constitute 22–28 percent of newspaper stories, "nearly three times as much attention as the presidency or the Congress or the state of the economy." And the most spectacular crimes—the stabbing of seven people in an upscale New Haven coffee bar, for instance—are likely to be the most "newsworthy" even though they are statistically the least likely. "The image of crime presented in the media is thus a reverse image of reality," writes sociologist Mark Warr in a study commissioned by the National Academy of Sciences.

36      Media coverage also brings us to another crucial political moral: The "seriousness" of crime is a matter of race and real estate. This has been pointed out before, but it can't be said too often. Seven people stabbed in a relatively affluent, mostly white neighborhood near Yale University—this was big news on a slow news night. It went national over the A.P. wires and international over CNN's *Headline News.* It was covered by *The New York Times,* and words of sympathy came to New Haven from as far as Prague and Santiago. Because a graduate student and a professor were among those wounded, the university sent representatives to the emergency room. The morning after, New Haven Mayor John DeStefano walked the neighborhood to reassure merchants and office workers. For more than a month the regional press covered every new turn in the case.

37      Horrendous as it was, though, no one was killed. Four weeks later, a 15-year-old girl named Rashawnda Crenshaw was driving with two friends about a mile from Audubon Street. As the car in which she was a passenger turned a corner she was shot through the window and killed. Apparently her assailants mistook her for someone else. Rashawnda Crenshaw was black and her shooting took place in the Hill, the New Haven neighborhood with the highest poverty rate. No Yale officials showed up at the hospital to comfort Crenshaw's mother or cut through red tape. *The New York Times* did not come calling; there

were certainly no bulletins flashed around the world on CNN. The local news coverage lasted just long enough for Rashawnda Crenshaw to be buried.

38      Anyone trying to deal with the reality of crime, as opposed to the fantasies peddled to win elections, needs to understand the complex suffering of those who are survivors of traumatic crimes, and the suffering and turmoil of their families. I have impressive physical scars: There is a broad purple line from my breastbone to the top of my pubic bone, an X-shaped cut into my side where the chest tube entered, a thick pink mark on my chest where the point of Silva's knife rested on a rib. Then on my back is the unevenly curving horizontal scar where Silva thrust the knife in and yanked it out, leaving what looks like a crooked smile. But the disruption of my psyche is, day in and day out, more noticeable. For weeks after leaving the hospital I awoke nightly agitated, drenched with perspiration. For two months I was unable to write; my brain simply refused to concentrate. Into any moment of mental repose would rush images from the night of August 7; or alternatively, my mind would simply not tune in at all. My reactions are still out of balance and disproportionate. I shut a door on my finger, not too hard, and my body is suddenly flooded with adrenaline and I nearly faint. Walking on the arm of my partner, Margaret, one evening I abruptly shove her to the side of the road; I have seen a tall, lean shadow on the block where we are headed and am alarmed out of all proportion. I get into an argument and find myself quaking with rage for an hour afterward, completely unable to restore calm. Though to all appearances normal, I feel at a long arm's remove from all the familiar sources of pleasure, comfort and anger that shaped my daily life before August 7.

39      What psychologists call post-traumatic stress disorder is, among other things, a profoundly political state in which the world has gone wrong, in which you feel isolated from the broader community by the inarticulable extremity of experience. I have spent a lot of time in the past few months thinking about what the world must look like to those who have survived repeated violent attacks, whether children battered in their homes or prisoners beaten or tortured behind bars; as well as those, like rape victims, whose assaults are rarely granted public ratification.

40      The right owes much of its success to the anger of crime victims and the argument that government should do more for us. This appeal is epitomized by the rise of restitution laws—statutes requiring offenders to compensate their targets. On February 7 the House of Representatives passed, by a vote of 431 to 0, the Victim Restitution Act, a plank of the Contract With America that would supposedly send back to jail offenders who don't make good on their debts to their victims. In my own state, Governor Rowland recently proposed a restitution amendment to the state Constitution.

41      On the surface it is hard to argue with the principle of reasonable restitution—particularly since it implies community recognition of the victim's suffering. But I wonder if these laws really will end up benefiting someone like me—or if they are just empty, vote-getting devices that exploit victims and

could actually hurt our chances of getting speedy, substantive justice. H. Scott Wallace, former counsel to the Senate Judiciary Subcommittee on Juvenile Justice, writes in *Legal Times* that the much-touted Victim Restitution Act is "unlikely to put a single dollar into crime victims' pockets, would tie up the federal courts with waves of new damages actions, and would promote unconstitutional debtors' prisons."

42     I also worry that the rhetoric of restitution confuses—as does so much of the imprisonment-and-execution mania dominating the political landscape— the goals of justice and revenge. Revenge, after all, is just another version of the individualized, take-out-the-bad-guys myth. Judith Herman believes indulging fantasies of revenge actually worsens the psychic suffering of trauma survivors: "The desire for revenge . . . arises out of the victim's experience of complete helplessness," and forever ties the victim's fate to the perpetrator's. Real recovery from the cataclysmic isolation of trauma comes only when "the survivor comes to understand the issues of principle that transcend her personal grievance against the perpetrator . . . [a] principle of social justice that connects the fate of others to her own." The survivors and victims' families of the Long Island Rail Road massacre have banded together not to urge that Colin Ferguson be executed but to work for gun control.

43     What it all comes down to is this: What do survivors of violent crime really need? What does it mean to create a safe society? Do we need courts so overburdened by nonviolent drug offenders that Daniel Silvas go untried for eighteen months, delays that leave victims and suspects alike in limbo? Do we need to throw nonviolent drug offenders into mandatory-sentence proximity with violent sociopaths and career criminals? Do we need the illusory bravado of a Schwarzenegger film—or the real political courage of those L.I.R.R. survivors?

44     If the use of my picture on television unexpectedly brought me face to face with the memory of August 7, some part of the attack is relived for me daily as I watch the gruesome, voyeuristically reported details of the stabbing deaths of two people in California, Nicole Brown Simpson and Ronald Goldman. It was relived even more vividly by the televised trial of Colin Ferguson. (One night recently after watching Ferguson on the evening news I dreamed that I was on the witness stand and Silva, like Ferguson, was representing himself and questioning me.) Throughout the trial, as Ferguson spoke of falling asleep and having someone else fire his gun, I heard neither cowardly denial nor what his first lawyer called "black rage"; I heard Daniel Silva's calm, secure voice telling me I killed his mother. And when I hear testimony by the survivors of that massacre—on a train as comfortable and familiar to them as my neighborhood coffee bar—I feel a great and incommunicable fellowship.

45     But the public obsession with these trials, I am convinced, has no more to do with the real experience of crime victims than does the anti-crime posturing of politicians. I do not know what made my assailant act as he did. Nor do I think crime and violence can be reduced to simple political categories. I do know that the answers will not be found in social Darwinism and atomized individualism, in racism, in dismantling cities and increasing the destitution of

the poor. To the contrary: Every fragment of my experience suggests that the best protections from crime and the best aid to victims are the very social institutions most derided by the right. As crime victim and citizen what I want is the reality of a safe community—not a politician's fantasyland of restitution and revenge. That is my testimony.

# PART II

## Exploring an Issue

The chapters in Part II offer different strategies for exploring sources and developing ideas for an issue of your choice. As you are preparing to write a paper, you may find several of these strategies helpful, regardless of what kind of paper it is. Each chapter, however, also corresponds to a chapter explaining a specific writing assignment in Part III.

# CHAPTER 7

# Entry Points

Up to now, you have learned how to analyze the argument of a single author. But to write about an issue, you need to consult more than one author. You need to learn about the ongoing conversation among the many people affected by the issue. This is not the same as learning facts about the issue. This is about finding points of controversy where people are deciding how to devote resources, develop policies, and take action.

You also need to find a reason to join the conversation—your personal angle on the issue, the aspect that you feel motivated to learn more about or do something about. The angle you end up with may not be something that you are aware of now. Many people find their personal connection only after digging deeper into an issue. In this chapter, you will begin to decide what issue to explore and you will learn how to conduct an authentic exploration.

This chapter will also give you three entry points to issues: personal experience, cases, and authors. These entry points will help you produce lists of related people, places, events, and concepts. In the next chapter, Chapter 8, you will learn strategies for using these lists to search in full-text databases, Web sites, newspapers, and magazines.

## Starting an Authentic Exploration

People become authors because they feel some personal urgency to do something about an issue: They feel bugged by the way an incident turned out or they feel a gut-level sense of injustice or caring.

Your strongest motivation for exploring an issue is likely to be an incident that you know about—from your hometown, school, workplace, organization, or church. You may know someone who got away with a crime—or someone who was badly treated for a seemingly minor offense. You may live in a place with a factory or business that has been accused of polluting the environment—rightly or wrongly. You may have been on a wilderness expedition that made you feel strongly in favor of increasing protection or increasing access.

To conduct an authentic exploration, you do not need to find completely uncharted territory, as Lewis and Clark did. Most public issues have been around for a long time so you will always find a great deal of relevant argument and information. You also do not need to start off in a direction that is completely unlike that of your classmates. If you follow your deepest interests and dig into the available sources, you are certain to come up with a completely different argument from your classmates, even if everyone happened to be working on the problem of ocean habitat off New England or the problem of youth crime in the San Francisco area.

To make your exploration authentic, remember to treat the issue as unsettled ground. If you go in convinced that the only problem is the wrongheadedness and obstinacy of your opponents, you are unlikely to produce a compelling argument. If you go in convinced of the obvious solution, you are unlikely to discover anything of value. It takes hard work and some courage to be an explorer, but that is the best way to become an author.

# Personal Experience

Many students begin their explorations from incidents they know about through personal experience. Rachel, a student exploring environment issues, came from a town near a large manufacturing plant that people in her town blamed for all kinds of illnesses. She decided to investigate health issues arising out of emissions. Scott, a student exploring crime issues, knew an honors student who was expelled and lost scholarships because his uncle had left a gun in the back of his pick-up truck. Scott decided to work on the issue of school safety.

You don't have to have this kind of personal connection in order to engage in an issue. But if there is some aspect of the environment or crime topic that you do care about, now is the time to explore it.

# Cases

Whether you are guided by personal experience or not, a good way to get into an issue is through cases (Chapter 3). A case is an instance of the category of problems that you want to address. The attack on the World Trade Center on September 11, 2001, is a case of terrorism, a category that includes other cases like the Oklahoma City bombing in 1995 and the siege at the Russian school in Beslan in September 2004. The tsunami in Southeast Asia in December 2004 is a natural disaster, a category that includes Hurricane Katrina, mudslides in California, and the flooding of the Mississippi River in 1993. The cases in a category shed light on issues of national security and environmental management. You hear about cases all the time from newspapers, TV, and Web sites: drunk driving cases, school violence cases, forest fires, oil spills, to name a few. Any one of these can be the starting point for your exploration of an issue.

Once you identify a case that you feel strongly about, you can dig further into the issue by investigating the details of that case and by finding other related cases. You analyze and compare these cases to understand the problem better, to explore what matters to you about it, and to find out about previously attempted solutions.

A case is an event, so it includes an **agent** who took **action** out of some **motive** with some **outcome.** "Cases" identifies these elements in Chivers and Castleman.

---

## CASES

### Environment: Chivers

Fishermen who use mobile gear for trawling and dredging (**agent**) scrape hard parts of the ocean floor (**action**) to catch more fish to send to grocery stores and restaurants (**motive**). They end up destroying sea-life habitats and removing fishing spots for traditional fishermen like Captain Taylor (**outcome**).

### Crime: Castleman

People who live in Noe Valley (**agent**) want to get on with their lives and concentrate on their families and jobs (**motive**). As a result, they cultivate ignorance about crime in the neighborhood, fail to get to know their neighbors, and fail to take safety measures (**action**), endangering everyone by increasing opportunities for crime (**outcome**).

---

A real-world case is not by itself a problem. The same events can be interpreted as good or as bad by different people. The way the outcome is described is the key to how the author sees it. If the outcome is portrayed as bad, then the case is being used as a **problem case.** If the outcome is portrayed as good, then it is being used as a good or **ideal case.** When you find a case, you are free to interpret it either way.

## Problem Cases

A problem case is a concrete situation whose outcome makes people dissatisfied or discontent. The description of a problem case is often used in an issue span (Chapter 2) as evidence for the existence of a whole category of similar problems.

"Problem Cases" provides and analyzes this type of case.

## PROBLEM CASES

### Environment: Tire-Tracks in Big Cypress

To get to the best hunting sites and fishing holes (**motive**), [avid outdoorsman Lyle] McCandless and his buddies (**agents**) from the Collier County Sportsman's Club near Naples drive their off-road vehicles (**action**) into the most remote sections of this 729,000-acre preserve [Big Cypress National Preserve, Florida], a vast undeveloped area of wetlands, cypress groves and protected wildlife. Environmental groups contend that the squat, fat-tired all-terrain vehicles are damaging wetlands and wildlife (**outcome**) by creating thousands of miles of deep ruts in the soil. (Canedy)

If you are an environmentalist who views the damage as significant and harmful, this is a problem case. Depending on what bugs you about this case, you can look for other cases of damage in parks by ATVs or for cases of damage to wetlands by sportsmen.

It is not a problem case for the sportsmen who can enter Big Cypress without restriction; for them it is a positive case of members of the public making use of a national park.

### Crime: Traffic Stops of Hispanic Youth

Recently three Latino young men came out to my home in the suburbs to pick up a couch and some clothes. Their van broke down on the expressway. Rather than getting assistance from the police (**agent**), the young men and all the contents of the van were searched (**action**). They had to walk a mile to call for help. While I was angry about what happened, they were not upset. They expected blatant discriminatory practices; they didn't look at the police as those who would help them but as those who would hassle them (**outcome**). (Brooks)

This is a problem case for Brooks, who believes that alienation from society ruins a human life. If you are like Brooks, you can look for other cases of young people in general being hassled or for cases of police profiling on ethnic or racial grounds.

For the police, this incident is not a problem case; it is probably seen as a routine traffic stop with no negative outcomes.

## Ideal Cases

An ideal case is an event with what you consider to be the best possible outcome, a situation that came out right. Of course, nothing is perfect; the outcome might not last or problems may emerge. But, even if it has some drawbacks, the ideal case should seem far preferable to the problem cases. "Ideal Cases" describes some real-world ideal cases.

# IDEAL CASES

## Environment

In order to prevent the extinction of the trumpeter swan (**motive**), the Fish and Wildlife Service (**agent**) established a winter feeding program at the Red Rock Lakes National Wildlife Refuge in 1932 and supported wild and captive flocks (**action**). The trumpeter swan population, that had declined to 77 breeding swans in Canada and 50 in Yellowstone, has increased to 16,000 today throughout the Pacific Northwest (**outcome**).

## Crime

In order to make subways safer and cleaner and collect more fares (**motive**), the New York City Transit Authority (**agent**) stopped using subway cars until they were clean of graffiti, increased background checks, and began arresting people for misdemeanors like fare-beating or spitting (**action**). As a result, crime and vandalism in the subways dropped dramatically between 1990 and 1994 (**outcome**).

Ideal cases are useful for many parts of a public policy argument. To show that a problem (or an opportunity) exists, you can compare the present situation to an ideal case that looks attractive enough to be worth achieving. Ideal cases are also helpful for identifying possible causes of a problem. For example, if several people became ill after eating at a picnic, then the sick people (the problem cases) might all have eaten something that none of the healthy people at the same picnic (the ideal cases) ate. You can also use an ideal case to show that a solution is possible or that it is likely to succeed. For example, suppose that a solution involves getting parents to be involved with their children's activities. To think up ways to increase parental involvement, you might look at another program where that is achieved, such as Head Start.

## Hypothetical Cases

Hypothetical cases are variations on real-world cases, imagining "what if it had happened this way?" You can create a hypothetical ideal case by imagining a positive outcome to a problem case; you can create hypothetical problem cases by varying the outcome of an ideal case or by changing some other aspect of the case. "Hypothetical Cases" presents hypothetical versions of the cases that you have already read in "Problem Cases" and "Ideal Cases."

## HYPOTHETICAL CASES

### Environment

**Creating an Ideal from a Problem Case**

For the environmentalists, the case of access to a Big Cypress would be ideal if the park managers had responded to their protest by banning ATVs or restricting where they could be ridden.

**Creating a Problem from an Ideal Case**

The reintroduction of the trumpeter swan in "Ideal Cases" would turn into a problem case if swan feathers became popular or if a new avian disease entered the area.

### Crime

**Creating an Ideal from a Problem Case**

For the police, a traffic stop like the one in "Problem Cases" would be an ideal case if they had found weapons or drugs because the goal is to follow suspicions to prevent crime.

**Creating a Problem from an Ideal Case**

An effort to clean up a subway system, like the one described in "Ideal Cases," would be a problem case if security became so strict that riders felt hassled and missed their trains.

To enter an issue, keep watch for cases that catch your interest and note their elements (agent, action, motive, outcome). These names, places, and technical terms provide you with search terms for digging deeper, finding related cases and background information, and identifying positions in the argument. You will learn more about searching with these terms in Chapter 8. You will learn more about using cases to explore a problem in Chapter 10.

# Authors and Stakeholders

In addition to thinking about your personal experiences and noticing cases in the news, a good way to enter an issue is to read something about it, especially an argumentative text that identifies allies and opponents. You have already read some articles and excerpts in this book that may have raised aspects of environment and crime that interest you. Keep watch for aspects of arguments that you find surprising, dubious, or outright wrong. Your reactions are clues to the knowledge, interests, and principles that will shape your own position.

Just as you note the aspects of an interesting case, you should list the key details that interest you in an article, especially names of people, agencies, places, and dates. Check the list of works cited to find related articles by other authors. You will learn to use these details to guide your search in Chapter 8.

Look for people who range in experiences, who play different roles in the problematic situation, and who have published information and arguments about it. These can include scholars, stakeholders, decision makers, and pundits. "People Involved in Issues" provides examples of each type.

---

## PEOPLE INVOLVED IN ISSUES

### Environment: People Involved in Dams

| | |
|---|---|
| **Scholars** | Ecologists, agronomists, hydrologists, engineers |
| **Stakeholders** | Environmental activists, recreational businesses, farmers, fishermen, city developers, electrical power companies |
| **Decision makers** | City- and state-level resource managers, U.S. Fish and Wildlife Service, National Park Service, Army Corps of Engineers |
| **Pundits** | Journalists, former officials |

### Crime: People Involved in Curfews

| | |
|---|---|
| **Scholars** | Lawyers, criminologists, sociologists, psychologists |
| **Stakeholders** | Parents, kids, neighbors, youth advocates |
| **Decision makers** | Mayors, police chiefs, government agencies, judges, legislators |
| **Pundits** | Journalists, former officials |

---

## Scholars

Just about any area of public life has been studied in some way by scholars trying to figure out how things work in the world and in society. Many scholars are professors at colleges and universities. Others work for companies or nonprofit organizations. A few decide to carry on an inquiry outside some other career simply out of intense curiosity or passion.

Scholars are not neutral observers (Chapter 6). Like everyone else, they have views about the issues they study. But scholars are expected to test those views very carefully against all the available evidence. They follow standards of evidence established for their discipline, standards that describe the kind of evidence that is needed before an author can state a claim with a high degree of certainty. If they publish in peer-reviewed journals, their conclusions and the methods they have used to reach them have been scrutinized by others in their field.

You can often find the names of scholars in articles you have encountered on your issue, including public opinion articles and academic articles.

"Scholarly Authors" lists scholars involved in the environment and crime issues among the articles you have read so far; some are authors of the articles and some are cited within the articles.

---

## SCHOLARLY AUTHORS

### Environment

- Arturo Gómez-Pompa and Andrea Kaus
- Canadian economist Laura Jones
- Peter Auster, science director of the National Undersea Research Center at the University of Connecticut
- Jeremy Collie, professor at the University of Rhode Island Graduate School of Oceanography

### Crime

- Gary Kleck
- Tracey Meares and Dan Kahan
- Wilbur Rykert, Ph.D., a former Michigan state trooper who directs the National Crime Prevention Institute at the University of Louisville in Kentucky
- Economists George Akerlof and Janet Yellen, a husband-and-wife team from the University of California at Berkeley

---

## Stakeholders

A problem is always a problem for someone. **Stakeholders** are people who are directly affected by a problem or by a proposed plan of action: those who are experiencing a problem, those whose actions or values are seen as the cause of a problem, or those affected by a proposed solution.

To develop a list of stakeholders for your issue, ask yourself: Who has a problem here? Who suffers by the problem directly? Who profits by it? Who cares deeply enough to get involved? Who will pay for its solution?

National or state-based groups are easy stakeholders to locate, including activist groups (such as Mothers Against Drunk Driving or the Wildlife Conservation Society), nonprofit organizations (such as the Heritage Foundation or the American Civil Liberties Union), and professional and trade associations (the National Association of Social Workers, Florida Police Chiefs Association, the Timber Producers Association, or the Association of National Park Rangers).These groups exist because they share viewpoints on issues that affect them. They often have Web sites and publish magazines.

Local stakeholders are harder to identify, including individuals, neighborhood associations, social groups, clubs, churches, mosques, and synagogues. Their stories are sometimes told in newspapers. If you choose to work on a local problem in your hometown, workplace, or college group, you probably know these people already. You can talk to them, interview them, and ask them about other local stakeholders and decision makers.

Stakeholders tend to sound more certain about their claims than scholars; they seem less open-minded or more biased. Keep in mind, however, that a stakeholder's arguments are not necessarily wrong or misleading just because he has something to win or lose. Stakeholders are excellent sources because they are motivated to gather and share valuable information about an issue; they often cite scholars, name decision makers, and describe cases. They provide important clues to the controversial parts of an issue. Finally, if the stakeholders can be persuaded to support a new solution to a problem, it is much more likely to happen.

Types of people who have are involved in the environment and crime issues are listed in "Stakeholders."

## STAKEHOLDERS

### *Environment*

- Cape Cod Commercial Hook Fisherman's Association
- Audubon Society's Living Oceans Program
- Captain Peter Taylor
- William Amaru, a small boat trawler out of Chatham, MA

### *Crime*

- The Sentencing Project, a Washington, D.C. organization specializing in criminal justice policy
- Highway Loss Data Institute, an insurance industry group in Washington, D.C.
- American Civil Liberties Association
- Residents elected to Local Advisory Councils at Chicago Housing Authority projects

## Decision Makers

In any public policy issue, a small number of people are authorized to make the decisions that can change the situation. These can include:

- Officials in local, state, or federal government, such as mayors, city planning boards, governors, state legislators, members of Congress, and the President.
- Officials in public departments, institutions, or agencies. At the local level, these can include the chief of police, the school board, or a principal. At a state or national level, these include heads of the Bureau of Mines, the National Park Service, or the Federal Bureau of Investigation. In addition to national directors, these agencies often have state or regional directors.
- Leaders of universities, hospitals, unions, and corporations.

These agencies often have Web sites that include official reports and mission statements. While these agencies may seem massive and faceless, they are staffed by people with very specific responsibilities. To find the officials who are most closely involved in your issue, look at an organizational chart or look closely at official reports for names and titles of decision makers. Another good place to look for the names and titles of relevant officials is in news stories.

Decision makers are good sources because they know a great deal about the situation and its history. They are often aware of different viewpoints on an issue because they have to juggle competing values:

- The U.S.D.A. Forest Service (www.fs.fed.us/) is in charge of balancing multiple uses and benefits in national forest resources such as water, forage, wildlife, wood, and recreation. Providing forage for domestic animals sometimes conflicts with protecting wildlife. Preserving forests sometimes conflicts with allowing recreation or managing fires.
- Police departments (dir.yahoo.com/Society_and_Culture/Crime/Law_Enforcement/Law_Enforcement_Departments/) are expected to catch criminals but they are also required to protect the rights of citizens, who are presumed to be innocent.

People who make decisions named in the readings are listed in "Decision Makers."

---

### DECISION MAKERS

#### *Environment*

- Richard Langton, Maine Department of Marine Resources
- New England Fishery Management Council

## Crime

- Richard H. Girgenti, New York State Director of Criminal Justice
- Judge Wayne Anderson, U.S. District Court for the Northern District of Illinois
- Chicago Housing Authority
- Chicago City Council

## Pundits

A **pundit** is a critic, often a journalist, whose job is to write opinion pieces for a popular magazine or newspaper every week or so. Pundits investigate current events, but also follow up their own interests on different issues. Pundits are rarely personally involved in the issue itself but may still have strong opinions. Television news and talk shows bring pundits together to talk, often convening people they assume will take widely diverging position.

**Is commentary ever really balanced?** © Harley Schwadron.

Pundits are useful sources because their articles are relatively easy to find; they frequently name and cite scholars, stakeholders, and decision makers; they explain technical, scientific, legal, and bureaucratic details in ordinary language; and they describe a wealth of cases involving stakeholders. (To find columnists in various newspapers, see dir.yahoo.com/News_and_Media/Columns_and_Columnists/Newspaper_ Rosters/.) Pundits who authored or are cited in the environment and crime readings include:

C. J. Chivers, a reporter from the *New York Times* who has covered crime and the wars in Afghanistan and Iraq;

Gregg Easterbrook, a senior editor at *The New Republic* who specializes in policy issues;

Dave Shiflett, a regular columnist for the *National Review* and a member of the White House Writers Group; and

Alexander Cockburn, a regular columnist for *The Nation.*

## Constructing a Conversation

The people you note from cases and readings can become part of a conversational group that you create. Participants in a face-to-face conversation respond directly to each other's arguments, but the people in the conversational group that you create may not even know that they are talking to each other. They are simply publishing their views to some audience that they know about. You are the one who will create the conversation by noticing shared and opposing views among the authors.

To construct the conversation, you will be searching for people who have a wide range of viewpoints about the same aspect of the issue that interests you. For example, in the readings about crime, Brooks is strongly opposed to curfews and gang ordinances while Meares and Kahan favor them; in the readings about environment, Shiflett's critique of jet skis differs dramatically from Kristof's endorsement of snowmobiles. Your conversational group should include positions as different as these. You can't avoid conflict or leave out opponents because you need to understand which points are controversial and why. You need to know what claims will be considered interesting and plausible. You need to know what claims have been made so often that they are no longer worth repeating, and what claims are generally accepted or rejected and why. Only then can you construct your own path of claims and decide how to support them.

You can find a wide range of viewpoints even among people who are on the same side of an issue. People who agree on a problem can have a wide range of views about what is causing it, what aspect of the problem is most important, and how to go about changing it. For example, everyone agrees that the United States must take action to prevent terrorism, but most strongly disagree on what to do.

"Varying Views among Allies" discusses the variety of viewpoints among allies on environment and crime.

## VARYING VIEWS AMONG ALLIES

### Environment

Few authors are in favor of pollution or hate wild animals. You will find controversies, however, over definitional questions, such as whether a species is endangered or whether an area counts as a wetland. Many people differ on priorities and values—whether scenery is more important than energy, whether the needs of today are more important than those of tomorrow, whether the recreational needs of the general public are more important than the preservational desires of those who value solitude. Many differ on what an acceptable amount of risk or damage might be. Allies can also be involved in causal controversies—whether land development will harm a species, whether logging will increase or decrease the risk of fire.

### Crime

Few authors are in favor of crime. However, crime fighters can disagree on definitional questions—what behavior is gang-related, whether a person with low IQ is competent to stand trial. Many people differ on priorities and values for dealing with crime—which crimes need the most attention, whether prevention is more important than arrest and conviction, whether catching the guilty is more important than protecting the innocent. There are also causal controversies—how crimes can be prevented, whether offenders can be rehabilitated.

You can find many clues for locating a wider group starting from one of the readings in this book, even one you strongly disagree with. If you see the author as an opponent, then the people named in concessions and rebuttals are potential allies. If you see the author as an ally, look at the people cited in support of the author's claims.

## EXERCISES

### Backtalk: What Do You Say?

Think of a high-profile local incident concerning environment or crime. In several paragraphs, describe what you know about the situation from your own experience. List as many stakeholders with different perspectives as you can. Describe sources of information you could consult to collect personal testimony, reports, and official documents. What aspect of the situation is most controversial and problematic for you?

## Recognize/Evaluate

Search closely through the pair of articles in your topic area listed below. List all the people referred to and classify them as scholars, pundits, stakeholders, or decision makers. Then write a brief comment: How does your pair of authors differ in the kinds of people they refer to? How do their choices affect your view of the author's credibility? Give reasons.

- **Environment.** Gómez-Pompa and Kaus; Easterbrook.
- **Crime.** Meares and Kahan; Brooks.

## Detect

Choose an aspect of the environment or crime issue that interests you, on which you have at least one argumentative article. Search the article to find specific individuals, including scholars, stakeholders, and decision makers.

## Produce

For the case in your topic area, narrate two versions; one a problem case and one an ideal case. The case can be real or hypothetical, but be sure to include details about the agent, motive, action, and outcome. For example:

- **Environment.** A rare species of salamander has been discovered living in Barton Springs, a popular natural swimming hole.
- **Crime.** A student who has been in the hospital is desperate to do well on the final test of the semester.

# CHAPTER 8

# Surveying the Terrain

In Chapter 7, you learned how to develop lists of the people, places, events, and concepts related to your angle on a case or topic of interest in environment or crime. In this chapter, you will learn how to use these lists to find informative and argumentative texts.

You are ready to use the strategies in this chapter if you are not starting from scratch. You should have already read two or three arguments with a specific focus like the readings in this book. You should also have done some written sketching or brainstorming about a specific interest or case. With this much to go on, you can begin your search with specific details and broaden it out.

The strategies presented here are designed to land you right in the midst of a complex issue with all the messiness of a controversy that matters. Whatever the angle or case that grabbed your attention, it will involve disputes over the facts, experts with contradictory testimony, and people who can't make up their minds. Your ultimate goal is to develop an informed position of your own, one that goes beyond describing or responding to what many people have already said. At this point, while you are exploring this issue, your goal should be to figure out the current status of the problem and where different parties stand. You therefore need a variety of sources for information and arguments that are up-to-date, including periodicals, Web sites, and books. Each type of source is useful for a different aspect of your exploration.

## Periodicals

Periodicals include newspapers, magazines, journals, and newsletters that are published on a regular schedule—in other words, periodically. The quality of the information depends on the periodical's publication schedule which may be daily, weekly, monthly, quarterly, or annually. Television news is periodical in the sense that it is broadcast hourly or daily. TV news is the most up-to-date, but may include material that turns out to be inaccurate. Sometimes the periodicals that appear the least often are the most prestigious; when only a few issues appear per year, the editors have to be especially selective.

After describing several types of periodicals, this section provides detailed strategies for finding articles using online library indexes and databases.

## Newspapers, TV News, and News Magazines

### Newspapers

Newspapers are excellent sources for finding recent cases, for updating information about past cases, and for identifying stakeholders, decision makers, and scholars.

The stories you find in major newspapers are considered very reliable; newspapers are an important part of the public record. Local newspapers are valuable for finding details about a local case. The most prestigious newspapers are those in big cities with many full-time journalists specializing in topics of national and international interest. These newspapers include:

- The *New York Times* (www.nytimes.com)
- *Washington Post*(www.washingtonpost.com)
- *Wall Street Journal* (online.wsj.com/public/us)
- *Los Angeles Times* (www.latimes.com)
- *Houston Chronicle* (www.chron.com)

While newspaper articles are helpful for building your argument, the stories are not themselves original arguments. So when you need to find conversational partners with different positions on your issue, reporters do not count as authors.

At first glance, a newspaper story can look like a public policy argument, reporting on disputes over problems and solutions. If the article is an opinion column or editorial, then it is an argument. But in a news story, the reporter's goal is to inform you about the different sides that are out there, not to formulate an original position.

If you are not sure whether an article is a news story or an argument, there are two good ways to distinguish them. First, as described in Chapter 6, the writing style in opinion pieces is very different from news stories. Second, consider how an author treats the parties involved in the incident. If the article simply reports on other people's conclusions and arguments, then the text is a news story. If the sources are used as evidence to support the author's own claims, then the text is an argument.

### Television News

Television networks provide information even more often than newspapers, with updates every hour. These stories are often based on eyewitness accounts of breaking news. Networks also provide discussions of the day's events by experts and pundits. Written versions of the news stories are often posted on network Web sites, which include:

- ABC (abcnews.go.com)
- CBS (www.cbsnews.com)
- CNN (www.cnn.com)
- Fox News Channel (www.foxnews.com)

- MS-NBC (www.msnbc.msn.com)
- PBS (www.pbs.org/newshour/)

Even though they seem to be as up-to-date as possible, television news programs are considered neither as reliable nor as authoritative as newspapers for public policy writing, because events are hard to understand as they are occurring. Television reporters who broadcast live on the scene have less time than newspaper reporters to gain perspective on the events over time or to seek out a range of witnesses and authorities. Even the spoken remarks of commentators on talk shows are considered less reliable than written articles because commentators have less time to consider the fairness and accuracy of their claims and gather appropriate evidence.

### News Magazines

Weekly news magazines provide valuable summaries of current events that give you the big picture of the issue: The stories are usually rich in photos, colorful in detail, and readable. These magazines summarize and expand on stories from newspapers. The writers have time during the week to consider a variety of sources and to see how a story develops over time. Many stories can be found on a magazine's Web site, for example:

- *Newsweek* (www.newsweek.com)
- *Time* (www.time.com)
- *U.S. News & World Report* (www.usnews.com/usnews/home.htm)

*"At this point, it's still not classified as a hurricane—
it's still being called a raindrop."*

**An event is hard to interpret as it is happening.** © The New Yorker Collection 2000 Liza Donnelly
from cartoonbank.com. All Rights Reserved.

Weekly news magazines, however, are considered less authoritative than newspapers because they provide less detailed support than either newspaper stories or journal articles. The magazines have fewer full-time reporters who are eyewitnesses to the events they describe; rather, the stories weave together reports from many other sources. Weekly magazines rarely publish arguments that reflect the original position of a specific author. In most academic and public policy writing, these sources are not formally cited.

## Monthly Literary and Political Magazines

Literary and political magazines, many of which are published monthly, are directed to people with similar cultural interests or political outlooks. Along with informative articles and reviews, they include argumentative articles on public policy issues written by pundits and sometimes by scholars. So when you are looking for authors to use as an ally or opponent, literary and political magazines are a good place to look. Literary and political magazines include:

- *The Atlantic* (www.theatlantic.com)
- *Boston Review* (www.bostonreview.net)
- *Mother Jones* (www.motherjones.com)
- *National Review* (www.nationalreview.com)
- *The New Republic* (www.tnr.com)
- *The Public Interest* (www.thepublicinterest.com)
- *Washington Monthly* (www.washingtonmonthly.com)

Many libraries subscribe to magazines like these, so you can look through past issues. A magazine's Web site will post the latest issue and many have searchable archives. Full-text magazine articles can also be located in a library's online indexes and databases.

## Scholarly Journals

Professors and other researchers use scholarly journals to argue for their latest theories and findings. Hundreds of journals in any major area of study, published monthly, quarterly, or annually, are available to you in college libraries and online databases. Various academic disciplines take different approaches to the same issue. For example, psychologists approach crime from a very different perspective than economists; ecologists approach the environment differently from anthropologists. Scholarly journals include:

- *Ecological Restoration* (www.wisc.edu/wisconsinpress/journals/journals/er.html)
- *Environmental Science & Policy* (www.environmental-center.com/magazine/elsevier/envsci/)
- *Crime & Delinquency* (cad.sagepub.com)
- *Criminal Justice Ethics* (www.lib.jjay.cuny.edu/cje/)

Articles in scholarly journals are considered reliable, especially those that passed a review from independent peers before they were accepted. Scholarly articles in some disciplines can be difficult to read because they are written for researchers who share the same intensive training and work on the same kinds of problems as the author. To get the most out of articles from scholarly journals, follow these strategies:

- Choose articles from your disciplinary major so that you can talk about them with classmates and instructors.

- Before reading a scholarly article, gain a clear overview from a story about this type of research in a newspaper or popular magazine.

- Focus on the introduction and conclusion sections because they are often more written in a general style.

## Trade and Professional Associations

In many controversies, the stakeholders include businesses, trades, or professions. It is important to understand the goals of this kind of group because you may eventually choose one as the audience for an argument.

Many trades and professions have associations that publish journals with stories of interest to their members. These journals often include news, position papers, opinion columns, and argumentative essays. You can often find full-text trade and professional journals in your library databases. Universities that offer degrees in agriculture, for example, are likely to subscribe to forestry and land management magazines. "Professional and Trade Association Journals" provides examples of such organizations, their Web sites, and their journal titles.

---

### PROFESSIONAL AND TRADE ASSOCIATION JOURNALS

#### *Environmental Organizations*

- *Land and Water* (www.landandwater.com)—journal directed at contractors, engineers, architects, government officials, and those working in the field of natural resource management and restoration

- National Association of State Park Directors (NASPD) (naspd.indstate. edu/research.html)—Web site collecting research relevant to state parks

- New Jersey Fishing (www.fishingnj.org)—Web site by and for New Jersey's fish and seafood industry

### Criminal Justice Organizations

- *Access Control & Security Systems* (securitysolutions.com)—Web site directed at dealers and installers of security systems, security managers, and architects
- American Correctional Association, *Corrections Today* (aca.org/publications/ctmagazine.asp)—professional journal published seven times a year for international readership in corrections and criminal justice.

# Finding Articles with Library Indexes and Databases

All types of periodicals are indexed, meaning that you can search for articles in online library indexes and databases by author's name, subject, date, and keyword. The results provide you with the citations of relevant articles, abstracts, and in many cases, the full text that you can download and print.

## Searching for Newspaper Articles

Newspaper stories from big cities and from hundreds of smaller cities and towns are available through online library indexes and databases such as:

- LexisNexis (web.lexis-nexis.com/universe/)
- InfoTrac Custom Newspaper (infotrac.galegroup.com)

LexisNexis is the most widely available tool for searching newspapers. To focus in on the most relevant articles for your angle on the issue, you will need to select among the search options available. Following are tips for using the Guided News Search option in LexisNexis (see Figure 8.1), with an example of an actual search in "Finding Local News Stories with LexisNexis."

*Tips for Using LexisNexis*

### National and Global Issues

**Search Mode:** Guided News Search

**News Category:** General News

**News Sources:** Major Papers

**Date Range:** [Adjust for your case]

**Search Terms:** Headline [for big news stories]; Full Text [for case details]

### State and Local Issues

**Search Mode:** Guided News Search

**News Category:** U.S. News

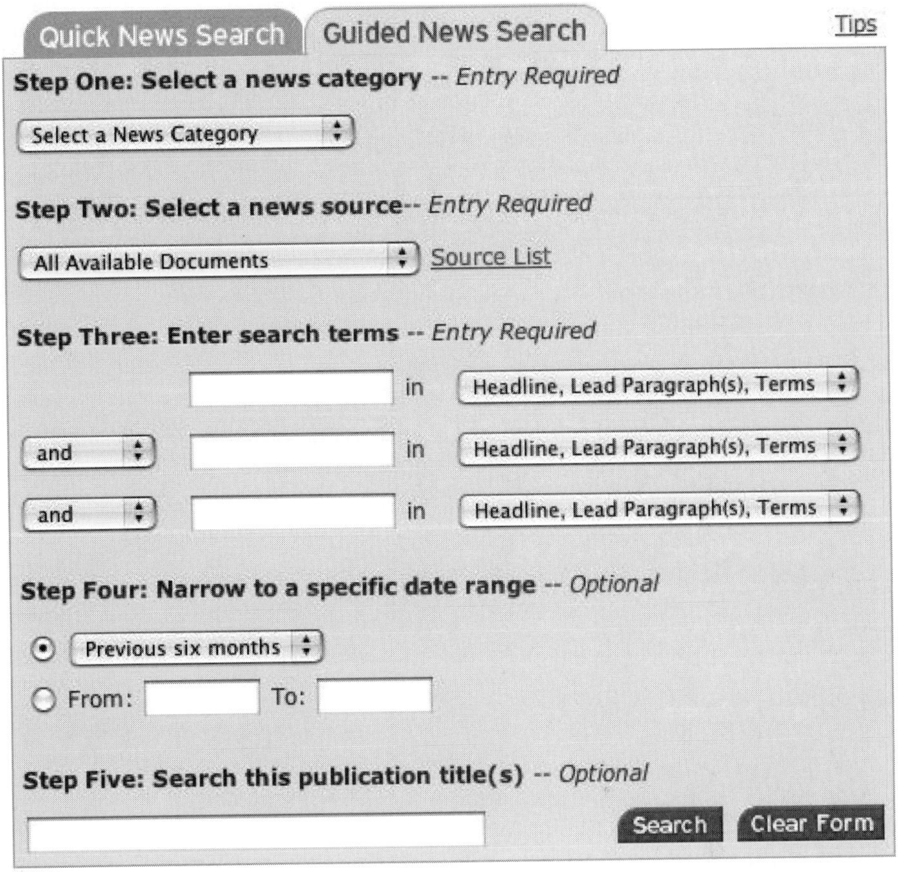

**FIGURE 8.1** LexisNexis guided search screen.
*Courtesy of •••••*

 

**News Sources:** [Select from list of regions and states]
**Date Range:** [Adjust for your case]
**Search Terms:** Headline [for big news stories]; Full Text [for case details]

### Editorials, Opinion Columns, Letters to the Editor

**Search Mode:** Guided News Search
**News Category:** General News
**News Sources:** Major Papers
**Date Range:** [Adjust for your case]
**Search Terms:** Headline: [Type in "opinion"]

Adjust the date range and search terms by consulting a list of stakeholder names, places, dates, and agencies, such as those discussed in Chapter 7. If many of the articles in the results list look off-topic, use "Edit Search" to add or change terms. If your search results in several hundred articles, use "Search in Results" and add another detail to narrow down the results.

Look through the results and mark the most relevant articles by clicking in the checkbox near the citation. The most useful articles will be longer than 100 words. At the end, you can e-mail yourself a list of all the citations you marked and the full text of the articles.

"Finding Local Stories with LexisNexis" shows a search for articles in a local paper about a specific case.

---

### FINDING LOCAL STORIES WITH LEXISNEXIS

The goal of this search was to find local updates on the shootings at Littleton High School. The following menu options were chosen:

**Search Mode:** Guided News Search

**News Category:** U.S. News

**News Sources:** Colorado

**Date range:** previous 2 years

**Search Terms:**

(Full Text) Columbine and Littleton
(Full Text) teenage and high school
(Full Text) violence and shooting

**Results:**

1. The Denver Post, October 25, 2002 Friday, 1st Edition, Pg. F-01, 995 words, SCORING a STRIKE Moore's probing, shocking 'Bowling for Columbine' also laced with humor, Steven Rosen, Denver Post Movie Critic

2. The Associated Press State & Local Wire, October 23, 2001, Tuesday, BC cycle, State and Regional, 437 words, Officials set to unveil the Colorado Anti-Bullying Project, DENVER

---

## Searching for Magazine and Journal Articles

College libraries often have a large number of indexes and databases, some general and some that specialize on a research area like business or psychology. For public policy issues and other broad-based topics, the best tools are those that cover many kinds of sources, including literary, political, scholarly, and trade journals. The most commonly used tools are these:

- Academic Search Premier (EBSCO) (search.epnet.com). Provides full text for over 3000 journals in arts, humanities, science, and social sciences.
- Expanded Academic ASAP (Gale Group) (infotrac.galegroup.com). Provides citations to articles from 2300 general news sources and scholarly journals in arts, humanities, science, and social sciences, with full-text articles or links to over 1300 journals.

These powerful tools allow you search across hundreds of indexed magazines for articles on a specific subject or those written by a specific author. Even more important, you can search for specific words anywhere in the full text of the articles. This feature allows you to narrow down your search far more precisely to the type of article you want to find. Below are tips for using the Advanced Search option in Expanded ASAP. The strategies for using Academic Search Premier are very similar. You will find a detailed comparison at the end of this section.

### Tips for Using Expanded ASAP
The success of your search depends on the combination of search terms you enter; with one combination of terms, you may end up with no listings (or hits) at all and with just a slight change, tens of thousands. The tips presented here are designed to locate a large number of somewhat relevant hits that you can narrow down to a few dozen highly relevant hits.

#### Narrowing-In Search Strategy

1. Use Advanced Search and the "Text Word" search field.
2. Start with a search on a single search term, such as a name or location. Each search produces a list of citations and a search record. To view the search record, click "Back to Search." You will see a numbered list of your searches and the total hits each one produced. See the Advanced Search screen in Figure 8.2.
3. To locate articles closely related to your case or angle, try searches with very specific terms such as "Klebold" or "Columbine" as well as searches with more general terms, such as "school shootings," or "school violence."
4. Continue with searches on different terms until your search record lists five or six searches that each resulted in a very large number of hits, in the tens of thousands or even over a million.
5. Combine terms to narrow down the hits to a manageable number.

#### Combining Searches
You can combine search records using logical terms such as "AND" and "OR." In only a few steps, search records of over a million hits each can be narrowed down to fewer than a hundred hits.

- Use "AND" when you want to narrow down your results by accepting only articles that have both terms. Of the 11,047 citations produced in the first two searches in Figure 8.2 (R1 and R2), only 949 contained both words, "Columbine" and "Littleton" (R4).

University of Texas at Austin
Expanded Academic ASAP

Advanced search

**Click in the entry box and enter search expression**

| Text Word (tx) | ⇕ | r1 and r2 | | AND ⇕ |
| Key Word (ke) | ⇕ | | | AND ⇕ |
| Key Word (ke) | ⇕ | | Search | Clear Form |

Select index then enter search term. Use AND OR NOT to connect the expression.

---

**Limit the current search (optional)**
☐ to articles with text
☐ to refereed publications
by date ⦿ all dates ○ before ○ on ○ after
○ between [     ⇕] [     ⇕] [     ⇕] and
[     ⇕] [     ⇕] [     ⇕]
to the following journal(s) [          ] ( Browse )
to entries containing the word(s) [          ]

---

**History**

---

R4 (tx (r1 and r2))
   View 949 Citations; Modify Search
R3 (tx (r1 or r2))
   View 10098 Citations; Modify Search
R2 (tx columbine)
   View 4652 Citations; Modify Search
R1 (tx littleton)
   View 6395 Citations; Modify Search

---

Expanded Academic ASAP has 12,951,341 articles and was last updated on Jan 17, 2005.

THOMSON
GALE   Copyright and Terms of Use

FIGURE 8.2   Expanded ASAP advanced search screen.
*Courtesy of •••••*

- Use "OR" in the early stages of searching on individual terms, when you want to broaden your results to accept articles that contain any one of a list of terms. In Figure 8.2, R3 shows the citations for articles that contained either "Columbine" or "Littleton." The result, 10,098 citations, is less than 11,047 because articles that contain both words are only counted once.

## Using the "Text Word" Search Field

The "text word" field is a powerful tool because it is extremely flexible for searching throughout an article. In contrast, the "subject" and "keyword" fields only search for terms that appear in the article title or terms that the indexer has assigned as major concepts in the article. By using text words, you can narrow down your results using any of the "Words to Watch For" listed in Chapters 1 through 6.

- To narrow down the results to articles that are likeliest to concern public policy, create a search record of all articles in the database that contain all the terms "problem," "solution," "claim," and "argue." Then combine that record with one that includes terms for your case.

- To narrow down to articles that are most likely to express an author's original position, create a search record of all articles in the database that contain all the terms "I," "my," "we," and "our." To find articles with refutation, create a search record with terms such as "disagree," "wrong," or "illogical."

- To find articles addressing moral values, add in search terms such as "morality," "justice," "fairness," or "heritage." To find articles addressing causes, add in search terms such as "cause," "effect," "factor," "blame."

### Using the "Subject" Field

Open the full text of the most promising article and scroll down to the end of the article. You will see a list of subject-heading links, such as the one at the top of Figure 8.3.

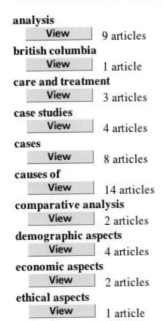

FIGURE 8.3   Expanded ASAP subject heading links.

To view all the articles that are in the same subject category, click on "View [number] Periodical references." To look for articles in related subcategories, click on "See also [number] other subdivisions." You will see a list of subcategories with the number of articles in each, such as the one at the bottom of Figure 8.3. If you are especially interested in finding cases of youth violence, click on "View" to see the listings for the eight articles.

*Tips for Using Academic Search Premier*
The strategies for using Academic Search Premier are very similar to those for Expanded ASAP. The main difference is the set-up of the search page.

The search page in Academic Search Premier is divided in half. The top has three spaces for searches. The bottom is for results organized under three tabs: "Refine Search," "Search History," and "Results."

When you enter a search command, such as "TX Klebold," the list of documents resulting from the search appears at the bottom of the screen. You can see the how many documents were found just below the "Refine Search" tab.

To combine the results of individual searches, click on the "Search History" tab. Your list of search commands appears at the bottom of the screen. You can type the identification numbers into a search space, in the same way as for Expanded ASAP. You can also check off the boxes next to the searches you want to combine and click "ADD." The terms will appear in the first space.

# Web Sites

You are probably already familiar with searching on the World Wide Web (WWW) with search engines such as Yahoo!, Google, or Alta Vista. This section will provide tips for finding stakeholder groups representing a wide range of positions on an issue, both advocacy groups and governmental agencies.

A categorical search engine, such as Yahoo!, is especially helpful for finding groups because you can scan categories under a topic area and narrow down to subtopics, geographical regions, and other categories of sites. While other search engines, including Google, have directory features, the examples here will refer to Yahoo!.

## Advocacy Web sites

Advocacy groups exist on all sides of a public policy issue. The members count as stakeholders, whether they are personally affected by a problem or not, because they care so intensely about the issue. Because advocacy groups represent a specific position on an issue, you have to judge the information they present carefully. Some advocacy groups try harder than others to provide extensive support for their claims and to treat opponents fairly.

However, you should not avoid advocacy Web sites just because they appear to be biased. Advocacy groups by definition have chosen a position on an issue.

Any advocacy group can give you insight into the values and beliefs at stake in the issue, even those that have extreme positions.

Many advocacy groups have Web sites and online magazines that provide historical information, position statements, news releases, graphics, and pleas for donations. The best sites are well-maintained and provide views on the latest developments on an issue.

You can begin finding advocacy groups related to environment and crime by visiting the Yahoo! directory page (dir.yahoo.com), clicking on "Society and Culture," and following subcategory links. For example, by clicking on a series of subcategory links, you can reach a category of student groups involved in environmental issues (dir.yahoo.com/Society_and_Culture/Environment_and_Nature/Organizations/Student/). From an advocacy group's Web site, it is easy to find others. The site is likely to provide links to the sites of allied groups.

"Finding Web sites of Advocacy Groups" provides a few links for environment and crime, each one following the link for the Yahoo! directory in which it was found.

## FINDING WEB SITES OF ADVOCACY GROUPS

### *Environment Groups*

**Yahoo! directory for trails groups:**

dir.yahoo.com/Recreation/Outdoors/Trails/Organizations/

**Listing under directory:**

www.americantrails.org—national trails advocacy organization working for the common interests of all trail users, including hiking, bicycling, mountain biking, horseback riding, water trails, snowshoeing, cross-country skiing, trail motorcycling, ATVs, snowmobiling, and four-wheeling.

### *Crime Sites*

**Yahoo! directory for law organizations:**

dir.yahoo.com/Society_and_Culture/Cultures_and_Groups/Gangs/

**Listing under directory:**

Gangstyle (www.gangstyle.com)—Gangstyle is not pro-gang. It is written by and for gang and ex-gang members from a Christian perspective.

## Government Publications and Web Sites

Public policies are set by local, state, or federal government agencies. So for many issues, officials from a governmental agency will be among the decision makers. The hard part is finding the appropriate agency for your issue. Some policies that affect your hometown are set at the local level, so supporters and opponents might start by appealing to a town council. But many local policies have to be consistent with state and federal policies, so they can sometimes be addressed at the state level and at the federal level.

In the Yahoo! directory system, many federal, state, and local government agencies are organized under a "Government" category, for example:

- U.S. Fish and Wildlife Service Divisions and Offices (dir.yahoo.com/ Government/U_S__Government/Executive_Branch/Departments_and_Agencies/ Department_of_the_Interior/Fish_and_Wildlife_Service/)

- Alaska State Offices Related to Fishing and Game (dir.yahoo.com/ Regional/U_S__States/Alaska/Government/Executive_Branch/Departments_and_ Agencies/Alaska_Department_of_Fish_and_Game/)

You may be surprised to discover how many agencies can become involved in an issue over time. "Government Agencies Involved in a Case" traces how different agencies became involved in two cases.

---

### GOVERNMENT AGENCIES INVOLVED IN A CASE

#### Environment: Sea Lions in Alaska

In Alaska, environmental groups and marine biologists became very concerned about Steller sea lions, an endangered species whose numbers were dropping rapidly. While the cause of the drop is a mystery, the activists argued that commercial fishing was harming the sea lion's habitat. Over time, the case has involved many agencies:

- In April 1998, three advocacy groups, Greenpeace, the American Oceans Campaign, and the Sierra Club, sued the NOAA's National Marine Fisheries Service (NMFS) (www.nmfs.noaa.gov) in U.S. District Court for not protecting the Steller sea lion.

- In July 2000, U.S. District Judge Thomas Zilly in Seattle (www.wawd. uscourts.gov) designated ocean and coastal areas as "critical habitat" for sea lions that trawlers could not enter.

- In December 2000, new restrictions on fishing were rejected by the North Pacific Fishery Management Council (www.fakr.noaa.gov/npfmc/). But the NMFS had final authority and submitted plans for restrictions to Judge Zilly.

- Alaska fishermen, seafood companies, coastal communities, and state officials complained to Alaska's U.S. Senator Ted Stevens (stevens.senate.gov) that the restrictions would hurt the local economy. In 2001, Stevens convinced Congress to budget millions of dollars to pay for sea lion research and to compensate local fisheries. The money was distributed by the Southwest Alaska Municipal Conference.

- In spring 2002, the NMFS began requiring fishing boats in federal waters off Alaska to carry satellite tracking devices to make sure they don't fish illegally in the restricted areas. The NMFS paid for the devices.

- In January 2003, researchers from the National Marine Mammal Lab (nmml.afsc.noaa.gov) and University of Alaska at Fairbanks Marine Advisory Program (www.uaf.edu/MAP/) began reporting their investigation of food, climate, and other factors to explain the drop in sea lion population.

- In October 2004, NOAA and the University of Alaska at Fairbanks hosted a research symposium at which many scholarly papers were presented (www.uaf.edu/seagrant/Conferences/sealions/prog.html).

- In July 2005, an animal rights group, the Humane Society of the United States, filed suit in federal court to protest the capture and hot-branding of sea lions by NMFS researchers.

  This case has been reported by the *Anchorage Daily News* and the Associated Press State and Local Wire. You can find the stories using LexisNexis by selecting the "U.S. News" category, setting the news source to "Alaska" and searching for "Steller" or "sea lion."

## Crime: Drug Dealing in Richmond, VA

The city of Richmond, Virginia, was quite concerned about how to get rid of drug dealers who were congregating at public housing complexes. The city decided to find a way to bar nonresidents, such as drug dealers, using a trespassing rule. The case was acted on by these decision makers:

- The Richmond Redevelopment and Housing Authority (RRHA) (www.rrha.org) worked with the city government (www.ci.richmond.va.us) in 1997 to create a trespassing regulation that police officers could enforce on patrol. In several apartment complexes where drug dealing was a serious problem, the government deeded the streets to the RRHA so that the regulation would apply anywhere around the complexes.

- In 1999, the manager of Whitcomb Court barred Kevin Hicks (a nonresident) from entering and a police officer arrested him when he came back. Hicks was convicted in a Richmond Circuit Court. The conviction was upheld in the Virginia Court of Appeals in October 2000.

- In June 2002, the Virginia Supreme Court (www.courts.state.va.us/courts/courts.html) overturned Hicks' conviction, deciding that the regulation was unconstitutionally broad.

- In June 2003, the U.S. Supreme Court upheld the trespass policy in *Virginia v. Hicks* (www.supremecourtus.gov/opinions/opinions.html). The court decided the rule did not violate the complainer's (Kevin Hicks) free speech because it did not apply to public speaking but to all activities.

- In October 2004, Richmond's voting registrar announced that the no-trespassing law did not apply to polling places located within Whitcomb Court because the state law on voting superseded the city law.

- In March 2005, the RRHA installed new lights, cameras, and fences in Whitcomb Court to make it harder for drug dealers to operate there. Now the RRHA plans to use the same approaches in other communities.

    Accounts of the case were first published in the *Richmond Times-Dispatch* and eventually in major newspapers such as the *New York Times*. You can find the local stories using LexisNexis by selecting the "U.S. News" category and setting the news source to "Virginia."

As an individual student, you may feel awkward when you imagine writing to a national decision maker. A good approach is to start with a local agency or a local chapter of an advocacy group.

If you or someone you know has a problem, you have the most influence at the lowest layer in the chain of command, where you count most as a resident or member of the community. As a community member, you can more easily find out about the history of the problem and its current status. You can also identify allies and relevant local agencies. If the problem is being debated at a higher level, you can find out what groups are involved at that level. If it is significant, even a local case may end up changing national policy and influencing scholarly research.

The strategy of starting at the local level is similar to complaining about a policy in a college class. If you think a policy has been applied unfairly, you speak first to your instructor who set the policy and knows the context of the case. If the instructor disagrees that the decision was unfair, you can speak to the department's undergraduate advisor. The instructor's class policy may be inconsistent with the policies of the department. If your complaints still aren't satisfied, you can often appeal to the department chair or someone in the college.

To find the local agencies that are involved in your issue, go to local newspapers for reports of a problem case that is similar to yours. Newspaper accounts will often identify the different decision-making agencies that are involved in a case, as they report on it over time.

Once you identify the governmental level you need, you can search for sites for relevant agencies. A cue to the type of site is often given in the URL:

- **Federal:** Sites with ".gov" in the URL, such as the URL for Supreme Court of the United States (www.supremecourtus.gov).

- **State:** Sites with the state initials in between the terms "state" and "us" in the URL. For example, official Alaska (AK) sites have URLs containing www.state.ak.us.

- **County:** Sites with the county name in between the terms "co" for "county" and terms for the state and us. For example, information about agencies in Cook County, Illinois can be found at www.co.cook.il.us/agencyList.php.
- **City:** Sites with the city name in between the terms "ci" for "city" and terms for the state and us. For example, official sites for Oakland, California, have URLs containing www.ci.oakland.ca.us/.

Unfortunately, not all cities and counties follow these conventions for naming their sites. You can also search for an agency using the name of the city or state in your Web browser.

Once you find an appropriate agency, you can use material about it in several ways. If you plan to write an argument to this agency, you will need information about its mission. If you are exploring for solutions, then you need to know how it has decided other, similar cases.

# Books

Books about issues are usually written by scholars or by pundits. They can be easier to read than scholarly journal articles because the authors have plenty of space to explain their ideas. However, it takes a long time for a book to be published. So the information in a book is not likely to be as up-to-date as in a magazine or newspaper. Books are especially useful if your issue has a long history and if the author is very well known. Some books have such a large effect on the way to see a problem that people refer to them for years.

- Aldo Leopold, a naturalist trained in forestry, died in 1948, but his *Sand County Almanac* was so influential in shaping wilderness conservation that it is still often quoted.
- French philosopher Michel Foucault's book *Discipline and Punish: The Birth of the Prison,* was published in 1972. It is cited often by allies and opponents because of its arguments about power and its effects.

If you find that an author such as Leopold or Foucault is cited in a large number of the articles you have found, it is a good idea to look for the book in your library. Scholarly books are a prestigious source of information because the selection process for publication is rigorous. However, as noted above, because of the lengthy time to publish, books are not necessarily the best sources for you to use in a public policy argument involving developing events.

# Selecting and Evaluating Sources

The most important strategy is to gather many relevant sources of different kinds and varying positions and then select from among them. Some students are satisfied as soon as they find one or two articles that are directly relevant to their case or their angle. But these one or two sources will not give you a broad enough view of your issue. Until you've looked at a larger number of relevant articles, you cannot evaluate their usefulness and quality.

Students who stop the search after finding only a few articles are usually frustrated. Maybe they became interested in these articles only after rejecting a variety of different general topics. Maybe they had trouble with the search tools and spent a long time looking at candidates that turned out to be off-topic.

This kind of burnout often results from starting with a vague and overly general topic area and trying to narrow it down, instead of using the strategies recommended here. If you begin with a specific case or an author's name, you should be able to find a dozen relevant news stories, Web sites, and arguments. If you haven't found anything relevant after an hour of searching with a library indexing and database tool, ask your instructor or a librarian for help.

Once you have many possible candidates, pick out the best ones according to their relevance to your case, uniqueness, document type, timeliness, and ethos (Chapter 7).

## Relevance

The most relevant articles are ones that have any of these features:

- Dealing with the same case or the same type of cases as other articles on your list.
- Referring to other authors, especially other authors on your list, no matter whether they treat them as experts, allies, or opponents.
- Describing cases with successful or unsuccessful outcomes.

Comparing related cases, positions, and outcomes will help you explore the nature of the problem and possible solutions.

## Primary and Secondary Texts

In public policy arguments, primary texts are considered more valuable than secondary texts as sources of evidence.

Primary texts are those that record firsthand accounts, including those that are:

- created whenever an event occurs, such as when you receive a receipt for a purchase or when you keep a copy of an e-mail message;
- produced during an event as a record, such as transcripts or minutes from a meeting; or
- produced from the author's own observation, such as when a news reporter views a scene and interviews eyewitnesses and when a researcher reports on the results of an inquiry.

Secondary texts are those that reflect on primary texts, by interpreting them, evaluating them, or combining information from them, including:

- news digests, such as in weekly news magazines;
- reviews of books or Websites; and
- fictionalizations in any medium: video, lyrics, novels, or short stories.

While secondary texts do include claims and evidence, they are not as credible as primary texts for evidence in public policy arguments.

## Timeliness

The authors you read will have used the most recent information available at the time they wrote. But their information is likely to be out of date as compared to when you are reading it. As an author, you are also responsible for finding timely sources.

Several kinds of source are timely:

- records of immediate reactions to an event
- records of the status of a problem or case at a certain historical moment
- records of the latest developments

This means that you need to check the historical context of the sources you use. Articles that you find in printed form or in a library index or database will always provide the date of publication. Websites are less reliable in providing the dates when a text was posted or changed. Online magazines will usually provide the date when an article was written. Advocacy sites may not.

## Ethos of a Forum or Web Site Sponsor

Every author bases an argument on information gathered by other people. To evaluate the credibility and usefulness of the information your find, you need information about the trustworthiness of the people who gathered it and wrote about it.

To judge the trustworthiness and usefulness of a source, you should look it over to see what information it provides about itself. Trustworthiness does not require neutrality; the participants in a public policy argument are very likely to have strong opinions that give you valuable insights into alternative positions. What matters is how clearly a source describes its goals and how responsibly its information is presented. For this reason, anonymous articles and Web sites with little background information are not as valuable as authored articles from periodicals.

### Periodicals

Information about journals and newspapers is available from many sources. The first step is to use a search engine such as Google or Yahoo! to look for an online homepage. Then look for links that say "about us" or "mission."

For example, the following is an earlier (2003) version of the mission statement for *The American Spectator,* posted on its Web site, www.spectator.org/aboutus.asp:

> The American Spectator Foundation is an independent nonprofit that publishes *The American Spectator* magazine, widely regarded as one of the most influential conservative publications in print today. Our mission: To publish *The American Spectator* and provide Americans with news and commentary on politics and culture, one that challenges the "political correctness" found in so many media outlets today and which advocates individual freedom, limited government, free markets, and traditional "Reaganite" foreign policy positions.

Some online library databases such as LexisNexis, Academic Search Premier, or Expanded ASAP also provide information about their sources. For example, Figure 8.4 shows the result of searching under "Sources" on LexisNexis for the "Columbia Journalism Review."

If you want detailed circulation information, or if the journal has no Web site, you can find online reference information at Ulrich's Periodical Index (www.ulrichsweb. com/UlrichsWeb/). Ulrich's entry on *The American Prospect* is shown in Figure 8.5.

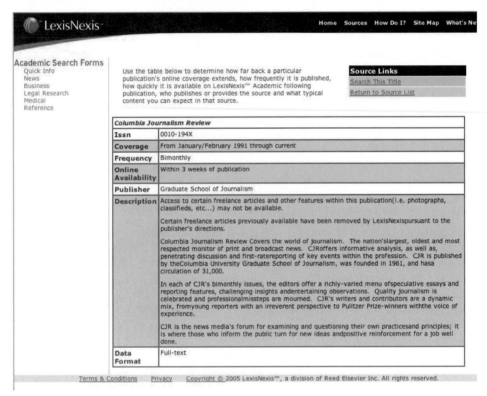

FIGURE 8.4  Source entry in LexisNexis for the *Columbia Journalism Review.*

## Web sites

If your article comes from a Web site, look for a link labeled "about us" or "mission." Dig around on the site to see who is in charge of the site and how well they maintain it. A Web site is more trustworthy if it:

- tells readers upfront about its points of view and goals;
- tells readers about the person or group responsible for the site, including contact information;
- gives readers details that allow facts and sources to be checked further;

## The American Prospect: a journal for the liberal imagination

◁ BACK TO RESULTS

◁ SEARCH MY LIBRARY'S CATALOG ▷

| Basic Description | Other Editions/ Formats | Abstracting/ Indexing & Article Access | Publisher & Ordering Information | Advertising, Rights, Demographics |
|---|---|---|---|---|

Click highlighted text for a new search on that item.

| | |
|---|---|
| **Table of Contents:** | **TOC** |
| **ISSN:** | 1049-7285 |
| **Title:** | The American Prospect: a journal for the liberal imagination |
| **Publishing Body:** | The American Prospect, Inc. |
| **Country:** | United States |
| **Status:** | Active |
| **Start Year:** | 1990 |
| **Frequency:** | 10 times a year |
| **Document Type:** | Magazine; Consumer |
| **Abstracted/Indexed:** | Yes |
| **Media:** | Print |
| **Language:** | Text in English |
| **Price:** | USD 19.95 subscription per year domestic<br>USD 29.95 subscription per year in Canada<br>USD 34.95 subscription per year elsewhere<br>(effective 2005) |
| **Subject:** | POLITICAL SCIENCE<br>LITERARY AND POLITICAL REVIEWS |
| **Dewey #:** | 320.51 |
| **LC#:** | E838 |
| **CODEN:** | APROEY |
| **Circulation:** | 55,000 paid and free |
| **Special Features:** | Includes Advertising, Book Reviews, Film Reviews, Television Reviews |
| **Editor(s):** | Harold Meyerson, Paul Starr, Robert Kuttner, Robert Reich, Scott Stossel |
| **Publisher(s):** | Robin Hutson |
| **E-Mail:** | info@prospect.org |
| **URL:** | http://www.prospect.org/web/index.ww |
| **Description:** | Offers political and cultural news and commentary for those who lead the liberal community. |

FIGURE 8.5  Entry in Ulrich's Periodicals Index for *The American Prospect.*

- allows readers to respond by providing e-mail addresses or discussion forums;
- maintains standards of public civility by publishing articles that set a tone of fairness and by setting rules for acceptable posts on discussion boards;
- gives details of particular problem cases and attempted solutions; and
- provides statistics in the text or in graphs and tables.

For example, here is the "about us" information for the National Center for Policy Analysis (www.ncpa.org/abo/):

> The National Center of Policy Analysis (NCPA) is a nonprofit, nonpartisan public policy research organization, established in 1983. The NCPA's goal is to develop and promote private alternatives to government regulation and control, solving problems by relying on the strength of the competitive, entrepreneurial private sector. Topics include reforms in health care, taxes, Social Security, welfare, criminal justice, education and environmental regulation.

This page also includes links to the NCPA's history, its board of directors, and its staff as well as contact information.

# Recommending a Source to Others

You may be asked to justify your choice of sources in writing, either to your instructor or to your classmates. Some classes vote on a selection of sources that everyone reads and writes about.

You can construct a evaluative argument about an source by judging it against the criteria described in the previous section: relevance, primacy, timeliness, and ethos. Most sources will score highly on a few criteria and weakly on a few others. Provide enough details about the source that a reader can understand your judgment without having seen the source itself. "Sample Nominations" provides descriptions that students posted for a class vote.

---

## SAMPLE NOMINATIONS

### *Environment*

Nealson, Christina. "In Wilderness, Don't Phone Home." *High Country News* 17 Aug. 1998: Vol. 30, No. 15. The author, who is an avid nature lover and adventurer, discusses her feelings on bringing technology into the wilderness. She believes that filling "solitude with instant access to the technological world" is disgraceful and defeats the purpose of wilderness itself. She takes a unique stance in pointing out that although she'll be wearing space-age fabric and such, cell phones cross the line. Christina Nealson is an author of a wilderness related book and a regular contributor to *High Country News. High Country News* is a "bi-weekly newspaper that reports on the West's natural resources, public lands, and changing communities." It's been around for 30 years and covers 11 Western states.

### Crime

Greenwood, Peter W. "Investing in prisons or prevention: the state policy makers' dilemma." *Crime and Delinquency*, January 1998. This argues the value of effective prevention rather than building more prisons. While DiIulio explored how best to structure prevention programs, Greenwood emphasizes the necessity of prevention. He relies mainly on logos and includes relevant statistics, but ethos strengthens his argument. Greenwood is the director of RAND's criminal justice program (a Californian nonprofit organization whose purpose is to influence governmental policymaking). Though the readers of the magazine are a select group (professionals in the criminal justice system), this is not difficult to read.

## EXERCISES

### Backtalk: What Do You Say?

Do you agree that newsmagazines and TV shows are less credible than articles from literary and political magazines and daily newspapers? Why or why not? In what situations would those sources be useful to cite?

### Recognize/Evaluate

1. Evaluate the strengths and weaknesses of these advocacy sites for relevance (to each other), originality, timeliness, document types, and ethos.

   - **Environment sites**

     Coral Reef Alliance (www.coralreefalliance.org)
     International Game Fish Association (www.igfa.org)
     SeaWeb (www.seaweb.org)
     New Jersey Fishing (www.fishingnj.org)

   - **Crime sites**

     Policing.com (www.policing.com)
     Critical Resistance (www.criticalresistance.org)
     The Fortune Society (www.fortunesociety.org )
     National Center for Policy Analysis Idea House
       (www.ncpa.org/bothside/crime.html)

2. Imagine your classmates submitted these nominations for articles that your group should read. Which nomination is most informative? Which authors are good choices for conversational partners? Why?

   - **Environment nominations**

     King, Michael. "Who's Poisoning Texas? Part Two: Voluntary
       Grandfathers and Big Dirty Secrets." *Texas Observer* 90 (May 8, 1998):

8–13. The article cites a published report that claims Texas has the most and worst amounts of air pollution of any state. The main contributor to pollution is found to be places that don't have to follow the current laws concerning air pollution. Texas citizens still don't think that enough is being done to help the situation; the State disagrees. (Sara)

Anonymous. "Killing to Be Kind: Why We Ought to Hunt Big Animals." *The Economist.* April 20, 1996 v339 n7962 p76(2). This seems like an editorial written by one person, and it's a good article even though we don't know his name. He argues against some wild life reserves because of animal over population and for hunting and other things.

Kennedy, Peter. "Position Paper on NPDES Permit." Georgians for Responsible Growth. 12 April 1999. This paper concerns the National Pollutant Discharge Elimination System Permit and how it will affect with water quality in Georgia. He outlines the concerns of the organization, why they disagree with the environmentalists, and lists some possible solutions. The article is useful because one can read about the environmental issue from the developer's point of view.

### ▪ Crime nominations

Messa, Christina, adds to the omnipresent debate regarding the gun control. Her article published in *Other Side of the News,* a conservative Christian magazine, states that gun control in the United States would only lead to an increase of innocent victims. Through use of statistics, examples of historical events, opinions and quotes from political figures and other journalists, the author presents a well-rounded argument. The author of this article seems, without hesitation, extremely supportive of her position. (Marisol)

Corbit, William Andrew, "Violent Crimes among Juveniles: Behavioral Aspects." *FBI Law Enforcement Bulletin* 69(6) 18–21. 2000 June. This article discusses the statistics involving juveniles in the past decade as well as discussing the behavioral aspects that contribute to their actions.

Myers, Jim. "Notes on the Murder of Thirty of My Neighbors." *The Atlantic Monthly,* March 2000. In this article, Myers, a journalist and author from Washington D.C., builds a very strong existence stasis but it does not propose a solution; however, Myers certainly engages the reader's attention. His purpose, one infers, is to ensure that the crimes he mentions will not be forgotten or ignored. He states, "But now I am battling against the inevitable: many of these cases will soon cross over into the netherworld of the forgotten." The disadvantage of this article is its length; it is four parts of about four pages each. (Alison B.)

## Detect

Using the search strategies in this chapter, find three articles or Web sites related to your case: an advocacy Web site, a scholarly journal article, and an argumentative article from a literary/political magazine.

## Produce

Write a brief evaluation of the usefulness and credibility of each article you found in the previous exercise. Use the sample nominations as models.

# CHAPTER 9

# Exploring by Responding

So far, you have worked on examining an author's point of view and finding out more about a problem that interests you. To explore positions that you might take, you now have to do more to examine where are you starting from and where you would like to go. If the issue is new to you, it may seem that you are starting from scratch, with no preconceptions at all—but this is rarely true. Once you begin thinking about related ideas and your reactions to the readings, you are likely to discover many relevant experiences, beliefs, and attitudes from your family life, school, or other activities. The act of writing your own claims and developing supporting appeals will lead you to think more about the problem and develop your own position.

In this chapter, you will learn several ways to express your reactions to an issue, either responding to another author's argument or exploring your own beliefs. Because this writing is exploratory, your goal is not to persuade someone to agree with you; that kind of writing can grow out of this exploratory step but it requires different kinds of planning and will be treated in later chapters. The goal here is to explore your attitudes and beliefs, connect the problem to your own experiences, identify the aspects of the issue that you care most about, and probe for weaknesses in another author's position. You will learn two approaches: narrating your own experience and generating responses to an author's points.

## Narrating a Case

A common response to a complaint is, "I don't see what there is to get all worked up about." Narrating a case is one technique for reflecting on what has made you "worked up" and for sharing that feeling with others.

The narrative you produce might end up in a formal argumentative paper, perhaps in the issue span (Chapter 2), perhaps as vivid support for a claim, or even in a short story. You have already seen how authors use cases in these ways. But an equally valuable reason to narrate a case is to explore the problem for yourself. Writing a narrative lets you put your ideas on paper, fill them out with details, and change them around.

Think of an audience to write to who is not exactly like you and your friends, so that you will remember to include details that you might otherwise consider obvious. But don't choose an audience of complete strangers. The audience should be familiar enough that you can imagine some of their beliefs and attitudes. For example, choose people your age who hang out with a different crowd, or people from your hometown who are in a very different age group.

Pick a public policy case that you want this group of readers to know about. The case needs to be one that could win the audience's attention and engage their values. Your goal should be to enable others to understand the problem that this case represents and to appreciate its significance. Try to choose a case that illustrates exactly the kind of problem you care most about.

To write a good narrative, you will need to learn to lay out vivid details—to evoke the frustration in a series of events or to raise positive expectations of an ideal case—and use literary stylistic techniques to show events happening instead of telling about them. "Narrating Strategies" analyzes these strategies for articles on environment and crime.

## NARRATING STRATEGIES

### Environment: Chivers

Chivers starts in the middle of an event, showing Taylor hauling in a net and later cleaning the fish with Taylor's comments interspersed.

#### Vivid Details

Forty-six miles south by southeast from Cape Cod's characteristic elbow . . . .

Captain Peter Taylor leans over the starboard gunnel of his 40-foot hook-and-line vessel, the *Sea Hound*, and grabs a bright orange buoy.

#### Similes and Metaphors

The rig sweeps along at four knots like an exaggerated butterfly net.

. . . greenish-brown waves so soupy that the late-morning sun penetrates only a few yards down.

#### Telling

Mobile fishing gear tended to "smooth out structures on the bottom" and "remove bottom fauna that contribute to sea floor complexity."

#### Showing

During one experiment I sat on the sea floor and watched a scallop dredge rumble by, and then swam into the path where the dredge had just passed to see much of the complexity of the sea floor removed. What was a complex of sponges, shells, and other organisms was smoothed to a cobblestone street.

## Crime: Shapiro

Shapiro begins his narrative in the middle of a frustrating event that happened when he had already recovered from his injuries, then jumps to the beginning (the evening of the crime), and then comes back to the present.

### Vivid Details

. . . writhing on an ambulance gurney, bright green shirt open and drenched with blood, skin pale, knee raised, trying desperately and with utter futility to find relief from pain.

### Similes and Metaphors

Suddenly there was chaos—as if a mortar shell had landed.

### Telling

The perpetrator would not have been deterred by tougher crime laws.

Not a single one of those 412 pages [of the crime bill] would have protected me or Anna or Martin or any of the others from our assailant.

### Showing

"Why are you doing this?" I cried out to Silva in the moment after feeling his knife punch in and yank out . . . . "You killed my mother," he answered.


## Laying Out the Details

In writing your narrative, include many vivid, concrete details about what happened, when, where, and to whom and how things looked, sounded, felt. To begin with, organize the events in a chronological order using time transitions. Later on, you can experiment with jumping from one sequence to another.

## Narrating the Frustration

Your goal should be to tell an engaging story that also brings readers to an understanding of your issue. You will be most successful if you can capture the tension in your problem cases through the story. Think of the problem cases in your list as a source of someone's frustration or outrage. Someone had high hopes and those hopes were dashed. Something happened to someone that was unjust or that led them to question their fundamental beliefs or values.

## Showing Instead of Telling

Devote extra space to details that reveal the causes of the tension and the outcomes for the individuals. In this way, you can paint pictures that *show* important points, rather than just *telling* the reader about them. Chivers puts readers on the boat with Taylor, listening to him describe changes in the ocean floor. Shapiro shows himself leaping up in front of the TV to make the point about how upset he was at how his case was being used. The showing strategy appeals to pathos because it evokes the reader's sensations, imagination, and emotions. "Student Case Narratives" provides samples of student efforts to use these strategies.

## STUDENT CASE NARRATIVES

### Environment

For the past five years, I have worked for an outdoor ministry that takes hundreds of students camping, canoeing, backpacking, caving, climbing, and repelling. We have two main objectives: to talk to them about Jesus and to get them out of the stale noise of our progressive world and allow them to appreciate and fall in love with the wilderness . . . . Of course, the best parts of those trips are when we see our objectives accomplished. There are two moments that result from this ministry that I would not trade for anything: when a student meets Jesus and when a student from the city looks up for the first time into a blanket of the darkest black he's ever seen, illuminated with more stars than he could ever imagine. Suddenly seventy-five junior high kids are willing to be still and quiet . . . . Whether you enter the wilderness to meet with God or go to simply get away from the noise of everyday life and taste nature's beauty, it is the act of being there that inspires passion and appreciation for the environment. (Katie)

### Crime

When you walk down the street, you can feel the anxiety and fear around you. The smell of easy money and a quick "high" being transacted instead of the business surrounding a normal suburban town. The streets I grew up in—you either were using drugs, selling, or were surrounded by it. It did not matter how old you were or how secluded you made yourself from it; you were always part of it. If you were against the life of drugs, you were always fighting it, always trying to refuse its tempting poison. A drug infestation in a community is a dangerous and perilous problem. The community becomes engulfed in it and seclusion from it is impossible. Drugs have a powerful high that destroys and ends lives in an unparalleled volatile manner. In the community of Compton, a residence of mine for many years, the drug problem has continued at high rates for multiple years. Drug dealers, users, and sellers encroach on every corner of every street in the neighborhood. Drugs can take over a community and change an environment with negative and deadly effects. (Ramin)

# Responding to an Author

If you have not had personal experience with a problem, a good way to explore your ideas is responding to an author. An author may have caught your attention as someone with whom you strongly agree or disagree. Or one author's angle on the issue may seem intriguing. Reactions such as these often provoke readers to write a response to the newspaper or magazine in which the author's article appeared.

The goal of a response can be to express solidarity with an author or to express rejection of an author's point of view; both goals can help you explore your reactions to specific claims in the author's argument. However, exploration does not happen automatically. Willingness to explore does not depend on whether you agree with the author or not. Exploration requires you to consider the evidence and reasoning separately from the personal characteristics of the author. "Responses from Readers" provides excerpts of published responses to articles you have read. The ones labeled "without Exploration" characterize people without addressing the evidence or reasoning.

---

## RESPONSES FROM READERS

### Environment: Responses to Kristof

Here are four responses to Kristof's "In Praise of Snowmobiles."

#### Agreement without Exploration

Snowmobilers merely want to preserve winter access to a very limited part of these great National Parks. This is what we do out West in the wintertime. I just wish someone from the anti-recreation community would accept our invitation to take one of the new technology sleds on a ride up to Old Faithful. I'm pretty sure they'd see snowmobiling in a new light. (Terry Manning, President of the Wyoming State Snowmobile Association, Dec. 24, 2002.)

#### Disagreement without Exploration

In his defense of permitting snowmobiles in Yellowstone National Park, Nicholas D. Kristof writes that when the roads are closed in winter, the only alternative to snowmobiles are noisy snow coaches. And he complains that peering through the fogged-up windows of a snow coach leaves one feeling far removed from nature. Here are two other suggestions for the traveler who wants to get into the winter woods: snowshoes and skis. (Philip Moustakis, Brooklyn, Dec. 24, 2002)

#### Disagreement with Exploration

Nicholas D. Kristof ("In Praise of Snowmobiles," column, Dec. 24) tries to snow readers into believing that snowmobiles are actually good for Yellowstone National Park. Tell that to the park rangers who have experienced breathing difficulties, headaches, nausea, dizziness and hearing loss from the extreme noise and pollution of these machines. Tell that to the imperiled species, such as grizzly bears, Canada lynx, gray wolves, and bald eagles, whose habitat is destroyed and polluted, and to the bison who use the 25-foot-wide trails cleared for snowmobiles to walk into Montana, where they're not protected and are often killed.

Our first and foremost national park has a mandate to protect wildlife and the ecosystem. Yellowstone is a national park, not a national playground. (Michael Markarian, President, The Fund for Animals, Silver Spring, Md., Dec. 24, 2002)

### Agreement with Exploration

It was a nice holiday surprise to read "In Praise of Snowmobiles," by Nicholas D. Kristof (column, Dec. 24). By saying President Bush "did exactly the right thing" to approve the use of new, environmentally friendly, four-stroke engine snowmobiles in Yellowstone National Park, Mr. Kristof rightly laments the decision of green groups and their lawyers to persist with their snowmobile eviction fight. Though interest groups and trial lawyers won't admit it, this case is illustrative of how government and the private sector should work together. Regulators identified a problem using sound scientific analysis, and manufacturers responded with an improved product that satisfies everyone except those with financial interests in further litigation, fund-raising and publicity. (Michael Baroody, Executive Vice President, National Assn. of Manufacturers, Washington, Dec. 24, 2002)

## Crime: Responses to Castleman

Here are four responses that readers offered to Castleman's "Opportunity Knocks." They illustrate different degrees of willingness to explore.

### Agreement without Exploration

. . . It was a relief to find that there are still some human beings who still sound like, think like, and feel like human beings. I don't think I've ever heard or read a more down-to-earth, thoughtful approach to the issue. As with all issues, the debate is fought between the loudest, most extreme faction of the left and right. Somewhere in the middle, the bulk of humanity gets lost. The reasonable approaches available to reasonable people during their day-to-day lives never get heard above the clamor. (John Arndt, San Anselmo, Calif.)

### Disagreement without Exploration

. . . Castleman premises the essay with a self-congratulatory note about his refusal to join the exodus of families from cities into the suburbs. His neighborhood, writes Castleman, is an urban oasis in which a diverse group of people live in harmony . . . . What follows, though, is an ode to a suburban mind-set in which everyone is seen as a potential thief, and the only reason to interact with neighbors is to form a group which agrees to keep its eyes peeled for outsiders. Even these neighborhood watch meetings are not truly safe, as Castleman suspects his fellow crime warriors to be criminals themselves. I would much rather live in the suburbs than have some paranoid guy hitch up his pants and try to get "neighborly" with me or my family in order to form an alliance against people who don't (nudge, nudge) "belong."

The article was clearly written for a white, middle-class audience and assumes a shared paranoia about crime, specifically at the hands of nonwhite, non-middle-class people. Castleman writes that he avoids young black men because he believes that they are more likely to attack him. He is unapologetic about his blatant stereotypical and racist attitude towards African-Americans, instead complimenting himself for the logic of his actions. It is clear that crime is on the minds of most Americans, but the fears of an upper-middle-class white guy do not belong on the pages of *Mother Jones*. (Edward Smock, Wesleyan University, Middletown, Conn.)

### Disagreement with Exploration

On the face of it, one might want to be neighbors with Castleman. He's straightforward, speaks his mind, believes in and acts for neighborly sociableness, and speaks honestly about the effects of violence in his life and upon his family. These are serious things and command respect . . . . Only when he begins to speculate about crime's causes does the not-in-my-parking-space indignation begin to leak . . . .

If Castleman is serious about organizing against crime, what about putting support into the school and other youth services? What about addressing the real estate practices and bank funding policies that make home ownership so exclusive? How about building alliances with community groups and activists to acknowledge the much larger common community interests? And how about taking a good hard look at your attitudes? You can't have a real neighborhood party based on fear. Nor one where the host checks the silver and the window latches after you leave. This article is not about hardening the target, but hardening the heart. (Allan Creighton, Oakland Men's Project, Oakland, Calif.)

### Agreement with Exploration

. . . [L]iberals and conservatives seem united in one assumption: With the correct policies, government could dramatically reduce crime. The fact is, government already has done most of what it can ever do to fight crime. Laws against nearly every conceivable offense have long been passed; it is hard to see how making punishments more severe will have much effect. Nor is it clear that government efforts to fight poverty and racism have done anything to make the country safer. Ultimately, all neighborhoods—affluent or poor—become safer or more dangerous because of the efforts of the people who live in them. Safe neighborhoods are organized. Liberals may be uncomfortable with the idea of citizens exercising any form of social control. But as crime rates rise, some force inevitably will step in to maintain order. Better concerned neighbors using peer pressure than a heavily armed government using courts and prisons. (Tucker Carlson, The Heritage Foundation, Washington, D.C.)

## Agreeing and Disagreeing

Many students find it difficult to explore an issue when the starting point is an article they agree with. It is hard to assess evidence and reasoning that you accept. However, expressing agreement can be exploratory because no two people ever think exactly the same way or have had exactly the same experiences. It is unlikely that any author has created a line of argument to a position that expresses everything you would have said yourself. By exploring with agreement, you can express solidarity with the author, bring in your own examples to support the author's claims, and even broaden the argument by making new claims that are consistent with the author's general position.

In some cases, an author will reach a final position that you agree with, but use a line of argument that you find unfamiliar or problematic. By examining each claim, you can explore opportunities for agreement and explore the strengths and weaknesses of the arguments. After this kind of exploration, you can end up with more and better reasons for your own position.

You can learn something from responding to any author, but you will probably learn the most by choosing an opponent rather than a close ally.

## Using Rogerian Argument

Carl Rogers was a psychologist who developed new techniques for mediating between hostile adversaries. He believed that we become hostile when we feel misunderstood and disrespected. When both sides are hostile, neither side has the freedom to grow, to explore which points are really important and which are not. Rogers's technique involved bringing the opposing sides into a room and having them take turns explaining their positions. For example, imagine a negotiation between a side that wants to adopt a plan (Adopters) and a side that doesn't (Resisters). After the Adopters state their position, the Resisters have to restate the Adopters' point before being allowed to make a response. The restatement must be accurate, phrased nonjudgmentally, and charitable, giving the Adopters the greatest benefit of the doubt. After the Adopters accept the restatement, the Resisters state their position. Then the Adopters must restate the Resisters' position before responding, and so on.

Rogers's approach is most effective when both sides are determined to reach a fair deal because neither side can remain passive. Rogers's approach works because it allows both sides to feel that their points have been heard. This means that the opponents' restatements may not be neutral or perfectly objective. Instead each side has to express the values of the other side accurately. The effort to put an opponent's position into their own words teaches both sides a lot about their own attitudes as well as those of the other.

When working with texts, you will seldom be able to ask another author whether she agrees with how you have stated her points, so it is good practice to ask yourself: Would the author accept my summary of her point? Am I representing her fairly? Have I made the most charitable interpretation possible?

To turn critical reading into a response, you have to turn your reactions into arguments. The thesis of your response will be to agree, partly agree, or disagree with the author, but you also have to say why—to give good reasons for your assessment. Coming up with these reasons is easiest if you know something about the issue and if you actively use your imagination.

Composing your response is an exploratory process because reasoning about someone else's position helps you reflect on your own. After writing a response, you may find that your position has become richer and stronger in some respects and weaker in others. You may end up searching for ways to defend the weaker parts of your position or even change them.

In Chapter 3, you learned about five types of claims: existence, definition, value, cause, and action. In Chapter 4, you learned that authors support claims by appealing to logos, ethos, and pathos. In the next two sections, you will learn ways to respond to each kind of claim and to each kind of support.

## Assessing Claims

As you saw in Chapter 3, each type of claim is developed with related claims: An existence claim includes many statements about the characteristics of an object or event; a definition claim includes claims about cases, categories, and characteristics; a value claim involves comparisons of cases against criteria or against each other; a causal claim involves a time sequence, agents, factors, and an object that changes; and an action claim involves the timing and nature of the action and the people responsible for acting. Each aspect of a claim is open to challenge by asking questions like these:

- **Existence claims.** Does the object or event really have the characteristics the author describes? Is it a unique case? If the author says something is impossible, is it really impossible?

- **Definition claims.** Is there an alternative category to which the case could be assigned?

- **Value claims.** Is the author's judgment appropriate? Is what the author considers "bad" really bad? (Is it bad for taxes to go up?) Is an action moral just because "everyone else does it"? or "someone else would have done it if I hadn't?" or "my intentions were honorable"? Has the author considered all the appropriate standards? (Why didn't the author consider efficiency?) Are the standards weighted appropriately? (Is freedom worth more than safety?)

- **Cause claims.** Is the cause factor actually adequate to produce the effect? Does the author explain how the factor leads to the effect? Could any other factor have produced the effect? Does that factor always lead to that effect?

- **Action claims.** Are the agents capable of taking the actions that the author recommends?

## Assessing Support

It is important to assess the believability of the author's appeals to logos, ethos, and pathos separately from the claim. You may be undecided about the truth of the claim because you find that the author's reasons are not convincing. Or you

"*I just think you're going to need a better rallying cry than 'Absence of evidence isn't evidence of absence.'*"

**Challenging an existence claim.** © The New Yorker Collection 2003 Robert Mankoff from cartoonbank.com. All Rights Reserved.

may believe that a claim is true, but for different reasons than the author has offered. To assess the support, there are two main questions to ask: Is it relevant and is it sufficient?

An author's appeal is irrelevant if your belief in the claim would stay the same no matter whether the support is true, false, probable, or unlikely. For example, suppose that Senator Smith proposes deregulating snowmobiles in Yellowstone and justifies the plan by saying that Old Faithful is the most spectacular geyser in the United States. You may feel that his evaluation of geysers is irrelevant to the merits of the snowmobile plan no matter whether Smith failed to compare Old Faithful to other geysers and no matter whether you agree that Old Faithful is wonderful.

Even if the appeals are relevant, they may still not be enough (or sufficient) to convince you of the truth of the claim because they account for only part of the conditions involved in the claim. "Insufficient Appeals" illustrates how a relevant appeal can fall short.

## INSUFFICIENT APPEALS

### Environment

Suppose an oceanographer looked at an area of ocean bottom and claimed that "Dredging was used here" because dredging destroys the sea bottom and the sea bottom here is destroyed. The reasons may both be true. But other factors might have been at work in this particular area (such as an underwater earthquake), so the claim could still be false.

### Crime

Suppose that a legislator argued that "We should eliminate sales at gun shows to eliminate school shootings" and supported this action claim with this appeal to logos: "Weapons bought at gun shows were used in shootings at twelve high schools." To test whether the support is sufficient, imagine a place where gun shows were banned. Then, if the action claim were true, you should be able to imagine believing this statement, "We have eliminated shootings in high schools." This statement still seems implausible because guns could enter a school from many other sources.

*"I still say it's only a theory."*

**Irrelevant support can be ruled out without affecting belief in a claim.** © The New Yorker
Collection 2005 David Sipress from cartoonbank.com. All Rights Reserved.

For controversial claims, authors can never provide enough support to convince all readers; they usually strive to provide the best support available at the time or the support they believe will be most persuasive for most of their readers. As an explorer, keep in mind that claims with insufficient or faulty support may still be true or partly true. Challenging the sufficiency of the evidence can help you recognize your own reasons for believing or disbelieving the claim. This process can also raise larger questions that are worth pursuing in your own argument:

- **Environment issue.** Does all dredging destroy the ocean bottom? Are other factors for ocean floor destruction worse than dredging?

- **Crime issue.** Are gun show sales the most important factor of crime to eliminate? Is shooting the worst form of school violence?

Each type of appeal offers different grounds for accepting a claim: because an authority says it is true (ethos), because you can identify with the claim in an emotional or imaginative way (pathos), and because of common sense or evidence from real-world observations (logos). Therefore, the appeals can each be challenged in a different way by asking questions such as these:

- **Challenging ethos.** Did the writer express the authority's view accurately and fairly? Is the question at hand within the authority's area of experience? Does the authority have a monetary stake in the outcome? A personal stake (e.g., attachments to people who might benefit)? An ideological stake (e.g., ties to groups that might benefit)? Do other authorities agree?

- **Challenging pathos.** Does the author seem sincere? Does the same concern extend through the entire argument? Would everyone involved in the situation describe it in the same way and feel the same emotions? If you felt milder emotions, would you still believe the claim?

- **Challenging logos.** Were the observations made by a qualified person? Were the conditions for observing good enough (e.g., visibility, distance). How many observations are reported? Does the case represent what usually happens? Has the author admitted the possibility of exceptions? Is the author justified in calling an opponent's position illogical or ridiculous? Is the author treating like cases alike?

## Playing Devil's Advocate

A helpful technique for finding ways to challenge an author's claims and support is to play **devil's advocate**. A devil's advocate is a friend who adopts the role of an opponent even if he or she really agrees with the claims or support. People who are "playing devil's advocate" are searching for the strengths and weaknesses in an argument by engaging in a hypothetical debate with an author, making challenges,

**Challenging a value claim with logos.**  © Scott Adams/Dist. by United Feature Syndicate, Inc.

imagining the author's possible responses, and coming up with challenges to those responses.

Playing the role of devil's advocate can be a lot of fun but it takes imagination. Beyond contradicting everything the author says, when acting as a devil's advocate, you must offer plausible alternatives. For example, if an author claims that a problem is significant, think of a problem that might be more urgent. If the author identifies a factor that causes a problem, think of an alternative factor. Or think of a case where the problem occurred even when that factor was absent. If the author presents solutions, propose alternatives (even far-fetched ones) to get at reasons the author might say his or her proposed solution is better.

Playing devil's advocate draws on the techniques for disagreement discussed in Chapter 5: identifying opponents, summarizing the alternative path fairly, making concessions, stating the rebuttal, and returning to the main path. When working with a partner, be sure to use all of these techniques. Deciding when to make concessions is especially important: if you concede too quickly, your partner will not have a chance to find ways to improve the point; if you are unwilling to concede, you will end up in a stalemate. "Devil's Advocate Exchanges" illustrates responses from a student to the author of a reading.

# DEVIL'S ADVOCATE EXCHANGES

## Environment

### Devil's Paraphrase
Jim DiPeso, the policy director for Republicans for Environmental Protections, argues that a new Department of Interior regulation will be disastrous because it will punch roads into wilderness areas and allow in reckless explorers with dirt bikes and ATVs.

### Devil's Response
The Bush administration was looking ahead when it enacted a law that may allow new roads to be contracted. With designated roads for ATVs and other forms of mechanical transport, people are less likely to try forging their own path through the fragile environment. People will travel where they wish if no road has been designated. They will make a road by repeatedly riding over dirt trails. They will continually choose new paths and disturb and even kill the plants and animals that inhabit the area they ride through. The American people will seek pleasure in the wilderness with their modern toys regardless of the consequences. But by enacting this regulation and opening up the possibility to making permanent trails that animals learn to avoid and plants grow away from, the Bush administration is actually saving the wilderness.

## Crime

### Devil's Paraphrase
Castleman rejects the liberal and conservative habits of blaming crime on family, racism, poverty, and bad morals. He argues that impulse, alienation, and opportunity are the true causes of crime among juveniles. To him, reducing opportunity is the "best bet for controlling crime," as compared to impulse and alienation.

### Devil's Response
Castleman claims that no one can ever rid us of criminal impulsiveness. He uses his own son's swiping some money as an example. But maybe his son is not like all young boys. Only a small fraction turn into street criminals. Even if we can't get rid of the impulse entirely, we are supposed to learn to control it or reduce it. That's what parents, churches, and schools are supposed to do. If we reduce opportunity without doing anything about impulsiveness or alienation, we just are changing where crime will happen not how much crime there is. Crime will keep moving to places where people can't reduce opportunity. It just takes a few slips to leave a window open. It's impossible to get rid of all opportunities.

# Imitating

Imitation is a very important way to learn to write because you can easily try out new ways to put an argument together. Artists and musicians often use imitation while developing their skills. They try out variations on themes from other artists before putting their own creations together. Imitation is an exploratory form of response because it requires you to look much more closely at the author's pattern of the argument, down to the words and phrases. Imitation makes it easier to identify passages that you find ineffective and figure out reasons why.

Imitation is both a natural and an unnatural activity. Psychologists have found that, even without noticing it, we pattern our sentences as we talk to match those of the people we are with. Some people have the sensation of thinking or talking differently after reading a book with a distinctive style, such as a British novel. However, creating a written imitation means deliberately crafting ideas to fit into a form, like writing a limerick or a rap. To do so, you have to search your memory imaginatively for ideas about a different topic to fit the pattern.

Choosing a good passage to imitate is important. It should be a passage that makes a point in a distinctive way. The author should be someone whose writing you admire, whose writing is different from yours in style or complexity.

For imitation to be effective, it must not be too mechanical. To create an imitation, follow the form of each sentence of the original passage while writing on a different topic. For example, where the original uses a value term to compare two items in a category, substitute a different value term and instances from a different category. If you succeed, you will create a fresh argument with a similar structure to the original. If the topic you choose is too similar to the original, or if you reuse too many phrases, the imitation will sound flat and you will be veering closer to plagiarism than to imitation. "Fresh and Flat Imitations" provides effective and ineffective imitations of a passage.

---

## FRESH AND FLAT IMITATIONS

### Original

One movie that really appealed to teenagers was *Star Wars*. It included countless zany, exciting special effects. One of the more impressive of these was a light saber. This lethal laser weapon once was used by awesome Jedi Knights. These Knights maintained truth and justice in their galaxies. But truth and justice were threatened by vile and ruthless creatures. These beings were led by Darth Vader, a sinister and merciless warlord. His goal was to destroy all the planets that refused to submit to him. The most important was Capricorn, the dune world. (vande Kopple)

### Fresh Imitation of Structure and Novel Topic

One type of music that really appealed to teenagers in the early nineties was grunge rock. It involved crunchy guitar, raspy vocals, and a sometimes-crazy onstage presence. One of the most inspired on-stage bands was Pearl Jam. This band was led by brutal front man Eddie Vedder. Vedder belted out sweet harmonies and mesmerizing lyrics in awesome performances. But these performances were soon threatened by weaker pre-fab bands. The worst of these was Creed, a band from Tallahassee that imitated Pearl Jam's sound. Creed's goal was to achieve fame that would come fast and produce maximum profit. The easiest path to fame was an appearance on T.R.L. (Ryan)

### Flat Imitation of Structure and Close Topic

One action figure that really appealed to little kids was He-Man. He fought countless zany, exciting battles. These battles were against evil enemies. One of the more dangerous of these was Skeletor. This lethal enemy was responsible for creating mass chaos in the world. This chaos would come to an end as He-Man comes to the rescue. (Matt)

## Arguing and Expressing

The end result of a good response is that you will have learned more about the issue and about your own beliefs. You should also have arrived at a position that is new from your own standpoint, one that expresses your own experiences, reasoning, and reactions. These kinds of outcomes are valuable in a society that cherishes the right of any person to express his or her ideas freely.

But free expression in itself is not enough to solve problems and arrive at difficult decisions. Even if all those involved in an issue had a chance to say what they think, there is no guarantee that they will then reach a good decision. In academic inquiry, the goal is to reach as far as possible toward the best or truest position, not the most popular one. In public policy debates, the goal is to make a decision that takes into account the interests of many parties and that is based on all the available evidence. What you write in a personal response will not necessarily be seen as a contribution in a public policy debate because it may not contain anything new for the stakeholders involved. It may not persuade readers to see the issue, the problem, or possible solutions in a new way. Writing that kind of contribution is the goal of later chapters of this book.

## EXERCISES

### Backtalk: What Do You Say?

Several readings use case narratives: on the environment topic, Chivers, Easterbrook, Kristof, and Shiflett; on the crime topic, Brooks, Castleman, and Shapiro. Which of these narratives do you find persuasive and vivid and which do you find cheesy and trite? How do the successful authors avoid turning off their readers?

## Recognize/Evaluate

The following are case narratives written by students. Identify their use of these strategies: using vivid details, narrating the frustration, and showing instead of telling. Then compare the narrative here to the one in "Student Case Narratives." Which one is more effective? Why?

### A. Environment

When I was a young child, I used to live at the edge of a beautiful, lush forest. I used to have picnics deep in the woods where no one could find me and I, also, had a tree house in a tall sycamore tree. I would spend every spare minute in the forest because it was my favorite place to be. I eventually moved away, but the vivid memories of my forest still remain intact. The fun that the children were having in my childhood play pen was an image that brought a smile to my face. This image was soon crushed when I visited my neighborhood a few years ago. In place of my childhood memory was a tall, somber office building and crowded parking lot. My forest had been destroyed by industrialization of the wilderness. The forest was not just a pleasant memory, but a home to many species, many of which may have been endangered. Colonies of species were wiped out by the construction and the land it sits on will never be the same. This construction is similar to what has been happening to our very own Yosemite National Park. Though the construction built in this place of natural wonders has been used to benefit its visitors and sightseers, the damage is still visible and dangerous. (Keri)

### B. Crime

On the morning of September 11, 2001, I walked into my economics class and took my seat. The class was its usual self, awaiting the professor's arrival, discussing last night's homework, or catching a few minutes of shut-eye. The professor walked in, set her books down, and said, "I'm sure that I am the first one to tell you . . . Two planes have been hijacked and have crashed into the World Trade Towers, collapsing both of them completely to the ground." At that moment, I didn't know what to think. I couldn't envision something like that happening; two planes, plowing into both towers, and both towers collapsing to the ground. The ninety minutes of class that day were useless; I could not pay attention. I had to get to a television to learn more. (Jeff)

## Detect

Which of the following passages use techniques of showing rather than telling?

## A. Environment

- In an informal survey, 15 people of a remote region of Durango, Mexico, were asked what the word *conservación* meant. None of them knew. "No," they replied, shaking their heads. "Qué será? (What would it mean?)" Earlier, one man from this group had pointed out ways in which he and his family were trying to protect the rangeland from the effects of drought and overgrazing and to protect the wildlife from poachers. When asked why, he turned in his saddle, viewing the range stretching away from him into the distance, and said, "Hay que cuidar, verdad? [You've got to care for it, don't you?]" (Gómez-Pompa and Kaus)

- One popular tropical conservation effort has been to encourage consumers to pay more for products that are cultivated or harvested in ecologically sensitive ways. Myriad international development projects have promoted these so-called sustainable practices in forests and farms around the world. Ordinary citizens in the U.S. and Europe participate by choosing to buy timber, coffee and other agricultural goods that are certified as having met such special standards during production. (Hardner and Rice)

## B. Crime

- In "Corktown," the district I studied, officers thought there were one, maybe two identifiable street gangs, but they felt that most of the so-called "gang calls" they were assigned to handle were unrelated to "real" gang activity. By "real," the police refer to activities that they believed to be gang activities, as opposed to the way the police organization expected them to report gang activities. (Meehan)

- The map categorizes each city tract; the darker the shading, the higher the crime rate. Each dot represents a liquor outlet. If one knew nothing about the city or what the shaded areas or dots represent and simply drew circles around the places where the dots are clustered, Milwaukee's poor, minority, high-crime, inner-city neighborhoods would be enclosed in those circles. (DiIulio, "Broken Bottles")

## Produce

### A. Devil's Advocate Interchange

Choose a partner who is prepared to role-play the author you want to challenge and respond as the author might respond. Choose a section (such as the problem span, Chapter 2) and challenge the author's points using the techniques of summarizing the alternative path fairly, making concessions, stating the rebuttal, and returning to the main path (Chapter 5). The author-player should be ready to defend the author's point with reasons, but may also end up making concessions or with you, an outcome that can help you identify your best challenges. After playing for 20 minutes, switch roles and focus on a different section of the author's argument (such as the solution).

## B. Case Narrative

Choose a case that you know a lot about and write a case narrative in which you provide many vivid details, narrate the frustration, and use strategies for showing your points.

# CHAPTER 10

# Exploring and Constructing a Problem

In Chapter 9, you explored your issue by formulating and expressing a personal response to another author. In this chapter, you will explore the nature of the problem itself by comparing cases and by analyzing the source of the tension.

At this point, you have collected a great deal of information about some aspect of the issue, so you may feel that you already understand what the problem is. But stating the problem in a productive way is harder than it seems. The following examples may seem to state a problem, but they do not:

"The problem is that we need to lower the legal drinking age." This states a solution; it says nothing about a problem.

"The problem is global warming." This names a phenomenon; it says nothing about what is wrong.

"The problem is frequent violence in schools"; "The problem is that tigers are disappearing." These hint at negative circumstances without spelling out why anyone should care about them.

For most issues, people disagree about what the "real" problem is because many factors contribute to a complex situation, not just one "real" problem and many "mistaken" ones. To find a meaningful and original angle on the problem, you may end up trying out several ways of describing it. This chapter offers several helpful strategies for developing and refining your descriptions.

## Two Strategies for Exploring the Problem

To build a persuasive argument about a problem that you want to solve, you will have to make claims at one or more stases (Chapter 3): that there is a problem (existence), that an incident should be counted in a category (definition), that the harms from the problem are significant (value), and that the problem has an identifiable source or effects (cause). For example, if you are concerned about the survival of a rare salamander found in a local swimming hole, you might have to argue that the salamander is there, that it belongs in the category of endangered species, that the danger is urgent, or that the salamander's rarity makes it extremely valuable, and that the danger comes from the way the pool is cleaned.

Alternatively, you may argue that opponents are wrong about a problem. In this case, you may argue that no problem exists (existence), that the phenomenon is not what an opponent thinks (definition), that the opponents' harms are trivial (value), or that the opponent's predictions are faulty (cause). For example, Kleck argues that there is no trend toward violent shootings in schools; that the problem is really one of media hype, not security; that the risks to school children are very low while the harms from hype are high; that opponents focus on irrelevant factors to explain the shootings; and that changing these factors would not prevent shootings.

To support claims that a problem exists, many authors rely on cases. As described in Chapter 7, a case is good evidence that the problem has happened at least once. A vivid enough narration of the frustration in the case (Chapter 9) can support a significance claim, as can multiple examples of cases. But piling up examples is not enough for identifying the factors that produce the problem; to tackle a problem, you have to figure out what is causing it.

Two good ways to figure out the cause of a problem are to analyze the nature of the conflict and to compare cases. These strategies are not guaranteed to lead you to the "right" cause, but they can help you identify some promising candidates. More importantly, they will help you find the aspect of the problem that you are most interested in pursuing.

## Stating a Problem as a Clash

As described in Chapter 2, problems are situations in which we need something that we don't have or we want to do something that we can't do. For example, you have a problem if:

- You have a job far from your home, but you don't have a car.
- You want to go to a concert, but you can't afford the tickets.
- Your sister is getting married this weekend, but you have midterms next week.

In these examples, it is easy to see what goal is desired and what keeps it from being achieved. These examples all concern personal issues. Public policy problems concern public resources (e.g., land, tax dollars, and information), public agencies (e.g., lawmakers, courts, and policing agencies), and public activities by ordinary people (e.g., citizens voting, business owners applying for a building permit, or clubs seeking to hold a lottery).

For both personal and public issues, a problem is a **clash** between what you want and what you have. A clash is a conflict or inconsistency involving tension and frustration; it creates a feeling of lacking or exigency. Your description of the problem should describe two parts of that clash. "Problem Statements with a Clash" illustrates problems in the environment and crime topics.

## PROBLEM STATEMENTS WITH A CLASH

### *Environment*

- (A) We want more people to visit our national park, but (B) we have no more room for camping or parking.
- (A) We want visitors to Yosemite to have access to trails with the best views, but (B) the crowds erode the trails, take artifacts, and litter.

### *Crime*

- (A) We want to jail every possible criminal, but (B) burglars hardly ever get caught.
- (A) We want innocent people to be left alone, but (B) Hispanic and African-Americans are often stopped by police for no reason.

To develop a full description of the two distinct parts that are in conflict, it is useful to separate them out as two separate statements, Statement A and Statement B, as in the template in Table 10.1. The statements in the following examples are short in length, but a statement in this template is not confined to a single sentence or phrase; sometimes it can take up paragraphs or pages.

The term **"A *BUT* B statements"** will be used for passages developed following this template. The key to creating a useful problem statement is ensuring that

**TABLE 10.1** **Problem Statement Template**

| | |
|---|---|
| Statement A | Describe an important goal, a desired state, or a value. The goal is often something we take for granted, but it is what is ultimately at stake or at risk. |
| BUT | Connect Statement A and Statement B with a conflict term such as "but," "however," "unfortunately." |
| Statement B | Describe a condition that prevents the goal, state, or value in Statement A from being achieved or realized at this time. It may be another feature of the situation. Or it may be a competing goal, desired state, or value. |

the values explicitly mentioned in Statement A are directly endangered by something else explicitly stated in Statement B. There are many kinds of clashes, but these three are most common.

- **Goal vs. Obstacle.** The goal (Statement A) is any desire or value. The obstacle (Statement B) is a physical barrier, a technical limitation, a rule.

- **Value vs. Value.** Sometimes satisfying one goal or desire (Statement A) means sacrificing another (Statement B) because they cannot both be achieved at the same time. Or two groups involved in a situation can have opposing values. The problem could be that neither group's goals are satisfied or that one group's needs (Statement A) are fully met while the other's are not met at all (Statement B).

- **Expectation vs. Observation.** What we expect to happen, based on prior experiences or theories (Statement A), can conflict with what we see happening (Statement B). Someone's goals or values (Statement A) can be endangered by her actions (Statement B).

"Three Kinds of Clashes" illustrates goal vs. obstacle, value vs. value, and expectation vs. observation clashes in problem statements from the readings.

## THREE KINDS OF CLASHES

### *Environment*

#### *Goal vs. Obstacle*

Shiflett: (A) People like me need silence to enjoy the majesty of nature in national and state parks. *BUT* (B) People who ride dirt bikes, ATVs, and jet skis in parks make a lot of noise, disturbing the people and the fish, in a pointless activity.

#### *Value vs. Value*

Easterbrook: (A) We need new energy sources to replace old, inefficient, and dirty power plants in order to make energy production in the United States cleaner and to satisfy the basic energy needs of impoverished people around the world. *BUT* (B) Many environmentalists want to preserve wilderness areas and ecologies in as pristine a condition as possible. They oppose building any kind of power plant in a wild area, even clean energy sources such as dams, because they alter the ecology.

#### *Expectation vs. Observation*

Gómez-Pompa and Kaus: (A) Western environmentalists, many of whom live in cities, want natural resources and wilderness ecologies to be preserved in their pristine state with as little trace of humans as possible. *BUT* (B) Nature is really a system that is continuously changing. Wilderness areas have been inhabited, modified, and managed throughout human history.

## Crime

### Goal vs. Obstacle

(A) Gun show dealers would like to comply with U.S. government laws that bar gun sales to felons, fugitives from justice, drug addicts, illegal aliens, individuals with dishonorable discharges, those renouncing U.S. citizenship, and mental incompetents. *BUT* (B) Gun shows run for only a few days in fairgrounds or rented space. So dealers do not have access to legal records or databases for background checks. So dealers can't tell if a gun purchaser is barred, unless he or she admits it on a form. Dealers would lose business if they had to wait.

### Value vs. Value

(A) Americans want to feel safe in their homes and to reduce neighborhood crime and violence. Some feel their homes and neighborhoods are safer without guns. *BUT* (B) Some Americans feel freer and safer from violence if they have a handgun so they can defend themselves if they are attacked.

### Expectation vs. Observation

(A) Most gun buyers want to keep guns for legitimate reasons, such as hunting, collecting, recreation, and self-defense. *BUT* (B) Some people who buy guns are felons, fugitives, drug addicts, and mental incompetents who are not supposed to buy them. Other buyers are responsible citizens who, in the heat of the moment or in a period of depression, use a gun to commit a homicide or suicide.

Stating the clash can take several tries and lots of refinement of the wording. To have a true clash, you have to identify two different aspects of the situation that are directly involved with each other. Statement B cannot merely paraphrase Statement A. Statement B cannot refer to a completely different situation from Statement A. For example, neither of these is a useful problem statement:

- (A) People of different ethnicities and religions need to learn to live together. *BUT* (B) They don't.
- (A) People of different ethnicities and religions need to learn to live together. *BUT* (B) No Hispanic has ever been President of the United States.

To come up with a good statement of the problem, think about the relationship of the A and B statements and the cause of the clash.

**State the clash clearly to keep allies on board.** © Scott Adams/Dist. by United Feature Syndicate, Inc.

## Stating Goals Explicitly

Statement A, which describes the goal, can be hard to state in words. A goal often involves values that we take so much for granted that no one bothers to express them. The importance of developing an explicit goal statement is to bring these values back into the open, so everyone is aware of exactly what is at stake.

The lack of an explicit goal is part of what is wrong with this effort to state a problem: "The problem is that tigers are disappearing." Even if the statement is true, it just describes the current state of the tiger population. There is no tension here. In fact, the statement "tigers are disappearing" could be good news to a rancher whose cattle are being eaten. The disappearance of tigers becomes part of a problem only when their absence conflicts with a goal that can only be achieved with tigers around, for example:

- (A) Farmers want to stop the growing wild pig population from destroying valuable crops and plant life. *BUT* (B) Tigers, the pigs' natural predators, are disappearing.
- (A) Traditional Chinese medical treatments need to make use of tiger parts such as bones, eyes, whiskers, and teeth. *BUT* (B) Tigers are disappearing.
- (A) We want wild animals to survive for the sake of biodiversity and tourism. *BUT* (B) Tigers are disappearing.

Specifying what is at stake, as in these examples, clarifies what you really care about; in the first example, what you care about is crops; in the second, you care about Chinese medicine; in the third, you care about wild animals in general and tigers in particular. Stating the goal as a question helps you investigate why the goal is in danger, the role of the obstacle. For example, asking "How can we keep wild pigs from causing destruction?" or "How can Chinese doctors continue treating their patients?" will lead you far away from the topic of tigers. But asking "How can we preserve diversity in the wild and support tourism?" enables a focus on tigers. If tigers are what you care about, write a statement starting with this version in Statement A.

# Exploring Possible Causes

To be worth exploring in writing, a problem has to be tough. A problem can be tough because the elements in the clash are hard to change. Another kind of tough problem is when commitments to clashing goals are strong, such as when two ethnic or religious groups claim sovereignty over the same land. To test the toughness of your problem, look first at the obstacle. If the obstacle is easy to get around, there won't be much extended debate over taking action. Next, consider the degree of commitment to the goal. If the desire is temporary or easily satisfied (such as "I want to have fun" or "I want to see El Capitan at Yosemite"), then the problem isn't much of a problem.

A problem can also be tough because its causes are complex or unknown (Chapter 3). For example, a healthy coral reef might suddenly start disintegrating or crime incidents might spike in a previously quiet neighborhood. At first, many factors seem plausible. The cause is what allows the problem to occur at all or what makes it worse. If you know a cause factor, then you can go on to explore a solution (Chapter 11) to figure out ways to change that factor and make the problem diminish or disappear. Elaborating on the clash can help you think of possible causes for the problem.

When you identify plausible causes, you can choose any of them as the most promising or the most interesting to address. "Exploring Causes" illustrates how agents have explored the causes of real-world problems.

---

## EXPLORING CAUSES

### *Environment*

Marine biologists in Alaska noticed a sharp drop in the population of Steller seals. Greenpeace and other environmentalist groups argued that fishing in their habitat was a plausible cause. Fishermen argued that they were not the cause because they weren't catching the kinds of fish that seals eat. The federal judge in charge barred fishing temporarily to test whether fishing was the cause.

### *Crime*

Castleman considered several causes for street crime at the social level, including poverty, racism, and morals. He gave practical reasons for not pursuing these—they were too hard to change. Then he considered causes at the level of individuals, including impulse, alienation, and opportunity. He concluded that reducing opportunity is something effective that anyone in any neighborhood can do. Other authors are free to reconsider the causes that Castleman rejected.

# Working Backwards from a Solution

Some students are so committed to a particular course of action that the only point they can make about the problem is that the solution they have in mind is not already in effect. If this is happening to you, try working backwards to think about what factors in the situation would be changed by your solution.

What desires or needs would the solution satisfy? What are the goals of those who oppose the solution? What would be changed if the solution were enacted? "Working Backwards" illustrates this technique.

---

## WORKING BACKWARDS

### *Environment: Snowmobiles*

(A) We need to ban snowmobiles, ATVs, jet-skis, and dirt bikes from national forests and parks. *BUT* (B) The government has overturned a ban on snowmobiles at Yellowstone.

This statement does not illuminate a problem because Statement A is a solution not a goal. To explore the goals that are at risk or in conflict ask questions about the ban such as these:

- What needs or desires would the ban satisfy?

  Environmentalists want animals to be left undisturbed, trails to be preserved, and air and water to stay clean. Some nature lovers who visit the parks and forests want to enjoy nature in silence.

- What are the goals of those who oppose the ban?

  Riders of snowmobiles, ATVs, jet-skis, and dirt bikes are tourists who love the outdoors and want to have fun. They might also be people who cannot or would not hike but want access to national forests and parks. The ban is also opposed by businesses that sell, rent, and manufacture these vehicles.

- What benefits might come if the ban were instituted?

  Less air, water, and noise pollution; less damage to trails; less disturbance to the animals. The ban would not totally eliminate these threats because people would still visit on foot and in cars. Other sources of pollution would not be affected.

- What harms might come?

  Fewer people would visit the parks and forests; they would go elsewhere on vacation. This would lower tourist business and possibly raise entrance fees. Some citizens will feel upset that U.S. land is not available for them.

These questions and their answers reveal two potential directions for exploration. First, the values of the people who want silence clash with those who want recreational fun. Both groups cannot be satisfied in the same place at the same time. Second, an area of common ground is that both groups love to be out in nature. So the snowmobilers' values (loving nature) may clash with their observed actions (causing pollution or damage). They may believe that the damage they cause is minor.

### Crime: Drinking Age

(A) We need to lower the drinking age. *BUT* (B) City officials won't do it.

This statement does not illuminate a problem because Statement A is a solution not a goal. To explore the goals that are at risk or in conflict ask questions such as these:

- What needs or desires does lowering the drinking age satisfy?

  Young people want to drink in order to let go, to fit in, and to flirt with danger. They want to be treated as adults in the decision to drink as they are in voting, holding a job, getting married, and going to war.

- What are the goals of those who want to keep eighteen as the legal drinking age?

  Parents and other adults want to reduce drunk driving accidents, date rape, and crime. They want young people to be safe and clearheaded enough to focus on their responsibilities.

- What benefits might come if the drinking age were lowered?

  The teenagers who want to drink would still drink but without a hassle. These teens might not find drinking as attractive anymore and drink less. Teens would have more respect for laws that are enforced effectively and fairly.

- What harms might come?

  More teens and younger kids might start drinking. These teens might not be able to handle drinking and get into trouble.

If the goal is reduced hassle for kids who want to get drunk, then your challenge will be to defend that as an important goal for public policy. If the goal is to get rid of ineffective or randomly enforced laws, then the obstacles to that goal need to be explored: too few police officers, lax bartenders.

## Analyzing Problem Cases

Another way to explore a problem is to analyze and compare problem cases. As described in Chapter 7, a problem case is a concrete real-world event whose occurrence makes people dissatisfied or discontent. Focusing on cases will help you see on a small scale the tensions that a large community might feel.

Using cases to describe a general problem is the basis for making claims for existence and definition. When you claim that a problem exists, you are saying that a set of cases with bad outcomes are all part of the same phenomenon and should be addressed in the same way. Identifying the tension in a case, the aspect that makes the outcome good or bad, is similar to identifying the clash using a problem statement. Exploring the tension is easier if you have found or invented several cases. A case consists of four elements: agent, action, motive, and outcome. "Case Aspects" illustrates these elements in problem cases from the readings.

## CASE ASPECTS: AGENT, ACTION, MOTIVE, OUTCOME

### *Environment*

#### Kristof's Cases

1. (agent) Nicholas Kristof (action) rented a snowmobile to ride around Yellowstone (motive) in order to see the park, be outdoors, find out if snowmobiles are really dreadful. (outcome) Had fun, saw two bull moose, got around the park efficiently.

2. (agent) Nicholas Kristof (action) took a snow coach ride around Yellowstone (motive) in order to get to Old Faithful, compare snow coach to snowmobiles. (outcome) Had trouble seeing out the windows, felt removed from nature.

#### Shiflett's Cases

1. (agent) Dirt bikers at Pike National Forest in Colorado (action) crowded out the hikers and made unbearable noise. (outcome) Dave Shiflett is distracted from contemplating nature as he hiked.

2. (agent) Jet skiers at North Carolina's Outer Banks (action) buzzed the pier, scared off the fish, and made unbearable noise (motive) for thrills. (outcome) Dave Shiflett and fisherman hanging out on fishing pier contemplate taking violent measures.

Comparing these cases may lead you to see factors they share. For example, Shiflett might approve of Kristof's motives for using a snowmobile while disapproving of the jet-skiers' desires for thrills. Another factor is the effect of the vehicles on other people. Kristof says nothing about whether the vehicles disturbed hikers, but he would agree with Shiflett that excessive noise is bad. On the noise criterion, Kristof claims that snowmobiles are better than snow coaches.

## Crime

### Shapiro's Cases

1. (agent) Daniel Silva (action) stabbed Bruce Shapiro and six others in a coffee bar near Yale University in New Haven, Connecticut. (motive) He acted randomly out of rage at losing his mother whom he mistakenly believed was dead when he couldn't find her in the hospital. (outcome) National and international media covered the attack with public comments from Yale and the mayor of New Haven and the story is reused by legislators promoting a crime bill. Victims are outraged by the coverage.

2. (agent) Unknown assailant (action) shot and killed 15-year-old Rashawnda Crenshaw who was riding in a car in the impoverished Hill area of New Haven, Connecticut (motive) while aiming to kill someone else. (outcome) Local media covered the story for about a week, without comments from mayor or representatives of Yale.

c. (agent) Colin Ferguson (action) opened fire in a train on the Long Island Rail Road, killed six and wounded 19 other passengers in 1993. (motive) Unknown. (outcome) Public is obsessed by televised trial. Courageous survivors become anti-gun activists and not capital penalty advocates.

Shapiro uses his cases in at least two ways. First, Shapiro uses his own and Crenshaw's cases to support the value claim that "the 'seriousness' of a crime is a matter of race and real estate." Like Kleck, Shapiro questions the attention paid to certain crimes by the media. This problem seems worth exploring further. Second, Shapiro presents the Ferguson incident as an ideal case showing that victims want speedy justice and not revenge. The issue of whether laws, like those requiring restitution, actually help victims and reduce crimes is worth exploring further.

Public argument arises when people can't agree on what cases are part of the problem or which cases are the most important to try to fix—the most typical cases that occur frequently or the most serious cases that occur rarely. They might not agree on which factors cause the majority of the problem cases. Or they might know of a case where a solution failed and argue that it is wrong for all cases.

## Collecting and Grouping Cases

Collect cases from sources, from your own experience, or through invention of hypothetical cases. To compare these cases, you need to be able to look at them all at a glance. Use whatever technique is easiest for you: Write each case on an index card or create a list of cases using a word-processing program or spreadsheet program.

## "The all-knowing Madam Zelda senses that you have a real problem with commitment."

**Seeing cases at a glance makes it easier to explore the problem.** *Courtesy of* Artizans.

Your attitudes and beliefs will draw you to count some events as cases of a problem but not others. To explore your understanding of the problem, use the cases to identify criteria for what counts as a problem case for you. As you explore a range of cases, try to describe the criteria, or underlying rules or principles, that determine whether a case is a member of the problem category.

Begin by comparing the cases and sorting them into groups. Do some cases seem to be more closely related than others? Write a general description of what is similar of the cases in the group. Write down differences you see between the groups. To explore the source of tension, try to identify the least problematic case with the least tension, the most serious case with the most tension, less serious cases that seem like part of the same problem, cases that don't seem part of the same problem, and cases that an opponent would consider serious but which you do not.

## Varying the Aspects with Hypothetical Cases

Any single problem case has a unique set of features. But public policy is about trying to treat whole classes of cases through rules, laws, and programs. Policies are formulated with possible future cases in mind. So a single case serves as the starting point for a general rule. For example, the attack on the World Trade Center on September 11, 2001, was not treated as a single isolated event. The U.S. government assumed that other terrorists might attack other sites. So the investigations and policy changes were based on imagining similar cases of attacks. Their goal was to decide what aspects of the attack might stay the same in possible future attacks, such as targeting major landmarks or using airplanes as weapons.

Similarly, you can explore a problem by choosing a case and then varying its aspects. Sometimes, by varying just one aspect, you change the overall tension. To vary the aspects, you play a series of mental "what if" games:

- What if the agent had been different? What kind of agent would increase the tension? What kind would decrease or eliminate the tension?

- What if the agent's motives had been different? Would the tension increase or decrease?

- What if the actions had been different? Would the tension increase or decrease?

If a change increases the tension, you can be sure that that aspect is important. Make up even more cases changing that aspect and describe its effect in writing. "Varying Case Aspects" illustrates this strategy by revising aspects of Shiflett's and Shapiro's cases.

---

## VARYING CASE ASPECTS

 **Environment:** *Shiflett's Case (Compare to version in "Case Aspects")*

- **Change agents.** (agent) Drivers on the way to their campsites OR a hiker with a boom box playing "Carmen" OR hikers talking, singing, and laughing (action) moved around Pike National Forest in Colorado making noise (motive) in order to contemplate nature. (outcome) Dave Shiflett is distracted from contemplating nature as he hiked.

- **Change setting.** (agent) Dirt bikers (setting) in a limestone quarry near Dave Shiflett's house (action) make unbearable noise for (motive) thrills. (outcome) Shiflett can't sleep on weekend mornings.

- **Change victim.** (agent) Dirt bikers at Pike National Forest in Colorado (action) ride around, crowding out the hikers, and making unbearable noise (motive) to have fun. (outcome) They drown out the voice of a forest ranger pointing out native plants to a group of kids and scare away birds and animals the kids were hoping to learn about.

By varying the agents, you may imagine that Shiflett could be frustrated by wilderness visitors other than the "yobs" he blames. If he still considers the bike riders the most serious offenders, then the tension probably does not derive from the amount or kind of noise but from their motives or their mode of transportation. If you take the problem more seriously when a group of kids is frustrated then, for you, the tension may come from seeing some activities as more "legitimate" than others (e.g., learning vs. having fun vs. contemplating nature) or some groups as more important than others (kids vs. adults).

### Crime: Shapiro's Case (Compare to version in "Case Aspects")

- **Change action.** (agent) Daniel Silva (action) punched Bruce Shapiro and six others in a coffee bar near Yale University in New Haven, Connecticut, (motive) acting randomly out of rage at loss of his mother whom he mistakenly believed was dead when he couldn't find her in the hospital. (outcome) Local media coverage disappears after a few days.

- **Change motive.** (agent) Daniel Silva (action) stabbed Bruce Shapiro and six others in a coffee bar near Yale University in New Haven, Connecticut (motive) because he had seen someone in the coffee bar attack his mother. (outcome) Widespread national and international media coverage on the attack with public comments.

- **Change agent and motive.** (agent) Unknown assailant (action) shoots and kills 21-year-old Bobby Gibson in the impoverished Bedford–Stuyvesant area of New York (motive) in order to keep Bobby from testifying to an earlier killing in his schoolyard. (outcome) Local media coverage for about a week. (Glaberson)

In these criminal cases, you may feel that motive is very important. You may feel that the tension in the Bobby Gibson case, where the motive is to subvert justice, is even higher than the Rashawnda Crenshaw case, where the motive was criminal but the shooting was accidental. Similarly, the tension may seem lower in the hypothetical case in which Silva acts out of revenge. You may also find the tension higher if the injuries to Shapiro and the others are less severe, but the media attention to these white middle-class victims stays the same.

As you explore cases, move between specific cases and more explicit statements of the problem in the *A BUT B* form. Your written statement of the problem should correctly identify the specific cases that you consider problematic and exclude cases that you do not consider problematic. "Problem Statements with Case Constraints" provides refined problem statements for Shiflett and Shapiro.

## PROBLEM STATEMENTS WITH CASE CONSTRAINTS

### Environment: Shiflett

(A) Respectable adults and children visit national and state parks to contemplate the glories of nature with quiet activities like walking, bird-watching, or fishing. BUT (B) Immature adults and kids who are out for thrills bring noisy vehicles and electronics to the parks that break the silence and scare away the wildlife.

Shiflett might exclude cases of people entering the park by car or making noise by talking and laughing. He might treat noise near his house as a different problem. He might include people bringing boom boxes, whether they are playing operas or hip hop.

### Crime: Shapiro

(A) Crime victims want to prevent random violent assaults from occurring and improve the efficiency of the justice system; they want officials and the media to give equal attention to victims in all parts of a city. BUT (B) The proposed legislation focuses only on punishment and restitution; money spent on it would be taken away from citywide institutions such as law enforcement, mental health clinics, and support agencies for victims.

Shapiro might exclude cases where the assault is not random, such as the Bobby Gibson case or the case of a woman stabbing her lover's wife. He might approve of anticrime legislation if it focused on prevention.

Such a statement is a key to defining what matters to you about the problem and communicating it effectively to others.

## Paradigm Cases

Your analysis may turn up a case that you find very compelling, a case that you want to put at the center of your work. This case can be called your **paradigm** case. A paradigm is an important example or model. Finding a paradigm case is likely to change the direction of your research and writing. This case may be the one that you use in your writing to help readers "see the issue." Or you may decide to center your efforts on changing the specific situation surrounding this case, looking for solutions that would work in that locality.

## Exploring Significance

To be worth addressing in a written argument, a problem has to be significant, closer to a crisis than to a nuisance. Exploring your problem also means figuring out what makes it significant. To persuade other people to take your problem seriously, you need to consider what values they care about and whether you can relate your problem to those values. By considering different stakeholders and their values, you can discover values that you didn't realize were at risk in your issue; adding these to your definition of the problem increases the significance of your problem to a wider audience.

In many public policy issues, the values listed on page 272 can be at risk. In general, the values near the top of the list are considered most important than those further down:

"Okay, so I'm not your <u>biggest</u> problem.
But, hey, I'm still a problem, right?"

**Problems must be significant to the audience.** *Courtesy of* Artizans.

- Life, health, quality of life, safety
- Money, resources
- Justice, fairness, pride
- Time, efficiency
- Enjoyment, happiness, recreation

There are four strategies for broadening significance. First, consider whether values at the top of the list are at stake in any way. Second, consider how many different values are at stake in any way; the more values, the more significance. In the environment topic, if bald eagles are considered an endangered species, then their lives are at stake, but so are the lives of their prey, the resources of tourist businesses, and the pride of U.S. citizens. Third, all other things being equal, a harm is more serious if the bad effects occur sooner rather than later, affect many people instead of a few, and last a long time instead of temporarily. For example, a false accusation may seem to endanger only a person's reputation. But it can have long-lasting effects: A person falsely accused of terrorism may get fired, may be denied access to assets frozen by the authorities, or live in fear of attack. Narrating a case about someone being falsely accused of being a terrorist may persuade readers that loss of reputation is a more important value than they had thought. Fourth, consider "opportunity" as a value: There may be no significant harms to the present situation but missing an opportunity to improve may put values at risk later on.

When you discover additional values at risk, add them to Statement A of your problem statement and explain what puts them at risk in Statement B. Be careful not to exaggerate the stakes or readers will think you are "crying wolf."

## EXERCISES

### Backtalk: What Do You Say?

Do you agree with the interpretation in "Varying Case Aspects" about Shiflett's and Shapiro's reactions to variations on their cases? Why or why not? Write an alternative problem statement that includes and excludes a different set of cases based on your interpretation of Shiflett's and Shapiro's concerns.

### Recognize/Evaluate

Which of the following problem statements has a direct clash between Statement A and Statement B? What kind of clash is it: goal vs. obstacle, value vs. value, or expectation vs. observation?

#### A. Environment

- The U.S. Forest Service has a policy of multiuse of resources that requires it to permit domestic livestock to graze in national forests. In the Targhee National Forest, sheep growers need to graze their herds in alpine wilderness areas as pastures lower down are eaten up and trampled. However, the Forest Service is also responsible for protecting wildlife, in this case bighorn sheep. Wildlife advocates want to bar domestic sheep from grazing in bighorn sheep ranges in alpine elevations. In other forests, domestic sheep transmitted a form of pneumonia to bighorn sheep populations and wiped them out.

- The passage of the 1990 Americans with Disabilities Act was intended to guarantee that disabled people have equal education, employment opportunity, and access to public spaces. But research clearly demonstrates that disability continues to be a significant barrier to employment. According to a nationwide National Organization on Disability/Louis Harris poll in 1998, only 29% of working-age (18–64) individuals with disabilities are employed full- or part-time, compared with 79% of nondisabled Americans.

#### B. Crime

- The population level of prisons has increased dramatically in the United States and the amount of spending on prisons has also skyrocketed compared to twenty years ago. Unfortunately, inmates are forced to suffer inhumane and unsafe conditions due to overcrowding. In some states, an inmate is guaranteed only food and clothing, but not a regular shower, medical care, or working toilets.

- The sealing of juvenile crime records was meant to allow the juveniles to be rehabilitated and make a new life for themselves, safe from the disgrace of errors of the past. However, in this process, family, friends, and school officials are deprived of facts that could endanger their safety in case the juvenile commits another crime.

## Detect

### A. Environment

A student working on the issue of campus ecology explored the problem of the destruction of plant life on campus. He generated the following cases. Which cases have the most tension? Why? What causal factors underlie these cases?

- The University creates additional student parking near the dorms by paving over an open lot with student-tended garden plots. The students are invited to grow plants in an unused greenhouse near the biology building.
- The University chops down a stand of cherry trees to replace the sewer pipes underneath. When the work is finished, they plant grass and bushes.
- After a number of large branches break off in a storm, the University chops down a stand of diseased elm trees and replaces them with grass and bushes.
- As a prank, fraternity members pour detergent into a pond and kill the fish and plants. They are photographed by a security camera and pay a fine. The pond is eventually cleaned and restocked.

### B. Crime

A student working on the issue of date rape explored the problem of how women respond to sexual advances. She generated the following cases. Which cases have the most tension? Why? What causal factors underlie these cases?

- A woman wants to stay involved with a man with some physical contact but no sexual intercourse. When the partner makes sexual advances, she does not resist physically or verbally and they have sex. He feels satisfied, but she feels violated.
- A man wants to get more involved with a female partner and have intercourse. He comes on to the woman who does not describe what she wants to do and does not resist. He breaks off without doing what either was willing to do. Both are dissatisfied.
- A woman and her partner have intercourse whenever they both want to but not if either he or she doesn't want to.
- A man wants to get more involved with a female partner and have intercourse. He comes on to the woman who tells him she does not want to have intercourse. He breaks off after some physical contact. She is satisfied, but he is dissatisfied.

## Produce

1. **Writing an A *BUT* B problem statement.** Consider the set of cases in your topic area in the Detect exercise. Write an A *BUT* B problem statement to describe the clash.

2. **Generating cases.** Choose one of the problem statements in your topic area in the Recognize/Evaluate exercise. Brainstorm to create hypothetical cases that vary the agent, action, motive, or outcome. Compose some cases with more tension and some with less.

3. **Exploring your problem.** Use your imagination to brainstorm answers to questions one and two, recording your work and reasoning. If possible, ask another member of your class to review and add to your responses, then switch roles.

   - Describe a specific problem case that you care about in terms of agent, motive, action, and outcome.
   - Vary the tension by changing the agent, motive, action, or outcome. Include hypothetical versions of the case where the tension seems much higher or much lower.
   - What other people (stakeholders) are affected by this situation? Who cares about it? Who is harmed by it in some way? Who is "in charge" of the situation? What goals or values are at stake in this situation?
   - Describe the problem in terms of an A *BUT* B problem statement. Are all the values at stake explicitly stated in Statement A? Which values conflict directly with the elements in Statement B? Consider Statement B closely to bring to mind new values that could be stated explicitly in Statement A. Write versions of the statement with different kinds of clashes: goal vs. obstacle, value vs. value, expectation vs. observation.
   - List the cases that your A *BUT* B statement covers and those it leaves out. Adjust the statement until all the cases you think are problematic are covered.
   - Describe the bad consequences of the problem. How could the significance of the harm be emphasized?
   - List some opponents to your views. How would they see the clash? What cases would they treat differently?
   - Where could you go to find more information on this problem area? Can you think of people in the area or relevant books or journals?

# CHAPTER 11

# Exploring and Constructing Solutions

This chapter will spell out in more detail the elements of a solution and the strategies for formulating one. You will learn how to come up with ideas for solutions, predict their effects on problem cases (Chapter 7 and Chapter 10), and evaluate their pluses and minuses. To use this chapter effectively, you should already have a problem in mind that you have begun exploring using the strategies in Chapter 10. But your work on the problem is probably not finished yet. Exploring solutions often leads to a change in your understanding of the problem.

To write a persuasive solution span, you have to make claims at several stases (Chapter 3): that one or more promising solutions exist or could be created (existence), that one or more solutions will cause the problem to go away or become less significant (cause), that one solution is better than the others in terms of cost, time, durability, and practicality (value), and that the solution should be implemented in a specific way (action).

At this point, you may have no idea what solutions could be used for the problem you want to address. Or you may already have a solution in mind with some ideas for constructing and supporting these kinds of claims. In either case, it is important to begin exploring solutions with an open mind.

## Facing the Unknown

A willingness to explore is especially necessary when considering solutions to problems. Actions and interventions in a problematic situation never have guaranteed results. No one can know exactly what will happen. The best ideas never work out just the way their advocates expect. Some actions have unexpected bonuses, but others create unforeseen complications. Even good ideas can be taken to excess. Some people call this "the law of unintended consequences" or "when bad things happen to good ideas." But many times doing nothing is worse than doing something that isn't perfect. When a problem is urgent, people have to make the best decisions they can and be prepared to deal with the consequences.

When authors propose solutions, they estimate as best they can what will happen. They look at what happened in other similar cases in the past, they try out plans on a small scale before tackling the problem as a whole, or they might even try to simulate what will happen using advanced computer programs. In the end, though, there is always uncertainty. That is why it is important to explore solutions thoroughly, anticipate what might happen, and write an argument that assesses the benefits, the costs, the risks, and the drawbacks fairly based on current information.

Because solutions are uncertain, most authors do not attempt to solve the entire problem all at once. Your goal should be to develop a small-scale proposal that you believe in, not a grandiose plan to eliminate the problem completely. A good small-scale solution is one that makes the situation better, reducing the significance of the problem enough to make it tolerable. A good small-scale solution addresses a key part of the problem or represents a single good first step that could lead to others.

Exploring solutions takes an investment of creativity to seek out a range of possibilities. Exploring means resisting the temptation to jump onto a **bandwagon,** a solution that appeals to a lot of people because it sounds simple and complete, such as legalizing marijuana, lowering the drinking age, banning abortion, saving the rainforest. Bandwagon solutions sound better than they really are because they reflect the views of only one set of stakeholders and ignore obstacles and risks instead of treating them.

## Generating Solutions from Problem Statements

In Chapter 10, you learned to express your problem in an A *BUT* B format that spelled out the goal and the obstacle that prevents it from being achieved. Once you have defined this kind of clash, you can begin asking yourself three kinds of questions, looking for ways to relieve the clash:

- **Changing the terrain.** Is there a way to remove the obstacle or get around it by introducing new technology, new rules, or new resources?
- **Changing goals or values.** Is the goal absolutely necessary? Is there room to compromise?
- **Adjusting expectations.** Is my expectation based on faulty information or reasoning? Is the observational evidence reliable?

"Questions Raised by Problem Statements" provides examples of the different kinds of clashes and the corresponding questions that are most likely to be productive for exploring solutions.

## QUESTIONS RAISED BY PROBLEM STATEMENTS

### Environment

**Robinson's Problem: Goal vs. Obstacle**

(A) Because we have so much impact on the world, humans should preserve the integrity, stability and beauty of our entire biotic community. *BUT* (B) The actions of both modern and traditional cultures degrade natural systems and reduce biological diversity.

#### Questions

**Changing Terrain.** What actions can be changed to have less impact? What policies can we pass to ban the most destructive actions? How can industries adopt technologies that have less impact? How can energy be produced and used more cleanly?

**Changing Goals.** Why are changes in ecology created by humans worse than ones caused by natural forces? Why are the needs of an endangered species more important than human needs?

**Adjusting Expectations.** How serious is the danger to biodiversity? How much degradation can we tolerate?

### Crime

**Kollin's Problem: Goal vs. Goal**

(A) Parents should raise their kids with enough instruction and monitoring to keep them from committing crimes. *BUT* (B) To avoid labeling a child for life, news executives have traditionally refused to pressure parents by publish the names of arrested juveniles, even though it is legal to do so.

#### Questions

**Changing Terrain.** What other agencies can prevent young people from committing crimes? What kinds of help do parents need? Can parents be reached without publicity?

**Changing Goals.** How can news executives be convinced that juveniles are not seriously harmed by exposure? That reducing crime is more important than protecting young people's reputations?

**Adjusting Expectations.** How much influence and control do parents have over their kids? How much impact would publishing names have on parents' behaviors?

## Changing the Terrain

For problems in which the clash stems from an identifiable obstacle, a good strategy for generating solutions is to think of ways to change the terrain. If you run into an obstacle such as a fallen tree or rockslide while on a trail, your first thought may be to try to remove it or get around it. Depending on the size of the obstacle and your resourcefulness, you have many possibilities to consider. Getting around an obstacle might mean applying more effort to go over it, taking a long detour around it, or building a bridge over it. Removing an obstacle might require team-work or special equipment. Considering the same range of options can help you brainstorm possible solutions to a problem.

Ask yourself what could possibly change or remove the factors creating the clash. Investigating a specific change in the existing rules or technology might help you find people who are working on something similar; your proposal can be to support that effort. You do not have to be an engineer or inventor to propose that a technological change should be explored. "Removing or Getting around Obstacles" illustrates how to brainstorm ways to remove or get around obstacles.

## REMOVING OR GETTING AROUND OBSTACLES

### Environment: Jet Skis and Snowmobiles

#### Problem

(A) People like Shiflett need silence to enjoy the majesty of nature in national and state parks. *BUT* (B) People who ride snowmobiles, dirt bikes, ATVs and jet skis in parks make a lot of noise, disturbing the people and the fish, in a point-less activity.

#### Solution Candidates

**Change A.** Help Shiflett avoid hearing noise: Use headphones, create separate demarcated areas for hiking, or designate times of day when vehicles are used.

**Change B.** Reduce noise: Take advantage of improved technology in snowmobiles (4-stroke engines); hire more rangers to prevent joyriding and buzzing. Eliminate noise: ban vehicles altogether, and promote activities such as hiking and swimming.

### Crime: Gun Safety

#### Problem

(A) Most gun buyers want to keep guns for legitimate reasons, such as hunting, collecting, recreation, self-defense. *BUT* (B) Some people can still buy guns even though they are not supposed to. Other buyers are responsible citizens who, in the heat of the moment or in a period of depression, use a gun to commit a homi-cide or suicide.

#### Solution Candidates

**Change A.** Convince gun owners to achieve goals in another way, such as hunting with bow and arrow, collecting swords, taking up martial arts, or installing an alarm system.

**Change B.** Increase gun safety: improve technology for background checks on buyers, develop technology to disable gun unless user is sober, pass laws to revoke licenses and allow seizure of guns from people whose mental or legal status changes.

# Changing Goals or Values

For problems in which one goal clashes with another, something has to give. For the problem to be resolved, one goal has to change or be abandoned, or both goals have to change. For example, a high school senior's goal of studying engineering may clash with her goal of attending a small liberal arts college close to home. She may have to consider another major or find the means to move elsewhere. When goals are in conflict, the solution may involve finding the best way to help the stakeholders recognize that one goal is unrealistic or that too much would have to be sacrificed to attain it.

Changing the goal is also worth considering when it is in conflict with an obstacle. This option is often overlooked because devotion to a goal is what makes a problem seem important in the first place.

People who argue vehemently about goals and values sometimes believe that positive and negative values are built-in to scales in absolute ways and that no reasonable person could see things differently. But to establish common ground with people we would like to convince, it is important to consider alternative value systems and see whether they are worthy of respect. For example, some people value nearness to their family over reputation of a school and choose to study at an institution close to home, whereas others reverse those values. It is usually possible to respect both value systems to some extent. Sometimes, however, values can come into conflict. A student might value reputation of the school over nearness to family, but the family might have the reverse weighting. If there is no reputable school within commuting distance, the different values conflict.

Common ground can sometimes be found in such cases by looking for shared values. The high school senior does value closeness to her family, so she might agree to come home for the weekends and schedule family visits to campus. In the environment topic, the fisherman's value of catching the greatest number of fish for the least money can conflict with the environmentalist's desire to preserve species diversity and habitat. However, sustaining fish populations at a healthy size is common to both sides. Together, they may come to agree on a solution even if separately, they went about evaluating the goals and solutions differently.

Being open-minded about value systems does not mean subscribing to "moral relativism" or to a philosophy that "anything goes." As you consider individual cases, you should look for situations in which even opponents would agree that one goal is more important than the other. You can then design a proposal for shifting values on part of the problem, the part that concerns the most serious cases.

For example, U.S. citizens cherish their civil liberties (freedom of speech, freedom of assembly, due process, etc.) but they also cherish living in safety and trusting national security. These values can come into conflict at times of war or terrorism. During normal times, we tolerate some risk to safety to allow members of the public to participate in rallies and to attend public hearings and court trials. But where certain kinds of speech could cause great physical danger (such as yelling "Fire!" in a crowded auditorium), we restrict it. After terrorist attacks or during wars, the public desire for security may increase to the point that it takes precedence over privacy or free assembly in more situations, though not in every situation. We may be willing to submit without protest to searches at airports or to limits on the size or location of a rally. However, restrictions in situations where safety seems less vulnerable (such as random house searches) may be hotly contested; there will always be disagreement about how much safety or liberty is reasonable to sacrifice.

It makes sense to consider abandoning or loosening a goal if it is not essential to a group's purpose or identity. In some arguments, a clash of goals represents only one possible interpretation of the problem. The solution to the problem may be to persuade the stakeholders to see the problem in a new way. "Changing Goals" illustrates ways to develop questions.

---

## CHANGING GOALS

### Environment: Energy vs. Conservation

#### Easterbrook's Problem

(A) We need newer cleaner energy sources to replace old, inefficient and dirty power plants. *BUT* (B) Environmentalists oppose new power plants because they want to preserve wilderness areas and ecologies in as pristine a condition as possible.

#### Solution Candidates

**Change A.** Energy Position: Are there any locations that even ardent power plant builders would agree should be off-limits for a new power plant? The Grand Canyon? The Everglades?

**Change B.** Conservation Position: Are there any types of power plants that even environmentalists would agree are benign enough to build: solar power? Wind power? Are there any places where environmentalists would be willing to put a newer, cleaner power plant: on the same site as an old polluting plant?

---

### Crime: Civil Rights vs. Neighborhood Safety

#### Brooks's Problem

(A) Everyone in the United States has rights to free assembly, free speech, and equal treatment under the law. *BUT* (B) Inner-city neighborhoods need to reduce risks from gangs and drug dealers, so residents support curfew and loitering ordinances that single out kids of certain ethnicities just for what they are wearing and who they are with.

#### Solution Candidates

**Change A.** Civil Rights Position: In what situations have the courts ruled that safety does outweigh civil rights? What kinds of ordinances are used in neighborhoods where ethnicity and race are not a factor? Have ethnic groups and racial minorities gained enough power in some cities that they should be allowed to restrict their own rights?

**Change B.** Safety Position: How can neighborhoods eliminate gangs and drug dealing without endangering the rights of innocent kids? In what situations are safety strategies, such as surveillance cameras or DNA tests, unacceptable? What kind of enforcement is unfair?

## Changing Expectations and Observations

In the natural and social sciences, a research problem is a question about how the world works. Scientists propose hypotheses that capture their expectations about what is likely to happen in an experiment (see cause section in Chapter 3) and collect observations about what actually does happen. If the observations clash with the expectations, then both parts need to be reconsidered. The method for collecting the observations may have been faulty, or the theory behind the hypothesis may need to be refined.

In a similar way, criminal investigators develop a theory of a case. Suppose a witness reported seeing the suspect somewhere other than the scene of the crime at the same time that it happened. The witness's observation clashes with the prosecution's theory of the case. The jury that is asked to decide the case has to question both parts, whether the eyewitness was mistaken or lying or whether the prosecutor's accusation is wrong.

# Generating Solutions from Cases

Having a set of problem cases (Chapter 10) on hand can also help you find or invent solutions. You may find cases in different locations where different solutions were tried. Then you can see if one of those would work in the case you are most interested in. Or you may see an analogy to a similar situation in another domain that you can try to import.

## Finding Previously Tried Solutions

Public debates over crime and the environment have gone on for such a long time that many different approaches have been tried in many different places. But the stakeholders in a particular case may not know about what has been tried elsewhere. So you can make a contribution to solving a problem by exploring whether that solution would work in the cases you are interested in.

If a solution already exists, then your main task in your argument shifts to the questions of cause and value. The fact that a solution worked in one place does not mean it will work in all cases. It may create different risks or benefits. The solution might also be too expensive or too difficult to accomplish in a new place. So proposing to adapt a solution involves careful comparisons of the situations and appropriate adjustments of what is implemented.

**Solutions should relate to the problem statement.** *Courtesy of* www.cartoonbank.com.

## Importing a Solution through Analogy

Creative authors sometimes see similarities among problems that don't have that much to do with each other. If the similarities are deep enough, then it might work to import a solution from an unexpected direction.

Consider Nicholas Kristof's proposal for solving the problem of gun safety in "Finding Solutions through Analogies." He imports a solution for dealing with guns from the issue of appliance safety; in particular, car design. To make a car solution work for guns, Kristof has to modify the solution to account for the different parts of a gun and what kinds of dangers they pose.

 ### FINDING SOLUTIONS THROUGH ANALOGIES

### Crime: Nicholas Kristof
### Lock and Load

. . . Since the Brady Bill took effect in 1994, gun-control efforts have been a catastrophe for Democrats. They have accomplished almost nothing nationally, other than giving a big boost to the Republicans. Mr. Kerry tried to get around the problem by blasting away at small animals, but nervous Red Staters still suspected Democrats of plotting to seize guns.

Moreover, it's clear that in this political climate, further efforts at gun control are a nonstarter. You can talk until you're blue in the face about the 30,000 gun deaths each year, about children who are nine times as likely to die in a gun accident in America as elsewhere in the developed world, about the $17,000 average cost (half directly borne by taxpayers) of treating each gun injury. But nationally, gun control is dead.

So it's time for a fundamentally new approach, emblematic of how Democrats must think in new ways about old issues. The new approach is to accept that handguns are part of the American landscape, but to use a public health approach to try to make them much safer.

The model is automobiles, for a high rate of traffic deaths was once thought to be inevitable. But then we figured out ways to mitigate the harm with seat belts, air bags and collapsible steering columns, and since the 1950's the death rate per mile driven has dropped 80 percent.

Similar steps are feasible in the world of guns.

"You can tell whether a camera is loaded by looking at it, and you should be able to tell whether a gun is loaded by looking at it," said David Hemenway, director of the Harvard Injury Control Research Center. Professor Hemenway has written "Private Guns, Public Health," a brilliant and clear-eyed primer for the country.

We take safety steps that reduce the risks of everything from chain saws (so they don't kick back and cut off an arm) to refrigerators (so kids can't lock themselves inside). But firearms have been exempt. Companies make cellphones that survive if dropped, but some handguns can fire if they hit the ground.

Professor Hemenway notes that in the 1990's, two children a year, on average, died after locking themselves in car trunks. This was considered unacceptable, so a government agency studied the problem, and General Motors and Ford engineered safety mechanisms to prevent such deaths.

In contrast, 15 children under the age of 5 die annually in fatal gun accidents in the U.S., along with 18 children 5 to 9 years old. We routinely make aspirin bottles childproof, but not guns, even though childproof pistols were sold back in the 19th century—they wouldn't fire unless the shooter put pressure on the handle as well as the trigger.

Aside from making childproof guns, here are other steps we could take:

Require magazine safeties so a gun cannot be fired when the clip is removed (people can forget that a bullet may still be in the chamber and pull the trigger). Many guns already have magazine safeties, but not all.

Finance research to develop "smart guns," which can be fired only by authorized users. If a cellphone can be locked with a PIN, why not a gun? This innovation would protect children—and thwart criminals.

Start public safety campaigns urging families to keep guns locked up in a gun safe or with a trigger lock (now, 12 to 14 percent of gun owners with young children keep loaded and unlocked weapons in their homes).

Encourage doctors to counsel depressed patients not to keep guns, and to advise new parents on storing firearms safely.

Make gun serial numbers harder for criminals to remove.

Create a national database for gun deaths. In a traffic fatality, 120 bits of data are collected, like the positions of the passengers and the local speed limit, so we now understand what works well (air bags, no "right on red") and what doesn't (driver safety courses). Statistics on gun violence are much flimsier, so we don't know what policies would work best, and much of the data hurled by rival camps at each other is inaccurate.

Would these steps fly politically? Maybe. One poll showed that 88 percent of the public favors requiring that guns be childproof. And such measures demonstrate the kind of fresh thinking that can keep alive not only thousands of Americans, but the Democratic Party as well.

*New York Times* (13 Nov. 2004).

# Testing a Solution with Cases

Once you have one or more solutions in mind, you have to challenge your assumptions about how it will work. Most people come up with a solution that probably would have worked for a single case but do not anticipate what would happen to other cases. The solution may not apply to some important cases and may cause unanticipated side effects in others. To satisfy your own goals and to anticipate the objections of opponents, consider how all your candidate solutions would work for a wide range of real and hypothetical cases. Even if your favorite solution turns out to be imperfect (as most are), understanding its limits will help you argue more persuasively that it is better than other alternatives.

## Predicting Effects on Problem Cases

As you saw in Chapter 10, problem cases vary in tension because of their agents, motives, actions, or outcomes. Because of these differences, a solution may reduce the problem more in some cases than in others. For example, a ban on trawling and dredging in an area where the ocean bottom is soft would not prevent the destruction of habitats, which only happens on hard bottom. Similarly, Brooks's plan to reduce gangs by coordinating Catholic volunteers was created with Hispanic youth in mind; it might not work the same way for young people in Southeast Asian neighborhoods.

Projecting how a solution would work is not the same as giving examples of how it has worked in other cases in the past. To create a realistic projection, you have to keep differences in cases in mind:

**Don't assume your solution is perfect.** © Harley Schwadron.

- Does the solution have the desired effect on the key cases?
- Would it have that effect in the case you are most concerned with?
- Is the solution too narrow, leaving out cases that need to be addressed?
- Is the solution too broad, applying to cases that it should not apply to?

For example, a zero-tolerance policy for drugs in school may be too broad if it punishes students who need to take asthma medication. But the same policy might be too narrow if it does not apply to unusual intoxicants such as aerosol sprays. Exploring the effects of a solution on different cases involves focusing on cause factors (see the discussion of cause arguments in Chapter 3).

## Evaluating Costs and Benefits

Apart from its effect on a problem, a solution has to be worth doing in other ways. Just about any action on a problem takes time, money, and effort. So decision makers have to decide whether the benefits (such as solving the problem) are worth the costs of enacting the solution. Authors may argue that one solution is worth its costs or compare the costs and benefits of several possible solutions. Exploring these aspects of a solution depends on value arguments, so review the discussion of strategies for comparing options against criteria in Chapter 3.

Several value dimensions are usually used for assessing solutions:

**Resources**    Time, money, equipment, staff, space

**Implementation**    Time before effect, maintenance needs

**Desirability**    Ethics, other priorities

For example, when buying a car, people consider cost, size, reliability, appearance, and gas mileage. No choice is perfect on all dimensions, so a believable argument weighs the results on all these scales. You can argue for a solution that has some drawbacks by arguing that these are minor compared to other solutions or compared to the harms of the problem.

## EXERCISES

### Backtalk: What Do You Say?

If you are considering the two candidate solutions described below, each with pros and cons, which would you choose and why?

**Solution #1.** It eliminates the problem in one location once and for all, but it is very expensive.

**Solution #2.** It reduces the severity of the problem in many locations and it is inexpensive, but you have to keep up the investment year after year.

### Recognize/Evaluate

For each of the following readings, decide whether the solution is designed to remove an obstacle, change a goal, or adjust expectations. Which author's solution addresses the problem best? Why?

| | |
|---|---|
| **A. Environment** | Chivers, Kristof, Gómez-Pompa and Kaus, Robinson, Shiflett |
| **B. Crime** | Brooks, Castleman, Kleck, Kollin, Meares and Kahan, Shapiro |

## Detect

For a problem case of your choice, search online newspaper databases (e.g., LexisNexis) for solutions that have been tried in other locations.

## Produce

Write a problem statement describing the clash in the set of cases in your topic area below, if you did not already do so in the exercises for Chapter 10. Then brainstorm several candidate solutions by changing the terrain, changing the goal, or adjusting expectations. Evaluate each solution: For which cases would it work well?

### A. Environment: Campus Ecology

A student working on the issue of campus ecology explored the problem of the destruction of plant life on campus. He generated the following cases:

- The University creates additional student parking near the dorms by paving over an open lot with student-tended garden plots. The students are invited to grow plants in an unused greenhouse near the biology building.
- The University chops down a stand of cherry trees to replace the sewer pipes underneath. When the work is finished, they plant grass and bushes.
- After a number of large branches break off in a storm, the University chops down a stand of diseased elm trees and replaces them with grass and bushes.
- As a prank, fraternity members pour detergent into a pond and kill the fish and plants. They are photographed by a security camera and pay a fine. The pond is eventually cleaned and restocked.

### B. Crime: Date Rape

A student working on the issue of date rape explored the problem of how women respond to sexual advances generated the following cases:

- A woman wants to stay involved with a man with some physical contact but no sexual intercourse. When the partner makes sexual advances, she does not resist physically or verbally and they have sex. He feels satisfied, but she feels violated.
- A man wants to get more involved with a female partner and have intercourse. He comes on to the woman who does not describe what she wants to do and does not resist. He breaks off without doing what either was willing to do. Both are dissatisfied.
- A woman and her partner have intercourse whenever they both want to but not if either he or she doesn't want to.

- A man wants to get more involved with a female partner and have intercourse. He comes on to the woman who tells him she does not want to have intercourse. He breaks off after some physical contact. She is satisfied, but he is dissatisfied.

# CHAPTER 12

# Mapping a Conversation

In this chapter, you will develop an understanding of the public debate about your issue, find a focal point for your own interests, and identify controversial points about the problem or potential solutions. Points of controversy are chances for you to contribute your own arguments. The exploratory strategy presented here involves synthesizing the positions of a variety of authors, a task in which you will characterize their views fairly and draw plausible inferences about how they might respond to challenges or questions.

Synthesis differs from analysis. Analyzing means taking apart the elements of an argument in order to look at its overall structure and find its strengths and weaknesses. You practiced analysis while working with the chapters in Part I; you may also have written an argument analysis using the strategies in Chapter 13. In contrast, synthesizing means creating something new by looking at a group of separate items and connecting them into a coherent pattern or map.

## Relating Your Position to Others'

If you think of a public debate as an expedition of individuals and groups, then synthesizing would be like taking a bird's eye view of the entire scene. Imagine that you are sitting on a hillside watching a crowd of people in a forest below searching for the way out. From the distance of your perspective, you can see where everyone is even though they may not be able to see each other. You can tell which searchers are closest together and which are furthest apart, which are headed in the same direction and which are covering old ground, who has wandered off and who is sitting waiting to be rescued. You can even pick out a promising spot that everyone has overlooked so far and identify who is "getting warmer."

You may never have considered the relationships among authors this way. Faced with a complicated array of positions on a controversial issue, you might be tempted simply to divide authors into groups, good guys against bad guys, or extremists against moderates. You might avoid authors whose views seem strange or ignore those points in an author's argument that would disrupt your neat picture. Public policy is not that simple. People who are opponents on one issue may be allies on another. Allies frequently disagree among themselves about what to do first and how to proceed.

In order to have your say taken seriously, you must understand how your position relates to those of many others involved in the issue. Only then will you seem informed and credible enough to deserve attention. Only then can you figure out which points your readers will find controversial, the ones that need the most development and support. Only then can you invent ways to make opponents more receptive to your ideas.

## Synthesis Defined

A synthesis is a form of argument, not a collection of dry information. Synthesizing an issue requires you to be imaginative, to think beyond the positions you have already taken on an issue. Even though you will write from a distanced perspective rather than arguing your own view from the ground, any map that you draw of an issue will be your description, made from where you are sitting, not some kind of cosmic photograph that accurately depicts every detail. No matter what your perspective is, you have reached it through a lifetime of experiences and lessons that were not shared by everyone else. From your viewpoint, you might not be able to see everyone; you might misinterpret where a group is headed; you may not know how things look from the ground. By synthesizing, you will focus on details you overlooked and seek explanations for points that seemed misguided or irrelevant.

Even though it will differ from how everyone else sees the debate, your synthesis can have value for yourself and for others. It will help you develop and articulate your position by highlighting the specific points on which you must decide whether you agree or disagree. A fully developed synthesis of an issue can also help everyone involved see more of the big picture; they may be convinced to accept your view and take your recommendations more seriously. Strategies for writing a full-length synthesis paper are presented in Chapter 15.

Writing a synthesis is also an important step if you plan to intervene directly in the debate by persuading the stakeholders to adopt your approach to the problem or the solution. The stakeholders will have already heard many arguments. To write convincingly you have to avoid rehashing positions that have already been rejected and address the disputes that are hot right now. Strategies for writing full-length problem arguments are presented in Chapter 16 and for solution arguments in Chapter 17.

You are ready to try the strategies in this chapter if you have already used one or more of the strategies in Chapters 8–11. You should have explored your own experiences and beliefs concerning the issue, searched a variety of sources to find out more about the issue, and searched out published arguments about the issue from a variety of authors and stakeholders.

Synthesizing requires that you develop a good understanding of each author's argument. Before you begin, you should read the texts carefully, following the strategies provided in Chapter 18 for segmenting an author's entire paper into spans (Issue, Problem, Solution), segmenting each span into stases (Existence, Definition, Value, Cause, Action), and each stasis into a series of points with claims and supporting appeals (Ethos, Pathos, Logos). You should then map out the main points of the authors' lines of argument. Following these strategies, you should end up with a rough sketch for each article like the ones provided for Castleman and Chivers in Figure 2.1 and Figure 3.3.

## Selecting a Relevant Set of Authors

The first step is to select authors to include in your synthesis. This chapter illustrates a synthesis of the six readings printed on each topic in this book.

You are likely to have a larger set of articles to choose from, including articles that you or your class have chosen. Ideally, the authors you choose will represent a wide range of positions, but almost any set of argumentative articles within your topic area will do. Select 6 to 8 articles using these strategies:

- Start with as many "on-topic" authors as you can find who directly address the specific issue that concerns you, articles from people they cite, and articles in which they are cited.

- Include additional articles that address any general points raised by the on-topic authors, such as prevention, human rights, or the role of the media.

- If you have not yet selected eight authors, choose from the remaining articles the ones with which you most strongly agree or disagree.

Do not hesitate to choose authors whose positions seem unrelated. Surprisingly enough, you can develop important new insights by synthesizing authors who are not explicitly addressing the same problem.

Next, compare the articles looking for points that most of the authors address. The most thorough way to find points of comparison would be to list out every point in every article and then draw connections, but this process is too burdensome. A better approach is to focus your attention on the points that matter most to you. The next sections offer strategies for using graphics to sketch out different connections and review them at a glance.

# What Are Synthesis Trees?

A synthesis tree is a branching diagram that illustrates groupings of authors. Each main branch represents a point on which a set of authors agrees. A group of allied authors all appear under the same main branch. Opposing groups are represented with their own main branches.

As a branch extends, it divides into smaller and smaller branches representing subgroups within a set of allies. The subgroups keep dividing until each author is represented on his or her own twig. Each branch separates authors who agree the most from those with other positions.

The synthesis trees discussed throughout this chapter are shown in Figures 12.1A–12.1F.

## Alternative Synthesis Trees

### Environment

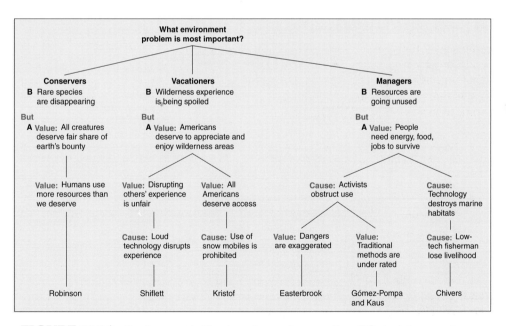

**FIGURE 12.1A  Environment:** Tree based on value question: What environment problem is the most important?

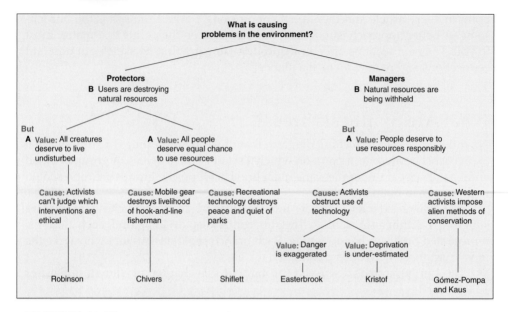

**FIGURE 12.1B   Environment:** Tree based on cause question: What is causing problems in the environment?

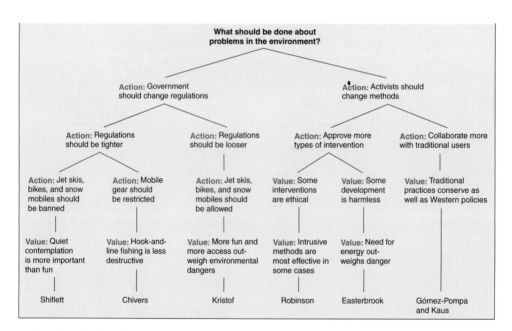

**FIGURE 12.1C   Environment:** Tree based on action: What should be done about problems in the environment?

*Crime*

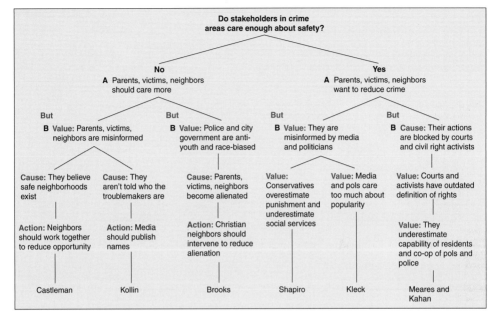

**FIGURE 12.1D  Crime:** Tree based on value question: Do stakeholders in high crime areas care enough about safety?

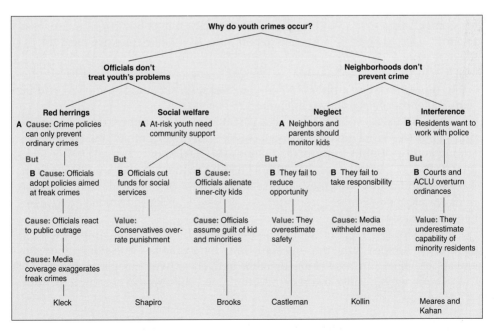

**FIGURE 12.1E  Crime:** Tree based on cause question: Why do youth crimes occur?

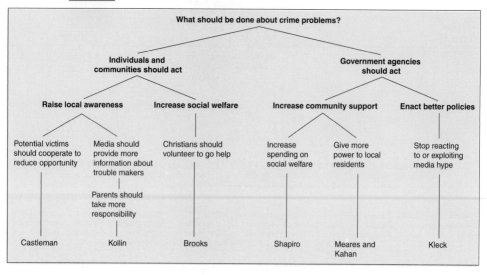

**FIGURE 12.1F  Crime:** Tree based on action: What should be done about crime problems?

A synthesis sketch looks like an inverted tree. Sketches like these are used by designers to summarize a lot of information in a small space. A similar type of sketch is the floorplan of a dreamhouse. Floorplans record different ways for dividing up the space available, for creating and connecting different types of rooms. Designers try out many alternative floorplans because they are easy to draw, easy to change, and easy to compare. Synthesis trees are used for the same reasons.

A synthesis tree can take many different shapes, especially as you try synthesizing more and more authors. When you start with six authors, you can end up with any of the shapes shown in Figure 12.2.

The most useful synthesis trees branch off at least two or three times. The more times your tree branches off, the more closely you are examining the connections among authors within a group. Of the trees sketched above, Tree a is far too shallow; it shows a collection of six authors lined up with no connections spelled out. Trees b, c, and d are better; they show separate groups of allies with no further relations among them. For any group of three, Trees e, f, and g show which two members are closest together.

To construct a tree, you will sometimes work by comparing authors to each other at the bottom of the tree and sometimes by posing key questions about general approaches to an issue at the top of the tree. These two strategies are explained in the next two sections. You may find that you prefer to use one strategy most.

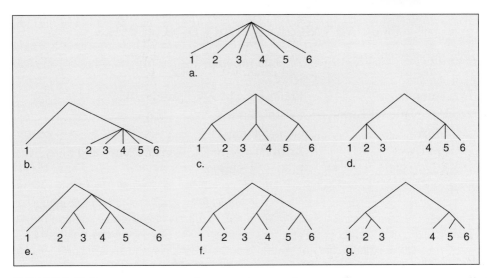

**FIGURE 12.2** Possible shapes of a tree with six authors.

However, the best way to use them is by working back and forth between the top and bottom levels. Whatever strategies you use, you must be careful to treat all authors fairly.

# Identifying Common Approaches

The easiest way to begin a synthesis is to select two or three articles that seem to be closely related and compare them. After you sketch out the common points and differences of a few authors, you will find it easier to consider additional articles and decide how they relate to the sketch.

## Grouping Authors

The first step is create some preliminary groupings of your authors. Try out a few sample groupings by asking yourself any of these questions: Which author or authors are your allies and which your opponents? Which authors agree with each other the most? Which authors address the most similar issues? Each question will lead you to create different clusters. Usually it will be easy to assign two or three authors to a cluster. Some authors will not fit easily anywhere; don't force them into a group. Some sample clusters are shown in "Preliminary Clusters of Authors."

# PRELIMINARY CLUSTERS OF AUTHORS

## *Environment*

| | |
|---|---|
| **Animals** | Robinson, Chivers, Easterbrook |
| **U.S. National Parks** | Kristof, Shiflett |
| **Crops** | Gómez-Pompa |
| **Pro-Use** | Kristof, Easterbrook, Gómez-Pompa and Kaus |
| **Anti-Use** | Robinson, Shiflett |

These alternative clusterings lead in different directions. The Pro- and Anti-Use groups address the same basic issue, use of resources, but from opposite sides. Within the Pro-Use group, the authors are all critical of restrictions called for by environmental activists. On the other hand, the Anti-Use authors Robinson and Shiflett agree that human activities can be harmful. This branching is likely to reveal differences among the allies on each side over which restrictions should be changed.

The clusterings around Animals, Parks, and Global Use topics do not build on basic agreements. Robinson and Easterbrook are not natural allies; Robinson is an environmental activist while Easterbrook criticizes "enviros." Shiflett and Kristof are direct opponents on using vehicles in park. None of these authors comment directly on the overall importance of the problems they address. This clustering, however, may still produce insights that lead to a valuable synthesis.

## *Crime*

| | |
|---|---|
| **Media** | Kollin, Kleck, Shapiro |
| **Civil Liberty** | Brooks, Meares and Kahan, Castleman |
| **Individualists** | Castleman, Kollin |
| **Governmentalists** | Kleck, Meares and Kahan, Shapiro |

These alternative clusterings lead in different directions. The Individualist and Governmentalist clusters address the same basic issue, responsibility for preventing crime, from opposite sides. The Individualists, Castleman and Kollin, agree that citizens should take action to prevent crime. On the other hand, the three Governmentalists believe that it is up to legislators to adopt better laws. This branching is likely to reveal differences among the allies on each side over which restrictions should be changed.

The remaining two clusters, Media and Civil Liberty, do not unite authors with basic agreements. While Brooks and Meares and Kahan focus on civil rights, they are not natural allies; Brooks is against curfews and gang laws while Meares and Kahan favor them. The authors in the Media cluster also disagree; Kollin favors more media coverage while Kleck and Shapiro consider media attention harmful. This clustering, however, may still produce insights that lead to a valuable synthesis.

No two authors will ever make exactly the same claims. But if the authors you have chosen are allies, then there are many points on which they would probably agree. They may share the same goals and disagree only on priorities and methods.

## Branching Out Groups and Subgroups

The branches in a tree signal disagreement over a claim. The group on one side agrees with the claim and the other group disagrees with it. Your branchings should represent the most central or important points on which your authors disagree. To branch out your tree, you will work creatively to compare authors and to articulate claims.

Of all your authors, ask yourself which two are in closest agreement. Write out some important claims on which this pair of authors agrees. Then consider the other authors one by one. An author who also agrees with these claims fits into a group with that pair; an author who disagrees does not. Considering the outsiders, create a group of authors who would agree to an opposing claim. As you continue, look at any grouping of three or more authors; try to generate claims to which two would agree and the third would not.

Using the strategies for inventing and naming groups in Chapter 5, write a descriptive term at each point where the tree branches.

Deciding which authors belong closer together along the entire tree is not easy. It takes persistence and creativity. However, that effort provides the key benefit of exploring with a synthesis. Expect the original groupings to change as you discover better or more important relationships.

"Reasoning about an Author's Assignment" illustrates different decisions on where to assign an author.

## REASONING ABOUT AN AUTHOR'S ASSIGNMENT

### *Environment*

In the clusters in "Preliminary Synthesis Trees," Chivers has not been assigned to either the pro- or anti-use clusters. He is close to the pro-users because he is allied with fishermen's organizations, but in wanting to preserve habitat and keep out destructive technologies, he is close to the anti-users. To be fair to Chivers, both aspects must be reflected in the synthesis.

Figure 12.1 shows two ways to assign Chivers. In Tree A, Chivers is grouped with the Managers because he is not for banning fishing or even banning mobile gear, just restricting where mobile gear is allowed. He is separated from the other Managers because he approves of environmental activism. In Tree B, Chivers is grouped with the Protectors who want to slow or eliminate the destruction of natural resources. Within this grouping, he is paired with Shiflett; both consider human use of the environment appropriate, within limits.

### *Crime*

In the clusters in "Preliminary Synthesis Trees," Brooks has not been assigned to either the Individualist or Governmentalist clusters. He is close to the Individualists because he is writing to churchgoers to urge them to volunteer to help kids; however, in opposing the passage of new curfew and gang ordinances, he is close to the Governmentalists. To be fair to Brooks, both aspects must be reflected in the synthesis.

Figure 12.1 shows two ways to assign Brooks. In Tree D, he is grouped with those who consider civil liberties to be important. Within this grouping, however, he is on his own in arguing that civil liberties violations increase crime. In Tree F, Brooks is grouped with the Individualists because he calls for personal intervention, not changes in the laws. Within the Individualists, he is on his own because he urges individuals (Christians) from outside the neighborhood to take action.

As you create groupings, you are likely to notice many points where authors in different groups share common ground. Keep track of these claims. Common ground is often the starting point for an author's proposal of a new way to see the problem or discover solutions.

## Drawing Fair Inferences

A crucial skill involved in synthesizing is drawing inferences about positions that your authors might take or assumptions that they might have made. Inferencing is necessary because the authors in your set are unlikely to address each other's points directly, unless you have chosen articles on a very narrow issue. To find points of agreement and disagreement, then, you have to infer an author's position. As you do so, an author comes to represent one case out of a category of very close allies who take the same approach.

For your synthesis to be of use in solving real-world problems, you must act as fairly as you can toward all the authors. If you mischaracterize an author, you open yourself to charges of demagoguery (Chapter 1), the willingness to use any means, including inaccurate and inflammatory claims, to win public support. Demagogues are good at stirring up allies and repelling opponents. However, their inaccurate descriptions of the problem lead to faulty solutions that fail to address its underlying causes.

The basic strategies needed for fair representations are the same as those introduced in Chapter 5 for disagreeing with an opponent: identify the authors, summarize their positions in a way they would agree is fair, make concessions, and state rebuttals. In a synthesis, your inferences describe the possible rebuttals that your authors would make to each other's arguments. Be prepared to support the plausibility of your inferences with evidence from the authors' own words.

"Representing Authors Fairly" provides examples of fair and unfair inferences drawn from the synthesis trees presented in this chapter.

---

## REPRESENTING AUTHORS FAIRLY

### Environment

In Figure 12.1A, Shiflett and Kristof are grouped together as agreeing on the importance of the wilderness experience.

#### Unfair Inference

Shiflett and Kristof think their own enjoyment as vacationers is more important than protecting endangered species. This makes them similar to the Managers who want resources extracted, no matter what the harm would be caused to the environment.

#### Fairer Inference

Shiflett and Kristof focus on the place of tourists in National Parks. They agree that a vacationer's enjoyment of the wilderness is important, even though they differ on what activities should be allowed. Neither of them says how they feel about the dangers to animal or plant life. However, because they both love being in nature, they probably disagree with the Conservers about the urgency of the dangers.

---

### Crime

In Figure 12.1C, Kleck is usually allied with Shapiro in criticizing current government approaches to crime.

#### Unfair Inference

Even though terrorists worldwide are usually turning out to be students, Kleck opposes the regulations that give federal investigators secret access to the library records, bookstore purchases, health records, and electronic communication of U.S. college students. He thinks the 9/11 bombing was a "freakish event," not an everyday, common occurrence; therefore, it is an inappropriate model for preventing terrorism. He would insist that universities be allowed to keep student records confidential.

### Fairer Inference

Kleck would probably agree that government action is needed for detecting potential terrorists in U.S. colleges. Nowadays, the most common perpetrators of terrorism worldwide are students; therefore, students deserve extra attention. But Kleck would probably oppose the regulations that give federal investigators secret access to the library records, bookstore purchases, health records, and electronic communication of U.S. college students. He would consider the 9/11 bombings to be a "freakish event" and an inappropriate model for preventing terrorism. He would support the colleges that want to keep student records confidential.

## Asking Argument-Based Questions

Another way to develop a synthesis tree is to treat each branching point as a question that authors must address in a public policy argument.

As you learned in Chapter 2, policy arguments often have three main sections, an issue span, a problem span, and a solution span. As you learned in Chapter 3, each span is developed with points about existence, definition, value, cause, and action claims. These points are the author's responses to questions such as these:

**Issue span**

| | |
|---|---|
| **Existence** | Has something happened? What is the current situation? Are there cases of a problem? |
| **Value** | Why is the issue worth attention? So what? Why should we care? |
| **Action** | What do we need to know about it? What new angle or approach do we need to take? |

**Problem span**

| | |
|---|---|
| **Existence** | Is there a problem? |
| **Definition** | What kind of event is it? Have cases of the problem been misclassified? |
| **Cause** | What causes it? How did it get this way? |
| **Value** | How serious is it? |
| **Action** | Should we try to solve it? |

**Solution span**

| | |
|---|---|
| **Existence** | Are any solutions possible? Have any solutions been tried or proposed already? |
| **Definition** | What kinds of solutions are they? |
| **Cause** | Will the solutions make the problem go away? Will they at least make the problem less frequent or less serious? |
| **Value** | What are the advantages and disadvantages of each solution? Which solution will cost the least and produce the most benefits? |
| **Action** | Who should act on the solution and how? |

Just as the points in a policy argument represent the views of one author on these questions, a synthesis tree captures the responses of groups of authors. The groups represent different approaches to a major question about the problem or the solution. The authors in each group share the same basic outlook on a major question but differ on specific points.

Focusing on these questions will help you decide on the most important ways in which authors disagree.


## Problem Trees and Solution Trees

A synthesis tree can contain points about both the problem and solution or it can focus on just one of these spans.

- **Environment.** Trees A and B in Figure 12.1 focus on the problem span: "What is environment problem is most important?" and "What is causing problems in the environment?" A synthesis tree can also focus on the solution span, like the tree entitled "What should be done about problems in the environment?" in Figure 12.1.

- **Crime.** Trees D and E in Figure 12.1 focus on the problem span, "Do stakeholders in crime areas care enough about safety?" and "Why do youth crimes occur?" A synthesis can also focus on the solution span, like the tree entitled "What should be done about crime problems?" in Figure 12.1F.

Your choice of a focus depends on the authors you are working with, the type of paper you are planning to write, and the aspects of the issue that interest you the most.


## Trees Based on Stases

The question that starts off a tree will itself represent a claim at one of the five stases: existence, definition, value, cause, or action. The claims at the major branches will also be at one of the stases.

As you can see in Figure 12.1, stasis labels can be attached to the question at the very top of the tree. The questions "What is the most important problem?" and "Do people care enough?" ask about values. The questions "What is causing the problems?" or "Why do problems occur?" ask about agents, factors, and changes. As you trace through the positions within a group, you will see that allies will often disagree on questions of value, cause, and action.

As you work on describing a disagreement between authors, it is helpful to ask:

Do they agree that there is a problem?

Do they count the same cases as problematic?

Do they have different priorities?

Do they appeal to different ethical principles?

Do they blame different factors?

Do they disagree on the effects of a change?

Do they recommend different actions?

Write down an inference describing how each author would answer these questions.

# Testing the Tree

Before finalizing your tree, it is important to test it to see whether you have characterized the authors' positions accurately and fairly, whether the tree captures different ways that groups would treat a problem case, and whether the tree is balanced and coherent.

## Role-Playing

In creating a synthesis tree, it is often helpful to imagine that the authors are all in a room talking. "Role-playing" presents part of a conversation among students who were asked to take on the role of an author, to ask questions that he or she would ask other authors and to answer their questions.

### ROLE-PLAYING

### *Environment*

**John Robinson**      What are our rights and obligations when having a wilderness experience? I think our obligation is to protect wildlife by any means possible.

| Dave Shiflett | We all have the right to enjoy the peace and serenity of nature. We are all also therefore obliged to respect the peace and serenity of others. |
| C. J. Chivers | I would recommend enjoying the wilderness and doing whatever you please as long as you do not destroy the wilderness permanently. |
| Nicholas Kristof | Robinson, by "any means possible," do you mean reducing our opportunity to enjoy the wilderness? Do you mean banning all transport? |
| Robinson | Kristof, if you mean limiting access, yes, if that is what it takes to protect a rare animal's habitat. Snowmobiles and mountain bikes allow access to otherwise unattainable areas where animals find sanctuary and scare them off into perhaps less beneficial areas. |
| Shiflett | Absolutely. We need to keep motorized vehicles out of our wilderness areas. |
| Gregg Easterbrook | Robinson, aren't you exaggerating the danger from these vehicles? Most animals would be fine after moving their habitats and other ones would come in to fill up in the gaps. |
| Robinson | It depends on which animals we are talking about. Individual animals that are not rare should still be available to the public even if they are harmed. Access to animals keeps people interested in their plight and willing to help preserve them. |

## Crime

| George Brooks | Castleman, I think we disagree in our assumptions about youth. Do you think we should treat every young person with suspicion? |
| Michael Castleman | Brooks, I do not think every young person should be regarded as a potential criminal or lawbreaker. I think you should take people as you meet and know them personally, just lock your doors at night. |
| Tracy Meares and Dan Kahan | Castleman, do you agree with us that people who live in high-crime areas need to cooperate more with the police? |
| Castleman | Yes. |
| Bruce Shapiro | I think the police do a lot to help crime in my neighborhood but not high-crime areas. What about |

| | placing the police in "hot spots" or specific areas where crime seems more prevalent? |
|---|---|
| **Meares and Kahan** | We think the *entire* American public should show some support for the enforcement of laws. This country is only as good as we [the public] allow it to be. We have no starting place without the ideas, support, and respect of the people. |
| **Brooks** | It is hard for someone to do that when your only interaction with the police is when they show up to take away your mother, brother, uncle, or best friend. |
| Castleman | Neighbors in any area can help change kids' lives; reducing opportunity in the first place reduces alienation and they won't commit the crimes. |
| **Joe Kollin** | I agree. Neighbors need to know which kids are the troublemakers. |

Role-playing conversations can help you discover points on which your authors agree or disagree, as long as the inferences underlying an author's response are fair.

When using these insights in your writing, be careful to signal clearly that these are hypothetical responses. Some useful phrases include "might argue," "might respond," and "would probably say."

## Testing with Problem Cases

A good way to test your tree is to select a problem case and infer how each group would treat it. For each group, try to answer these questions: Is this case relevant to their position? Would it be seen as an ideal case or a problem case?

## Looking for Coherence and Balance

Once you have finished a sketch of a complete tree, test it for coherence. Read through the sequence of claims leading from the top of the tree to each individual author's position. The sequence should make sense for each author. General points should precede specific points. An author's position on one claim should lead naturally to the claims following it.

To check the tree for balance, read across the branches at each level. The claims at a single level should all make sense as alternative answers to the same question. The branches should come in a sensible sequence so that the authors who agree the most are closest together and the ones who disagree the most are farthest apart.

# EXERCISES

## Backtalk: What Do You Say?

Come to class prepared to pretend to role-play one of the authors your class has been discussing. Reread the author's article carefully. Prepare a list of one or two questions your author would ask the other authors. Write a list of questions that you anticipate an author might ask you.

## Recognize/Evaluate

### A. Environment

Consider each statement in the following role-playing conversations. Which statements are fair to the authors who are speaking and which are unfair? Support your answers by referring to passages in the authors' articles.

1. **Kristof:** OK, Shiflett, I agree with you that the wilderness can be a serene place where silence is golden. But how are we to enjoy these places if we can't get to them? There are thousands of miles of trails in other parts of the country. Would it be okay if the transportation users stayed in areas designated for them?

2. **Shiflett:** If you can enjoy it without ruining it for anyone else, more power to you. But if technology disrupts other people's enjoyment, then the person using that technology is in the wrong. You have to be concerned with other people's wilderness experiences, not just your own. It's impossible to keep loud mountain bikes from ruining trails for hikers.

3. **Easterbrook:** Since when are mountain bikes loud? The wilderness can rebuild itself, so what about having trails in a kind of rotation system where every year a different bunch of trails is opened while some remain closed?

4. **Robinson:** Does one person's enjoyment cancel out the other's ruined experience? A resounding NO. Snowmobilers and mountain bikers can enjoy nature just as well from the ground without causing harm. Why not just take the simple route and say no to snowmobiles?

5. **Kristof:** Because they are fun. We all want to have fun in the wilderness, right? What about the people who do not want to rough it or who are disabled or out of shape? Don't they have the right to enjoy the wilderness?

6. **Shiflett:** The mountain bike itself isn't loud. The person enjoying his ride with his buddies is loud. So get rid of the people and leave the bikes, as long as I don't trip over them and ruin my experience or something.

7. **Chivers:** How can the wilderness unpave a paved road? Even with bikes, it would take more than a few years to erase the marks on the trails. Simply switching trails every few years would not leave nature enough time to properly heal herself.

8. **Easterbrook:** Agreed! Humans have to go in and restore trails. There is nothing wrong with filling in ruts with rocks and topsoil. It does not harm a thing. After a couple of years it will be back to the way it was before it was torn up by human contact.

## B. Crime

Students in this role-playing exercise were asked to respond to a case as they inferred their author would. Consider each statement in detail. Which statements are fair to the authors who are speaking and which are unfair? Support your answers by referring to passages in the authors' articles.

*How do you respond to this problem case: A seventh-grader brought a can of beer to school and gave it to a classmate. The classmate was caught drinking from the beer and expelled from school, due to a zero-tolerance policy for drugs and alcohol.*

1. **Kleck:** Harsh zero-tolerance policies are another misguided attempt provoked by media coverage and resulting public pressure due to the Columbine tragedy. Administrators and the public waste time overreacting instead of looking at individual cases and specifics. By overreacting to the situation (just one sip of alcohol, and by accident), the system drives kids to an all or nothing mentality on alcohol.

2. **Brooks:** This case shows a clear example of bias against a completely undeserving, innocent young woman. Her civil rights were obviously violated. If a boy had done the same, the punishment wouldn't have been nearly as severe. Zero-tolerance policies are like curfew laws in that they do nothing to curb crime while hurting young people. Instead we should put mentoring programs in place to prevent the problem of underage drinking altogether.

3. **Meares and Kahan:** Certainly the punishment was unfair in this particular case, but perhaps in agreeing to go to public school students must give up some rights. Appropriate suspensions and even zero-tolerance policies may be necessary to keep schools safe.

4. **Castleman:** The policy is foolish in the first place and likely won't prevent kids from drinking because it's often an impulse decision. Parents should instead team up to watch their children's behavior and stop drinking. The severity of this punishment smacks of the conservative let's-put-all-our-eggs-in-one-basket approach to sentencing.

5. **Shapiro:** This exemplifies why harsher regulations won't work. We need to work within the school systems to make sure kids don't fall through the cracks and start new antidrinking and violence programs in schools.

## Detect

### A. Environment

1. Edward Abbey, an environmental activist, wrote an article entitled, "The Damnation of a Canyon." An excerpt of this article can be found in the exercises in Chapter 5. After reading the excerpt, fit Abbey into one of the trees in Figure 12.1. To complete this exercise, you will probably have change the branchings and relabel them.

2. Read the following description of a problematic case concerning a rare species of seal in Alaska:

> Marine biologists in Alaska noticed a sharp drop in the population of Steller seals. Greenpeace and other environmentalist groups argued that fishing in the seals' habitat was a plausible cause. Fishermen argued that they weren't catching the kinds of fish that these seals eat. The federal judge in charge barred fishing temporarily to test whether fishing was the cause.

Choose one of the trees in Figure 12.1. For each group, write a brief description of what the authors would probably say about this case.

### B. Crime

1. Nicolas Kristof, a pundit for the *New York Times*, wrote an article entitled, "Lock and Load," proposing a different approach to gun control. The text of this article can be found in Chapter 11. After reading the excerpt, fit Kristof into one of the trees in Figure 12.1. To complete this exercise, you will probably have to change the branchings and relabel them.

2. Read the following description of a problematic case concerning racial profiling:

> A group of teenagers playing a pick-up game of basketball got into a shoving match. A police officer driving by stopped the fight. He searched the trucks of the two Hispanic players, found a weapon, and arrested Roberto for possession of a firearm in public. Roberto, a high school senior and member of the basketball team, had never been in trouble before. He was kicked off the team and eventually expelled from school.

Choose one of the trees in Figure 12.1. For each group, write a brief description of what the authors would probably say about this case.

## Produce

Draw a synthesis tree for a group of six authors. At least three of the authors should be different from the ones discussed in this book.

# PART III
## Having Your Say

### Chapters

Part III of *Having Your Say* describes how to become the author of papers in which you have your say about individual authors, the state of the debate on the issue, and issues themselves. These writing assignments represent the major types of contributions that authors make to ongoing public policy debates.

# CHAPTER 13

# Having Your Say
# on an Author's Argument

The essence of argument is to hear, assess, and respond with evidence and reasons to the positions of other authors. The authors in a discussion are more or less friendly rivals, each seeking to regain the floor in the discussion.

The most basic contribution that authors can make to a discussion is to analyze and evaluate the arguments of their rivals. Authors write about a rival author's argument when they think it is important to bring to the attention of the community, whether they agree with it or not. If the rival is an ally, an author may be acting as a teammate, seeking to test the argument for weak spots in order to improve on it. If the rival is an opponent, analyzing the argument is an important way for allies to gain insight into their opponent's beliefs and values. Analyzing a rival's argument is also a way for an author to help uncommitted readers see its strengths and weakness as preparation for making a response.

Writing an analysis of an author's argument is different from writing a response essay. In a response essay, described in Chapter 14, you give reasons for agreeing or disagreeing with the author's argument. In an analysis, you interpret the author's goals and evaluate how well these goals are met by the text that the author has produced. Both kinds of essays involve identifying strengths and weaknesses in the author's argument. But in an argument analysis, the strength of a point depends on how well it is argued, not on whether you agree with the point or not.

You are prepared to write a critical analysis of an author's argument if you have practiced recognizing the basic components of a policy argument in Chapters 2–6 and if you have studied the critical reading processes described in Chapter 18.

Your instructor may assign you an argument to analyze. Or you may have the opportunity to choose an argument relevant to your issue. If you choose your own argument, try to choose a text you disagree with; you will find it easier to make interesting points about the argument. To be sure that you have selected an original argument by an author, rather than a news story about other people's arguments, review Chapter 6 on style and Chapter 8 on types of periodicals.

Before reading further, read one of the essays in "Sample Argument Analysis Papers":

■ **Environment:** Monica Maxwell's "Shiflett's Show"

■ **Crime:** Shay Gilmore's "Solutions to Corporate Crime"

These sample papers will be used to illustrate the approaches to writing an argument analysis throughout this chapter. Note that they follow the MLA documentation conventions (Chapter 22).

---

## SAMPLE ARGUMENT ANALYSIS PAPERS

### *Environment*: *Monica Maxwell*
### *Shiflett's Show*

1   In "Parks and Wreck," published in the *National Review* on March 19, 2001, Dave Shiflett argues that the government should ban motorized vehicles in state parks. For the audience to which Shiflett is writing, it is a persuasive argument. With his appeals to their values and emotions, they would most likely overlook his lack of appeals to credible authority and logic.

2       Shiflett writes to conservatives who love nature and look down on others who don't agree with their views. To prove that he is one of them, he expresses his dislike for [President Bill] Clinton, approving the fact that he is "being generously lashed for his efforts on behalf of swindlers, tax cheats, crack merchants, traitors, and other well-connected felons." He refers to his readers as right-wingers who "tend to side with industrial interests," but he asks them to reconsider Clinton's decision in this case, "on truly conservative grounds." Shiflett also assumes that his readers "love the majesty of nature," because then they must "see these people (motorized vehicle riders) for what they are." But Shiflett does not assume his readers are environmentalists. He argues that "environmentalists traffic in hysteria." He sees environmentalists as fanatics who wreak havoc as opposed to those who love the peaceful beauty of nature. Shiflett's audience also seems to be somewhat elitist, looking down on those who ride motorized vehicles. He implies that his audience has refined taste by saying things like "One can no more enjoy a walk in the forest with one of them around than one can enjoy an opera while sitting beside a barking dog."

3       Shiflett does a lot to define motorized vehicle riders. He argues that they are loud, rude people who don't appreciate nature and ruin it for others. They believe that "scenery is for saps." He sees them as a nuisance to others in nature, as "national pests" who "should be kept out of national parks." He calls them "slothful vandals," "subspecies," and "wankers." He compares them to other pests, saying that they have "the mindset of the adolescent yob who gets his thrills passing gas in elevators, setting off cherry bombs in movie theaters, scaling the walls of convents, and otherwise strutting his ignorant stuff any place he can put one foot before the other."

4    Shiflett's knowledge of the topic comes from some research he has done. He quotes a study by Bowe Marketing Research to argue that the "average PWC (personal watercraft) operator is not who you think he is." The majority are married, middle-aged, educated white-collar workers.

5    But Shiflett bases his argument mostly on his own experience of run-ins with jet skiers and dirt-bikers. The first one was in Colorado where he found himself "wishing for a few long strands of piano wire to stretch between trees at roughly Adam's apple level." He describes Pike National Forest as a place where "in some sections at least, one can be run down by dirt-bikers—many of whom no doubt have a jet ski and a snowmobile back in their garage." As a result, "Thanks to their efforts, this beautiful stretch of forest sounds like downtown Los Angeles on the Fifth of May."

6    Shiflett thinks that because he has had these bad experiences, that they must be completely telling of what all motorized vehicle riders are like. His grounding is too anecdotal, based on individual testimony. He assumes all people's experiences are just like his. He uses the rhetorical fallacy of pars pro toto, assuming that his opinion is the universal opinion of motorized vehicle riders. He is simply not fair-minded in thinking that all people should agree with him. Maybe others don't agree that one has to have silence in order to enjoy nature. He makes no attempt to see things from a different point of view.

7    Shiflett also uses the emotions from anger to humor to persuade his audience of elitist conservatives interested in nature. He uses the emotion of anger by making it seem like these motorized vehicle riders take away his rights and those of nature lovers. He appeals to anger when he wishes for the piano wire. He expresses his anger, which encourages the anger of his audience. He also disguises his anger using sentences like "At this point, let me abandon the neutral fair-minded tone that has marred this essay thus far," letting his audience enjoy the ridicule of motorized vehicle riders.

8    It seems that Shiflett just amplifies the feelings that already exist in his audience. In order to be persuaded by Shiflett, one has to already have these feelings at some level.

9    He doesn't say this but the main goal of his argument is to put the value of his experience over the value of the motorized vehicle riders' experience. He encourages his audience to feel superior to this group. The owners of PWCs "reject all sensible notions of beauty, order, and civilized behavior." He implies that his audience members live noble lives, upholding these values. He also refers to these riders as adolescents saying, "True right-wingers have historically known how to handle adolescents: Be sweet, but also be firm." He persuades his audience to feel like they are much more mature and sophisticated than the riders. He implies that the riders and his readers are different, when in reality, both groups of people are the same age and share the same white-collar educated background. So not only does Shiflett

10    do a good job appealing to emotion, but he also appeals to the value of superiority with his audience.

Overall, Shiflett's ethos suffers because he's extremely biased against those with different opinions. He narrows his potential audience to conservatives who also find humor in name calling. His article would be very persuasive to upper-class conservatives. The strengths of his argument, using emotions of anger and humor and appealing to the value of superiority, outweigh the weaknesses of lacking a strong logical basis or a fair-minded presentation.

### Crime:  Shay Gilmore
### Solutions to Corporate Crime

1    Along with increases in wealth and superior technology, the corporate world has experienced rapid increases in crime with new angles that are more difficult to detect. In "Beating Bolder Corporate Crooks," published in *Fortune* on April 25, 1988, Brian Dumaine addresses the issues involved with corporate crooks, summarizes the problems that are occurring, lays out a detailed campaign to help diminish this type of criminal offense, and explains methods for dealing with the perpetrators. *Fortune* magazine provides investigative editorials such as this, as well as advice and ideas, to leaders in corporate America and to the country's top entrepreneurial thinkers. Dumaine's main challenge in this editorial is to convince readers that crime by employees is very serious and that corporations themselves are responsible for letting it happen.

2    Brian Dumaine has the authority to blame his own readers. He is currently the editorial director of *Fortune Small Business (FSB)* sector, and a graduate of Amherst College. Dumaine helps shape the editorial content of the magazine, is the chief editorial spokesperson, and has the responsibility of extending *FSB*'s brand into new target audiences and arenas. He has written numerous cover stories that have affected corporate America as well as investigative pieces on marketing, investing, technology, and corporate crime. However, Dumaine still needs to persuade readers to reject their own practices.

3    Dumaine begins the issue span by highlighting the existence of the temptations faced by employees: Technology is a necessary asset to businesses, but also makes it easier to compose fraudulent documents that frequently go unnoticed. Dumaine captures the readers' attention by vividly describing instances of executives downloading millions into Swiss bank accounts, ways our culture encourages employees to hunt and lust to be wealthy, and cases of indictments and convictions in corporate crimes. He ends with the causal claim that the victims of these crimes sometimes bring it upon themselves by not taking proper security precautions.

4    Dumaine then defines the main problem of corporate crime by magnifying the inability and negligence of companies to protect themselves. This value section is brief, but it is interesting to see how Dumaine worsens the criminals' actions by recognizing that these cases bring humiliation to all parties, including the convicted parties' families. He also lifts some of the blame, turning it toward the corporate firms for making it so easy to steal, for example when addressing the crook's "after-the-fact" remorse.

5    Dumaine uses logos to support his value claim that these crimes are a huge problem. Statistical logos appeals are effectively placed, such as the following: "The U.S. Chamber of Commerce figures dishonesty costs U.S. business at least $ 40 billion annually, which shows the value of these situations" and " . . . a company can lose 1% to 2% of its sales to crime, mostly committed by insiders. In a company the size of IBM, that amounts to at least $500 million a year."

6    Now that Dumaine has established the issues and problems with corporate crime, he goes into the solution span. With several stases involved, he separates it into three parts: keeping criminals or potential criminals out of the company (definition); preventing and detecting crime among employees (cause); and handling a criminal once he is caught (action).

7    Characteristics of criminal employees can be detected by watching out for job candidates who want dramatic increases in salary and by thoroughly checking employer references. He also recommends recognizing employees who seem to be living outside of their means and may have troubling lifestyles.

8    Dumaine then uses common sense techniques to prevent crime. First, he states that it is important for the company's top guns to set a good example. If employees hear of superiors and top authorities making ethical compromises, it is that much more tempting for them to participate in foul play of their own. Second, Dumaine uses an ethos appeal by citing Jerry Wernz of Boise Cascade Security; he "believes that employees can be the most effective weapon in battling crime. We tell employees how crime actually affects them, how it might make their division less profitable and therefore their jobs less stable." Once the guilty party is suspected, it is very important to verify that the facts are true. Dumaine explains that if a person may be falsely accused, lawsuits could occur.

9    Once an crooked employee is detected, the next course of action is to confront him in the presence of other security people and more than likely a confession will soon follow. Dumain argues that the criminal should be exposed because preventing crime is more important than saving face.

10    Dumaine considers and rejects some alternatives on cracking down on corporate crime when he supports the outlawing of lie detector tests. He recognizes that these tests are not legally reliable and can sometimes infringe on the employer/employee relationship. Dumaine also considers another alternative to his argument when mentioning how many com-

panies would rather absorb losses caused by an employee than move to press charges and ultimately have a media scandal. He states, "Most companies will sweep the crime under the carpet and quietly fire the crook, reasoning that if news leaked out, the ensuing publicity could hurt more than the crime itself." Dumaine's rebuttal is done by reminding readers of the failure of the companies' previous reactions to corporate crime that are listed above. This is effective because it enhances his main point, how important it is to crack down on this issue. Without these alternatives, opponents of his stance could consider him biased and skewed.

11      The author's solution plan is very reasonable and practical. I think it would be foolish of any company not to implement these tactics into their current precautionary methods. Together, with help from all angles of a company, the employees, employers, and accounting personnel should be able to help diminish losses in a short amount of time.

12      I agree with Dumaine's thesis that corporate crime is a problem not to be taken lightly. Dumaine does a thorough job presenting associated drawbacks and effects of the crime, and gives detailed suggestions for company executives, employees, and auditors to execute. His argument is only somewhat persuasive because it presents achievable solutions, but does not give any evidence of their success. However, I find this argument viable because of the repercussions for corporate companies, employees' autonomy, and possible ripple effects throughout the economy.

# Planning Purpose and Audience

Authors who write an analysis essay are usually aiming at readers of academic journals or at readers of literary and political magazines. They include stakeholders and decision makers as well as authors and potential authors. These readers are interested enough in the issue to want to keep up with developments in the public conversation about it. An analytic essay, which often comes in the form of a lengthy review of a new book by an important author, helps readers keep informed about new positions and decide what to read. An argument analysis also helps them discover ways to challenge an opponent's argument or strengthen their own.

As a student, you will analyze an article rather than an entire book. However, you can write with this kind of audience in mind. Or you may aim your analysis at classmates who are reading and writing about the same topic as you. In either case, it is best to assume that your readers are unfamiliar with the article you are analyzing. Assuming that readers don't know what the article says will help you provide an appropriate amount of detail about the author's argument; readers need a detailed description to understand the guts of the author's argument and how it is made. Details raise a reader's confidence in you; they show that you have studied the argument thoroughly and that you are treating the author fairly.

Your purpose is *not*, however, to present a close paraphrase or summary of every bit of the argument as you may have done when writing simple book reports in grade school. A school-level book report is usually designed to show your teacher that you read and understood the book. In an argument analysis, by contrast, you are creating your own interpretation of a complex argument and evaluating its success. Your goal is to address questions such as these:

- What choices do you believe the author made to make his or her argument persuasive to intended readers?
- Where has the author spent the most time? Why might he or she have chosen to focus on those points?
- What strategies for making claims and appeals does the author use most often? Why might he or she have chosen to rely on these strategies?
- How well do you think these choices succeeded (for you and especially for the intended readers) and why?

Answering these questions involves constructing your own argument because any text can be interpreted and evaluated in more than one valid way.

## Planning Your Line of Argument

After following the critical reading process described in Chapter 18, you should have a good outline of your author's argument. But this outline will not necessarily serve as an outline for your paper. Your paper is itself an argument about the author's main strategies and their effectiveness. This means that you have to construct a thesis about the key aspect of the author's argument. The evidence for your claims will come in the form of references to the text, including paraphrases and brief quotations. "Reasoning about Thesis and Audience" illustrates how Monica and Shay reasoned about a thesis and decided who to address.

---

### REASONING ABOUT THESIS AND AUDIENCE

#### Environment: Monica's Reasoning

The key aspect of Shiflett's argument, for Monica, was his use of so much insulting language. Because she was offended by some of this language and disagreed with some of his political views, she wondered how he could have expected to have his argument taken seriously. So she took as her goal to figure out, first, whether Shiflett was actually presenting a good argument apart from the insults and, second, what kinds of conservatives might find the argument more convincing than she had. She decided to keep in mind readers who would agree with Shiflett's politics but disagree on this policy.

#### Crime: Shay's Reasoning

Shay was intrigued that Dumaine blames his own readers, corporate executives, for letting crooked employees commit crimes. He decided to focus on how Dumaine conveys such a negative message without turning off his readers. Shay highlights these strategies all along the line of argument. He addresses his argument to members of the public like himself who are unlikely to identify with corporate executives.

# Allocating Space and Planning the Arrangement

While you are responsible for describing the author's argument in some detail, the length and focus of your paper should not mirror it exactly. That is, you do not necessarily need more pages to analyze a long article and fewer pages to analyze a short one. If the text you are analyzing is long, you can focus on larger sections and overall patterns in the argument. If the text is short, your analysis can go deeper into the details of each point.

You have several choices for arranging your paper including:

- **Following the author's sequence.** Starting with the issue span and working through all its levels (stases, appeals, rebuttals, style), then doing the same for the problem span and the solution span.

- **Working top-down.** First analyzing all the points at the highest level (the spans), then addressing the stasis claims within each span, one at a time, starting with the first span, then moving to the stases in the second and third spans, then the appeals, then rebuttals, and then, finally, style.

- **Organizing by argument types.** Providing an overview of the entire line of argument, then analyzing the most important or most frequent type of point (such as causal arguments) with its typical forms of support, then another type of point (such as rebuttals), then the next.

- **Organizing by topics or themes.** Reviewing the entire line of argument, then analyzing the most important topic, such as the media, then the second most important, such as the government, and so on.

Each structure has its own consequences. Following the author's sequence produces a structure that is easy for readers to follow, but it is harder to build an argument evaluating the article as a whole, rather than a play-by-play commentary on many minor aspects. This arrangement is hard to use for very long articles.

Working top-down is also easy to organize, with a section about each level of argument. By dealing with the spans first, you provide an overview of the argument as a whole. It is easy to point out an author's habits, such as heavy reliance on causal claims or appeals to ethos. The challenge of this arrangement is to provide a clear picture of the construction of important points and how they build to the author's conclusion. You must avoid writing a superficial analysis with a set of disconnected examples.

Organizing by type of argument or by topic both require you to take a bird's eye view of the entire argument. This arrangement is easiest for presenting your interpretation and evaluation of the author's approach; however, it also requires you to come up with a clear structure of points that build up to your conclusion.

Another aspect of arrangement to consider is your twin goals of analysis and evaluation. If you react strongly to the article, you may be tempted to focus on giving your critique while giving little attention to analyzing what the author has actually done. However, to come across as fair to the author, especially one you disagree with, it is a good idea to position your evaluation *after* your description of a strategy. This way, readers can see what you are talking about before you judge whether it is good or bad. Postponing your evaluation does not mean waiting until the end of your paper, but only until the end of a paragraph or the end of a section, wherever you can logically include it.

## Adopting an Analytic Style

Writing an analysis and evaluation requires an analytic style. This style is different from one you might use to respond to the author or change a stakeholder's position. An analytic style is one that is appropriate for an academic journal or for a literary and political magazine. Of the styles described in Chapter 6, students usually adopt a blend of academic and public opinion styles.

An analytic style involves focusing on the author and what he or she did, not on your own positions and judgments. Here are some techniques to use in creating an analytic style:

- **Author as topic of sentences.** "Castleman argues that youth crimes will always happen. He chooses opportunity as the one that we can address ourselves."
- **Attributions to author.** "According to Shiflett"; "For Castleman, this is a myth."
- **Identification of argument components.** "Castleman adds to his 'ordinary Joe' ethos by admitting to crimes he committed when he was young"; "This section addresses three possible causes for youth crimes: impulse, alienation, and opportunity"; "Castleman backs up this claim with both statistics and personal testimony"; "Castleman finally gets to his solution in paragraph X. His solution is simple: 'Be like me.'"

"Choosing an Arrangement and Style" illustrates how Monica and Shay chose to arrange their points and construct an analytic style.

### CHOOSING AN ARRANGEMENT AND STYLE

#### *Environment: Monica's Choices*

Monica did not see clear divisions into spans in Shiflett's essay. She realized that Shiflett's point was not to argue about the existence of a new problem but to support a solution that already existed, one proposed by President Clinton. To Monica, the main goal of Shiflett's essay was to persuade people to see motorized vehicle riders as he did so that they would support the solution he supported.

She also realized that Shiflett's readers in the *National Review* were being contrasted to the vehicle riders. So she opened her essay by focusing directly on these readers and what she could tell about them from the essay. Then she presents Shiflett's definitional claim and the kinds of supporting appeals he offered.

Because she was accusing Shiflett of being biased and unfair, Monica adopted an analytic tone rather than a personal tone. She also took care to illustrate her claims with many snippets of Shiflett's own language.

### *Crime:* Shay's Choices

Shay found it easy to divide Dumaine's argument into spans and stases, so he follows Dumaine's arrangement in his paper. Within each span, he identifies the stases of the main claims and explains how they are supported with appeals. Shay adopts an analytic tone because he had no personal perspective on corporate crime to draw on. He provides few direct quotes because Dumaine relied so little on appeals to pathos.

## Criteria for an Argument Analysis

Keep the following set of criteria in mind as you write and review your draft. Picture yourself as "the writer," and the author you are analyzing as "the author." Picture a member of your audience as "the reader."

### Reasoning and Content

- The writer understands the social and historical context of the argument (Chapter 6).
    The author being analyzed is identified and his or her credibility assessed (Chapter 5).
    The journal or publication site of the article is identified and its readership is described in detail. The author's choice of this venue is evaluated (Chapter 8).
- The writer understands the author's line of argument (Chapter 18).
    The article is divided into plausible spans (Chapter 2).
    The writer describes the major claims (existence, definition, value, cause, action) within each span (Chapter 3).
    The writer describes the author's use of support (appeals to logos, pathos, ethos; concession and rebuttal) for major claims (Chapters 4 and 5).
- The writer evaluates the author's choices of:
    Where to devote the most space;
    How to address allies and opponents (Chapter 5); and
    Language, tone, and style (Chapter 6).
- The writer provides sufficient evidence from the article.
- The writer treats the author fairly.

### Purpose and Audience

- The writer provides enough detail that someone who has not read the article can understand the argument.
- The writer has an original claim about the key strategy in the article.

## Organization

- The essay consistently follows an organizational plan.
- A reader can easily find the places in the article that the writer refers to.
- Sections of the paper are created with groups of paragraphs; paragraphs are divided into coherent topics or subtopics.

## Expression

- The writer uses an analytic style.
- Sentences focus on what the author "did," not on what he or she said.
- A reader can distinguish between the author's claims and the writer's claims

"Assessment of Student Papers" evaluates Monica and Shay's essays along these criteria.

---

### ASSESSMENT OF STUDENT PAPERS

#### Environment: *Monica's Analysis*

Monica's introduction effectively illustrates her personal identification with Shiflett's problem, which, despite her critique of Shiflett's argument, is echoed in her conclusion. In par. 2, she identifies Shiflett clearly as a conservative pundit writing in a conservative journal, taking an interesting opposing position to his allies. She provides an overview of her overall argument in par. 3, allowing readers to anticipate the points to come. She efficiently addresses each span in its own paragraph, within which she points out major claims, using paragraph numbers to make these easy to locate in the article. She uses another two paragraphs to discuss Shiflett's typical appeals. Much of her evidence comes in the form of brief, well-chosen quotes from Shiflett. Monica's own style is analytic but colorful; she comes across as fair to Shiflett without softening her criticism.

#### Crime: *Shay's Analysis*

Shay analyzes Dumaine's line of argument (spans, stases, and appeals) effectively and clearly. Within each span, he shifts smoothly between Dumaine's main points and their support. His concise paraphrases usually convey the content with well-chosen details. Shay does not mention Dumaine's use of space or his style.

Shay states his thesis clearly in par. 1. He uses this thesis effectively to assess Dumaine's credentials and choice of journal. In other places, however, the relationship of his analysis to the thesis is not fully developed.

Shay's introduction and conclusion are functional but not attention-grabbing. He could have strengthened these by relating Dumaine's article to current headlines such as misdoings at Enron or by reacting as a potential corporate employee. Elsewhere, however, his neutral stance establishes a sense of fairness and confidence.

# Peer Review Guidelines

The following are suggestions for helping a classmate improve the draft of an argument analysis. You may also find them helpful for planning and reviewing your own draft. Your advice will come across as more helpful if you address the writer directly, using "you."

1. Suggest information that your peer should add about the author/publisher, journal/site and assumed readers of the text.

2. After reading your peer's paper, see if you can able to identify the article's main sections (spans) and the main claims under each span (stases)—even without reading it. What parts seem underdeveloped or confusing? Ask questions about how the article is put together.

3. Suggest ways your can peer improve his or her analysis of the rhetorical strategies listed below. Which ones should your peer look for? Which ones need to be explained more or supported with better examples? Which ones need more evaluation? What should be changed?

   ■ Identifying author's spans (seeing issue, defining problem, choosing a solution).
   ■ Author's claims at the stases of existence, definition, cause, value, and/or action. Has your peer left any out? Does your peer point out any that are missing from the article?
   ■ Author's appeals to logos, pathos, or ethos. Has your peer left any out? Does your peer point out any that are missing from the article?
   ■ Author's fairness in use of concessions and rebuttal.
   ■ Author's use of pictures, graphs, or tables in the published article.
   ■ Author's style: academic, public opinion, journalistic; hectoring, preachy, smart-alecky.

4. Help your peer create a more consistent structure. Can you see a pattern for the paper—by sections in the text? By rhetorical strategies? Other? Which paragraphs seem out of place? Which paragraphs repeat points discussed elsewhere? Which paragraphs shift around among different topics?

5. Suggest ways your peer can improve the introduction or conclusion and make them work together.

6. See if your peer's overall evaluation is based on a personal reaction or on the probable effect of the article on its intended audience. If the audience is not considered, suggest places to add analysis. Consider whether your peer's evaluation is fair, accurate, and persuasive. Explain why or why not.

   For advice on giving your classmate the most helpful response, review Chapter 21.

# CHAPTER **14**

# Having Your Say by Responding to an Author's Argument

You may write a response paper for a variety of reasons: to draw attention to an aspect of the issue that you believe an author has overlooked or gotten wrong, to test the author's approach in a new situation, or to add on to it by looking more deeply into an aspect the author has raised. In a response, you may express strong feelings about an issue, whether from your own experiences or from reacting to what you have read. To prepare for writing a response, you should explore your own views on the issue, using the strategies in Chapters 7 and 9.

Writing a response essay is different from writing an analysis of an author's argument. In an analysis, described in Chapter 13, you interpret the author's argument and evaluate its success for its intended audience. In a response essay, you develop your own position on the issue by agreeing or disagreeing with at least one other author. To be fair to the authors you discuss, it is important to be sure that you understand their lines of argument. Thus you should not write a response until you have read the article(s) critically, using the processes described in Chapter 18.

Before reading further, read one of the following sample student essays in "Sample Response Papers":

**Environment:** Katie Kucera's "Loved to Death: A Response to C. J. Chivers"

**Crime:** Lauren Downey's "Blue Crime,"

These sample papers will be used throughout this chapter to illustrate the approaches to writing a response paper. Note that they follow the APA documentation conventions (Chapter 22).

## SAMPLE RESPONSE PAPERS

### Environment: Katie Kucera
### Loved to Death: A Response to C. J. Chivers

1    I work for Homeward Bound, an outdoors organization that takes students into nature to rescue them from the noise and distractions of modern life so they can enjoy the untouched beauty of creation. We take them into the mountains of Colorado, the rivers of south Texas, and our most frequent venue, Enchanted Rock, a beautiful dome of solid pink granite in central Texas. We usually have a group of about 60 to 90 people.

2    Two years ago, the founder of Homeward Bound asked the staff if we would come up to Enchanted Rock one weekend when we didn't have a group and help rebuild some of the trails. Once a month, a small team of devoted folks labor to repair and maintain the trails of the park. That weekend, I realized what a toll my outfitter must take, rotating hundreds of kids over those paths week after week. The park is designed to accommodate around 200,000 visitors a year but currently attracts well over 300,000 a year. From that point on I began to notice how worn-down and trampled the trails were. In five years, I had seen the topography of the park change as the flora got thinner and the erosion worsened. Enchanted Rock is still as majestic as ever and can still take my breath away, but if not for that trail team, it would be even more sadly stripped and barren.

3    This forced me to ask myself a hard question: What takes priority, our desire to be immersed in the wilderness or our responsibility to preserve it? I love the natural, undisturbed tranquility of the wilderness. The problem is that by simply being in nature, I change things; I stress the trails by walking them; I unintentionally weaken nature's defenses against erosion when I leave the path to become completely engulfed and, until recently, I didn't even realize it.

4    In his article concerning deep-sea trawling and dredging, C. J. Chivers (2000) addresses a similar problem. Chivers finds that most fishermen are unaware of how much damage they cause and are too quick to assume that they will have little impact in the grand scheme. However, as Chivers points out, this all adds up to substantial damage. Hikers are the same way. People believe the effect they have is so miniscule and the environment is so resilient that they have nothing to worry about. This would be true if only a few people visited the state and national parks, but this is not the case. With the number of people drawn to the parks, our impact, even just hiking around, is quite significant.

5    Although degradation of state and national parks and of the ocean floor are much different, they both deal with overuse, indifference, or unawareness toward the problem. Both involve a value argument pitting right of access against responsibility to conserve.

6    Chivers (2000) offers several possible solutions. The first is no-fishing zones, areas where use is simply not allowed. Applied to the wilderness, this would mean that areas would be off-limits to people altogether. This approach is necessary to preserve a shred of truly wild earth and some completely isolated wildlife refuges. However, it is hard for me to support extensive use of an off-limits conservation solution. After all, a large amount of my sentiment concerning conservation comes from my selfish desire to enjoy it.

7    Chivers's (2000) second solution is regulation of gear and catch limits. The San Juan National Forest in Colorado and most other National Parks have some similar methods of regulation. Groups of more than four or five people have to register with the public lands office and rent camp space. They are only allowed a certain number of nights on the trails. In this way, the park can monitor how heavily trafficked its trails become. This seems to work quite effectively; the forests are so large that most of the park remains fairly well preserved.

8    At places like Enchanted Rock, however, this is not the case. It is easily accessible and not nearly large enough to support its tourism, with 100,000 more people than it was designed for. So would regulation solve the problem at Enchanted Rock or even be reasonable? Currently, the park staff closes admissions after a certain number of people enter the park. But this is on a day-to-day basis and is more a preventative measure against overcrowding than a way of promoting conservation. Could they limit the number of visitors per year? That would help but it would mean that fewer people get to enjoy it. Regulation should be a part of the solution but, again, it is not enough.

9    The solution Chivers (2000) seems to favor most is also the most difficult to implement. He seems to believe that the best way to protect the ocean floor is through the personal choices made by fishermen. Chivers meets a traditional fisherman named Captain Taylor who holds to his gentle, yet less-efficient fishing methods in order to protect his source of income and his source of life. By being deliberate, and going a little out of the way, Captain Taylor maintains the habitats of his harvest, insuring their reproduction and the survival and longevity of his business.

10   How would this approach apply to Enchanted Rock? The last time I was out at Enchanted Rock, I saw a group of kids taking golf swings at cactus with a branch they had just pulled off a tree. This kind of behavior will eventually make Enchanted Rock and other parks eroded and barren. Acting in the same deliberate manner as Captain Taylor would give us a good start to the preservation of nature. But Captain Taylor had a lifetime's experience on the sea. Most of the kids we take on trips have little to no experience in the wilderness.

11   I believe that appreciation grows out of time spent in the wilderness and that the right level of respect is not present at the beginning. So teaching is a challenge. Logistically, we haven't the manpower or resources to run our

trips as intimately as we'd like. Monitoring kids has never been an issue on our smaller trips. It only becomes a problem when we have seventy-plus kids. If only we had more staff and could take smaller groups of students, then we could teach respect more effectively. But we meet only a fraction of the visitors to Enchanted Rock.

12      I agree with Chivers (2000) that we should balance use of the wilderness with its preservation. The problem of damage to popular, easily accessible nature spots, however, is not easy to solve. The approaches that he proposes are not enough.

### References

Chivers, C. J. (2000, February). Scraping bottom. *Wildlife Conservation*, 103, 46–50.

### Crime: Lauren Downey
### Blue Crime

1    Tony Martinez, dead at 19, was killed five days before Christmas, 2001. In December of last year, here in Central Texas, Tony's door was broken down during an early morning raid by a SWAT team serving a warrant on his uncle. The results of the raid left Tony lying on the couch dead, along with many unanswered questions. A review by a Travis County grand jury did not indict Derek Hill, the deputy involved.

2    My brother-in-law, the only officer in our family, told of a local county sheriff chastising anyone not meeting a certain quota of tickets or arrests. My sister was arrested and not told why until 24 hours later. A long-time friend was arrested when leaving a convenience store with alcohol, even though he is 23 and always carries identification. Another friend was pulled over by four police cars, then pulled out of his car by several officers when trying to reach for his insurance card. Recently, police intimidation hit home for me when driving on the freeway with an officer riding my car so closely I could see his face. It might go without saying, but seeing these actions in my limited world makes me question and imagine the worst of the big picture.

3    Many cases exist today of police forces abusing power and acting against their code of conduct. Certainly a reasonable amount of leeway is needed if used with discretion. Misconduct is not necessarily typical for most officers. But it happens more than one might expect.

4    The problem is that police misconduct exists but it is either not dealt with adequately or no one knows how to prevent it. In some places, members of minorities are the most likely to be harassed, as in the cases that

George Brooks (1997) describes. He tells of Hispanic kids in Chicago who were driving a van and pulled over under suspicion of burglary. Maybe there is some underlying issue that causes the problem. It would help to collect more examples of police misconduct and see what they might have in common.

5    Gary Kleck (1999) might find the media guilty of exaggerating police misconduct by dwelling on cases like Albert Louima or Amadou Diallo or Rodney King. But the police are a normal part of our lives. If we ignore their crimes, then crime itself, whether common or not, would take on a whole new meaning. In that sense, Kleck might agree that police crimes are fairly typical and deserve society's attention after all.

6    I feel that part of the solution has to come from understanding how to avoid conflicts between oneself and an officer. Michael Castleman's (1995) ideas are applicable in that crime is everywhere and may be closer to home than one thinks. Crime could happen to anyone. I agree with Castleman that we are not safe from crime if we are ignorant, especially if the offense comes from those who we think not to suspect—such as police officers. Just as Catholic families never suspected that a priest might mistreat a child, we pay too little attention to the possibility of misconduct from the police.

7    Castleman is also right that we should reduce opportunity, in this case by educating ourselves on constitutional rights. We have to know our rights and the rights of the officers. We need to know what we are required to do by law versus what we are told to do. If people are prepared for situations, it will be less likely that they are taken advantage of or abused. We should all be aware of our surroundings. For example, a person who is pulled over alone on a dark bare street could refuse to get out of the car. When an officer comes to a home, the resident should make sure there is a warrant, and so on.

8    Another step towards the solution of this problem would be punishing those officers who misbehave. Even if we can't prevent all abuse, at least victims would know that their rights are respected when the offending officers are disciplined. If these cases go unacknowledged, the same officers are allowed to continue without regard to whether they will act inappropriately again. Regardless of a person's status in the world, committing a crime should be punished. What kind of example does it set that crime is excusable if it is committed by the police?

9    I like to picture how I first thought of police officers, when I knew that they were there to help, not to suspect me or to show prejudices towards age, race, sex, or status. I liked knowing there was safety. It was nice to know that criminals would be out of the neighborhoods. By now, that is harder to imagine. I am not saying that all police are untrustworthy or even that most are. I am sure that overall, they are upstanding examples. I would like to return to when a few negative cases did not cloud the positive ones.

### References

Brooks, G. (1997, March). Let's not gang up on our kids. *U.S. Catholic,* 62.3, 18–20.

Castleman, M. (1995). Opportunity knocks. *Mother Jones,* 20, 26 + . [Available online *Mother Jones Interactive.* www.motherjones.com/ commentary/columns/1995/05/castleman.html (4 Apr. 2002).]

Kleck, G. (1999). There are no lessons to be learned from Littleton. *Criminal Justice Ethics,* 18 (1999): 2 + .

## Planning Purpose and Audience

Your response is not simply a personal reaction. It is instead an informal version of a policy argument, based on one or more readings, knowledge of current events, and personal experience. Its purpose is to move readers to see the issue in a new way, as you do.

Authors who write a response essay are usually aiming at readers of academic journals or literary and political magazines. For example, the *Boston Review* (www.bostonreview.net) publishes the "New Democracy Forum" in which 8–10 authors publish responses to an essay; the essay author then has a chance to respond to the responses. In most cases, however, an author of a response essay cannot assume that everyone has read the articles that he or she is addressing.

The readers of response essays are interested enough in an issue to want to keep up with developments in the public conversation about it. These readers are not simply sitting on the sidelines; they include stakeholders and decision makers as well as authors and potential authors. So writing a response is taking a turn in the conversation.

As a student, you can address this kind of audience. Or you can address class-mates who are reading and writing about the same topic as you. Your first task is to raise readers' confidence in you; you must show that you have thought carefully about the issue and that you are treating other authors fairly, not simply blowing off steam. See Chapter 20 for more on finding new ideas that readers will take seriously.

"Reasoning about Thesis and Audience" illustrates how Katie and Lauren chose a position and authors to whom to respond.

### REASONING ABOUT THESIS AND AUDIENCE

#### *Environment*: *Katie's Reasoning*

In developing a response to the environment issue, Katie had years of experiences in national and state parks to draw on. She believed strongly in the benefits of bringing young people to visit the wilderness. She wanted to keep up the visits but she also wanted to preserve the places for future visits. When she read C. J. Chivers's article

"Scraping Bottom," she saw his position on fishing as similar to hers. So she used her response as a way to explore for solutions to the problem she was most interested in.

Because fishing and hiking would seem completely different to most readers, she planned to develop the comparisons as fully as possible, all the way from talking about the problem to considering the solutions.

### Crime: Lauren's Reasoning

Lauren's reaction to the crime issue was sparked by reading George Brooks's description of the police pulling over some Hispanic teenagers driving a van with items they were moving. She was reminded of several encounters with the police in her small town that she considered unfair. Her position was that the problem of police misconduct was being neglected. She saw two other authors as relevant to her position, Gary Kleck and Michael Castleman. Both were potential opponents, so Lauren's response considered whether they could be enlisted as allies.

## Planning Your Line of Argument

Because a response paper is a form of policy argument, it is appropriate to plan sections for seeing the issue, analyzing the problem, and considering solutions.

After exploring positions using the strategies described in Chapters 7 and 9, you should be aware of cases that matter a great deal to you. You should also have detected points of agreement and disagreement with a number of authors. Pick out the points that are most important to your view of the issue and the ones that are likely to be most controversial. In planning your line of argument, your goals should be to take a position that you develop across the essay as a whole, choose compelling cases that will also appeal to readers, choose authors whose points are relevant to your position, and make fair but effective rebuttals to opponents' points.

### Responding Strategically

When you respond to another author, choose the most important points to respond to. If you feel compelled to "set the record" straight on every small inaccuracy, you will distract attention from the main points. You may leave the impression that you are simply out to show up your opponent instead of to explore the issue.

While choosing points to challenge, be sure to weigh your evidence. Choose points to which your response is strongest and for which you have good evidence. Sometimes it is easy to weigh your evidence against the author's: The evidence on one side has flaws that the other side does not suffer from. It is more difficult to resolve conflicts between evidence when each side is supported by some strong evidence. Having conflicting evidence is very common because policy arguments deal with complicated issues. It is extremely rare, if not impossible, for an author to make an important claim with enough support to forestall all possible objections or responses. If it were easy to come up with enough reasons and evidence to satisfy all current and future readers, then arguments of policy would be resolved after two or three turns from different perspectives. But they aren't.

When your evidence conflicts with an author's, your best option is to admit it and make some concessions. This does not mean that the question is undecidable; you can still argue that your position should be given greater consideration, that is, treated as if it were true and your opponent's as false. You can consider the consequences of adopting each position and the risks of each side. For example, many people dispute the existence of global warming. Think of the risks of acting as if there is global warming, even though there might not be. One risk might be harm to the economy through needless regulation of some industries. Then consider the risks of acting as if there is no global warming, even though there might be. The risks may include climate changes, destruction of species, and so on. You can ask for greater consideration for acting as if there is global warming if you can make a strong value argument that risk to the economy is less serious than the risks to the climate and species.

## Allocating Space and Planning the Arrangement

With these ideas in mind as you draft, decide how much space to allocate to the three spans (Chapter 2) and which stases must be developed within each span (Chapter 3). Like any author, you should give the most space to the points that are newest and most controversial.

When you respond to several points that an author has made, choose an arrangement for the points:

- **Agreement toward disagreement.** Begin with points where you and the author agree and where you can make concessions. Then introduce points where you disagree. This arrangement increases chances that you will seem fair and open-minded.

- **Disagreement toward agreement.** If it seems obvious that your position and your opponent's are very far apart, describe the points of disagreement first. Then introduce points where you may share more ground than may be expected.

"Choosing an Arrangement" illustrates how Katie and Lauren allocated space and arranged their points.

## CHOOSING AN ARRANGEMENT

### *Environment: Katie's Reasoning*

Katie uses a vivid personal narrative to describe how she became aware of the issue. Her testimony about her own case establishes her ethos as someone who is caught up in the issue, both as a user and a preserver of the environment. She devotes two paragraphs to supporting her analogy between hiking and fishing. Once Chivers's approach is established as relevant, she spends the rest of the essay considering how Chivers's solutions might be adapted to her own problem case, Enchanted Rock. She takes care to describe his solutions fairly and explains why it makes sense to consider them. Even though she ends up rejecting Chivers's solutions, her objections seem fair because they are based on details of the situation at Enchanted Rock.

### Crime: Lauren's Reasoning

Lauren's response paper focuses consistently on police misconduct. To provide a vivid view of the issue, she opens with a series of cases that involved her family and friends. She establishes her ethos by providing personal testimony and by acknowledging that readers might initially see her concerns as paranoid. The remainder of her space is divided almost equally between the problem and the solution. In discussing the problem, she compares her problem cases to those that Brooks and Kleck might raise. In discussing the solution, she considers Castleman's approach but moves further to emphasize the need to punish offenders, even if they are police officers.

## Adopting an Appropriate Style

As described in Chapter 6, authors adopt a writing style that is appropriate to the readers they are addressing. Because a response paper is most appropriate for an academic journal or for a literary and political magazine, you can choose an academic style or a blend of popular opinion and academic styles.

You may find it interesting to experiment with a provocative style in all or part of your essay. If you do, be sure that your claims are fully developed and well supported, as Shiflett and Brooks do. Otherwise, you run the risk of having your response dismissed as a closed-minded rant instead of a contribution to a conversation.

Some students find it difficult to signal where their own position differs from that of the author they are discussing, especially if the author is an ally. The following techniques can help you:

- **Author as topic of sentences.** "Castleman argues that youth crimes will always happen. He chooses opportunity as the factor that we can address ourselves."
- **Attributions to author.** "According to Castleman"; "For Castleman, this is a myth."
- **Concessions and refutation.** "Castleman is right that . . . "; "But I disagree with him on . . . "; "He forgets that . . . ."

For more insights into creating a rhetorical style, review Chapter 6.

# Criteria for a Good Response Paper

Keep the following set of criteria in mind as you write and review your draft. Picture yourself as "the writer," and the author you are responding to as "the author." Picture a member of your audience as "the reader."

## Reasoning and Content

- The writer's position relates to central aspects of the issue.

    The writer takes a clear position on the issue.
    The writer introduces relevant cases to illustrate the problem.
- The writer relates his or her position to one or more authors.

    The response is not a play-by-play of reactions during reading.

## Disagreement (Chapter 5)

- The writer reaffirms or challenges important claims.

- Counterexamples and opposing appeals are sufficient.

- The writer acknowledges the social and historical context of the argument.

    The writer identifies authors as potential allies or opponents.
    Cited authors are identified; their credibility is assessed; their choices of
        where and when to publish are evaluated.
    Differences in the situations of writer and authors are described

- The writer treats authors fairly.

    The writer provides sufficient details and quotes from other articles.
    Authors would agree with the positions attributed to them.
    Inferences about the authors' motives are plausible.

## Purpose and Audience

- The writer develops an angle of the issue that would interest others.
- The writer establishes an effective persona or ethos for the audience.
- The writer provides enough detail for readers who are unfamiliar with the issue and the readings.

## Organization

- The focus of the response is the writer's view of the issue.
- The essay consistently follows an organizational plan.

    Paragraphs stick to one clear point or subpoint.
    Topic statements and transitions are used appropriately.
    Space is allocated to fully develop important or controversial points.

- The introduction grabs the reader's attention and provides cues to the focus.
- The conclusion readdresses the issue as a whole.

## Expression (Chapter 6)

- The writer mixes popular opinion and academic styles appropriately.
- The writer describes most cases with vivid and specific details.
- The writer uses personal testimony effectively.
- The writer avoids antagonizing readers into not taking the essay seriously.
- The writer documents sources accurately in the text and in Works Cited or References (Chapter 22).
- The essay looks professional; it has been carefully proofread and edited.

"Assessment of Student Papers" assesses Katie's and Lauren's essays according to these criteria.

---

### ASSESSMENT OF STUDENT PAPERS

#### Environment: *Katie's Response Paper*

Katie positions herself as allied with Chivers on the type of problem, but parting on the choice of solution. She comes across as fair to Chivers because she compares their positions in detail, points out areas of agreement and disagreement, and acknowledges differences in their cases. Katie's ethos (Chapter 4) is established by her use of vivid personal testimony, and her acknowledgement of changes in her thinking. Her style is both personal and analytic.

#### Crime: *Lauren's Response Paper*

Lauren's position criticizing the police is a controversial one. She opens with a series of attention-grabbing problem cases from her personal knowledge. However, she comes across as fair because she avoids exaggerating the problem and does not take a hostile tone. To explore the problem and solutions, she enlists Castleman, Brooks, and Kleck as allies, though she gets less bang for her buck by omitting their credentials. The essay is easy to follow and smoothly blends personal and analytic styles.

## Peer Review Guidelines

The following are suggestions for helping a classmate improve the draft of an argument analysis. You may also find them helpful for planning and reviewing your own draft.

1. Suggest ways the writer's position be made stronger, clearer, or more interesting.

2. Identify places where the writer refers to authors you have read.

   - Suggest ways the writer can treat these authors more fairly.
   - From your own reading, suggest other relevant authors. Note their connection to the writer's issue.

3. Look at the writer's use of cases: problem cases or ideal cases.

   - If no concrete, specific cases are spelled out, brainstorm and describe one or two, from the news, your experience, or imagination.
   - If the writer includes a case, suggest ways it can be explained better or more vividly. What other cases should the writer consider?

4. Estimate (by percentage) how much space in the essay is devoted to the issue, problem, and solution spans (Chapter 2). How should this proportion be changed?

5. Help your peer create a more consistent structure. Number the paragraphs. Identify any paragraphs that seem out of place, that repeat points discussed elsewhere, that shift around several different topics.

6. How can your peer improve the introduction or conclusion?

For advice on giving your classmate the most helpful response, review Chapter 21.

# CHAPTER 15

# Having Your Say on the State of the Debate

In this chapter, you will learn how to write a synthesis of positions on an issue of your choice, giving your interpretation of the current state of the debate. The usual audience for a synthesis of this kind are readers of monthly literary or political magazines or scholarly journals. You are ready to begin writing about the state of the debate if you have created one or more synthesis trees following the strategies in Chapter 12.

Your goal in this paper is to contribute something "new" to a public policy debate by providing insights about the big picture. The perspective you offer on the debate will reflect your own position on the issue, but your main purpose is not to argue for your position. Rather, your goal is to persuade others to reconsider the sources of controversy by pinpointing questions on which the authors agree and disagree. Write on the state of the debate in these situations:

- When an important point is being overlooked or misunderstood;
- When you see ways to bring opponents closer together; or
- When a new development might lead the parties to rethink their positions.

In this chapter, you will learn to present your synthesis clearly and fairly to maximize the chances that all sides will take it seriously as a positive contribution.

A clear interpretation of the current state of the debate is valuable because most issues are complex and evolve over a long period of time. Authors with important approaches may not know about each other's ideas because they are separated by time and distance. Authors are often unable to see relationships between the cases they care about most and those of other participants. As a result, participants in a debate often argue at cross-purposes, not realizing how close their positions may be and what the important points of disagreement are.

You can make a valuable contribution by taking a messy array of positions, creating plausible groups of allies, and analyzing why these groups agree and disagree. At the same time, you can argue powerfully for your own perspective by relating these groups, or *approaches,* to your *paradigm* case (Chapter 10), the case that represents the aspect of the problem you care about most.

A state of the debate paper is similar to a response paper. In a response paper, you interpret the position of an author, making reasonable inferences about how he or she would treat the cases that you care most about. The purpose of a response paper is to establish your own position, not simply to provide a running commentary of your reactions to an author's argument. Similarly, a state of the debate paper involves establishing your own position. But instead of responding to individual authors, you respond to approaches within which authors with similar positions are grouped together. A state of the debate paper is not a running commentary on a set of articles. Instead, you draw inferences about how authors would respond to each other's positions as well as to your own.

Before reading further, read one of the sample student essays in "Sample State of Debate Papers." These sample papers will be used throughout this chapter to illustrate the approaches to writing a state of debate paper. Note that they follow the MLA documentation conventions (Chapter 22).

**Environment:** Michael Choate's "Technology in the Wilderness"

**Crime:** Andrew Loomis's "Who is Responsible for Crime?"

*"We'll return in a moment with full coverage of our analysts analyzing other analyst's analysis of this issue."*

**Can there ever be too much analysis?** *Courtesy of* Artizans.

# SAMPLE STATE OF DEBATE PAPERS

## *Environment: Michael Choate*
## *Technology in the Wilderness*

**Audience: High Country News**

1   I am an avid and competitive mountain biker and was initially resistant to Michael Carroll's suggestion of keeping mountain bikers off wilderness trails. As a biker, I considered myself a true conservationist, like every mountain biker I know. Then I began reading that mountain biking speeds up erosion and scares off wildlife, sometimes to places where there might be a lack of food and other resources necessary for survival. I began questioning the effect I was having on the wilderness I so enjoy. It had simply not occurred to me that when I saw a deer cross the trail, I had forced that animal to move to another part of the park due to its fear of me.

2       My behavior is a microcosm of the problem of technology in the wilderness: I want to experience the wilderness, be it on bike, on snowmobile, or on foot. However, my choice of transportation might be disrupting many natural processes.

3       The heated debate on the role of technology in the wilderness has permeated the outdoor adventure and recreation community for years. The debate has three main camps. The first camp, the By-All-Means camp, believes that modern technology should be unregulated in the wilderness. This approach would open up places like our state and national parks to off-road vehicles, snowmobiles, jet skis and countless other recreational vehicles, as well as high-tech and mechanical devices. The second camp, the Segregation camp, agrees that technology increases enjoyment of the wilderness. They believe that mountain bikes and other mechanized vehicles can be used in our state and national parks, but only in strictly designated areas. This camp also believes that limited uses of communication technology, for safety reasons only, are acceptable. The third camp, the Purists, believes that modern technology, such recreational vehicles, communication technology, and devices such as dams or tramways have absolutely no place in the wilderness.

4       The By-All-Means camp seems to have the upper hand in most of these debates, due to the fact that it has the entire Bush administration on its side. However, a good argument can be made in favor of unregulated use of recreational vehicles in our national parks system. In a recent *New York Times* opinion from December 24, 2002, Nicholas D. Kristof states the mission of this group: "[O]ur aim should be not just to preserve nature for its own sake but to give Americans a chance to enjoy the outdoors." He argues that many Americans, especially those with disabilities, would not be able to enjoy the

great outdoors if it was not for the mobility that many recreation vehicles provide. He also argues for snowmobile designs that pollute less and create less noise. However, Kristof does not say what is clean enough or quiet enough. He also does not propose any ways to ensure that people will only use these models or that they will use them in non-destructive ways. Kristof comes off as interested only in his own recreation.

5      There are, however, others in the By-All-Means camp that are easier for the reader to relate to. Jim Hasenauer of the *Denver Post* is an avid mountain biker. He discusses how his riding through the wilderness on his bike "renews his commitment to public-land preservation." I can personally relate to his argument that the beauty that he experiences is enough to encourage anyone to develop and maintain a stronger respect for the outdoors. This respect will in turn recruit many more people to the effort of the conservation of our vanishing American landscape. His views differ from those of Kristof only in the sense that Kristof is supporting a new policy to loosen current regulations on motor vehicles while Hasenauer is against a proposal to start regulating human-powered vehicles. They both believe that technology enhances the outdoor experience and helps the environmental movement.

6      The Segregation camp is like the By-All-Means camp in seeing technology as a way to enhance recreation, but differs in thinking more about how technology can be harmful. Michael Carroll is another *Denver Post* journalist and avid mountain biker who lives in Durango, Colorado, which is considered by many as the mountain biking capital of the world. Most of his biking experiences have been on the road, but recently he has begun spending more time on the trails. His article is a direct response to Jim Hasenauer and was published on the same day. Carroll does enjoy mountain biking but he argues that "there are some places my bike doesn't belong, and ranking first is wilderness." He does not argue that there should be absolutely no mountain biking at all; he just believes that bikers should stay clear of our protected wilderness. I agree with his analysis of the situation. He is right that there are places that are too fragile to risk tearing up with the potentially destructive force of a mountain bike. He also describes seeing the erosion caused by bikers, including the ones who stay on trails and the ones who want to go where no biker has gone before.

7      Another Segregationist is Mark Grisham, a columnist for the *High Country News*. Grisham works as an outfitter in the Grand Canyon. He does see the use of some technology as "selling out." However, he believes that safety precautions must be taken while in the wilderness. Of all the arguments he has had with his colleagues, the one they all agree on is carrying a cell phone. They all believe that the ability to contact emergency services is vital. He describes the case of a woman who had fallen from a cliff and who would have died had it not been for a radio that was used to contact an overhead plane that in turn contacted the air-traffic control center in Los Angeles, that

then contacted the Grand Canyon National Park emergency services. Had it not been for the radio, which is unarguably an advanced piece of technology, this woman would have died a very painful death at the bottom of a 40-foot ravine. Grisham admits that technology can change the wilderness experience but he counters that wilderness is about freedom, including the freedom to choose the kind of experience you want.

8     My position is close to the Segregationists. I believe that the overuse of technology in the wilderness has its adverse effects, but the complete lack of technology makes the wilderness almost too dangerous to enjoy. My main opponents are in the Purist camp who are against any and all technology. Now I am not saying that the Purist side of the argument is completely wrong, because I agree with a lot of the points they bring up. The Purists agree with both of the other camps that experiencing wilderness creates love for the environment. They agree with the Segregationists about the effects that technology can have. However, it seems as though some members of this camp are asking a little too much.

9     One definite purist is Edward Abbey, a naturalist writer whose name is often heard in the same breath as the names of Aldo Leopold and Henry David Thoreau. His magnificent writing style grabs the reader from the very beginning. He pours on so much pathos that it is almost impossible to reject his cause. In his article, "The Damnation of a Canyon," Abbey vividly describes how the building of the Glen Canyon Dam transformed a stretch of beautiful river into what his opponents call "our nation's newest, biggest and most impressive 'recreational facility.'" Abbey points out that it is hard for anyone to learn to love cement. His concern lies solely with bringing back the aesthetic beauty of what Glen Canyon once was. He does not care much about the amount of cheap and environmentally friendly energy the dam provides, not to mention the large tourist revenue the reservoir produces yearly. He even calls himself a "butterfly chaser, goo-gly-eyed bleeding heart and wild conservative." I believe that Abbey's heart is in the right place. However, his argument is one-sided and aimed only at an audience that chooses the same way of experiencing the wilderness as he does. So he does not address Hasenauer's safety point or his freedom point or Kristof's mobility point.

10     Another outdoor enthusiast in the Purist camp is a writer named Christina Nealson. Her book *Living on the Spine* is a journal of her life as she spent five years in the Sangre de Cristo Mountains in Colorado. Nealson is the main opponent to cell phones and GPS devices. In fact, Grisham wrote his article to respond to her article, "In Wilderness, Don't Phone Home," in the *High Country News*. Nealson argues that any form of modern technology (except guns, whistles, and other camping necessities) tames the wild. It turns wilderness into a place where all the mystique and danger have vanished. Nealson asserts that "I go to the wilderness to leave linear time behind." She chastises those who bring along their electronic helpers by

saying, "I also leave behind the world of instant access, where phones, e-mail, cars and airplanes provide fast contact with anyone in the world." She believes that a step into the wilderness is supposed to be a step into the unexpected. Without that danger, there would be no wilderness. Her position is better than Abbey's because she does care about people's experiences and not just aesthetics.

11　　My question to her is the same as to Abbey: What about those of us who are not outdoor aficionados such as yourself? What about those of us who choose to experience the excitement of the wilderness without the risk of death or severe injury? Nealson is thinking only of those like herself who are actually able to navigate on their own and not those of us who are less experienced, but still equally enthusiastic about the wilderness. Both Abbey and Nealson think that their own ways of experiencing wilderness are the only acceptable ways.

12　　For some Purists, the greatest concern above aesthetics and danger is the adverse effect technology will have on the environment. This is an issue that Jim DiPeso of the *San Francisco Chronicle* takes head on. In his article, "New Rule of the Road," DiPeso laments the fact that "the Bush administration announced a new administrative rule that any 19th century burro trail or wagon track could be routinely approved as a highway right-of-way on public lands." He argues that the initiative is very shortsighted. Roads can be used for recreation and for business purposes. DiPeso uses pathos as he lists the adverse effects: "Roads mangle watersheds, erode soil, wreck fisheries, and damage streams." Out of all the people staking claim to the Purist camp, Jim DiPeso makes the most logical and least insulting argument for the complete absence of recreational vehicles and other modern technology throughout the wilderness.

13　　Dave Shiflett, a columnist for the *National Review*, takes the same stance as Jim DiPeso in stating that motorized recreational vehicles have no place in the wilderness. He is unhappy because of the constant noise and ruckus that these combustion engines create. In his article, "Parks and Wreck," Shiflett spends most of his time chastising those who use recreational vehicles and using his personal annoyance as evidence of their effect, calling the people using the vehicles "subspecies" and "circle jerks." Dave Shiflett makes a passionate cry for a ban of motorized recreational vehicles from the wilderness. I agree that, while in the wilderness, I want to have my peace and quiet. However, Shiflett's argumentative style is quite flawed. He ends up sounding even more selfish than Kristof. He goes even further than Abbey and Nealson in insulting people who don't choose his form of experience. If his goal is to get people to quit using these vehicles then he cannot go around insulting them. I do not believe many of these "circle jerks" are going to change their "evil" ways through the persuasion of Mr. Shiflett.

14    I have never been known as a middle-of-the-road guy, but on the issue of technology in the wilderness, I am going to camp with the Segregationists who believe that technology deserves a limited role in the wilderness. Hasenauer and Grisham have the right idea when they argue that these devices, if used responsibly, can enhance and protect one's outdoor experience. After reading their articles there are two things that I will now do: (1) I will not take my mountain bike into fragile parts of the wilderness where it can cause irreversible damage, and (2) I will always carry a cellular phone with me while in the wilderness, because there is no telling when I will take a 40-foot fall into a ravine and have no other way to signal for help. The wilderness is something that everyone should be able to enjoy, but it is something that everyone should respect and strive to enjoy responsibly and safely.

### Works Cited

Abbey, Edward. "The Damnation of a Canyon." *Beyond the Wall*. New York: Henry Holt and Company, 1984. 95–105.

Carroll, Michael. "Do Mountain Bikes Belong in Wilderness? No: We Can Prevent Trail Degradation." *Denver Post* 12 Jan. 2003: E4.

DiPeso, Jim. "New Rule of the Road." *San Francisco Chronicle* 10 Jan. 2003: A27.

Grisham, Mark. Letter. *High Country News* Midwest ed. 28 Sept. 1998: p. NA.

Hasenauer, Jim. "Do Mountain Bikes Belong in Wilderness? Yes: Cyclists Respect Environment." *Denver Post* 12 Jan. 2003: E4.

Kristof, Nicholas D. "In Praise of Snowmobiles." *New York Times* 24 Dec. 2002: A23.

Nealson, Christina. "In Wilderness, Don't Phone Home." *High Country News* 17 Aug. 1998: p. NA.

Shiflett, Dave. "Parks and Wreck: Against Jet Skiers, Snowmobilers, and Other Louts." *National Review* 19 March 2001: p. NA.

### *Crime: Andrew Loomis*
### *Who Is Responsible for Crime?*

**Audience: The Atlantic Monthly**

1    Journalist Jim Myers has a unique perspective on the crime issue. The same poor, crime-infested area in Washington, D.C. that Myers writes about is also the neighborhood he calls home. In Myers's neighborhood, crime and violence have become so overwhelming that merely going outside can be life-

threatening. This was the case when Myers tried to organize a neighborhood watch group. Within a short time, the patrol abruptly disbanded after gunfire rang out. The group had no power to prevent the death of twenty-one year-old Michael McIntyre. In Myers's account, McIntyre's fate is becoming normal for residents (especially young males) of poor, inner-city neighborhoods. By allowing a portion of the population to live surrounded by violence and apathy, we are creating a generation of criminals that poses a threat to us all. There must be a way to create a better environment for future generations growing up in these areas.

2     Myers himself describes the situation without ever pointing out a specific reason for the crime or advocating a solution. Myers is a white man married to a black woman who lives in PSA 109, a mostly-black, poor neighborhood in Washington, D.C. His article, "Notes on the Murder of Thirty of My Neighbors," is especially poignant because it is about his friends and their children. While describing case after case of unsolved deaths, Myers hints at many problems that lead to crime: police ineffectiveness, poor parenting, violent influences in the media, alienation. However, the most compelling argument that Myers makes is for the value of his neighbors' lives as human beings, not just the victims but also the criminals themselves. Myers depicts a world in which crime and violence are the only ways to feel accepted and important. Perhaps Myers knows that there is no one solution to the problem but a series of societal and governmental issues that need to be addressed.

3     For politicians and legislators, as well as community activists and residents, to understand how to proceed, it is important to examine solutions that have already been tried and ones that have been suggested. For this purpose, I have analyzed authors who are concerned with solving similar societal problems. The authors can be divided into two major schools of thought. The first group, the Individualists, focuses on solutions that put the responsibility on individuals. The second group, the Institutionalists, puts the responsibility on the administering body (the U.S. government, school boards, etc.). Within these schools of thought, authors differ in the types of crime they address and whether they emphasize prevention or punishment. Exploring the positions of these authors is useful for gaining insight into the issue of crime itself and for my goal of finding a solution to crimes in neighborhoods like Jim Myers's.

4     The Individualists all agree that a solution to crime requires the individual to change, but they differ in targeting punishment or prevention. This group includes Michael Castleman and Tracey Meares and Dan Kahan.

5     Writer Michael Castleman is not a crime expert; he has mostly published books on health. Instead, he represents the common man's take on the issue. Castleman targets neighborhood crime and focuses on prevention, advocating citizen involvement in their own neighborhoods. He arrives at this conclusion after dismissing many possible causes and set-

tling on opportunity as the factor most possible to change. He actually discusses implementation of a neighborhood awareness program as his main solution. But in a situation like Jim Myers's, the same type of prevention has proven futile. Maybe neighbors cannot be responsible until after more drastic measures have been taken.

6    Two experts in this group are Tracy Meares, a law professor at the University of Chicago, and Dan Kahan, a law professor at Yale. Unlike Castleman, they attempt to isolate the cause of crime in violent, inner-city neighborhoods. But they agree with Castleman on neighborhood action. The group they argue against is the ACLU that has taken actions to disband crime prevention measures such as random building searches, curfews, and anti-loitering ordinances. The ACLU felt that the residents' civil rights were being compromised, even though it was the residents themselves who lobbied for these ordinances. In their article, "When Rights Are Wrong: Chicago's Paradox of Unwanted Rights," Meares and Kahan describe how society has changed since the 1960s, while the civil rights laws have stayed the same. Their stance on this issue shows that they advocate programs that are aimed at preventing crime and believe that they are necessary in neighborhoods like Jim Myers's PSA 109.

7    Meares and Kahan hold the administration (the government) responsible for the problem, but they emphasize the individual's importance in solving it. They believe the government should support the individual residents' requests for increased protection, even at the expense of civil rights. I believe that Meares and Kahan have hit on something very important. I agree that the residents' value hierarchy should be respected because extreme situations (like PSA 109) warrant extreme solutions. However, before this approach could be applied to PSA 109, the relations between the police and residents would have to improve drastically.

8    The second faction of authors is the Institutionalists who place the responsibility for crime on those who are in charge, the administrations and governments. This faction is represented by Brian Dumaine, the editorial director of *Fortune Small Business* and John J. DiIulio, a professor of politics, religion, and civil society at the University of Pennsylvania.

9    In "Beating Bolder Corporate Crooks," Brian Dumaine writes about a different aspect of the crime debate: white-collar corporate crime, but his views are applicable to crime as a whole. Dumaine holds the administration responsible, in this case executives and corporate security personnel. He discusses several steps to prevent hiring crooks, detect them if they are hired, and punish them when they are caught. Executives, however, already exercise more power over their employees than the government does over citizens. In Myers's neighborhood, the problem is that the police don't use any power at all to solve most of the crimes.

10    John J. DiIulio has written two articles on crime. In one, "Unlock 'Em Up: A Lock 'Em Up Hard-Liner Makes the Case for Probation," he discusses

the current state of the parole system and its effectiveness. After considering the lack of funding and the recidivism rates, DiIulio concludes that parole must either be disbanded or radically changed. He places the responsibility on the criminal justice system in parole boards, and argues that they must reform, letting more nonviolent criminals go with better supervision. In focusing on prisons, DiIulio emphasizes punishment, but he emphasizes it as a means of prevention. The people he targets as eligible for parole is broad so it may include residents of inner-city neighborhoods. But I believe that he is not addressing the root of the problem. Society should concentrate on preventing crime at a much earlier stage.

11    In his second article, "Broken Bottles: Alcohol, Disorder and Crime," DiIulio focuses more directly on the prevention aspect of crime by showing the relationship of alcohol to crime. Here he also focuses on the same types of inner-city neighborhoods and individuals that Myers discusses. DiIulio argues that certain individuals, who are already prone to commit crimes, are even more likely to do so under the influence of alcohol. DiIulio thus directly relates violence to alcohol and to the presence of establishments that sell alcohol. This is particularly relevant because often in neighborhoods like Myers's PSA 109, there is an abundance of both alcohol advertisements and liquor stores. DiIulio admits the importance of the community and the individual in creating an environment that does not condone alcoholism, but he concludes that it is the government's responsibility to fix the problem. He suggests that increased bans on alcohol advertisements and improved zoning and property laws are necessary to lessen the influence of alcohol in inner cities. DiIulio is targeting a better cause and solution in this article than in his other, but solutions could still work at a deeper level. If there were programs that improved the quality of life for inner-city youths and improved the prospect of their future, they would be able to resist alcohol on their own terms.

12    The violence that occurs in inner-city neighborhoods is undeniable and it is steadily getting worse. Reviewing the positions described here shows that not one particular cause or solution sticks out as the right one. Instead it is clear that a series of circumstances leads to this situation. DiIulio is correct in his correlation of violence with alcohol, Castleman's solution of increased neighborhood involvement would be beneficial, and Meares and Kahan are right that residents need more control to be involved. But all of these are too specific. The general underlying cause of the violence in these areas is hopelessness and apathy. Only Myers gets at the meat of the issue. These poor violent neighborhoods are spawning generations of hopeless, and in their own minds, worthless youth. To subvert alcoholism, school violence, workplace crime, and societal rejection, these youths need to know their importance and their value to society. Only after we have a new attitude can we foresee changing violence and crime.

## Works Cited

Castleman, Michael. "Opportunity Knocks." *Mother Jones* 20 (1995): 26 + . Available online. *Mother Jones Interactive.* www.motherjones.com/ commentary/columns/1995/05/castleman.html (1 Apr. 2002).

DiIulio, John J., Jr. "Broken Bottles: Alcohol, Disorder and Crime." *The Brookings Review* 14.2 (1996): 14 + . Available online. Gale Group, Expanded ASAP.

DiIulio, John J., Jr. "Unlock 'Em Up: A Lock-'Em-Up Hard-Liner Makes the Case for Probation." *Slate* 20 Dec. 1996. slate.msn.com/?id = 2409. April 1, 2002.

Dumaine, Brian. "Beating Bolder Corporate Crooks." *Fortune* 117.9 (1988): 193 + . Available online. Gale Group, Expanded ASAP.

Meares, Tracey L. and Dan M. Kahan. "When Rights are Wrong: Chicago's Paradox of Unwanted Rights." *Boston Review* 24.2 (April/May 1999) Available online. bostonreview.mit.edu/br24.2/meares.html (1 Apr. 2002).

Myers, Jim. "Notes on the Murder of Thirty of My Neighbors." *The Atlantic Monthly* 285 (2000): 72–86. Available online. www.theatlantic.com/issues/2000/03/myers.htm (1 Apr. 2002).

## Planning Purpose and Audience

Your state of the debate paper will be of value to two audiences: people who are new to the issue and people who have been too deeply involved in the debate to see the big picture. You can reach both audiences by aiming at the readers of a monthly literary or political magazine. Most readers are interested in policy issues but not deeply invested in any particular one. Among these readers, however, are activists, public officials, and pundits (Chapter 7).

To gauge how much to say to these readers, assume that they know much less than you do about the issue; no one will have read everything you have been reading and no one will have been thinking about it as much as you have. In order to inform these readers, make good use of overviews and summaries.

"Reasoning about Thesis and Audience" illustrates how Michael and Andrew reasoned about their choices.

### REASONING ABOUT THESIS AND AUDIENCE

#### Environment

Michael considered two audience options, *High Country News* and the *Denver Post.* Both had published arguments about technology in the wilderness. He chose *High Country News* because it focuses specifically on environment issues. To come across as credible to this audience, Michael drew on his own experiences as an active mountain biker who was experiencing a clash of values between enjoyment and preservation. It was important to Michael to come across as committed to both values, not as someone unable to make up his mind.

### Crime

Andrew's interest in inner-city neighborhoods had been sparked by reading a long and compelling article by Jim Myers, "Notes on the Murder of Thirty of My Neighbors." He was dissatisfied, however. Myers created a sense of urgency without exploring solutions. For this reason, Andrew aims his paper at the same audience, *The Atlantic Monthly*, and attempts to pick up where Myers left off. Throughout the synthesis, Andrew uses the case of Myers's neighborhood to assess alternative approaches. Without personal experience related to the issue, Andrew attempts to come across as knowledgeable, concerned, and fair.

## Planning Your Line of Argument

The major sections of a state of debate paper are related to the issue, problem, and solution spans (Chapter 2) of any public policy argument. The opening span should grab your readers' attention and establish the urgency of the issue that you will synthesize. For a synthesis to be worth reading (or writing), you must persuade your readers that the issue is important and controversial enough to warrant sorting out all the positions.

The main span of your paper will be based on a synthesis tree that you create following the strategies in Chapter 12. The tree will set out two or three main top-level approaches that represent different answers to a question. In addition to describing each approach, you will give your interpretation of why the authors within it differ.

In the final span, you will evaluate the strengths and weaknesses of these approaches from your own perspective. You might find that one approach is superior overall, that all the authors have missed a key aspect of the issue, or that opponents have more in common than they realize.

### Choosing a Paradigm Case

An effective way to integrate your perspective into your synthesis is with a paradigm case (Chapter 10). A paradigm case is one that, for you, sums up or epitomizes the problem and why it must be addressed. Describing the case vividly in your introduction is a good way to grab readers' attention. Referring to the case throughout the paper is a good way to establish a line of argument that will add up to the evaluation in your conclusion.

Your choice of paradigm case will affect many aspects of your paper, including what authors you choose to include and how you group them. Your goal should be to represent as many plausible approaches toward handling your case as you can.

**Different fields often take different approaches.** © Harley Schwadron.

## Describing Approaches

An approach is a belief, goal, or method that a large group of authors adopts for handling similar problems. For example, one approach to environmental issues is to leave wild areas entirely untouched; another is to weigh possible damage against benefits from use. One approach to the war on drugs is to prevent drugs from being produced or sold; another is to prevent people from using them. In a synthesis tree, the major approaches are represented as the top-most branches.

Using the techniques in Chapter 12, draw a tree of approaches centered on your paradigm case. Create branches representing approaches that take different views on the major spans, questions of seeing the issue, defining the problem, choosing solutions. Your tree will probably change as you work on your paper.

## Describing Positions within an Approach

Under each main branch in your tree, create smaller branch-points to represent groups that disagree on an important point, as in the following examples:

- In Figure 12.1A–C, environmental authors grouped under the managerial approach all seek to use resources responsibly. Within the managerial approach, however, are those who differ about what is preventing responsible use: a high-tech group and an activist group.
- Castleman distinguishes between the liberal and conservative approaches to crime. The conservatives attribute crime to lax enforcement and light punishment. Within the conservative approach, however, are those who want punishment to be more severe and the "thoughtful conservatives" who want it to be swifter and more certain.

To create your tree, you will probably work back and forth between the approaches at the top of the tree and the individual authors at the bottom. In writing your paper, however, start at the top so that your insights extend beyond the exact authors you have chosen. That is, describe an approach and then locate authors within it, rather than describing authors and then joining them up into a position. In this way, it is easier to treat the authors as representatives of an approach or as cases within a category, not as the only people in the world who feel that way.

"Paradigm Case and Synthesis Tree" describes the choices that Michael and Andrew made.

## PARADIGM CASE AND SYNTHESIS TREE

### Environment

Michael's paradigm case concerned the use of mountain bikes in the wilderness: Technology enhances our enjoyment of nature, but it can also be harmful to nature. The following depicts part of the tree:

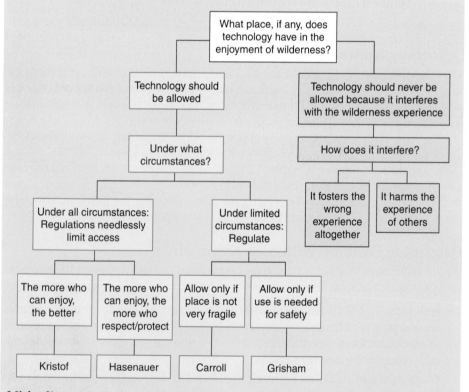

**Michael's tree**

The approach in the left branch considers situations when technology is allowable; the right branch focuses on the harms of allowing technology.

## Crime

Andrew's paradigm case concerned crime and violence in inner-city neighborhoods. He defined approaches to the issue based on whether individuals or institutions were seen as the primary agents who should implement solutions to the problem. The following depicts part of the tree:

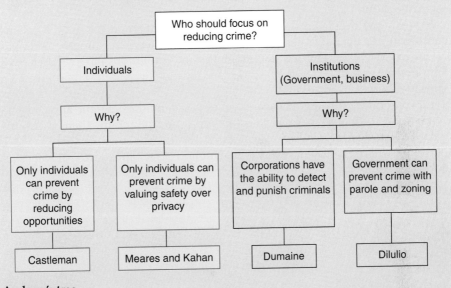

**Andrew's tree**

The approach in the left branch emphasizes responsibility of individuals; in the right branch, institutions.

# Allocating Space and Planning the Arrangement

You will decide the order in which to introduce the approaches and the order of individual positions within each approach. Your decisions should be based on leading readers clearly through the debate so that they end up understanding the position you prefer and why. Some common arrangements are **chronological, merit-based,** and **controversy-last.**

A chronological arrangement is effective when many approaches have been tried over time, each leading to new, unsettled issues. For example, in the environment debate, a chronological sequence would start with early environmental successes, then Easterbrook's critique of enviros in the 1990s, followed by setbacks occurring more recently. Similarly, in the crime debate, Brooks's support for the earlier views of civil rights would come before Meares and Kahan's new conception of rights.

A merit-based arrangement is one that "saves the best for last." A simple merit-based sequence puts approaches in a worst-bad-good-best order. This order is based on your own preferences and those of your readers. That is, a sequence from the far political left to center to the right is appropriate if you see yourself and your readers as conservative. If you see yourself as a moderate, you can use another merit-based order, means-extremes, with the far-left first, the far-right second, and the middle ground last.

If you are writing to an audience that does not share many of your views, then a controversy-last arrangement can be effective. Begin with approaches that your readers prefer most, point out their strengths and limitations fairly, and end with an approach that you believe is best that your readers would have been unwilling to consider at first.

As you build your tree, you may end up with an idiosyncratic approach that doesn't seem to fit anywhere. If it seems important to include, then discuss this approach first, clearly pointing out its unusual nature. Then move on to one of the other sequences. "Choosing an Arrangement and Style" illustrates Michael's and Andrew's decisions.

## CHOOSING AN ARRANGEMENT AND STYLE

### Environment

In his preliminary analysis of technology in the wilderness, Michael had identified three camps. The By-All-Means and Segregationist groups were closest together in agreeing on some uses for technology. In his paper, he discussed these positions first and ended with his opponents, the Purists. In some ways, this order creates an anticlimax, ending on a rejection. Other effective arrangements are also possible. He might have used instead a means-extremes arrangement, describing By-All-Means first and the Purists second and ending with his allies, the Segregationists. Or he might have chosen an arrangement of increasing merit: Purists, By-All-Means, Segregationists.

### Crime

Andrew begins with the position that he thinks has the most merit (Myers) because he gets at the heart of the problem, then moves to discuss a series of authors, all of whom have less merit because, according to Andrew, they do not get at the root cause of the problem. He concludes by identifying a need to work on changing what he sees as the root cause. His arrangement would be stronger if the middle approaches clearly increased in merit, creating a sequence of "better but still not quite good enough" rather than "bad to good."

# Adopting an Analytic Style

The style of a state of the debate paper can be that of an academic article or a personal opinion essay, depending on the audience you address. Your rhetorical style will be analytic as you compare approaches and authors. It will be personal as you establish the cases you care about and use them to judge approaches. This section will offer a variety of ways to talk about distinctions among approaches.

In order to talk about a set of approaches you need to name them. To come up with descriptive names, use the techniques in Chapter 5. Easterbrook, for example, invented these names for environmental activists: "enviros," "unviros," and "eco-realists." Kleck referred to these groups: "news media," "analysts," "journalists and other writers of every ideological stripe," "pro-gun people," "pro-control people," and "those who propose preventive measures."

As you develop your tree, think of words or phrases that are short, memorable, and catchy. Choose a phrase that can be used both as a noun to name the groups ("the ecorealists") and as an adjective to describe the approach ("the ecorealist approach"). Choose names that echo each other in sound and meaning, such as "Puritans," "Libertarians," and "Communitarians."

To create coherent paragraphs about approaches and authors, use these techniques:

- **Attributing views to groups.** Use group names in sentence subject position with a verb of attribution: "The Crime Is Here to Stay camp assumes that kids will always commit crimes." Use group names before the main clause: "According to enviros . . . "; "For hard-core enviros, this is impossible."

- **Associating groups within an approach.** "Purists and recreationists share a concern for . . . "; "Both would reject . . . ."

- **Distinguishing between approaches.** "Safety-firsters believe . . . but most libertarians believe . . . ."

- **Distinguishing among allies.** Set up a contrast: "Almost all enviros believe that . . . . Yet Chivers thinks . . . "; "Putting recreation above preservation is typical for conservatives, except for Shiflett, who argues that . . . ." State a disagreement: "Chivers and Laurence disagree when it comes to . . . ."

- **Evaluating approaches.** Use adjectives and adverbs to characterize the position: "A stronger position would be . . . "; "Castleman takes a less extreme position."

- **Describing hypothetical responses.** Use indefinite pronouns: "One could respond that . . . "; "Everyone understands that . . . "; "No one denies that . . . ."

# Criteria for a Good State of Debate Paper

Keep the following set of criteria in mind as you write and review your draft. Picture yourself as "the writer," and the author you are responding to as "the author." Picture a member of your audience as "the reader."

## Reasoning and Content

- The writer motivates the reader to learn about the issue. The writer presents realistic and significant cases or a problem statement.
- The writer presents the main approaches clearly and fairly.
- The writer distinguishes among positions clearly at each level of branching.
- The writer treats all authors' positions fairly. The inferences the writer draws about what an author would say are plausible and well supported.
- The writer takes a clear position, evaluating the approaches effectively from his or her own perspective.

## Purpose and Audience

- The writer explains the debate for readers who have not read the same texts.
- The writer offers helpful insights for readers involved in the debate.

## Organization

- The organization is based around groups of authors; it is not a series of unrelated summaries.
- The sequence of groupings is effective, both for authors within a group and for groups within a branch.
- The paragraphs and sections each develop one clear topic. Use of overviews and transitions make the paper easy to follow.
- The introduction and conclusion are appropriate in tone and strategy.

## Expression

- The writer maintains a strong voice throughout the paper, keeping quotes short, using verbs of attribution, and paraphrasing effectively.
- The writer comes across as critical but fair.
- Sources are documented appropriately, both in the text and in Works Cited or References.
- The paper looks professional; it has been carefully proofread and edited.

"Assessment of Student Papers" evaluates Michael's and Andrew's papers by these standards.

## ASSESSMENT OF STUDENT PAPERS

### Environment

Michael's perspective on the debate comes across clearly throughout the paper. He adopts a personal style that immediately establishes his ethos as an outdoors enthusiast and allows him to evaluate approaches and authors along the way. He uses overviews and transitions skillfully to move along his line of argument.

He clearly distinguishes among major groupings and among authors' positions with thorough comparisons and consistent challenges. He provides sufficient summary that readers gain a good sense of each author's argument.

In the overall sequencing, Michael leaves the Purists, his strongest opponents, for last. He created this sequence because he saw himself in the middle. However, this placement creates an anticlimax because it comes after he identifies himself as a Segregationist.

### Crime

Andrew's personal perspective comes across most clearly in the vivid language he uses to describe the problem of inner-city crime. Because he lacks direct standing on this issue, Andrew adopts a somewhat formal and distant style. His rationale for writing follows directly from his description of Myers's argument as lacking in solutions.

Andrew sets up a clear set of approaches for addressing inner-city crime that he consistently relates back to the case of inner-city crime. Authors within an approach are identified clearly and treated fairly. He provides sufficient summary that readers gain a good sense of each author's argument. However, the authors within an approach should be compared to each other more thoroughly.

Andrew sees strengths in both the Individualist and Governmental approaches, but ends up raising apathy as a factor that they both neglect. This argument could be strengthened by inferring how each author would treat apathy and alienation along the way. By raising apathy as a stumbling block only at the end, Andrew's conclusion seems less solution-oriented than he intended.

# Peer Review Guidelines

The following are suggestions for helping a classmate improve the draft of an argument analysis. You may also find them helpful for planning and reviewing your own draft.

1. Consider the choice of authors and how they are described. How relevant are the authors to each other on the topic? Which authors, if any, would you replace? Which would you use instead?

2. Consider the writer's groupings of authors. Sketch a tree that the writer seems to have had in mind. How can the writer improve the description of major points of disagreement between opposing groups? How can the writer distinguish more clearly among the positions of allies within a group? Which aspects of a policy argument should the writer consider more closely: Problem/solution? Stases (existence, definition, value, claim, action)?

3. Consider how the writer refers to other authors. How fully are they identified by name and credentials? How can the writer represent each author more fairly and accurately?

4. Consider the writer's perspective and insights. What cases does the writer raise in discussing the authors' approaches? If no cases are discussed, brainstorm and describe some, from the news, your experience, or imagination. If cases are used, how can the descriptions be made clearer or more vivid?

5. Suggest ways for the writer to make the organization of the paper more effective and easier to follow. How can the writer improve the use of group names? The sequence of authors within groupings? The sequence of groupings?

For advice on giving your classmate the most helpful response, review Chapter 21.

# CHAPTER 16

# Having Your Say on the Problem

In this chapter, you will learn to write a problem-based paper on an issue of your choice to an appropriate audience. You are ready to begin writing a problem-based paper if you have gathered material about the problem from a variety of sources (Chapter 7 and Chapter 8) and explored your views on the problem (Chapter 10).

Your goal in this paper is to make your own contribution to a public policy debate. You can contribute something "new" to a public policy debate by establishing that a problem exists, by defining it in a new way, by raising or lowering its significance, or by identifying new causes. You should choose to make a problem-based contribution in any of these situations:

- When you really want to talk about the problem;
- When it seems important to change your readers' minds about the problem itself; or
- When you have ideas for the problem but lack a clear idea of what to do to solve it.

In this chapter, you will learn to match your message to an appropriate audience so that you have the highest chance of changing your readers' minds. See Chapter 20 for more on finding new ideas that readers will take seriously.

When you write a problem-based paper, most of your space will be devoted to the issue and problem spans (Chapter 2). While your solution span will be brief, it is important to point to what needs to happen next.

In some cases, the problem is so little understood that it is premature to propose specific solutions. Debate over the nature of the problem in these cases can be very helpful. If you have concluded that the community does not understand the problem, you try your best to convince readers to see it your way so that they do

*"I'd rather be a huge part of the problem than a tiny part of the solution."*

**Is your position problem- or solution-based?** © The New Yorker Collection 2002 Leo
Cullum from cartoonbank.com. All Rights Reserved.

not pursue solutions that won't work. For example, Kleck argues that people concerned about school violence were focusing on the wrong kinds of crime: extraordinary rather than ordinary; he does not offer specific solutions to ordinary crimes. Gómez-Pompa and Kaus argue that environmentalists' attitudes toward traditional agriculture are wrong, but they do not offer specific solutions for how to change the environmental agenda. The purpose of these arguments is to encourage other authors to take the next step toward finding possible solutions.

In other cases, the solution will seem obvious if people see the problem the way you do. For example, if pro-life advocates persuade the public that abortion is murder, the solution is obvious: We already have a system for prosecuting and punishing murderers. If environmental advocates are convinced that dredging and trawling are equivalent to clear-cutting a forest, they will already know how to protest.

Before reading further, read one of the student sample essays in "Sample Problem-Based Papers":

- **Environment:** Eileen Dudzik's "The Rainforest is in Houston's Backyard"
- **Crime:** Anna McGaha's "Prostitution is a Feminist Cause"

These sample papers will be used throughout this chapter to illustrate the approaches to writing a problem-based paper. Note that they follow the MLA documentation conventions (Chapter 22).

---

## SAMPLE PROBLEM-BASED PAPERS

### Environment: Eileen Dudzik
### The Rainforest is in Houston's Backyard

**Audience: Houston Chronicle**

1   Everyone knows about the controversy over the future of the Amazon rainforest. Most Americans think of the loss of rainforest in terms of "they": How could "they" allow such destruction? What most Houstonians do not realize is that for us the term to use is not "they," it's "we." Believe it or not, the fate of the Amazon rainforest is right in our own backyard.

2   At some level, anyone at all can be seen as involved in the issue. The entire international community is involved because the loss of rainforest could have severe consequences for global climate change and the availability of medications. But Houstonians are involved at a much deeper level than this because our city is home to companies such as the El Paso Corporation, North America's leading provider for natural gas services. El Paso is the majority shareholder of the two largest generating plants that would benefit from pipelines built in the Urucu and Jurua gas fields in the Brazilian Amazon. (El Paso Corporation) By applying the pressure of public opinion on American companies such as El Paso, Houstonians can have a significant effect on the Brazilian rainforest.

3   The Urucu-Pôrto Velho and Coari-Manaus gas pipelines are part of Brazil's $45 billion dollar project, Avança Brasil. Avança Brasil is a collection of economic development projects proposed by the Brazilian government and approved four years ago by Brazil's National Congress. Its goals are developing Brazil's agriculture, mining, and timber industries. It calls for building roads, repaving roads, redirecting waterways, and deforesting lands needed for these industries. The amount of damage that this project would cause was calculated by William Laurance, a research scientist for the Smithsonian Tropical Research Institute. Laurance and colleagues fed in data to create computer-generated maps of the effect on the rainforest by the year 2020 if Avança Brasil is fully or partially implemented. These maps show that there will be extensive fragmentation in the Brazilian Amazon. The forest becomes fragmented when any road, whether a highway or a pipeline, is built.

4   According to Laurence, the fragmentation is the most dangerous aspect of the project. A rainforest depends on a canopy of the top

branches and leaves of its ancient trees. Above the canopy, climate stays relatively hot all year round because the Amazon is located at the equator. However, below the canopy the temperature is much cooler and the canopy traps moisture for the living forest below. The Amazon receives almost half of all the precipitation that falls on land and this, along with the canopy, allows for the lush environment in the rainforest (Rainforest Action Network). By simply cutting down one tree and creating a hole in that canopy, you open up the forest to the heat above. One small hole can cause acres of forest damage, which builds on itself by killing plants and trees at their roots below when moisture is zapped, and the environment beneath the canopy dries up. This is a very unforgiving process simply because replanting trees does not recreate the canopy needed for plants to survive in the immense heat. Therefore, it is actually more harmful to cut through the rainforest and destroy large areas of intact land than it is to cut trees from the outskirts of the rainforest.

5      This is exactly why the Urucu-Pôrto Velho and Coari-Manaus Gas Pipelines are the most controversial aspect of Avança Brasil. The plan is for two pipelines to be built through the Urucu and Jurua gas fields. The first gas pipeline will extend from the Urucu gas fields to the major Amazon city of Pôrto Velho at the cost of $175 US million. The building of the Urucu-Coari is not active because it violates national environmental law. The second pipeline will stretch from the town of Coari to the largest Amazon city of Manaus at an estimated cost of $275 US million. The Coari-Manaus pipeline began when Avança Brasil was first implemented but then stopped in the summer of 2001 when the program went under environmental review, according to the Amazon Financial Information Service and Friends of the Earth ("Urucu," also see "Lack"). So far, political pressure in opposition to the project has stalled the two pipelines, however, the deadline is rapidly approaching. In August of this year the Brazilian National Congress will be presented with the results of latest environmental study that could allow the projects to start back up (Friends of the Earth, "Environmental").

6      Most of the major environmentalist groups that oppose Avança Brasil are already planning the legal action in case the National Congress passes Avança Brasil a second time. The international federation of national environmental organizations, Friends of the Earth, is planning lawsuits against the major stakeholders that will be profiting from the program, which are mainly Brazilian companies like Petrobras. This approach could be counterproductive because it ignores the goals and methods of the Brazilian government. Lately, Brazil has taken a very strong position on dealing with their problems on their own, even on issues with international consequences such as the Amazon. In fact, Brazil has even turned down programs that would grant them millions

of dollars in exchange for not developing any further into specific regions of the Amazon, most notably, areas like Urucu and Jurua. After William Laurance's article appeared in *Science*, the Minister of Planning José Silveira responded on behalf of the Brazilian government. He argued that Brazil's current, more democratic government is committed to keeping the damage to the environment as minimal as possible in relation to the real needs of the poor populations of this region. Brazil is running its own show as a democratic capitalist society.

7    So what can people do who want more protection for the rainforest than Brazil? They can look to their own backyards. As a democratic capitalist society, Brazil allows in international companies. One such company is the El Paso Corporation. Although the pipelines will be built by Brazilian companies, Petrobras and Electronorte, these companies are in agreement with the Houston-based company whose headquarters can be seen in the heart of downtown off Louisiana Street, the El Paso Corporation. According to its Website, El Paso controls over seventy-six percent of the electricity generated in the Brazilian state of Amazônia and is about to become the leading energy provider for the state of Rondônia. These are the two states that the pipelines will cut through. El Paso is the majority shareholder of Termonorte I and Termonorte II, the two largest generating plants in the Amazon (Friends of the Earth, "Urucu"). The gas pipelines of the Urucu-Pôrto Velho and Coari-Manaus projects will be directed to the El Paso Corporation's generator plants, which include the Termonorte plants. Therefore, El Paso is just as much as a key player in the destruction created by Avança Brasil as the companies actually cutting the forest to build the pipeline.

8    Here is where Houstonians can make a difference. By applying pressure to the company in our own backyard, the El Paso Corporation, Houstonians can change the fate of the Amazon. If we can persuade El Paso to disassociate from the Avança Brasil program and Petrobras, then it would be difficult or pointless for Petrobras to build a pipeline. Petrobras would not have a generator plant for the pipelines to connect to and therefore would not be able to process and distribute the energy taken from the gas fields. At this time there is only a general agreement between the two companies, but no binding legal document. Without El Paso's plant, Brazil would have to find the funding to build another plant, and with all the revenue and billions of dollars already going into the overall aspect of Avança Brasil, the government would most likely just drop the Urucu-Pôrto Velho and Coari-Manaus pipeline projects instead of putting in the time, effort and most importantly money, into looking for additional funding. Houstonians need to let El Paso know that we do not support its partnership with Petrobras or its placement of the Urucu-Pôrto Velho and Coari-Manaus pipelines.

9    The vitality of our city depends on the world around us. We cannot ignore the effects of American companies in other nations. As in the case of the Brazil, their nation becomes our backyard; destruction of one part affects the whole. The people of Houston have a chance to preserve the most valuable region of land in the world and all we have to do is appeal to a company right here in our own town.

### *Works Cited*

Amazon Financial Information Service. "Red List Risk Profile: Urucu-Pôrto Velho & Coari-Manaus Gas Pipelines. Amazônia and Rondônia." *Redlisted.com*. 25 Jan. 2001. redlisted.com/brazil_urucu.html (20 Apr. 2003).

Amazon Watch. "Amazon Watch Launches Mega-Project Report: New Pipelines Threaten Intact Amazon Rainforest in Brazil." *Amazon Watch Newsroom*. 10 Aug. 2001. amazonwatch.org/newsroom/view_news.php?id = 314 (20 Apr. 2003).

El Paso Corporation. "El Paso Energy International Announces Phase II of Brazilian Termonorte Project." 19 May 2000. www.elpaso.com/press/newsquery.asp?sId = 2037 (28 Apr 2003).

Friends of the Earth. "Environmental Impact of the 'Avança Brasil' Programme Evaluated." *Amazônia*. 6 Aug. 2002. www.amazonia.org.br/noticias/noticia.cfm?id = 19260 (20 Apr. 2003).

Friends of the Earth. "Urucu-Pôrto Velho Gas Pipeline." *Amazônia*. www.amazonia.org.br/english/guia/detalhes.cfm?id13365&tipo=6&cat_id=88&subcat_id=1 (20 Apr. 2003).

Greenpeace. "Brazil: Rainforest under Siege." *Greenpeace Annual Review*. 26 July 1996. archive.greenpeace.org/~comms/cbio/brazil.html (8 Mar. 2003).

"Lack of Consensus over Construction of Gas Pipeline in Amazônia." *ComCiência*. 17 Jan. 2003. www.amazonia.org.br/english/noticias/print.cfm?id = 56029 (20 Apr. 2003).

Laurance, William F., et al. "The Future of the Brazilian Amazon." *Science* 291 (2001): 438–439.

"Mapa Do Brasil." Brasil Tur. geocities.yahoo.com.br/brasil_tur/mapa_bra.htm (30 Apr. 2003).

Rainforest Action Network. "Brazil." *RainforestWeb.Org*. rainforestweb.org/Rainforest_Regions/South_America/Brazil/ (7 Apr. 2003).

Silveira, José Paulo. "Development of the Brazilian Amazon." *Science* 292 (2001): 1651."Striving to Save the Forest." *Upstream Newsletter* 11 Feb. 2003. www.upstreamonline.com (18 Apr. 2003).

## Crime: Anna McGaha
## Prostitution is a Feminist Cause

*Audience:* **NOW Times** *Newsletter posted on NOW.org*

1    Preventing violence against women has always been a feminist cause. Therefore, an important part of the feminist cause should be preventing violence against a specific group of women: prostitutes. The recent murder of Kirschalyn Jones, a 15-year-old prostitute on April 18, 2002, illustrates why we need to rethink our approach (Glenn). The most support that prostitutes have gained from our community is access to programs for escaping prostitution. For example, feminist Melissa Farley, contributor to the *Prostitution Research and Education* Website, proposes ways to help the women who want to escape prostitution. These may be great programs, but they won't help the women who can't or won't leave prostitution and those who are most vulnerable to murderous acts.

2    The feminist movement owes more to women than neglecting them for staying in prostitution. Let the rest of the world pick and choose who is deserving of help and let us help *all* women. Some of us believe that prostitution is the choice of the woman, while others of us believe that its existence perpetuates a sexist world. Either way, one factor is clear: Women still choose to be prostitutes and are often in situations where they are the victims of rape and murder. Essentially, if we want to say that we represent the freedom and safety of women, then we must agree that the violence to which prostitutes are subjected is our problem. The first step to seeing this problem in the right way is to understand the overall vulnerability of prostitutes.

3    Our culture makes prostitutes more vulnerable by using degrading words that make them seem as though they are not really human. Even some feminists refer to a specific woman who is a prostitute, as "that prostitute" instead of "that woman." This sort of language implies that the woman is no longer a woman, but only a prostitute with no other identity. Other instances of dehumanizing language have been noted by Linda Fairstein, author of *Sexual Violence: Our War against Rape*. She found that when prostitutes reported rape or murder to police in California, the police would stamp the report with the letters "NHI," meaning "No Human Involved."

4    Our goal has always been to keep women safe. Prostitutes are vulnerable women like the other vulnerable women that we feminists care about. Prostitutes are the target of rape, murder, beatings at the hands of their pimps, and arrest by police officers. Their lives and identities are not disposable.

5    Prostitutes are also women who are treated unfairly just because of their gender. Prostitutes are punished more than men for the same act. Prostitutes are arrested for soliciting sex while their male customers are not. In Seattle,

for example, 2508 prostitutes were arrested from 1991–1993, but only 500 men, according to the Seattle Women's Commission (Weitzer). Prostitutes are branded as nonhumans for selling sex but the men are simply treated as shoppers; there seems to be nothing wrong with trying to find sex for sale. As long as prostitution is a crime, it should be illegal for both parties, rather than only for the women.

6      Prostitutes are vulnerable because they tend to have psychological problems and have been victims of sexual abuse during some time of their life. A large percentage of prostitutes have been abused. According to the 1991 Annual report of the Council for Prostitution Alternatives in Portland, Oregon, 85% of prostitute/clients were sexually abused in childhood, with 70% reporting incest (Dunn). Many prostitutes are also in poverty. The idea that they are adults consenting to sex seems far-fetched. If they are choosing to be prostitutes as a last resort, then it is not that much of a choice and not very moral for their customers to engage in sexual acts with them.

7      The fairest way to help prostitutes is to make it riskier for the men. Oregon has taken steps to restrict men's access to prostitution by taking impounding the cars of men who try to get prostitutes. They trap the men with undercover police pretending to solicit sex. The penalty that the men have to pay for solicitation is high and they also have to pay to get their cars back. This approach would be similar to Michael Castleman's strategy for reducing street crime in his neighborhood. In Castleman's terms, Oregon is increasing the certainty and the severity of punishment, which makes the customer fear trying to get prostitutes. They are trying to limit prostitution from the demand end. As long as there is demand, there will be women who are willing to sell sex. If the demand lessens, so will the supply. The problem with this tactic is that it is impossible to eliminate demand. This is similar to Castleman's argument that the impulse to commit crimes will never go away completely. Men might try to find other places to look for prostitutes where the risk is less. As long as officials keep after the customers, however, it may scare enough people to significantly reduce prostitution.

8      In conclusion, it is very important that we learn to look at prostitutes as people; until this happens, it will be difficult to protect them. The programs our feminist organizations have already established, such as helping prostitutes escape their job, only treat part of the problem. We must be willing to support plans to increase the risk for men and to help the safety of prostitutes, whether they decide to leave the job or not. A mixture of programs could ultimately lead to the safety and freedom of the discarded women in our society: prostitutes.

### Works Cited

Castleman, Michael. "Opportunity Knocks." *Mother Jones* 20 (1995): 26 + . [Available online. *Mother Jones Interactive.* www.motherjones.com/ commentary/columns/1995/05/castleman.html .]

Dunn, Katia. "Prostitution: Pro or Con?" *The Portland Mercury* 9–15 May 2002. www.portlandmercury.com/2002-05-09/feature.html.

Fairstein, Linda. *Sexual Violence: Our War against Rape.* New York: William Morrow, 1993.

Farley, Melissa, ed. "Prostitution: Fact Sheet on Human Rights." *Prostitution Research & Education.* 2 Apr. 2000. www.prostitutionresearch.com/factsheet.html.

Glenn, Mike. "Murder Suspect is Arrested in Stabbing of Teen Prostitute." *The Houston Chronicle* 27 Apr. 2002.

Weitzer, Ronald. "Prostitution Control in America: Rethinking Public Policy." *Crime, Law and Social Change* 32.1 (1999): 83–102.

# Planning Purpose and Audience

As a student, your greatest concern may be your ethos (Chapter 4), your standing and credibility in the eyes of your readers, so the most challenging part of writing a problem-based argument may be deciding on your audience. Take some time to consider your possible messages and your possible audiences. Choose an audience that needs to hear your message with whom you have standing (Chapter 20).

You have standing with stakeholders in any group to which you belong: the town where you live, the school you attend, the business you work for, the church you belong to, the places you shop, the clubs you join, the parks you visit, the organizations concerned about your interests. Brainstorm a list of choices by using the strategies provided in Chapter 7 and find out more about them using the research strategies in Chapter 8.

Once you choose an audience, you can decide what claims need fullest development; what appeals to logos, ethos, and pathos are appropriate; and what style to adopt. "Reasoning about Thesis and Audience" illustrates Eileen's and Anna's decisions.

## REASONING ABOUT THESIS AND AUDIENCE

### *Environment: Eileen's Reasoning*

During her research on new plans for development in Brazil, Eileen discovered that a local company was deeply involved. She felt eager to protest to this company because she had standing as a member of the local community. She considered writing a letter directly to the company but she realized that they already knew about her most startling piece of news, the company's own involvement. If she wrote to the company, she would have to convince them to pull out by making an argument for the value of the rainforest. That argument was not new enough to be interesting to her. She decided instead to write to potential allies who might feel the way she did when she found out about the company. So she addressed the *Houston Chronicle*; her goal was to convince Houstonians that they are partially responsible for the future of the rainforest because a key player was located in Houston.

### Crime: Anna's Reasoning

Anna was shocked to discover in her research that police used the phrase "No Human Involved" in cases involving prostitutes. She considered arguing for solutions that would lead to more humane treatment of prostitutes. However, she had trouble thinking of an appropriate audience. She found that the decision makers were officials at the city level but she didn't have a particular city in mind. She also did not want to argue for the morality of prostitution. When she searched for allies, she was surprised to find that the National Organization of Women Website said very little about prostitutes. She knew that NOW was already active in preventing violence to women. After more digging, she decided that NOW might be neglecting prostitutes because the members didn't think of them as women. So she decided to try to convince NOW to expand their definition of women.

As described in Chapter 20, one effective way to establish standing is to share your background with your readers, either by choosing a case narrative that affected you or people you know or by describing your membership in the same group as the reader. Neither Eileen nor Anna has personal cases to share relating to their issue, but both describe their shared affiliation with their readers. Eileen calls the readers of the *Houston Chronicle* Houstonians, continually refers to Houstonians as "we," and focuses on influencing a local company. Anna refers to the readers of the NOW Web site as feminists and refers to feminists as "we."

Chapter 20 also describes how to establish ethos through your selection of information to include, by cutting obvious details or signaling your awareness of old news. However, do not cut reminders to the values at stake in the issue; these are vital for establishing the significance of the problem. For example, it is worthwhile for Eileen to remind Houstonians that the rainforest affects their own climate and health and for Anna to remind NOW that "preventing violence against women has always been a feminist cause."

## Planning Your Line of Argument

A key to planning your line of argument is to identify your main contribution. Your main contribution will probably center on one of the five stases (Chapter 3). If you want to talk mainly about existence or definition, you may have little to say about cause or value. But to focus on cause or value, you should have a problem whose existence is well recognized.

Arguments about problems are so common that our culture has many expressions, called **commonplaces,** for summing them up. The commonplaces below can guide you toward identifying and developing your main contribution. Consider how each one could be relevant to your problem, then review Chapter 3 to figure out how to develop arguments at that stasis.

## Problem Commonplaces

*Existence*

- Crying wolf.
- If it ain't broke, don't fix it.
- Houston, we have a problem.

*Definition*

- If it looks like a duck and quacks like a duck . . . .
- Calling a tail a leg doesn't mean a dog has five legs.
- They're like two peas in a pod.

*Cause*

- Barking up the wrong tree.
- Where there's smoke, there's fire.

*Value*

- It's later than you think.
- That's making a mountain out of a molehill.
- We have to draw the line somewhere.
- What's sauce for the goose is sauce for the gander.

*Action*

- Get used to it.
- Let sleeping dogs lie.
- It is better to light a candle than to curse the darkness.

To make the best use of these commonplaces, you don't have to state them verbatim in your draft. Instead, write out an analogy assigning aspects of your problem to terms in the commonplace, as illustrated in "Brainstorming with Problem Commonplaces."

## BRAINSTORMING WITH PROBLEM
## COMMONPLACES

### *Environment*

- **"Houston, we have a problem":** In my case, Houston would be the city council and the astronauts would be the power plant operators.
- **"If it ain't broke, don't fix it":** The policy isn't broken because the tribe has gotten a lot of jobs and money from having the waste dump on the reservation and there's no sign of pollution. I could also use "Ain't nobody's baby" to say that Native Americans don't need environmentalists to tell them not to allow a new waste dump to be built. They are not babies and they don't need to be treated as such.

### *Crime*

- **"Barking up the wrong tree":** The dogs chasing the intruder are city council members who desire to lower juvenile crime by instituting curfews at 10:00 p.m. However, since most youth crime occurs immediately following school, their solutions becomes irrelevant and the nighttime is, in a sense, " the wrong tree." They don't understand the real problem.
- **"They're like two peas in a pod":** Some might excuse the NBA brawl by comparing basketball to other sports where fights are common, like hockey or boxing. I'll explain why basketball isn't the same kind of pea as the others by pointing out that boxing has a lot of fights but also training and equipment. Hockey players have helmets even if they're not trained to defend themselves. I think I'll use a lot of definitional arguments here.

While commonplaces are very helpful to your planning process, use them sparingly in your writing; repeating many of them verbatim makes your writing sound trite and cliché.

## Allocating Space and Planning the Arrangement

You should plan to give the most space to points at stases where readers lack knowledge or are likely to disagree with you (Chapter 3). If the problem has not been recognized, then existence arguments may occupy most of your paper. If the problem is well recognized, you can simply remind readers of points of common knowledge and agreement to show your readers that you know about the problem. Similarly, you can decide whether to remind or develop points on cause and significance. "Choosing an Arrangement" describes the decisions Eileen and Anna made.

## CHOOSING AN ARRANGEMENT

### *Environment: Eileen's Planning*

Eileen spends little space on the issue span, signaling that the rainforest issue is very familiar. Her biggest task is to change Houston readers' attitudes that "it's not my problem." To do so, she has to make a chain of causal arguments in her problem span linking a local corporation to the destruction of the rainforest canopy; over half the essay (par. 4–7) is devoted to this point. Along the way, she makes brief value arguments: The pipelines are the most harmful parts of the plan; action is urgent because a decision is coming up; the Houston corporation is a major player in the pipelines. Assuming that environmentalists in Houston know how to register concerns, Eileen devotes little space to her solution span ("apply pressure," "Let El Paso [the company] know that we do not support their activities.")

### *Crime: Anna's Planning*

In writing to NOW, Anna realized that she did not need to devote much space in her problem span to arguing that violence against women existed, was an important problem, or could be prevented. Instead she had to convince them to treat prostitutes just like other women. So her lengthiest point (par. 3–6) is a definition argument that prostitutes are women who are covered by NOW's mission. She develops three definitional criteria: dehumanization, gender discrimination, and susceptibility to abuse. In her solution span (par. 7–8), Anna introduces one promising approach that NOW members might not be aware of, supporting it with an audience-appropriate appeal to equal treatment of genders.

During her planning process, Anna was well aware that her readers would have moral objections to prostitution and would see prostitutes as maintaining an image of women as sex objects that violates feminist beliefs. She spent a long time debating whether to address these objections at length in her paper and ended up deciding to mention them briefly (in par. 2) in her definition argument.

## Criteria for a Good Problem-Based Argument

Keep the following criteria in mind as you write and review your draft. Picture yourself as "the writer," and a member of your audience as "the reader."

## Reasoning and Content

- The writer contributes something "new" by challenging readers' views of the nature of the problem at one or more stases.

  The writer argues convincingly that a problem exists or does not exist.

  The writer reasons about the problem by comparing cases, by presenting an A BUT B problem statement, or both.

  The writer provides a good definition of the problem that distinguishes between cases that are and are not included.

  The writer accounts for changes in the problem by examining causal factors and agents

  The writer makes effective value arguments raising or lowering the significance of the problem.

- The writer provides good appeals to pathos, reasons and observational evidence, and credible sources (both allies and opponents) throughout the argument.

- The writer anticipates where the readers will disagree with his or her way of seeing the problem. The writer considers these views fairly and responds with concessions and refutations.

- The writer offers or points toward a solution, if appropriate.

## Purpose and Audience

- The contribution is addressed to a specific readership whose beliefs, attitudes, or actions are important to the debate.

- The writer addresses readers in a way that will encourage them to take the ideas seriously, whether they are allies or opponents.

- The writer has chosen a specific audience, either stakeholders in a specific problem case or authors/activists who have addressed this or similar cases.

- The entire text is oriented toward this readership.

## Organization

- The argument focuses on the issue and problem spans.

- Space has been divided appropriately among the sections of the text, with the most space given to the newest or most controversial claims.

- The introduction grabs the readers' attention effectively and prepares for the contribution.

- Each paragraph develops a coherent point; paragraphs on the same point are clearly related.

- Topic statements, headings and transitions are used effectively.

- The conclusion draws conclusions: It is not merely a restatement, nor does it make completely new points.

## Expression

- The writer conveys understanding of the reader's expectations, using appropriate vocabulary, style, examples, and format.
- The writer does nothing unintentional to antagonize the readers whom he or she wants to persuade.
- Sources are documented appropriately, both in the text and in Works Cited.
- The essay looks professional; it has been carefully proofread and edited.

"Assessment of Student Papers" evaluates Eileen's and Anna's essays according to these criteria.

---

### ASSESSMENT OF STUDENT PAPERS

#### *Environment: Eileen's Essay*

Eileen's discovery of a local connection is a valuable contribution to the rainforest issue. She singles out one specific case of rainforest damage, fragmentation from piercing through the forest with a pipeline. She appeals skillfully to her fellow Houstonians throughout and displays no hostility to Brazilians or to the power company. Her central causal argument is presented fairly and in detail. She summarizes fairly and rebuts an alternative nonlocal approach, pressuring Brazil directly. Her focus on the problem span is appropriate and the essay is well organized and easy to follow.

#### *Crime: Anna's Essay*

Anna's discovery that NOW was neglecting a portion of its constituency gave her an opportunity to make an original contribution. Anna confidently establishes herself as an ally of NOW and places her goal squarely in line with NOW's stated goals. She singles out the case of women who stay prostitutes as the ones in need of help and develops an extended definitional argument. She also identifies a key factor causing the problem, the lenient treatment of men, and develops an analogy to Castleman's opportunity factor. Her solution addresses that factor directly, with evidence of a case where the solution is being tried out. As a national organization, NOW has the means to promote Oregon's approach more widely.

---

## Peer Review Guidelines

The following are suggestions for helping a classmate improve the draft of a problem paper. You may also find them helpful for planning and reviewing your own draft.

1. Part of your goal is to respond like a real reader from the audience your peer has selected.

   - Describe in detail a real or hypothetical person (age, gender, job, hobbies, education) who might belong to this audience.
   - Read through the entire essay with this person in mind. What claims will this reader find most controversial? What are some legitimate reasons why this reader might disagree?

2. Estimate (by percentage) how much space in the essay is devoted to the issue, problem, and solution spans (Chapter 2). How should this proportion be changed?

3. What stases (Chapter 3) of the problem span do you see addressed in this paper: existence of the problem, analysis of problem cases, definition of key concepts, significance of the problem, and/or causes of the problem? Which need to be developed more fully? How?

4. How appropriate is the tone that the writer takes towards this audience? Why? Indicate which of the following the writer should do: stop yelling at or blaming the reader, respond more to readers' concerns, be fairer to opponents. What could the writer do to achieve these goals?

5. Suggest ways that your peer can improve the introduction or conclusion.

For advice on giving your classmate the most helpful response, review Chapter 21.

# CHAPTER 17

# Having Your Say on the Solution

In this chapter, you will learn to write a solution-based paper on an issue of your choice to an appropriate audience. You are ready to begin writing a solution-based paper if you have gathered material about the problem and current solutions from a variety of sources (Chapters 7 and 8), explored the problem (Chapter 10), and explored possible solutions (Chapter 11).

Your goal in this paper is to make your own contribution to a public policy debate by challenging the current approach to solving a problem, by challenging someone else's proposed solution, or by promoting a different kind of solution—a new technology, a new policy, or an adaptation of an existing solution. You should to write a solution-focused contribution in these situations:

- When what you really want to talk about is the solution;
- When there is widespread agreement about the significance and causes of the problem; or
- When it seems important to change your readers' minds about the solutions currently being used or proposed.

See Chapter 20 for more on finding new ideas that your readers will take seriously.

In a solution-focused paper, most of your space will be devoted to the solution span (Chapter 2). However, you will also need to do some work in the issue and problem spans to justify reconsidering the current solution. If there isn't agreement that the current solution is problematic, you will need to develop this part of your argument in the issue and problem spans.

Before reading further, read one of the essays in "Sample Solution-Based Papers":

- **Environment:** Jackson Blair's "How to Sustain Southern Bluefin Tuna"
- **Crime:** Jeff Corbett's "Identifying Underage Drinkers"

These sample papers will be used throughout this chapter to illustrate the approaches to writing a solution-based paper. Note that they follow the APA documentation conventions (Chapter 22).

---

## SAMPLE SOLUTION-BASED PAPERS

### Environment: Jackson Blair
### How to Sustain Southern Bluefin Tuna

**Audience: Japanese Members of the Commission for the Conservation of Southern Bluefin Tuna (www.ccsbt.org)**

1   As the members of your Commission know, the onslaught of unchecked fishing from around the globe has reduced the Southern Bluefin population to below ten percent of their 1970's population (McVeigh, 2000). This rapid decline is clearly due to the change in fishing technology. The majority of tuna is no longer caught with short lines or small multi-hook lines. Instead, they are harvested with long lines (that can be over thirty kilometers long with thousands of hooks), pair-trawlers, driftnets, or purse seines (Greenpeace Australia Pacific, 2001). These techniques are paired with radio buoys, high power sonar, satellite technologies, GPS, fish tracking devices, and powerful ships that can stay at sea for weeks (Trivedi, 2002). The current fishing practices, technology, and approaches create a system in which sustainable populations of Southern Bluefin tuna (SBT) cannot be maintained. As a result, the International Union for Conservation of Nature and Natural Resources (IUCN) (2002) listed the Southern Bluefin as "Critically Endangered" on its Redlist for threatened species. There is a real possibility that commercial SBT fishery will collapse in the Pacific unless catches are reduced.

2   All members of the Commission for the Conservation of Southern Bluefin tuna (CCSBT), including you, acknowledge that the Southern Bluefin tuna is an extremely valuable fish economically, as well as ecologically. All the members of your group are also concerned with the future stocks of the tuna.

3   As the Japanese representatives of the CCSBT, you have taken the position that protecting the economy, which relies profoundly on the Southern Bluefin Tuna, is more important than increasing the Bluefin population. Therefore your country is not taking steps to protect the Southern Bluefin from overfishing. Your values are completely justifiable. Suddenly placing extreme limits on the amount of tuna that could be harvested would cause job loss and economic problems. However, I am not advocating a system in which Southern Bluefin could not be harvested at all nor one in which they could only be harvested from farming aquariums.

4    I am proposing that steps be taken now to ensure the recovery of the Bluefin to a biologically sustainable level so that there would be no need to use abrupt, last-minute efforts to fix the long-building problem. The result would be having a strong economy longer because the tuna will not disappear.

5    Only by adopting a plan like this will the Southern Bluefin continue to play a vital role in your country's economic well-being. Japan should avoid the mistakes of others. The actions taken by the Canadian government leading up to the North Atlantic cod collapse are remarkably similar to the actions currently being taken by the Japanese government dealing with the Southern Bluefin industry. Canada's inaction led to the loss of over 40,000 jobs, and caused great harm to their economy (Greenpeace, 2002).

6    As of course you know, the Bluefin is a staple of almost all sushi bars, which play such an important cultural role in Japanese society. The Bluefin currently provides thousands of fishermen, middlemen, and restaurant and sushi bar owners a valuable way to earn a living. If the Southern Bluefin were to become extinct or so rare that they could not be harvested economically, many of these people would lose their means of support. A significant aspect of Japanese culture would be lost forever. Why choose such a path when it could easily be avoided by responsible harvesting?

7    Another reason to reconsider your actions is Japan's foreign relations. The IUCN has recommended reducing the allowable Southern Bluefin catch immediately. But this is the opposite of what your government's "experimental fishing programs" are doing, according to Australian Foreign Affairs Minister Alexander Downer (Downer & Vaile, 1999). The experimental programs are based on controversial scientific evidence about which other members of the CCSBT strongly disagree. Past stock projections have been criticized as overly confident (Hayes, 1997). Of course it would be logical and prudent to use firm, scientific data when considering an increase in quotas on Southern Bluefin. Before the IUCN's quotas are expanded, more research and nonlethal experimentation should be conducted by an internationally recognized team of experts. Representatives of the CCSBT from Australia and New Zealand agree with this approach.

8    It would be helpful to Japan to be in more agreement with the CCSBT. Being isolated as the only country that disagrees about the impact of environmental policies can create diplomatic and trading tensions. For example, the United States was the first of the few countries that refused to sign the Kyoto Accord that was negotiated in your country. This refusal caused the respect for the United States of many other countries to deteriorate. Although Southern Bluefin policy is on a much smaller scale, actions such as experimental fishing programs can create problems for Japan similar to what happened to the United States after failing to compromise on the Kyoto Accord.

9      As members of an agency that can influence government policy, you should promote a plan that would reduce the number of Southern Bluefin caught so they can once again reach a biologically sustainable population level. Once a sustainable population has been achieved, fishermen will be able to harvest Southern Bluefin at a higher level without fearing a sudden loss of the fishing stock from overfishing or a natural disaster.

10     Of course Japan is not entirely to blame for the tremendous decrease in Southern Bluefin populations since the 1960s, but Japan is a responsible party. Because Japan is such an influential and a powerful country, both politically and economically, I am trying to convince you to lead the way and set an example for other countries to follow.

11     An ideal plan would target both the direct and indirect causes of the Bluefin decline while simultaneously trying to hold economic difficulties to a minimum. Such a plan would focus on limiting the amount of Bluefin that could be legally harvested by Japanese fishermen and decreasing the public's demand for Bluefin tuna.

12     To attain a smaller Southern Bluefin catch, I propose that you lower the legal Southern Bluefin harvest limit by at least thirty-five percent. This decrease in the catch will give the Southern Bluefin a seventy-five percent chance of recovering to their 1980 level by 2020 (Hayes, 1997). A greater decrease in legal catch would increase chances to accomplish that goal, but a thirty-five percent decrease is a necessary first step.

13     To reduce demand, you should start an advertising campaign to educate the Japanese public on the Southern Bluefin's situation. Along with this step, you should introduce a "seal of approval" or "certification" that eating establishments could receive if they did not serve Southern Bluefin.

14     To minimize the economic effects of this plan, you should also strongly promote substitutes for Southern Bluefin. These include other species of tuna and other large game fish that are not endangered and domestically raised Southern Bluefin (although at present, domestically raised Southern Bluefin are not readily available). This would allow people and businesses that were adversely affected by the reduction in Southern Bluefin to recoup some of their losses.

15     The next action in creating a lasting solution would include the creation of ocean reserves. These reserves would be a haven for Southern Bluefin as well as any species of sea life that was in the area. They would need to be created in vital Southern Bluefin locations, such as spawning areas, migration routes, and feeding grounds. These reserves allow fish that mature slowly, such as Southern Bluefin, to reach the full potential and greatest size.

16     Reserves would help directly in increasing the Bluefin population. According to Callum Roberts, a marine conservation biologist at the University of York, female fish produce exponentially more eggs as they grow larger (qtd. in Trivedi, 2001). Therefore, the reserves would help create faster population increases for Southern Bluefin. The reserves

would also protect the ocean floor. This would give sea bottom creatures, such as crabs, clams, and mussels, a chance to recover from destructive harvesting techniques. In previous trials of fish sanctuaries, the results have been spectacular. Harvest size increased tremendously in fishing areas surrounding an ocean reserve near St. Lucia (in the Caribbean). In some areas two to three times more fish were caught (Trivedi, 2001). The trials also showed great promise for sea-floor creatures, on which the Japanese economy depends heavily. After some areas of Georges Bank off the coast of New England were turned into reserves, the following years' harvests produced scallop catches that had not been matched since the early 1980's (Trivedi, 2001).

17    Marine reserves sound ideal but there could be difficulty in obtaining international approval from some countries in which the reserves would be located. With Japan's leadership and the help of your fellow CCSBT members Australia and New Zealand, you could create Southern Bluefin sanctuaries that would create the greatest benefits.

18    By taking these steps the CCSBT could return the Southern Bluefin to a biologically sustainable level. Once at this level, increased fishing could take place. Fishermen would no longer have to travel as far or work as long to catch the same amount of Southern Bluefin. The fishing economy would be enhanced thanks to a greater number of Southern Bluefin and ocean floor animals that could be harvested. Your organization would also gain respect from scientists and environmentalists for bringing Southern Bluefin back from such low levels.

19    I am looking forward to witnessing the active role the Japanese members of the CCSBT have in the recovery of the Southern Bluefin.

## References

Downer, A., & Vaile, M. (1999, June 1). Japan's decision on southern bluefin tuna unacceptable. *Australian Government Department of Foreign Affairs and Trade.* www.dfat.gov.au/media/releases/foreign/1999/fa059_99b.html.

Greenpeace Australia Pacific. (2001, April). Southern bluefin tuna in crisis. www.greenpeace.org.au/oceans/bluefin_tuna/bluefin_2.html#facts.

Greenpeace. (2002). Canadian Atlantic fisheries collapse. *Greenpeace Annual Review.* archive.greenpeace.org/comms/cbio/cancod.html.

Hayes, E. (1997, July). A review of the southern bluefin tuna fishery: Implications for ecologically sustainable management. (Executive Summary). *TRAFFIC.* www.traffic.org/factfile/tuna_summary.html.

International Union for Conservation of Nature. (2002). *The IUCN red list of threatened species.* www.redlist.org/search/details.php?species = 21858.

McVeigh, T. (2000, September 10). Overfished tuna "near extinction." *Guardian Unlimited.* www.guardian.co.uk/fish/story/0,7369,366715,00.html.

Trivedi, B. (2002, February). Cold War military technologies have devastated global fish populations. *National Geographic News.* news.nationalgeographic.com/news/2002/02/0225_0225_TVnomorefish.html.

Trivedi, B. (2001, December 4). Marine reserves found to boost nearby fishing grounds. *National Geographic News.* news.nationalgeographic.com/news/2001/12/1204_TVmarinereserves.html.

### Crime: Jeff Corbett
### Identifying Underage Drinkers

**Audience: Public Management *magazine*
(www.icma.org/pm/info/about.cfm)**

1    I will never forget what happened my first night on a college campus last year. The events of that night can be summed up in one word: alcohol. I have never seen so many people so disgustingly drunk before in my life. Students were throwing up in bushes, on stop sign poles, even in the middle of the street, all the while attempting to locate their cars to drive home. I would estimate that night there were over two hundred people at the party, with at least half of them driving home legally intoxicated.

2    My own family was affected by problem drinking. My father was hit by a young drunk driver when he was 18 years old. He was initially pronounced dead on the scene by the first authorities to arrive, but once he was pulled from the wreckage, he was still alive. Today, he has two huge scars on his chest from the accident and a nose that hardly resembles the one shown in his senior yearbook. Cases like these happen all over the country everyday, often caused by a youth who is legally intoxicated, like the one in my father's case.

3    Excessive drinking and drunk driving are important problems at college campuses around the country. Mothers Against Drunk Driving (MADD) (2002) cite a recent Harvard study that found that binge drinkers, those who consume five drinks or more in one night, are responsible for more than 70 percent of all college alcohol consumption. Fifty-seven percent of these binge drinkers report having driven home after drinking. MADD also cites a study by Dr. Ted Miller, professor at the Pacific Institute for Research and Evaluation, which found that alcohol kills 6.5 times more young people each year than all other illicit drugs combined. With a problem this serious, we have to ask where are the hiccups in the system that prevent it from being solved?

4    One source of the problem is that it is easy to get alcohol without getting caught. As everyone knows, the legal age to purchase and consume alcohol is 21 and valid ID must be shown in order to finalize the sale. For

many youths who choose to drink, getting around this requirement is a walk in the park. Fake IDs have become frequent inhabitants of underage drinkers' wallets. With access to scanners, digital cameras, photo editing software, and take-home lamination kits, almost any computer-literate person could produce a fake ID that is virtually impossible to detect. Some students also turn to ID professionals, who have the exact same materials that the state uses to produce legal IDs, such as black-light sensors and hologram logos.

5    Another source of this problem is the liquor stores themselves. Some store owners and clerks feel they can tell who is underage and who isn't. Many youths will send the oldest looking friends to buy the alcohol because the chances are the clerk will believe they are over 21 without checking the ID. Some clerks are afraid that carding will annoy or embarrass the customer. Most customers are in a hurry and find it annoying to take out their ID to show the clerk. Clerks also fear embarrassing the customer. While this reason may sound silly, it is very true. I was once with my uncle who was in his early 30's when a clerk asked to see his identification. When we left the store, my uncle was shocked that the clerk asked him to see his ID. I remember him saying, "Do I look like a boy?"

6    Of course there are clerks who want to obey the law, but have a hard time doing so. While it is reasonable that a clerk would be unable to detect a professionally made fake ID, most fake IDs have many errors. While most liquor store clerks do a reasonable job of detecting these errors, many do not. The cause: a lack of training. Many do not know where a fake ID could have telltale flaws and even if they do know, they may have a hard time detecting them.

7    Minors caught with fake IDs are charged with a misdemeanor of falsifying a government document. However, underage drinking is very rarely punished. MADD (2002) reports that of the 35.6% of college students that admit to have driven drunk, only 1.7% were arrested. This means that only 1 out of 20 drunk drivers is caught. This is scary to imagine, but it is reality and must be dealt with to remedy the problem.

8    I believe that alcohol must be stopped directly at the source, any store that sells liquor. The way to go is to make it easier to detect fake IDs using current technology.

9    In America today, almost anyone with a bank account has an ATM card. ATM's are a convenient way to withdraw money from a bank account from any of millions of locations around the world. An ATM card carries your personal banking information, including your account number, on the magnetic strip on the back. The ATM then communicates with your bank electronically to confirm that your account has the necessary funds. If not, the ATM machine will deny your transaction, leaving you cashless.

10    I suggest that a method similar to this be used for IDs, using the magnetic strip on the back of a driver's license. The magnetic strip would include the date of birth of the individual. I propose making it required

to swipe the driver's license upon purchasing alcohol into a verification system in order to complete the purchase.

11      Some doubters may think this would be no better than a clerk asking to see ID. One advantage is that it would work at any store or restaurant where liquor is sold. When someone buys alcohol, most stores scan the UPC barcode to determine the product's price and to maintain the store's inventory. A verification system could be easily designed to link this scan with the cash register. If the UPC barcode identifies that the product is alcohol, the system could place a halt on ringing up the alcohol until the driver's license is verified.

12      This method eliminates fake IDs from the equation. Since the verification system will not ring up the price, a proper driver's license must be used because only this would be accepted by the licensing database. Have you ever heard of a case of an individual creating a fake ATM or credit card magnetic strip to scam their way into free goods and money? Of course not. Therefore, fake IDs could not be created to purchase alcohol.

13      This does not yet address the cases in which a valid ID is borrowed by a minor. What about minors who use the license of an older individual who somewhat resembles the minor? A remedy to this problem is simple. Once an individual turns 21 years of age, their old identification card should become invalid. Similar to the expiration date on a credit card, once time expires, it is required that a new card is obtained. It could be required that a new driver's license be attained every four years. When a license is expired, the individuals would lose the right to purchase alcohol, creating an incentive to renew licenses quickly and helping police and other law enforcement correct the problem of out-dated licenses. When an individual renews a license before the expiration date, the old identification card should be deactivated, similar to when a credit card is lost or stolen. This would prevent minors from using a lost or stolen ID that has not expired. By taking these measures, a minor would find buying alcohol with false identification next to impossible.

14      This still does not yet address another set of cases in which adults purchase alcohol for minors. Because the purchaser is using valid identification and is allowed to purchase alcohol, these cases are difficult to detect. However, the verification system could include a deterrant. The personal database, which would be created as a result of this system, could keep a record of individuals who have been caught distributing alcohol to minors. When an individual is caught and the police report has been filed, that information would be inputted into the personal history of the individual in the database, barring the individual from purchasing alcohol for a given amount of time. The individual loses his or her right to purchase alcohol until the time has expired. Repeat offenders would receive longer time restrictions.

15      This approach could also have advantages beyond preventing illegal distribution of alcohol to minors. The method of "tagging" an individ-

ual's history in a verification database could help decrease crime by placing restrictions on the purchasing of alcohol by criminals who have committed a crime under the influence of alcohol. Professor John J. DiIulio Jr. (1996) claims that alcohol use is directly proportional to crime. He refers to a classic 1990 study that found that sixty-three percent of those convicted of homicide had been drinking before the offense. Anywhere from thirty to ninety percent of convicted rapists were drunk while committing the crime. DiIulio concludes that alcohol plays a huge role in the decision making of a criminal.

16    With my approach to tagging in place, police could prevent criminals who broke the law while drunk from purchasing alcohol by placing a time restriction on their personal database. This could apply to any crime, such as driving under the influence or assault. Also, this method could be applied towards alcoholics. On a voluntary or court ordered basis, those who need to stop drinking, but struggle with the habit, could be restricted from purchasing alcohol. This way if the individual had an uncontrollable urge for alcohol, he would be prevented from purchasing it.

17    The biggest problem with this solution is obviously its infrastructure. This method would require that every alcohol outlet have a verification system. But similarly to requiring a liquor license, the government could require that a verification system is mandatory to sell alcohol to the public. If the store or business chooses not to comply, it will lose its liquor license. The only equipment needed for this system to work is a standard electronic cash register and a phone line. For the locations that do not have this technology, the government could assist in providing the necessary equipment.

18    The problem of underage drinking has plagued our society for many years. Even though there are responsible minors who call a cab or use a designated driver, there are far too many irresponsible minors that put potential lives on the line. Controlling the decisions that youths make is almost impossible to accomplish. So we must develop solutions to prevent them from drinking to keep the lives of the innocent free from harm. I believe my solution to this problem is a worthy alternative to mend the flaws of current underage drinking policies. The lives of many are at stake when an irresponsible youth chooses to drive home. It is our moral duty to protect the ones who cannot control their decision.

### References

DiIulio, J., Jr. (1996). Broken bottles: Alcohol, disorder and crime. *The Brookings Review,* 14.2, 14 + .

Mothers Against Drunk Driving. (2002, April 29). Stats and resources. *MADD Online. www.madd.org/stats/.*

# Planning Purpose and Audience

In a solution-based paper, your main task is to make a fully developed argument for adopting your approach to someone who can take action. You will choose a reader (or readers) who is involved in the issue; one who differs from you on important points (Chapter 20). To keep these readers in mind, you'll have to figure out specifically what objections they will have to your position, make concessions, and refute opposing claims.

Your aim will be to present your case responsibly and in a way that helps the audience understand and consider implementing it. Keep in mind that you are not expected to eradicate the entire problem when you propose a solution. A partial solution is worth proposing if it softens the effects of the problem, if it reduces the number of people affected by it, if it represents a reasonable first step toward a more ambitious goal, or if it would be significantly better than keeping things the way they are.

If you have written a state of the debate paper (Chapter 15), you may think that a solution-based paper is the same thing because both involve assessing the approaches of others from the perspective of your problem cases. However, a solution-based paper is different in two important ways. You will be writing to a stakeholder audience, instead of an academic audience or the readers of a literary and cultural magazine. As a result, you will focus much more on the practicalities of solving specific cases instead of analyzing commonalities among alternative positions. An audience of stakeholders knows a lot about their situation and doesn't care at all about the full range of positions being debated. They want to know the costs and benefits of taking action and the reasons for taking the action you propose.

Your purpose must be to give as fair and accurate an assessment of the alternative actions as you can. Much more is at stake in recommending a solution than in analyzing the problem. Both kinds of arguments address a harmful situation that is going untreated; goals and values are at stake. However, taking action brings about both good and bad consequences; a solution has its own costs in time, money, and, sometimes, lives. A solution-based paper, therefore, has at stake both the goals threatened by the problem and the investment required by the solution.

The first readership you may think of for a solution-based argument may be a "general audience." However, writing to a general audience makes it far too easy to overlook or dismiss the possible objections of those directly involved with the problem. It is difficult for writers to imagine a general audience that knows more than they do or that has a significantly different viewpoint on the problem. More importantly, the public is not usually capable of taking action to enact a solution.

The second readership you may think of is a high-level official, such as the President or the governor of your state. Sometimes this audience is appropriate. For example, Albert Einstein launched the Manhattan Project during World War II by writing to President Roosevelt about the need to counter German research into atomic weapons. In this case, the reader was powerful enough to take steps to change the situation and was convinced to do so by a single author. But individual authors rarely have the standing of an Albert Einstein. And unless an official is directly in charge of the situation, he or she may not be able to act as quickly and decisively as Roosevelt.

Writing as a college student, you must choose an audience that will consider your viewpoint important. As described in Chapter 7, many authors address officials at a local level. For example, engineers address local water management officials about what kind of dam to build and where to put it. Neighborhood residents address the local police chief about where and when patrols are needed. In these cases, the author already has a relevant relationship to the reader: the engineer is working on a project approved by the local authority; the police chief is answerable to the people who live and vote in the neighborhood. If you are working on a problem in a particular place that you know about, you can claim this kind of standing (Chapter 20).

Authors also try to amplify their message by appealing to others for **grassroots** support. They aim their messages to a wide audience that includes potential allies, the general public, and even potential opponents. Their goal is to reach as many readers as possible. If many people are persuaded to voice their support to the authorities, their collective position may be taken more seriously.

Therefore, your goal should be to choose readers who are closely related to the problem but who approach it in a way you don't like:

- Decision makers who are directly involved in evaluating and implementing solutions (whether allies or opponents)
- Advocacy groups that are already concerned about the problem (whether allies or opponents)
- A segment of the population that is affected by the problem, who could be persuaded to contact decision makers
- Other authors who have argued about either the problem or the solution.

"Reasoning about Thesis and Audience" illustrates Jackson's and Jeff's efforts to choose readers whose decisions and actions were relevant to carrying out the solution.

---

## REASONING ABOUT THESIS AND AUDIENCE

### Environment: Jackson's Reasoning

Jackson found a personal connection to the environment issue from his ordinary life. He had heard that his favorite fish to eat, the Bluefin tuna, was in danger of disappearing. He found many sources on the dangers to the Bluefin population, so he knew that the problem was recognized internationally. He found out that international fishing policies had been proposed to restore the Bluefin population. But Japan, the country with the biggest harvest and consumption of the Bluefin, was circumventing these policies. At first, Jackson wanted to find a way for the United States to pressure Japan into changing its ways. But he couldn't figure out what he could propose, who to propose it to, or how to make Americans care that much about the Bluefin, when it is not commonly eaten here. During his research, Jackson found out that the Commission for the Conservation of Southern Bluefin Tuna had Japanese representatives. Jackson decided to address his argument to the

Japanese members of the Commission, to convince them to follow the Commission's policies by responding to their concerns directly. Apart from his dining preferences, Jackson has no personal case to narrate to the Japanese commissioners and does not share their affiliation in any group; his main opportunity to establish ethos is to emphasize his knowledgeability and fairness.

### Crime: Jeff's Reasoning

Jeff agreed with classmates who argued that the regulations against minors' drinking were "a joke" because students easily got away with drinking without being caught or punished. The class also agreed that even if they did not like them, the laws would be fairer if they were enforced consistently. In exploring solutions, Jeff decided that a big obstacle to enforcement was the use of fake IDs. Then he came up with some ideas about a system that would detect fake IDs more easily. He thought about writing to a college newspaper because students are interested in the issue, but they were not capable of enacting the solution. Then he looked into decision makers and found that enforcement decisions are made in city or county governments. He didn't want to write to just one city council because he didn't think one city could carry it out alone. Then he found a Website (www.icma.org/pm/info/about.cfm) for a journal, *Public Management*, that published articles on "issues of common concern to local government managers" for the International City/County Management Association. He decided to write his paper as an article for this journal.

## Planning Your Line of Argument

A key to planning your line of argument is to identify your main contribution, the part that is newest to your readers.

If you have come up with a new approach, that is, a new idea about the steps to take to solve the problem, then your solution span begins with the existence stasis, an argument that this approach is available (Chapter 3). Plan to devote a considerable amount of space to describing the plan in detail and showing that the necessary technology and resources are available. Then your argument continues through the cause, value, and action stases to predict what effects your plan will have, what it will cost, and how it should begin.

In many cases, stakeholders have already considered a variety of solutions, including some similar to yours. In this case, you need only remind them of its key aspects. If they oppose this approach, think of ways to convince them to reconsider. If they are considering several other approaches, think of ways to convince them that your approach is better. If you are proposing a change to a plan they like, think of flaws in the current approach and ways that your approach will address them.

A crucial part of a persuasive solution span is conceding limitations and drawbacks to your proposal. Readers know that no realistic plan will resolve all cases perfectly. Presenting your solution as a **panacea**, or cure-all, will only generate skepticism.

**Feasibility is more important than cost.** © Scott Adams/Dist. by United Feature Syndicate, Inc.

A comparative analysis of solutions typically has three parts. First, you have to make causal arguments about the changes that the solutions will cause, their effect on the problem itself. Second, you have to make value arguments about the costs of the solutions, including money, time, and reputation. Finally, you have to make value arguments about which alternative works best at least cost and whether the changes are worth the costs.

Arguments about solutions are so common that our culture has many expressions called **commonplaces,** for summing them up. The commonplaces below can guide you toward identifying and developing your main contribution. Consider how each one could be relevant to your solution, then review Chapter 3 to figure out how to develop arguments at that stasis.

## Solution Commonplaces

*Existence*

- There's nothing new under the sun.
- Let's not reinvent the wheel.

*Definition*

- We have to draw the line somewhere.
- This will separate the sheep from the goats.
- Let's call a spade a spade.

## Value

- They paved paradise to put up a parking lot.
- The cure is worse than the disease.
- An ounce of prevention is worth a pound of cure.
- That's using a sledgehammer to kill a fly.
- Don't change horses in the middle of the stream.
- You can't make an omelet without breaking a few eggs.
- No pain, no gain.
- Rome wasn't built in a day.

## Cause

- That dog won't hunt.
- Borrowing from Peter to pay Paul.
- Treating the symptoms, not the disease.
- That's throwing good money after bad.

## Action

- Let's cross that bridge when we come to it.
- A journey of a thousand miles begins with a single step.

While commonplaces are very helpful to your planning process, use them sparingly in your writing; repeating many of them verbatim makes your writing sound trite and cliché.

To make best use of these commonplaces, you don't have to state them verbatim in your draft. Instead write out an analogy assigning aspects of your solution to terms in the commonplaces, as illustrated in "Brainstorming with Solution Commonplaces."

---

## BRAINSTORMING WITH
## SOLUTION COMMONPLACES

### *Environment*

- "Rome wasn't built in a day" and "A journey of a thousand miles begins with a single step": The deer overpopulation problem cannot be solved overnight and building blocks are needed. The different solutions that I present in my paper (such as putting contraceptives in food and spraying to kill fleas and ticks) can be the first steps to solving it even though they won't show any effect for 2–3 years. If the sprays turn out to be harmful, then an opponent might say, "The cure is worse than the disease."

- "Let's not reinvent the wheel." I know my solution isn't really new. I just want to spread the "dolphin-safe tuna" labeling idea to go along with the types of advertising that already exist for coffee beans. My "rainforest-safe" coffee label isn't new but I'm using it in a new place. "An ounce of prevention is worth a pound of cure." In my case, doing this little step to get growers to change pesticides would be easier and less expensive than paying for health problems later on.

### Crime

- "No pain no gain": In my solution, parents have to take "pains" to block time out of their busy days to attend the weekly seminars on the proper techniques in dealing with drinking and driving for their children, but they get the gain of less worry. "That's throwing good money after bad": I talk about how I don't think that M.A.D.D should spend money pushing for zero-tolerance policies when those obviously aren't working.

- "The cure is worse than the disease" describes my argument against zero tolerance. I say that the policies cause more harm than good by uncovering only a few kids with drugs yet still violating many innocent kids' basic rights. "We have to draw the line somewhere": The policy I am opposing forces juveniles convicted of a crime to transfer schools. My argument is that the policy does not use enough discretion and lumps all violators together. A boy who steals bread so his family can eat should not be treated as a murderer would be.

## Allocating Space and Planning the Arrangement

When writing to a stakeholder, keep in mind that officials of any kind are busy people who have so many demands on their attention that they can only spend a small amount of time on any one problem. To grab the attention of this kind of reader, you must establish your ethos as someone worth listening to. To keep his or her attention, you must be very selective in the information and arguments you make. Chapter 20 describes how to establish ethos through your selection of information to include, by cutting obvious details or signaling your awareness of old news. However, do not cut reminders of the values at stake in the issue; these are vital for establishing the significance of the problem. For example, it is worthwhile for Jeff to remind the commissioners of the economic and ecological value of Southern Bluefin tuna and for Jackson to remind state and local officials of lives at risk from drunk drivers.

A big portion of any solution-based paper is devoted to describing and comparing the current way of doing things to one or more alternative solutions. Each solution must also be evaluated against a set of criteria, such as feasibility, degree

## TABLE 17.1

| *One-at-a-Time* | *Criteria-Based* |
|---|---|
| **Yugo** | **Cost** |
| Cost: low | Yugo: low |
| Durability: low | Honda: low |
| Gas mileage: high | Explorer: high |
| Passenger space: low | **Durability** |
| **Honda Civic** | Yugo: low |
| Cost: low | Honda: high |
| Durability: high | Explorer: high |
| Gas mileage: high | **Gas mileage** |
| Passenger space: moderate | Yugo: high |
| **Ford Explorer** | Honda: high |
| Cost: high | Explorer: low |
| Durability: high | **Passenger space** |
| Gas mileage: low | Yugo: low |
| Passenger space: high | Honda: moderate |
| | Explorer: high |

of effect on the problem, costs, and benefits. When you have a combination of alternatives and criteria, you can make use of a comparison-contrast arrangement.

To create a comparison-contrast arrangement, you can follow either of two basic sequences, the one-at-a-time arrangement or the criteria-based arrangement. These arrangements are illustrated in Table 17.1 using the task of buying a family car.

In a one-at-a-time arrangement, start with one solution and discuss all of its qualities, then take the next solution and discuss all its qualities, and so on. At the end, you sum up the strengths and weaknesses of each approach and argue for the one you think is best. This arrangement is often easiest to write and easiest for readers to follow. For this arrangement to be successful, it is important to create a pattern of qualities that you follow through on for each solution. If you fail to consider each quality of each solution, you may come across as biased or careless. It is also important to introduce the solutions themselves in a clear sequence (from weakest to strongest, oldest to newest, or least favorite to most favorite).

In a criteria-based arrangement, you start with one criterion and evaluate all the solutions against it. Then you take the next criterion and evaluate all the solutions against it, and so on. At the end, you sum up the most important and least important criteria to find the best solution. For this arrangement to be successful, it is important to create a sequence of solutions that you follow for each criterion. It is also important to introduce the criteria in a clear sequence, such as most important to least important. A criteria-based arrangement is not quite as easy to read. However, it allows readers to compare the solutions easily. It is also more efficient when your solutions are not all viable contenders, because you need not say much about the weak solutions.

Space will not be allocated evenly in either arrangement. The most space should be devoted to the most controversial points. "Choosing an Arrangement and Style" describes the decisions of Jackson and Jeff.

---

## CHOOSING AN ARRANGEMENT AND STYLE

### Environment: Jackson's Planning

Jackson knew that his readers, as members of the Commission for the Conservation of Southern Bluefin Tuna, would already know a great deal about the fish and would care about its survival. He realized that he did not have to convince his readers in his issue span (par. 1-2) that the problem was significant, but that he understood the problem. He decided that he had to address the Japanese directly in his problem span (par. 3-10) and appeal to Japan's values instead of yelling at them.

Jackson devotes a substantial amount of space to Japan's current approach (par. 3-8), describing what is at stake for Japan's key values: the strength of the economy, the endurance of cultural heritage, and good foreign relations. His basic theme is a causal argument, that Japan's approach defers the economic harms to the future, "Borrowing from Peter to pay Paul."

Jackson devotes even more space to his solution span (par. 11-19), detailing the four recommended actions and predicting their effects on the tuna population. The basic theme here is a value argument that small steps now will avoid big harms later, "An ounce of prevention is worth a pound of cure." The last step, creating reserves, is treated as the most controversial; three paragraphs are devoted to evidence that it helps restore populations and to concessions that implementing it will be difficult. Jackson ends by summing up the advantages of his plan.

### Crime: Jeff's Planning

Jeff's essay consists of a brief issue span (par. 1-2), a longer problem span (par. 3-7), and a long solution span (par. 8-18) that uses more than half the space in the paper.

Jeff understood that local officials appreciated the significance of underage drinking. He decided to open with a personal case to show his own credentials for being involved in the issue, even though he is a college student himself.

His problem span focuses on the exact cause that his solution will eventually address: the widespread use of fake IDs in the current situation. He details several factors: the ease of making IDs, lax enforcement of ID checks, and lack of training in detecting fakes. He ends with the result that underage drinking is rarely detected. His theme is a causal argument that the current approach does not address the key factor, "treating the symptoms instead of the disease."

In his solution span, Jeff describes his basic plan for using existing technology in a new way. He explains in a common sense way how the plan would eliminate the use of fake IDs. Jeff's exploration of problem cases led him to consider several different ways in which minors get alcohol even without fake IDs: minors borrowing the IDs of adults and adults buying alcohol for minors. In his solution span, he explains how his basic plan could be adapted to cover these cases as well. Finally, he argues that the system would help reduce crimes in cases completely different from underage drinking. Jeff concedes some difficulties with implementing the plan, though he does not consider other disadvantages to his plan, such as privacy concerns or the fact that not all adults have driver's licenses. However, he concludes that the plan is feasible and worthwhile overall, considering the significance of the problem.

# Criteria for a Good Solution-Based Argument

Keep the following criteria in mind as you write and review your draft. Picture yourself as "the writer," and a member of your audience as "the reader."

## Reasoning and Content

- The writer demonstrates that he or she understands the significance and causes of the problem.

- The writer contributes something "new" by challenging the current approach to the problem, by challenging someone else's proposal, by inventing a new approach, or by adapting one from a different area.

- Possible solutions are fairly compared with arguments at one or more stases:

    Whether they already exist or are feasible to bring about and what steps would need to be taken;
    Which cases they would treat;
    Whether they would reduce the significance of the problem or eliminate it and whether they would create negative side effects;
    Whether they are worthwhile in terms of cost, time to completion, difficulty; and
    Who should take action.

- The writer anticipates which points in the argument will be controversial for the readers. The writer considers these views fairly and responds with concessions and refutations.

- The writer provides good appeals to emotions (pathos), reasons and observational evidence (logos), and credible sources, both allies and opponents (ethos), throughout the argument.

## Purpose and Audience

- The writer addresses his or her contribution to a specific readership whose decisions and actions are relevant to carrying out the solution.
- The writer addresses this audience in a way that will encourage them to take the ideas seriously, whether they are allies or opponents.
- The entire text is oriented toward this readership.

## Organization

- The opening section(s) grabs the readers' attention effectively and conveys understanding of the problem.
- The argument focuses on the solution span.
- The most space is devoted to the newest or most controversial points.
- Alternative solutions are ordered in a logical sequence, such as "saving the best for last."
- The solutions are analyzed systematically and the analyses are presented in a consistent pattern.
- Each paragraph develops a coherent point; paragraphs on the same point are clearly related; topic statements, headings, and transitions are used effectively.
- The conclusion draws conclusions: It is not merely a restatement, nor does it make completely new points.

## Expression

- The writer conveys understanding of the readers' expectations, using appropriate vocabulary, style, examples, and format.
- The writer does nothing unintentional to antagonize the readers whom he or she wants to persuade.
- Sources are documented appropriately, both in the text and in Works Cited.
- The essay looks professional; it has been carefully proofread and edited.

"Assessment of Student Papers" evaluates Jackson's and Jeff's papers according to these criteria.

---

### ASSESSMENT OF STUDENT PAPERS

#### Environment: Jackson's Paper

Jackson uses many persuasive strategies for addressing his main opponents, Japanese officials who have blocked steps to protect the tuna. He appeals to their own values to establish the significance of the problem and treats their concerns respectfully. The novelty of Jackson's contribution is the combination of steps he offers to address Japan's economic and cultural concerns. The series of steps he proposes are developed in detail, with evidence of effectiveness and suggestions for minimizing costs. The essay is well organized and easy to follow.

### *Crime: Jeff's Paper*

Jeff addresses an audience of policy makers. He uses personal cases to establish his ethos as a witness and victim of the problem. He combines the cases with statistics as evidence of the significance of the problem. As a student, he has the opportunity to offer a detailed analysis of the causes of the problem that officials might miss. Then he uses existing technology to propose an ID-checking system that gets around the obstacles. Jeff does not appeal directly to his readers and their concerns, but he does address several drawbacks and limitations of the system. Jeff also refers respectfully to those contributing to the problem: students who use fake ID and lax store clerks. The paragraphs in the essay are coherent but their internal sequence and conciseness could be improved.

## Peer Review Guidelines

The following are suggestions for helping a classmate improve the draft of a solution-based paper. You may also find them helpful for planning and reviewing your own draft.

1. Part of your goal is to respond like a real reader from the audience your peer has selected.

   - Describe in detail a real or hypothetical person (age, gender, job, hobbies, education) who might belong to this audience.
   - Read through the entire essay with this person in mind. What claims will this reader find most controversial? Why? What are some legitimate reasons why this reader might disagree?

2. Estimate (by percentage) how much space in the essay is devoted to the issue, problem, and solution spans (Chapter 2). How should this proportion be changed?

3. What stases (Chapter 3) in the solution span do you see addressed in this paper: existence of alternative solutions, definition of key concepts, effect of solutions on problem cases, side effects of the solutions, costs in money and time, implementation details? Which need to be developed more fully? How?

4. How appropriate is the tone that the writer takes toward this audience? Why? Indicate which of the following the writer should do: Stop yelling at or blaming the reader, respond more to readers' concerns, or be fairer to opponents. What could the writer do to achieve these goals?

5. Suggest how your peer can improve the introduction or conclusion.

   For advice on giving your classmate the most helpful response, review Chapter 21.

# PART IV

## Reading and Writing Resources

### Chapters

Most students come to college with ways of reading and writing that have served them well in school. However, the challenges of authorship, of reading and writing to make your own contribution to a debate, often require students to expand the set of strategies they normally use.

It is helpful to think of ways to read and write as a toolkit: Some methods are specialized for particular tasks and others can be used for a lot of different jobs. Reading and writing are skills that can continue to grow across your entire life, as you take on new purposes for writing in new situations.

The chapters in Part Four are designed to help you add to your toolkit. Most of the processes recommended here are ones that experienced readers and writers have been observed using. Other strategies are those that people who have trouble reading and writing have found helpful. Many combinations of tools can serve your purpose; the choice of tools is up to you.

# CHAPTER **18**

# Critical Reading Process

Many students read texts looking for valuable nuggets of information to remember for an exam or to use in a writing assignment. To argue on an issue, however, you need to read actively and critically, with multiple goals in mind:

- To formulate a position of your own, not simply to find information.
- To find allies and opponents to respond to, instead of looking for quotes to fill out your paper.
- To find important points of dispute, instead of points the experts all agree on.

To understand a complex argument thoroughly, you will have to read it more than once. You might end up reading parts of it five or six times, looking at different aspects each time. This chapter will give you ideas for what to do while preparing to read, reading a text for the first time, reading to deepen your understanding, reading to map out the argument, and following through after reading. These strategies focus on different goals; the best ones to follow depend on how difficult you find the article and what you want to do with it.

These strategies are used every day by professionals, academics, and successful students. Using them does not guarantee that you will develop perfect understanding of the text; because texts allow for more than one reasonable interpretation, you can't check an answer key to see if your interpretation is right. But these strategies will help you build a thorough and coherent interpretation. Along the way, you may consider and reject several shaky ones.

## Preparing to Read

The best way to learn something new is to connect it to something you already know, something that you already have in mind. When you are first starting to read a new article, you may not have anything in mind that relates to it at all. You may be thinking about dinner or about an assignment in another class. So some good strategies before you read are to start thinking about the article in advance and to build up some expectations about it. The strategies in this section will help you focus on the topic, notice aspects of the text, and decide how much effort you will need to invest. Two of the best ways to prepare are to preview the text and to check out the author and the forum.

## Previewing

Previewing the text is a quick and easy strategy. It begins with glancing through the text, looking for clues about what conversation the author is joining and what the author wants to say. Read the title carefully. Look at the authors' names. Look at the title of the journal and the date when the article was published. Look for headings and read them carefully. Look for a list of references or works cited and see what kinds of articles or books are included. (For types of articles and books, review Chapter 8.) Look at any pictures or diagrams. Read an abstract if it is available.

Then, form some hypotheses about the author, the kind of article this is, its probable audience, and its topic. Scan your memory to think of things you already know or feel about this topic or about people like the author and probable readers. Recalling what you know activates the most relevant areas of your mental knowledge base and makes the new information in the article easier to understand and remember.

Finally, set some expectations. What do you think the author will say about the issue? The problem? The solution? Will this be an easy read? An interesting one? Are you likely to agree with this author? Setting expectations helps you notice both the strengths and weaknesses of the argument as you read.

## Checking

To understand the author's point of view, you need answers to these questions: Who is the author (name, job, stake in the issue, age, etc.)? What inspired him or her to enter the conversation at this particular time? How does the author's background relate to his or her position on the issue? Who are the author's allies and opponents? Who are the intended readers of this article?

To find information about the author, look for biographical information in a note at the beginning or end of the article, or on a separate "Contributors" page in a book or journal. Or search for the author's name on the Internet. (Review Chapter 8 for search strategies.) "Check Out the Author" illustrates the types of biographical information to look for.

---

## CHECK OUT THE AUTHOR

### Environment: Easterbrook's Background

Gregg Easterbrook has been a contributing editor at *Newsweek* and *U.S. News & World Report*. A senior editor of *The New Republic* and a contributing editor for *Atlantic Monthly* and *Washington Monthly,* Easterbrook is a two-time winner of the Investigative Reporters and Editors Award and a distinguished fellow of the

Fulbright Foundation. He is the author of several critically acclaimed books, including *Beside Still Waters: Searching for Meaning in an Age of Doubt*. This information was found at the Website "Gregg Easterbrook: Beliefnet Columnist," www.beliefnet.com/author/author_78.html.

### Crime: Kleck's Background

Gary Kleck is a Professor in the School of Criminology and Criminal Justice at Florida State University. His research centers on violence and crime control with special focus on gun control and crime deterrence. Dr. Kleck is the author of *Point Blank: Guns and Violence in America* (Aldine de Gruyter, 1991), which won the Michael J. Hindelang Award of the American Society of Criminology, for the book which made "the most outstanding contribution to criminology" in the preceding three years. This information was found at the Website "Who is Gary Kleck?" www.guncite.com/gcwhoGK.html.

To check out the forum where the article appeared, use the strategies described in Chapter 8. Find out as much information as you can about the aims and goals of the periodical or Web site and evaluate its trustworthiness. Remember that a forum can be trustworthy and useful even if it takes a strong stance on one side of an issue.

With all these recollections and ideas in mind, you will find the article easier to understand. The topics and approach won't all seem new and unexpected. You will also find it easier to respond to the author and to assess the strength of her arguments. The strategies described here work best in advance of reading, but you can also use them at other times. For example, you will use these strategies to find and choose additional sources.

## Reading a Text for the First Time

The first time you read an article, don't try to work out every detail. Plan to give yourself more opportunities to keep refining your understanding of the argument. Follow these strategies:

- **Focus on the big picture.** Read to get the main ideas of the argument. Check the expectations you set before reading. While some of your expectations were probably right, others may have been off-target. Adjust your expectations. Don't worry if the argument doesn't all make sense right away. Stop and reread as needed to follow the main ideas.
- **Note questions.** If you are having trouble understanding some passages, write questions (or even just a question mark) in a nearby margin. Similarly, mark any passage or section that seems pointless or irrelevant. Then you can come

back to these sections later to see if they make more sense after you have additional information provided further on in the article.

- **Note surprises, frustrations, and unmet expectations.** It is important to note these experiences early, while they are fresh in your mind. Perhaps you are picking up on a point that the author should have included or on a tone that turns you (and other readers) off.

Trust your reactions to the text. All readers, even experts, invest effort figuring out the meaning of confusing passages. Any passage can be confusing because any piece of writing allows multiple interpretations, because authors don't always explain themselves clearly, and because readers differ in what they know and why they are reading. What is clear to one reader can confuse another.

Later on, if you are writing an analysis of the argument or a response to the author, these points may give you important clues to weaknesses in the article.

# Reading to Deepen Your Understanding

An initial reading is enough to give you a good picture of the author's entire argument. However, to analyze the argument, you need a deeper understanding of how the argument is put together.

Begin by reading the article again more slowly. Slowing down gives you more time to think about what you are reading. Think about how the current point fits in with the ones that came before. Think about how the points relate to your own knowledge of the topic.

Then return to any passage you had marked as confusing. Try summarizing or restating it in your own words. Here is how one reader used this strategy to figure out a confusing technical passage about a car recall. Below is the original passage. The second paragraph is a transcript of the reader saying out loud everything he was reading and thinking. The words that he is reading from the text are printed in plain typeface and his comments and paraphrases are in italics:

**Original passage:**
This plate (front suspension pivot bar support plate) connects a portion of the front suspension to the vehicle frame, and its failure could affect vehicle directional control, particularly during heavy brake application.

**Example of a person reading and thinking aloud:**
This plate (front suspension pivot bar support plate) *I guess that's another way of saying what this plate is*—connects a portion of the front suspension to the vehicle frame, *OK the plate connects the suspension to the vehicle frame*—and its failure could affect vehicle directional control, *so if this plate messes up, you lose the ability to steer I suppose*—directional control *I guess means steering*—particularly during heavy brake application . . . *so when you apply the brakes you could lose control of the car if you have a problem with this plate hmm—*

This reader restates the difficult phrases as a story about a real person experiencing the problem. His paraphrase is actually much clearer than the original and would be a good basis for a revision of the passage.

Depending on the article, you may have to read it several times in its entirety to understand the main points of the argument. While you do not need to understand every word or idea, you should see a purpose to every section. Going on to map the argument will also help you understand it.

# Reading to Map Out the Argument

Mapping out the line of argument means identifying a sequence of sections and claims that the author has laid out to steer the reader towards her destination. No matter where an article is published, authors face pressures to be as concise as possible, so you can assume that the author has a reason for including every passage. A good approach is to treat the article as a puzzle. Your job is to figure out how each section of the text contributes to the author's overall purpose. Two useful techniques for mapping the argument are annotating the text and creating a sketch.

## Annotating the Text

Annotating is the familiar process of writing in the margins, circling or underling text, or using a highlighter. For this process to be effective, be selective in what you mark.

- Highlight references to authors, experts, witnesses, and groups. These references will help you identify the author's allies and opponents.

- Highlight descriptions or references to real-world cases in which a problem has occurred, including place names, dates, and names of officials and agencies. These references will help you later on as you explore the problem and invent possible solutions.

- Write a brief phrase in the margin that sums up the main topic of a paragraph or group of paragraphs.

## Creating a Sketch

Your goal is to create a sketch that divides the text into the major sections of a public policy argument, the spans (issue, problem, and solution) described in Chapter 2 and the stases (existence, definition, value, cause, and action) described in Chapter 3. Your sketch can look like the ones provided for Castleman and Chivers in Figures 2.1 and 3.3. To create such a sketch, follow these steps:

1. Number the paragraphs in the text.
2. Write a list of the numbers on a separate piece of paper.

3. Draw a line between the paragraph numbers to represent the breaks between the issue and problem spans and another for the break between the problem and solution spans.

4. Look at consecutive paragraphs within a span to see if they are about the same topic or point. Paragraphs on a topic repeat important phrases. Draw a bracket around these paragraph numbers on your list and label it with a descriptive word or phrase. Include a stasis label if you see many of the "Words to Watch For" listed in Chapter 3. For example, in the Castleman article, the repetition of the term "street criminals" in par. 9–12 creates a grouping. This grouping could be a definition passage.

5. Join up consecutive groupings if they all belong to the same stasis. For example, in the Castleman article, a large causal argument runs from par. 17–29, made up of subgroupings for liberal and conservative causes (such as the family or punishment) and for Castleman's causes, impulse, alienation, and opportunity.

Remember that a grouping may be very short or very long. Authors pick and choose among the possible stasis points, spending more time on some than others. An author spends most time on the points he or she thinks are most important and most controversial at the moment.

By the end of this process, every paragraph should belong to a topical grouping under a stasis, the set of stases should extend across an entire span, and the spans should extend across the entire article.

With so much flexibility in the framework, mapping out the line of argument is a real challenge. It is not a matter of clear-cut right or wrong answers; instead it takes reasoned interpretation about what makes sense.

## Identifying Spans and Passages within Spans

Figuring out the size and shape of a passage takes informed judgment. The important clues to the purpose of a passage are those that you can point to by underlining words or phrases. Review the "Words to Watch For" in Chapter 3 and keep those pages handy as you read.

As noted in Chapter 4, the appeals that support a claim can themselves be claims. For this reason, the process of identifying passages becomes frustrating if you try to classify units of text that are too small, such as individual sentences. Here are several strategies for looking for spans and passages:

*Supersize It*

- Don't try to classify each sentence; you will lose sight of the big picture. Start by looking for spans and then for stases within a span.

- For spans, look at big units of text, as short as a paragraph and as long as several pages.

- Assume for the time being that the issue span starts with the first paragraph of the article. Find the halfway point in the article. Look near or before it for the start of the problem span. Look near or after it for the start of the solution span.

- Assume for the time being that a span is a sequence of passages developing each stasis: existence, definition, value, cause, and action. Consider whether a passage is developing an idea related to a stasis. For example, definition claims develop ideas about cases and categories, value claims compare cases within a category to each other or to a standard, and cause claims involve items that change over time due to factors.

- Within a span, look for a paragraph that contains several of the "Words to Watch For" for a particular stasis. Then highlight or underline all the terms that you can find in the paragraph.

- Look at the neighboring paragraphs to see if they are about the same stasis. Group together the biggest possible number of connected sentences or paragraphs on one stasis before assuming that you have entered a passage on a different stasis.

## Find the Edges

- Read headings and subheadings to see if they signal the beginning of a span or a stasis.

- Look for the solution span first; it is often the easiest to find.

- Find a clear case of a span or stasis; then work forward and backward to find where it starts or end.

- Within the spans, work back and forth to find text segments at the stases. Once you spot keywords for a stasis in one paragraph, see if the surrounding paragraphs are about the same topic and belong in the same segment. Then look for a new segment before or after that one. The stasis segments should cover all the paragraphs within the span.

- Mark where segments begin and end by drawing lines or writing a label in the margin. Draw these in pencil so you can change your mind.

## Allow for Absences and Extras

- Be sure that your proposed spans cover the entire article. Be sure that every segment within a span relates to a stasis or purpose.

- Don't assume that you will find all three spans. Some issues don't need much introduction. At times, analyzing a problem is more useful than trying to solve it.

- Don't assume that you will find every kind of stasis. Not all stases are used equally often. An issue span may simply be one big existence claim. Definition arguments are relatively rare.

- Spans and stases can be used more than once. You might find a sequence of alternative series of solutions, each with its own existence-cause-value claims, before one is recommended.

## Tying It All Together

Once you have identified passages and labeled them at least tentatively, you can begin working out the puzzle of how every passage contributes to the author's overall conclusion.

- Assume that the line of argument has to make sense—that it all fits together. Look for a consistent theme or position that connects all the segments. Figure out what happens to topics raised at the beginning. If the argument starts with a problem case (Chapter 7), figure out how the solution would affect it.

- Look for connections at the level of stases (existence, definition, value, cause, action) to get to the guts of the argument. Some articles seem easy and clear at the top level of spans; the stases are where the real action is.

- Sometimes, a passage that seems irrelevant to you may be aimed at a specific audience. Look again at the information you found out about the journal or Web site. Why would the author think that this audience would need to read this passage?

- Summarize the argument in your own words to test the coherence of your interpretation. Be sure to use span and stasis keywords. Consider whether the author would agree that your summary or interpretation is fair. Do you exaggerate any of the author's claims? Adjust your summary to make it sound fair.

# Following Through After Reading

Critical reading doesn't end when you put down an author's article. Even after you stop looking at it, you should continue thinking about it from time to time. Tell a friend or relative about an interesting point. Keep an eye out for related information on the news, in conversation, or in other class discussions. Jot down any new ideas or new sources of related information. These follow-up strategies are valuable, no matter whether your goal is to remember the article for an exam, to learn background information on an issue, or to write your own argument on the issue.

When you read about a controversial issue, you may feel as if you are in a room with a lot of people arguing, talking quickly, getting off track, answering some questions and not others. To figure out how to jump in, you need a way to keep the authors and their positions straight by actively creating a mental reminder for each author.

Find a memory hook for each article. Come up with a catch phrase that sums up the topic of the article and the author's position. Concentrate on associating the phrase with the author's name. The goal is to remember the main line of the argument whenever you hear or think of the author's name.

- **Environment.** Chivers: dredging the ocean floor; Shiflett: jet skis and dirt bikes; Gómez-Pompa and Kaus: Western and non-Western conservation.

- **Crime.** Castleman: street crime and opportunity; Shapiro: being stabbed on TV; Meares and Kahan: civil rights, curfews, Chicago.

Try to remember a case that the author cares a lot about. Try to remember what he or she talks most about. If you have more than one article from the same author, come up with another catch phrase and another case to set it apart.

When you read an article from a different author, take time to compare the two authors. Try to remember an earlier author by recalling your catch phrase. Then think about where these authors would agree/disagree.

# CHAPTER 19

# A Repertoire of Writing Processes

A repertoire is a set of skills that a person can choose from in different situations. The goal of this chapter is to help you build up a repertoire of writing processes.

If you have a way of writing that has worked very well for you in the past, you may not think you need any other. But even now, you probably use different processes without being completely aware of it. Do you use a different process for writing e-mail or instant messages than you do for writing a school essay? You write in so many different situations that it would make no sense to use the exact same process in each.

Writing is a skill that can keep developing over your whole life. Expert and professional writers pick up many different writing skills as they write for different audiences and purposes. As you progress through college, your writing assignments will probably become longer and more complex. The processes you have used until now may not work very well for these assignments

If you have never had much success at writing, then trying out different processes may help you find strategies that work better for you. But don't think that there is some way to write that will produce good results every time. Writing well is almost always hard work. Fully formed arguments do not flow effortlessly from any writer's fingers. A writer who struggles to write and rewrite is not deficient in some essential gift or genius that "good writers" have.

Writers can use many effective ways to get from a blank piece of paper to a successful text. As compared to other skills, writing is unusual. For most skills, such as diving into a pool, practicing over and over makes performance more "automatic," reducing the time and effort needed to execute the skill successfully. But more experienced writers do not always speed up; they tend to invest greater time and effort than do inexperienced ones. Believe it or not, experienced writers don't let the process become automatic. They willingly think about the demands of each writing situation in order to adapt to it and to improve their skills. They raise the standards for their own writing. They are motivated by having their writing succeed and by rewards in the process itself, the pleasure they get when an idea or phrase finally clicks.

# Writing Process Components

Observing writers has led researchers to identify several components to the writing process:

| | |
|---|---|
| **Planning** | Deciding what kind of text to write, to whom to write it, what to say, and how to arrange it; making notes and lists; changing plans as a draft develops and new ideas occur. |
| **Drafting** | Expressing ideas in writing in connected sentences and paragraphs; adding more text anywhere in the draft. |
| **Evaluating** | Comparing the draft to the goals set during planning in order to detect and diagnose mismatches. |
| **Revising** | Changing the draft by deleting, moving, and recasting in order to match the plans more closely; editing to make corrections. |

Writers differ so much in the way they use these components that researchers have concluded that there is no prescribed order of what should be done first, second, or third—instead these components seem to be recursive. Any component can lead to any other one: Drafting can lead to planning or to revising; revising can lead to drafting or to more planning. Evaluating can take place at any time along the way or in a deliberate review.

It is impossible to tell from looking at a finished text what sequence of processes the writer used to produce it. But it is possible to find out about processes by observing writers as they work, by questioning them, and by looking at their drafts. Researchers have found that many experienced writers adopt a characteristic approach to writing. Here is a brief description of three common approaches:

- **Spew-and-reviser.** Prefers to "let loose" and write nonstop before deciding what to keep. Doesn't mind throwing away long passages and likes to tinker with the language. Finds it difficult to keep from focusing on wording and style before generating ideas and evaluating the emerging argument. Finds it difficult to switch early and often enough to evaluating and planning to create a clean arrangement.

- **Planner.** Prefers to think out all or part of a text before drafting. Consults plans often during writing; changes plans when necessary. Finds it difficult to switch to drafting early enough to carry out the plans and allow revision of the draft.

- **Skipper.** Prefers to write one piece at a time, but doesn't write in order from the beginning of the paper to the end. Finds it difficult to switch to planning often enough to connect up the pieces into a line of argument and to switch to revision early enough to smooth out the transitions.

You may recognize yourself in one of these descriptions. If your current approach is frustrating, feel free to "try on" another style. The only ineffective approaches are ones that leave out an important component entirely or ones that you follow too rigidly.

# Planning

Planning is an important component that many beginning writers neglect. Experienced writers usually spend time planning before drafting connected prose. They often return to planning after starting to draft, sometimes making very drastic changes in the purpose or direction of their text.

A plan is not a miniature summary of your paper. Making a plan is like sketching a floor plan for a dream house, not like creating a blueprint. A blueprint is an extremely detailed and precise set of diagrams that must be followed exactly down to the smallest piece. A plan is meant to be easily changed.

Planning lets you put symbols on a page and move them around. The symbols in a floor plan stand for objects that, in the real world, are bulky and complicated, like bathtubs or walls. It is much easier to move them around in a drawing than it is on a blueprint or construction site. Similarly it is much easier to move around a case narrative or a candidate solution in a plan than in a full text.

Plans come in many forms, including simple lists, diagrams, and formal outlines. Using one of these graphic formats makes changing a plan easier. Writers cross items out and add new ones. They put stars by items they think are important. They use numbers or arrows to move items into a different order. You can use the same types of plans for units of text of any size, from the whole paper to a paragraph, from a problem section to a set of examples.

In addition to thinking of what points to make, it is important to consider how to arrange them. Some writers like to plan out parts of the arrangement before they start drafting. Others put off thinking about arrangement until they have drafted some text. In either case, it usually works best to switch off between these processes.

Your final arrangement of points will probably be quite different from the sequence in which the ideas occurred to you because your readers should benefit from your experience. If you took a long, steep, and twisty path to figure out your final position, you might lose your readers if you make them follow the exact same steps. If your beliefs and attitudes are different from your readers, then you need to build on what they believe and find an order that will be persuasive for them, not just for yourself.

At some point in the process, you have to plan the arrangement from your reader's point of view. This topic is discussed in detail in the next chapter. In the meantime, here are some useful arrangement strategies to consider:

- **Best-for-last.** Present one or more alternatives that you reject before presenting the choice you prefer.

- **Merit-based.** Present the most important, the strongest, or the most positive points first.

- **Sequential/chronological.** Present points in order of size, location, or timing.

While most writers do a lot of their planning early in a project, experienced writers reconsider their plans frequently along the way. You may have changed your mind, forgotten a goal, or added a goal. The ideal text you had in mind when

*"It's plotted out. I just have to write it."*

**It helps to coordinate your planning with your drafting.** © The New
Yorker Collection 1996 Charles Barsotti from cartoonbank.com. All Rights Reserved.

you started planning may have turned out to be too big or too hard to handle. So
it is just as important to be willing to evaluate and revise your plan as your draft.

# Drafting

Drafting means carrying out your plans by putting your ideas into words, sentences, and paragraphs. You can start drafting whenever you like with any section
of a text that you prefer. Lots of writers find the introduction the hardest section to
write, so they begin writing a paper somewhere in the middle.

The goal of drafting is to get ideas onto the page in connected sentences and
paragraphs. While you may consult a plan as you write, you should also let ideas
come to you. Often it is only during drafting that you figure out what you really
want to say.

Some students dislike drafting because they don't think they have enough
things to say. This is unlikely if you have been reading and thinking about your
issue. You do have ideas even if the sentences don't flow easily. Other students have
lots of ideas but have difficulty putting them into words or deciding among all the
possible things they could say.

Most successful writers face these difficulties at some point. Even professional writers can dread looking at a blank page. Some strategies that experienced writers use to put material on the page are freewriting, talking it out, and generating from a schema.

## Freewriting

To freewrite, you have to turn off your internal critic, the one that says "No, that's no good, that will never work." You have to be willing to write down many more ideas than you will end up using, even ideas you think are half-baked. Thinking about one idea makes it easier to think of related ideas or memories. So the more ideas you write down, the greater the chances that you will come up with ideas for connecting them into a point and supporting it.

Start by skimming an assignment sheet or a text about an issue that interests you. Then begin writing and keep writing in sentences or phrases. If you run out of ideas to write down, reread what you have and circle ideas that seem good to you. Then begin writing again with those ideas in mind. In the end, look over what you have written to see where you have the most ideas or the best ideas. Look for ideas that go together and start arranging them.

## Talking It Out

The simple act of saying your ideas out loud makes them easier to write down.

Call or get together with someone you trust who is willing to act as a sounding board. Then tell the person about the assignment, or about what you found out about your issue, or about the section you are working on. Ask your friend occasionally to sum up what you said or ask questions about what you are trying to do—not to give suggestions. When you find yourself saying something new or interesting, pause to write it down.

Without a partner, you can talk it out by treating your research process as a story that developed from the time you got the assignment, including ideas you had along the way, and changes in your position. The writing that you produce from this process is not yet a rough draft of your paper. Getting this story on paper simply gives you the raw materials of sentences and phrases that you can arrange into a line of argument.

## Using Generic Storyboards

Genres are categories of texts that share many features in common: They have similar goals, appeal to the same kinds of readers, and follow roughly the same sequence of development, which we might call a common storyboard. For example, a common genre in books and movies is the triumph of the underdog athlete or team. The storyboard shows the team in trouble, facing more powerful opponents, and getting help from an inspired coach, one who is usually seeking redemption as well. The team overcomes obstacles to arrive at the finals and come out on top. Recognizing that a text belongs to a familiar genre helps readers understand and analyze it because they can anticipate how the storyboard will develop. A storyboard creates some predictability but is also flexible enough to allow countless variations and twists. For an author who wants to write an underdog sports story, the storyboard can serve as a set of reminders of the kinds of characters and situations you need to include.

This book has described the genre of public policy argument with components that you can use as a storyboard to guide the development and arrangement of your ideas. Looking at the "Words to Watch For" in Chapters 2–6 can remind you of your options, from the larger units down to sentences. Below is a less detailed listing of these options.

### Templates for Policy Arguments

- Policy arguments call for issue, problem, and solution spans (Chapter 2).
- A span can be developed with passages at a sequence of stases: existence, definition, value, cause, and action (Chapter 3).
- Each stasis claim calls for a different kind of development:

  Existence passages are about the characteristics of cases.

  Definition passages are the categories to which cases might be assigned.

  Evaluation passages compare cases within a category to each other or to some standard.

  Cause claims are about how cases change: what causes them to start or stop existing, become a different kind of thing, or become more or less significant.

  Action claims are about the agents who might bring about a change and what they should do.

- A claim can be supported with appeals to ethos, pathos, and logos (Chapter 4) as well as concessions and rebuttals (Chapter 5).
- Each type of appeal has several options.

  Logos appeals can be based on witness testimony, common sense, or direct observations of the world.

  Ethos appeals are about the credibility of authors, experts, eyewitnesses, or cultural icons.

  Pathos appeals evoke imagination, emotions, and sensations and can be made with vivid description, emotion terms, or sensory terms.

- Claims can also be developed by responding to opponents (Chapter 5). A response can involve naming the opponents, summarizing their views fairly, admitting when they are right, signaling disagreement, stating challenges to a claim or its support, and restating the main point.

To use this list as a storyboard, start by jotting down concepts related to your issue. Then look at the terms on the list and write down whatever comes to mind relating to your issue. "Brainstorming with a Storyboard" provides some sample notes.

# BRAINSTORMING WITH A STORYBOARD

## Environment: Sea Turtles

**Jason's Notes**

Sea turtles dying—world ⎫

causes—eggs trampled, bright lights, shells colleted, hunted for meat, ⎬ Issue
dogs & raccoons, plastic bags

values—old species, biodiversity, beauty of shells ⎭

Case—Broward County, FL ⎫
brought home eggs with friends from beach ⎬ paradigm case

definition—green and leatherback endangered (Atlantic and Gulf) ⎫

action—fines, sea turtle hotline, marine patrols, public education ⎬ Problem

cause—tourists on beaches at night (OK), beach houses lit too bright (OK),
sky-glow from construction sites (big), raccoons (big) ⎭

how to keep raccoons out? how to stop construction lights ⎬ Solution

## Crime: Gang Violence

**Carlo's Notes**

Paradigm Case—Liberty High School—teen killed for stealing shoe ⎫

violent teenagers cause risk to themselves, neighbors, bystanders ⎬ Issue

values: lives, property, safety, future of America

Columbus ⎭

causes—graffiti, unsafe parking lot, not enough police, guns, rivals, ⎫
Castleman—impulse, alienation, opportunity, BUT ALSO racism, poverty

value—US problem signif. (stats), Cincinnati—most homicides in 14-yrs in ⎬ Problem
2001, Columbus?

Options— ⎭

Castleman—reduce opp (not enough) ⎫

Dilulio—remove liquor stores (not enough)

Toby—HS optional. Bad move: case of PJ dropping out of school—was his right ⎬ Solution
but ended up in jail

new approach—anti-gang program in Chicago: surveillance, anti-violence
groups, reduce 25% ⎭

Think of even more ideas by using the storyboard. Use the "Words to Watch For" as a set of reminders or questions for ideas to consider, not as a formula that must be followed exactly. Then jot down phrases or sentences in response to every argument keyword on your list. For example, if you think you need a value argument, try to craft sentences that include phrases like "is better than," "costs more than," "is reliable enough," or "fails the safety requirement."

In the end, look over the ideas you have jotted down to see where you had the most good ideas and start arranging them. Start writing about the ideas you find most interesting or the ones you think will be easiest to write about. Write something about every part you think you need. Then go back and expand each part.

# Evaluating

Evaluating means looking for places where your draft needs improvement. To evaluate your text accurately, you need to compare what is on the page with what you had planned or imagined the text would be like. Finding a mismatch between the text and the plan is harder than it seems. When you have been caught up in researching and writing about an issue, your mind easily fills in connections and explanations that don't actually appear on the page.

To bring your plans and goals to mind, take another look at the assignment sheet, read a model student paper if it is available, or reread a published text that is central to your argument.

To detect what is really on the page, you need to get some distance from your draft. Print out the text if you have been composing online, then put it away for a few days. When you look at it again, pay attention to moments when you are unsure of what you meant or your ideas no longer sound as good as they did before. These are spots where your written text doesn't match your intentions.

Another distancing strategy is to read your draft aloud or ask a friend to read the draft aloud to you. Suddenly your own words will sound strange. Your partner may pause or stumble over your wording. These spots are candidates for revision.

A third distancing strategy is to write out a list of goals for your paper, such as "I want to sound well-informed," or "I don't want it to be wordy and boring." Keep this list in front of you as you reread your paper and you will begin noticing spots where these goals have not been achieved.

## Detecting

All writers have expectations for texts that help them detect certain errors or gaps, but not everyone's "error detector" is set off by the same problems. The hard part is to find places that would set off someone else's detector. But how can you find problems that you don't know are problems?

The best way to detect these problems is to get feedback from another reader. This approach is described in Chapter 21. In this section, we will present some techniques to find problems on your own.

A good approach is to concentrate on one aspect of the paper at a time. In a systematic evaluation, a writer reads through the paper, focusing just on the argument, or the organization, or the readability.

- To evaluate the structure or arrangement, write an outline based on the current division of your draft into paragraphs. Or look at one paragraph at a time to make sure it is focused on one coherent topic. Mark any material that strays from that topic.

- To detect sentence-level problems in word choice, spelling, and mechanics, try reading the text backwards, from the last sentence to the first one.

- To detect problems in the use of sources, do one pass to check that every source mentioned in the text appears on the Works Cited or References list (Chapter 22). Then do a separate pass to check that every item on the Works Cited References list is mentioned in the text.

Even if you revise in several passes, you won't find everything that is worth changing without feedback from another reader. It is much easier to see the weaknesses in someone else's paper than in your own.

## Diagnosing

After you detect a difference between your text and your plans, you need to decide what is wrong before you decide what to do. Try to describe what is wrong in words. Here are a few sample diagnoses:

- I don't want to do that after all.
- I guess what I really want to do is . . . .
- This doesn't say everything it needs to.
- I don't know why this is here.
- This doesn't connect up to what comes before.
- I've said this already.
- This is getting wordy.
- I can't think of how to say this.

# Revising

Once you have detected problematic areas, you need to decide what to do about them. Should you change the text or the plan? What kind of change should you make?

The most frequent action that beginning writers take while revising is to delete. Deleting is appropriate when a passage simply restates an idea that was already expressed elsewhere. But in many cases, beginning writers delete passages that contain important ideas because they don't know how to make them clearer or fit them smoothly into their paper.

The purpose of revision is to improve your draft by working through these rough patches. Revision does not mean changing the topic. Revising literally means re-seeing to figure out what you want to say. The processes of evaluating, detecting, and diagnosing will help you discover options that fit the situation. You may end up adding, moving, or changing your arguments in significant ways. Here are some tips for improving the structure of your paper at the passage and paragraph levels:

*Revising Passages and Paragraphs*

- **Section Level.** Insert headings to divide your text into spans. Insert additional headings within each span that group together all the paragraphs about the same point. You may keep the headings in your final draft as aids to your readers.

   If a set of paragraphs about a topic is interrupted by one on a different topic, move it to a different section.

   If it is difficult to find a sequence of paragraphs all about the same point, try moving paragraphs around to create two or three coherent sections.

- **Paragraph level.** As you read through each paragraph, write a word or two in the margin as a label for its main claim. Then read the sentences to see if they all relate to that claim.

   If you find sentences on a different topic in the middle, you may need to move them into a different paragraph.

   If you find sentences at the end of the paragraph that shift to a different claim, then you may need to break the paragraph.

   If you can't come up with any single claim that a paragraph is about, you may be trying to cover a lot of different claims, none of which is fully developed.

# Editing at the Sentence Level

Editing is the process that focuses most closely on the language in the draft. Like revising, editing often works best when you look for one thing at a time. The aspects of language to consider include: word choice, redundancy, wordiness, grammar, punctuation, spelling, and flow.

You can detect and correct some of these language features through careful rereading. You will notice others only when a classmate or your instructor points them out.

To deal with aspects of the language skills that you can't improve on your own, use a handbook. When a peer or instructor points out a specific problem, look through your entire text to see if there are other instances to fix.

# Deciding When to Revise and Edit

You can make use of the revision process at any time, not just when you are close to finishing your paper. Revision may lead you back to reconsider your plans for the paper, even your main conclusion. It may lead you to change passages significantly or to write new passages. It may lead you to rearrange sentences or paragraphs or delete material altogether. It can take place at any time up until you have a final draft and even days, weeks, or months afterward. Outside the typical school environment, an author's earlier writing is often reshaped as the basis for later texts.

So there is no ideal time to revise. Many writers find, however, that revision is easier after some time has passed, when they have gained some distance from their draft. This may happen because the author forgets enough about the paper to read it as if someone else wrote it.

# Getting Stuck and Unstuck

Lots of authors get stuck while writing. Getting stuck is not a sign of laziness or lack of talent. In many cases, nothing is wrong with the process that the writer is using; instead, the process simply starts too late or a step in the process turns into a barrier.

Many students put off working on a paper because they are reluctant to dive into the messy process of assembling ideas, putting ideas into words, and shaping the argument. The disadvantages of this kind of procrastination are obvious: you don't have time to find the resources you need, let your ideas develop, and create a position that you really care about.

Some procrastinators find that when they really become tired and desperate, something clicks and the writing seems to pour out. What happens at 2 a.m. is not a visit from the writing angels. Instead, you are finally able to loosen some of the "rules" for how you "should" write.

Writers get stuck when they turn a flexible strategy or guideline into an iron-clad rule or standard. Writers get stuck when they create an insurmountable hurdle that must be surpassed in a certain way before any other work on the paper can be done. Any strategy or guideline can be transformed into a counterproductive rigid rule.

## Loosening Rigid Rules

- You DO NOT have to know your thesis before you can begin to research or to write.

- You DO NOT have to complete your research before you start to write.

- You DO NOT have to write a perfect introduction before you can write anything else.

- You DO NOT need a new topic when the going gets rough.

- You DO NOT need a certain number of points or examples or paragraphs.

- You ARE ALLOWED to put in your own opinion and to use "I" and "me."

- You ARE ALLOWED to disagree with experts and to point out ways that they disagree.

The best way to get unstuck is to give yourself permission to write something flawed and incomplete. Let "Get something down on paper and improve it" be your mantra. Worrying too early about the quality of your idea or correctness of the sentences can be counterproductive. It breaks your train of thought and diverts attention away from your ideas. It is much better for an early draft to contain many ideas written in a haphazard style than only a few ideas written elegantly.

## Permission Giving

- Tell yourself that you are going to write one full page before stopping, no matter what.
- Title your draft "HorribleDraft.doc."
- Skip over a spot where you can't think of the right words. Write a related word or insert the phrase "[FIX THIS]" and then come back to it later.

The best way to write is to allow yourself to depart from templates, to break the rigid rules, and to follow out the ideas that really interest you. Then revise to make it all look smooth and orderly. Don't be a Procrustes towards your own paper as illustrated in "The Procrustean Bed."

Vase painting (470 BCE) of Greek hero Theseus killing Procrustes. Erich Lessing/Art Resource, NY.

### THE PROCRUSTEAN BED

Procrustes was a legendary Greek villain who forced his "guests" to sleep in an iron bed that was guaranteed to fit each occupant. The bed turned out to be a torture device. If a victim was shorter than the bed, he would be stretched with a rack until he fit. If he was longer than the bed, his legs would be cut off.

Moral: Avoid the Procrustean bed! Don't stretch out a text to fit an ideal length. Don't pummel ideas into the shape of an argument type that you think it is "supposed" to have. Do not truncate your ideas just because you have reached the page limit.

# CHAPTER 20

# Rhetorical Planning

Rhetorical planning involves finding something new and relevant to say to your readers. The best way to do so is to view your message from the reader's current perspective and use the resulting insights to shape what you have to say and how you say it.

**Show you understand the reader's perspective.** © Harley Schwadron.

# Asking What's New

To contribute to a policy debate on an issue, you have to have something new to say. It is not enough to present everything you have found out in an organized report, even if it is peppered with your reactions. What counts as new depends on the situation in which you are writing; newness is judged in relation to what the people who care about the issue have been doing and talking about.

This means that an idea is not necessarily new even if it is something you have just learned or just thought of for the first time. To be new, the idea has to be something your readers see as an addition, a different perspective, or a challenge to what they already believe. It is impossible to say something new without knowing what is old.

If you've ever heard the old adage, "There is nothing new under the sun," you know that saying something new does not mean coming up with something that no one in the world has ever thought of. The hardest problems have a long history of attempted solutions. So even if an idea has been around for a while, it can count as new if it is adapted to a different setting. For example, the idea of enacting gang curfews is not new for neighborhoods in Chicago, but it might be new for Topeka because every setting is different. For you to recommend Chicago's approach to curfews, you must reason about the differences between the two cities and consider how the approach would have to be changed to apply to Topeka.

In order to say something new, you do not necessarily have to add to what is known; you can also contribute to the discussion of an issue by challenging the current viewpoint or creating doubt.

Because saying something new depends so much on the context in which you say it, you have to consider your choice of audience early in your planning. You have to ask yourself what different groups of readers already know about the issue, what they care about most, and what you have to contribute that they will find new.

Most importantly, of all the new ideas that you could write about, you have to choose something that you really want to say. Writing becomes an empty exercise if you don't take an active role in the conversation. It is easy to sit on the sidelines to summarize and comment on what other people are saying. It takes some courage to have your say.

Authors rarely know exactly what they have to say at the beginning of the writing process. Like them, you will probably consider approaches for several possible audiences. The message that you really care about making may not emerge until you have completed a draft.

Once you decide what to say and who to say it to, you may need to revise your draft substantially. The decisions you make will influence every aspect of your argument, from the space you devote to different sections, to the tone you adopt. In this chapter, you will learn how to plan with a rhetorical situation in mind.

# Relating to an Audience

Most students write with either their instructor or a "general" audience in mind. But your instructor is unlike most of the people who have a stake in your issue. Your instructor knows more than the stakeholders about some aspects of the problem and less on others. And the general public is a hard audience to write for; most students do not accurately gauge what people in general know or care about. So writing to these audiences is like a ballplayer taking batting practice. The ball is easy to hit, but a hit does not score any points that count.

Relating to an audience in a specific situation is like being at bat in an inning with opponents on the field and, perhaps, some allies on base, and lots of spectators with different allegiances. The situation can change quickly. You need to be ready to recognize opportunities and adjust your stance accordingly.

## Adopting an Authoritative Role

As a student, you may feel that you cannot take on an authoritative role in a conversation because of a lack of knowledge or standing. But, as you can tell from radio or TV talk shows, you don't have to be an expert to have your say. As a graduate of the local school or a member of a local club, for example, you have valuable knowledge and experience that policymakers may lack about a problem in your town, school, or workplace. For aspects of the issue that you do not know enough about, you can do as the pundits do, explore the issue (Chapter 7). After doing some digging and exploring, you may have important points to make. For example, Jackson Blair who wrote about Southern Bluefin tuna (Chapter 17) and Anna McGaha who wrote about prostitutes (Chapter 16) based their arguments on extensive research.

Similarly, you need not be a decision maker to have standing. Your standing may come from being directly affected by an issue or knowing people who have been involved. You also have sufficient standing if you belong to a relevant organization, live in a politician's district, or make use of a relevant product or service. For example, Katie Kucera (Chapter 14) draws on her experiences in an outdoors ministry to write about damage to wilderness areas. Jeff Corbett (Chapter 17) draws on his familiarity with students, store clerks, and customers to explain the difficulties of enforcing the laws on under-age drinking.

Narrating a personal case is an effective way to establish your standing early in your paper. Several student papers in this book include vivid personal cases. For example, Lauren Downey (Chapter 14) described a series of negative encounters with the police and Jeff Corbett (Chapter 17) described his father's car accident with a drunk driver. Other students used effective strategies to signal membership. For example, Michael Choat, writing to wilderness enthusiasts out West, describes himself as an avid mountain biker. Anna McGaha (Chapter 16), writing to the National Organization of Women, describes herself as a feminist.

## Writing to Insiders or Outsiders

A basic question about audience is whether to write to insiders or outsiders. Insiders are people who already know something about the situation. They include stakeholders, decision makers, authors, and pundits who have already written on the issue. When writing to an insider audience, it is important to show that you have done your homework—that you share their awareness of what has been happening. Writing to insiders may allow you to move more quickly to the changes in attitudes, beliefs, or actions that you think should happen. You can choose to write to a single individual, to an agency or organization, or to a trade magazine or journal aimed at your readers.

Outsiders are people who may have some interest in the issue but little direct knowledge. They may include readers of a popular magazine, such as *Mother Jones, National Review,* or a local newspaper. In writing to outsiders, it is important to show readers how they are or could be affected by the issue. For example, Eileen Dudzik, writing to fellow Houstonians, spells out in detail the connection between a local energy company and the Amazon rainforest.

Insiders consider it impolite for a newcomer to barge into their conversation and try to change its course. To join an inner circle, you must follow its conversation for a while. Then by referring knowledgably to the group's values and previous efforts at addressing the problem, you show that you care about the very questions that motivate this community and that you have done your homework. Only then can you identify some shortcoming and make the case that you have something to add that is fresh, worth people's time, and capable of filling a gap.

You may also write to a complex audience that includes both insiders and outsiders. This can be a very effective choice because you may inspire other people like you to make their own arguments. You can reach a complex audience by writing in the style of journals like *The Atlantic Monthly* or *Wilson Quarterly* that are marketed to policymakers and academics as well as the public.

## Writing to Allies or Opponents

Another basic choice is whether to write to allies or to opponents. Both choices are reasonable because you may easily find yourself disagreeing with allies and agreeing with opponents. You may want to persuade allies to take a more effective approach to an issue or to become aware of some aspect of the problem that they are neglecting. While it is unlikely that reading one argument will completely change the minds of opponents, you may help them to see the issue in a new way or to recognize alternatives. When writing to allies, refer often to shared values and goals and signal your membership with personal pronouns such as "we," "us," and "our."

Phrases such as "I understand that you . . . ," "I know that you . . . ," and "Obviously, you are well aware that . . . " acknowledge how an opponent is likely to feel about your idea: worried, angry, receptive. Instead of dismissing these concerns as false or foolish, show that you understand the reasons for these feelings. Then respond as best you can while remaining honest. Point out benefits to the solution that reader might not have thought of, acknowledge and praise steps that they have taken, and/or acknowledge that there are alternatives besides yours.

# Addressing Readers

Figuring out how to address your audience can help you imagine yourself in an appropriate role, which in turn can help you plan what to say and how to say it.

## Using "I" and "You"

If you are writing directly to a specific stakeholder or decision maker, using "you" makes sense. If you can count yourself as a member of the same community or group, then addressing allies as "we" can sound more natural than "they" or "you." But addressing opponents as "we" may sound phony.

　　If you are writing to a complex audience, you can adopt a voice that expresses more than one kind of relationship, as in these examples:

- "Because we all understand the importance of preventing school violence, it is important for each of us to do our part. School officials should keep it in mind when they vote on the budget. Parents should discuss the new policies with their children. And my classmates and I should be ready to report anything suspicious."

- "As leaders, you are responsible for both our town's economy and the state of the wetlands we all enjoy. Until now, you have treated these as opposing interests. My goal is to show you how maintaining the wetlands can improve the economy."

## Signaling Shared Knowledge

Addressing readers also involves selecting the right amount of detail. Busy readers can be turned off by long passages describing events or policies that they already know about. To make appropriate choices, you need to find out as much as you can about the reader.

　　To exhibit selectivity, either cut out information that the reader will find obvious or signal that you are aware that the reader knows it.

- **Cut obvious details.** Judge what is obvious by considering the readers' areas of expertise. There is no need to tell an official from the Department of Transportation that "drunk driving severely impairs your ability to operate any kind of machinery, slows your reaction time, impairs your senses, and makes you tremendously hazardous on the roadway."

- **Signal awareness of old news.** When you are not sure what to cut or when you must repeat familiar information to the reader, use signals such as "as you know," "I know you believe that . . . ," "clearly, this fact is well-known to you," "you have already taken steps in this direction," "everyone knows that . . . ," and "to the readers of this journal, it is no surprise that . . . ."

- **Retain reminders of values at stake.** For example, it is effective to tell the Austin City Council that "we are fortunate to have one of most environmentally concerned city councils in the country."

## Avoiding Pejoratives

When you have chosen an issue that you care about and are writing to an opponent, it is easy to adopt a critical tone so sharp that your reader will see it as hostile and stop reading. Writing the paper may vent some of your feelings, but it will not narrow the gap between your position and that of your opponent. While you should not leave out any important points of disagreement, you can present them in ways that avoid alienating your reader.

One important way to come across as fair is to put points of agreement before points of disagreement, whether in a paragraph, a passage, or an entire span. Similarly, if you have both descriptive and evaluative points, put the descriptive parts first, phrased in calm language, then introduce the most critical points of disagreement.

In phrasing your points, avoid using accusatory terms and phrases such as "Their deaths will be on your head," "It's all your fault," "People like you care more about money than other living things," or "There is no reason for what you are doing."

## Allocating Space

When we began identifying the spans in published articles (Chapter 2), you learned that the sizes of the spans vary from article to article. That is, the issue, problem, and solution spans do not each deserve 33 percent of the space available. Points about existence, definition, value, cause, and action do not divide up neatly into one paragraph apiece. The relative proportions of the spans do not come about completely by accident. Authors decide how to allocate their space with their purpose and audience in mind. In the same way, you must think about what aspects of your argument will need the most development and support.

The sketches in Figure 20.1 illustrate some ways you can allocate space. A problem-based argument, on the left, is appropriate when the existence, significance, or cause of the problem is controversial. A solution-based argument, in the middle, is appropriate when there is widespread agreement about the problem, but not about how to address it. A more evenly distributed argument, on the right, is necessary when all aspects of the issue are unsettled.

By planning out how you will allocate your space, you are more likely to stay on track as you draft your paper.

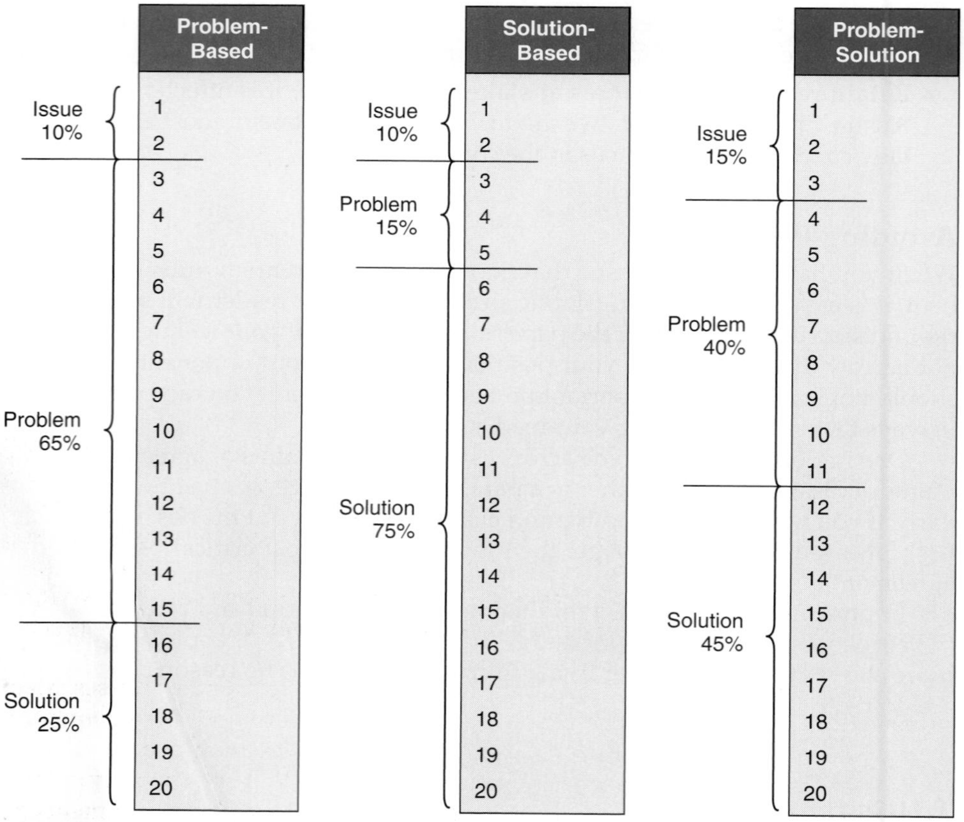

FIGURE 20.1   **A few ways to allocate space.**

# Making Plans Flexible

The kind of planning described in this chapter is open for adjustment during the entire writing process. Your plans may change as you discover new information, change your mind, and receive feedback. A good plan is one that makes it easy to make changes, not one that rules them out.

# CHAPTER 21

# Collaborative Evaluation and Revision

When authors write in the workplace or in private or civic organizations, their text will be seen and used by many other people. If no one wants to read it, the author's text will not accomplish any work in the world. If the text is unclear or unpersuasive, its author could miss a chance to be hired for a job, have a proposal turned down, or cause confusions and delays for clients.

When a lot is at stake, authors ask for feedback throughout their writing process. Before they send a text out to do its work, they want to be sure it is as accurate and persuasive as possible.

You have probably participated in peer review activities in other classes. Most students find these activities valuable. Some students learn more from commenting on someone else's paper than from receiving comments on their own.

The benefits of reviewing a peer's paper are obvious. Reading a variety of texts written for the same assignment gives you a better idea of how the assignment can be approached. You may notice strategies that you can adopt in your own paper. It is easier to detect weaknesses in someone else's paper than in your own.

Commenting on someone's writing gives you a skill that becomes more and more valuable as time goes on. You and your friends may comment on each other's personal statements for school or job applications. The higher your status in an organization or business, the more likely it is that you'll comment on someone's writing. As a tutor or even as a parent, you may find yourself helping students with their schoolwork. By learning how to talk about writing, you'll feel more confident in those situations and you will provide more useful advice.

Why does it seem better to give than to receive comments? One reason has to do with commenting itself: Peers sometimes write comments that writers can't use. Another reason has to do with the authors; they sometimes dismiss comments instead of revising with them in mind. In this chapter, we will focus on ways to make the comments you write as helpful as possible and on ways to apply a peer's comments to your own paper.

# Taking on a Helpful Role

The most helpful comments come from peers who are acting as an engaged audience member, as a teammate, or as an open-minded opponent. In any of these roles, you can help the author see the argument from another point of view, one that he or she didn't think of. Then the author can improve the writing by making changes that readers like you would find more persuasive.

Taking on one of these roles requires imagination. So if you have limited time to respond to your peer, you may not be able to respond thoroughly to the whole paper. In this case, read through the entire paper before making any comments. Then select two or three aspects to comment on that you think need the most improvement.

# Giving Helpful Feedback

The most frequent comments that students write on a peer's paper fall into the following categories:

| | |
|---|---|
| **Praise** | "I liked how you ... "; "This looks good" |
| **Instructions** | "Change this wording"; "Add some examples" |
| **Descriptions** | "This is really interesting/vague/unclear/ organized" |

All these comments have value. Praise is something that everyone appreciates; it encourages authors to do more of the same and take more risks. Instructions are efficient for small-scale corrections at the word, sentence, or paragraph level. Descriptions give an overall impression.

But useful feedback consists of more than comments like these. A peer reviewer who only praises, instructs, and describes is not helping the author improve the argument and its presentation.

In addition to taking on a helpful role, you should also give more helpful types of comments. The best comments challenge the author to explain and defend his or her position as well as possible. They are very specific and focus on a particular passage. Useful comments relate to the process of evaluating described in Chapter 19:

| | |
|---|---|
| **Detect** | Explain what made you stop to comment on this particular passage and what reaction you had while reading it. |
| **Reflect** | Describe what you think the writer was trying to do in the passage. |
| **Diagnose** | Explain what might be causing the problem or give reasons why other readers might have trouble with this passage. |
| **Suggest** | Come up with one or more ways to fix the problem. Phrase them as options rather than commands. |

## Detect

Detection is an attempt to describe the problem from your point of view. Any engaged reader can make this kind of comment by pausing frequently and asking "Does this make sense?" or "Why is this here?" Here are some examples:

- "I found this section hard to follow—I had to reread it three times."
- "I was expecting a solution, so I was surprised that you ended so abruptly."
- "I am not sure why you put cost as the first criterion."
- "If I were your opponent, I'd just stop reading right here."

## Reflect

A reflective comment describes what you think the writer actually meant to do in the passage. Any peer can be reflective, no matter what you know about the topic. It is very useful for a writer to see what a reader thought the goal was. If you are right, then the author will know that the intended message is coming through. Reflection is even more helpful if your hunch is wrong. If you don't get the point, then it is likely that other readers will have the same trouble. Your comment will help the author see what is actually written on the page and not what he or she only intended to put there.

Reflection is often combined in a comment with detection:

- "I am a little confused by the fourth paragraph. The problem you are addressing is the fact that crime and violence are on the rise in America and you say this is a result of the lack of religion in American life. So maybe the values that you are arguing should exist are not present in American life because of the obstacles you list: ineffective church systems, failure to communicate to children, etc. It sounds like a problem with religion in America in general and not so much with crime. Maybe crime is the obstacle that religious values must overcome? I think this is confusing for me because the paper starts out with the problem of crime and finishes with the problem of religion. Is this where you are going?"
- "I think you are saying that laws exist to keep minors from drinking, but they do not do much to stop underage drinking. As a college student I think it is important to you because underage drinking is common among college students. I don't see you describing the negative effects of underage drinking. Maybe you just want to show that the present laws are not working to stop underage drinking."

## Diagnose

You may detect a passage that trips you up but have trouble explaining why. One of the following descriptions may apply to the passage:

- "This is confusing."
- "This claim is questionable."
- "This gives the wrong impression."

- "This makes you seem unfair."
- "This is a big leap."

Another useful way to come up with a diagnosis is to identify the kind of argument in the passage (e.g., a value argument or an ideal case). Then refer to the guidelines for that type of argument in Chapters 2–6. What is supposed to be there that might be missing from the paper? Look for things that don't belong. Play devil's advocate.

- "The paper was somewhat short and lacking in a few areas, especially a conclusion. A good conclusion would really pull the paper together and help to sum up all the ideas discussed up to that point."
- "I don't see any ethos appeals."
- "Your tone is not right. An expert in evaluating arguments would be more confident in the analysis and get more critical of what is wrong. You don't take a position."
- "You don't say anything about DiIulio's solutions. I tended to see his solutions as an important part to discuss because they do seem like viable options. Not including them, I think, can severely distort one's outlook on his article."

## "Look at all these typos! Haven't you ever heard of 'spellcheck?!'"

**An unhelpful peer comment.**    *Courtesy of* Artizans.

## Suggest

The difference between a suggestion and an instruction is more than just a nicer tone. Giving a suggestion acknowledges that there is more than one good way to make an argument. In contrast, giving an instruction implies that yours is the only acceptable approach. That is why instructions work well for word-, sentence-, and pararaph-level corrections, but not for improving the argument.

The most helpful suggestions are specific and include a reason.

- "Add some citations to experts who agree with you because otherwise it's all your personal experience."
- "The claims and the appeals go back and forth in the same paragraph. If you separate them, you can keep me on one subject in each paragraph. In other words, keep the ethical portions in one part of the paragraph instead of jumping around."

## Comments to Avoid

The least useful comments either are too harsh or go overboard with praise. Comments that are too vague are also unhelpful because they give the author no clue about what to do or where to do it. Here are examples of each kind:

*"Let's change 'brink of chaos' to 'Everything is wonderful.'"*

**Avoid suggestions that alter the author's meaning.** © The New Yorker Collection 2004 David Sipress from cartoonbank.com. All Rights Reserved.

| | |
|---|---|
| **Personal attacks** | "You obviously didn't work very hard on this"; "I can't believe you think this way." |
| **Exaggerated praise** | "It seems perfect to me. I can't think of anything that needs to be fixed"; "Once you find some evidence, it will be fine"; "No one could possibly disagree." |
| **Vague, timid, or nonspecific comments** | "You don't use any sources but maybe we don't have to"; "It sounded vague in places"; "I didn't like this part, but I don't know anything about your topic." |
| **Suggestions that alter the author's meaning** | "This part doesn't make sense but you have plenty without it"; "I was always told not to be this personal." |

# Using Feedback During Revision

Many students pay little attention to their peers' comments because they find them unhelpful, irrelevant, wrong, or clueless. If all the comments you get are praise or vague descriptions, then you may be right to ignore them. But if your peer has tried to give helpful comments, then you should take them seriously.

The key to getting the most out of a peer's comments is to treat your peer as the exact person you are trying to convince. If your peer misunderstands you, then it is up to you to make your point clearer. If your peer brings up counterarguments, then it is up to you to add concessions or rebuttals to your paper.

Some students ignore comments because they don't understand why the peer made that comment or what he or she meant. In this case, you need to do some work to figure out how the comment could be helpful. Here are some common complaints about peer comments and suggestions for interpreting them.

- *If you're thinking:* "What she wants is already in the paper."

  Assume that your peer read carefully. If the peer can't find an example or an appeal that you think is there, then maybe you need to highlight it by moving it or providing a better transition. Or the peer may be asking for more examples or better ones than you provided.

- *If you're thinking:* "He just doesn't understand my point"

  Don't just ignore the comment; other readers might have the same reaction. Instead, jot down some reasons for why the comment is off-base or wrong. For example, "It's obvious that I'm talking about kids in middle school here." You may find that you have drafted persuasive or explanatory material that you can add to the paper itself.

- *If you're thinking:* "The comment doesn't make any sense"

Don't assume that your peer is stupid or incapable of understanding. Instead, assume that there is a reason for the comment. Ask yourself, "How can this comment make sense? What must my peer have thought I was saying? "

- *If you're thinking:* "I explained this in class."
  If you've answered this orally, you have satisfied one reader or even the instructor but not all the other readers who might have the same reaction. Make the explanation in your paper.

In addition to reading your peer's comments charitably, think about whether there are other places in your paper where they may apply. For example, if your peer points out a need for transitions in the problem span, check on the quality of your transitions elsewhere, too.

## Giving Feedback to Reviewers

To improve your skill as a reviewer, you need two types of feedback. First, if more than one student reviewed the same paper, you should exchange reviews to see where your comments overlapped. Did another reviewer see more or less to comment on than you did? Were your comments more or less specific? Second, you should receive some feedback from the writer whose text you reviewed. Which of your comments did the writer find the most useful?

Giving and receiving comments help you become a better reader and a better writer. While most people would rather not have to rework a paper, doing a major reworking is one of the most powerful ways to improve your paper.

# CHAPTER 22

# Documentation Conventions

Documentation conventions guide the way you refer within your text to sources of information and arguments by other authors. They also shape your presentation of publication information about these sources in a list at the end of your paper. These conventions make it easy for readers to go and look at any of the sources you used, in order to judge their credibility for themselves. They might want to see when and where a source was published, find out more about what the author said, or see if you stated the author's point fairly.

Following the rules for documenting sources is like knowing what to wear when you go out. Showing up at church wearing party clothes is just as bad as showing up at a party wearing church clothes. Conventions for documenting sources signal what academic discipline a writer belongs to, if any at all. So following these conventions, even the ones that seem arbitrary and nitpicky, is an easy way to establish your ethos (Chapter 20), your credibility, with your readers.

In this chapter, you will learn the basics of two of the most widely used conventions. The MLA style, which is widely used in the humanities, is governed by the Modern Language Association (http://www.mla.org). The APA style, which is typical for social science disciplines, is governed by the American Psychological Association (www.apastyle.org). Each organization publishes a handbook that will give you more complete information than you will find here.

The MLA and APA styles reflect the research methods and publishing habits of their academic disciplines. In the humanities, authors often refer to older texts, such as books by well-known writers. The MLA style emphasizes the author's name by spelling it out in full and deemphasizes the date of publication by putting it at the end. In the sciences and social sciences, authors try to refer to the most recent available research, often published in quarterly or even weekly journals. So the APA style emphasizes the date of publication by placing it at the front of the reference, immediately after the author's name. It also deemphasizes authors by using initials instead of first names.

# Two Parts of Documentation: In-Text Citations and Lists of Sources

Documentation conventions have two parts, first a short reference in the text (called an in-text citation) and second a full record of publication information in a list at the end of the text. These two parts work together:

- All the sources on the list must be mentioned explicitly somewhere in the text.
- Every source that is mentioned in the text must appear on the list.

The MLA style and APA style differ in many small details both in the in-text citations and in the list of sources. To make these details easier to spot, we present the two styles one above the other in "Source Lists for MLA and APA Styles."

## SOURCE LISTS FOR MLA AND APA STYLES

MLA Works Cited    Miller, Arthur. "Civil Rights & Hate Crime Legislation: Two Important Asymmetries." <u>Journal of Social Philosophy</u> 34.3 (Fall 2003): 437–44.

---. "Confidentiality, Protective Orders, and Public Access to the Courts." <u>Harvard Law Review</u> 105.2 (Dec. 1991): 427–502.

Rachuba, Laura, Bonita Stanton, and Donna Howard. "Violent Crime in the United States: An Epidemiologic Profile." <u>Archives of Pediatrics & Adolescent Medicine</u> 149.9 (Sept. 1995): 953–61.

"Stats and Resources." <u>MADD Online</u>. 29 Apr 2002 <http://www.madd.org/stats/> (1 May 2004).

APA References    Miller, A. (2003). Civil rights & hatecrime legislation: Two important asymmetries. *Journal of Social Philosophy, 34,* 437–444.

Miller, A. (1991). Confidentiality, protective orders, and public access to the courts. *Harvard Law Review, 105*(2), 427–502.

Rachuba, L., Stanton, B., & Howard, D. (1995). Violent crime in the United States: An epidemiologic profile. *Archives of Pediatrics & Adolescent Medicine, 149*(9), 953–961.

Stats and resources. (2002). *MADD Online.* Retrieved May 1, 2004, from http://www.madd.org/stats/

By comparing the entries in "Source Lists," you can see that the MLA style and APA style differ in heading, punctuation, capitalization, and the placement of items of information. In fact, the two styles differ in more than ten ways. You will learn how to create a list of sources later in the chapter. For now, refer back to the entries in "Source Lists" as we explain how to cite them in a text.

# In-Text Citations

You can mention a source in your text in two ways, either by direct reference, referring to the author by name as you develop your claim, or by parenthetical citation, inserting the author's name in parentheses as an aside.

## Direct Reference Citations

In Chapters 4 and 5, you learned how claims are supported with references to other authors, both allies and opponents. These references include the author's name, identify her status or source of expertise, and use verbs of attribution to characterize her position. When you use an author's name in this way, you are making a direct reference citation. To see how direct references differ in MLA and APA styles, see "Direct References," which is based on the entries in "Source Lists."

### DIRECT REFERENCES

#### Direct Reference with Direct Quotation

| | |
|---|---|
| MLA | Laura Rachuba, Bonita Stanton, and Donna Howard, health researchers at the University of Maryland, found that "the highest rates of violence and the highest increases in violence are occurring not among adults but among children." (956) |
| APA | Rachuba, Stanton, and Howard (1995), health researchers at the University of Maryland, found that "the highest rates of violence and the highest increases in violence are occurring not among adults but among children" (p. 956). |

#### Direct Reference to an Author with Two or More Articles on the Source List

| | |
|---|---|
| MLA | Arthur Miller raises the possibility that hate crime legislation increases resentment ("Civil Rights"). |
| APA | Miller (2003) raises the possibility that hate crime legislation increases resentment. |

## Indirect Parenthetical Citations

Using a parenthetical citation such as (Miller, 2003), you can credit another author as the source of your information without mentioning the author by name in your discussion. A parenthetical citation provides just enough information for readers to find the full publication information on your list of sources. The essential information is the author's name. But MLA and APA styles differ on what other information to provide. Compare the entries in "Parenthetical Citations," which are based on information in "Source Lists."

Parenthetical citations are easier to use than direct citations, because you can insert them without rewording your sentences. However, they are also less persuasive, because they provide no extra ethos support for your claim. Parenthetical citations say nothing about the author's status and give you no chance to interpret the author's claim yourself, so they provide very little "bang for the buck."

## PARENTHETICAL CITATIONS

### Parenthetical Citation to an Author with Two or More Articles on the Source List

MLA

Even in the 1990s, some lawyers opposed giving the public greater access to legal documents (Miller, "Confidentiality").

APA

Even in the 1990s, some lawyers opposed giving the public greater access to legal documents (Miller, 1991).

### Parenthetical Citation to Two or More Authors

MLA

The risks of violence faced by minorities are widely acknowledged (Miller, "Civil Rights"; Rachuba, Stanton and Howard).

APA

The risks of violence faced by minorities are widely acknowledged (Miller, 2003; Rachuba, Stanton & Howard, 1995).

## Citations to Sources with Unknown Authors

Some texts (such as postings on Web sites or newspaper editorials) do not identify a specific author.

- **Direct Reference.** If the author of an article is unknown, then substitute the name of the organization publishing it (such as the *New York Times* or the National Rifle Association).

- **Parenthetical Citation.** In place of the author's name, put the name of the organization or the first words of the article title.

See entries in "Citations to Articles with Unknown Authors," which are based on the entries in "Source Lists."

## CITATIONS TO ARTICLES WITH UNKNOWN AUTHORS

### Direct Reference to Unknown Author

MLA

Among other "Stats and Resources," the Mothers Against Drunk Driving (MADD) Web site lists a 2002 Justice Department finding that frequent binge drinkers make up only six percent of the U.S. population but drink 50 percent of all the alcohol consumed.

APA

Among other "Stats and resources" (2002), the Mothers Against Drunk Driving (MADD) Web site lists a 2002 Justice Department finding that frequent binge drinkers make up only 6% of the U.S. population but drink 50% of all the alcohol consumed.

### Parenthetical Citation to Unknown Author

MLA

Frequent bingers make up only six percent of the U.S. population but drink 50 percent of all the alcohol consumed ("Stats and Resources").

APA

Frequent bingers make up only 6% of the U.S. population but drink 50% of all the alcohol consumed (Stats and resources, 2002).

# Lists of Sources

In addition to requiring references to sources within the text, MLA and APA styles also require a list of the publication information for every source. In MLA style, this list of sources is titled "Works Cited." In APA style, it is titled "References." In both styles, the list is arranged alphabetically by the author's last name and appears on a new page after the text of the document.

Entries on the list differ according to the type of document you have cited. Most students cite documents of one of these four basic types:

- Books and book parts
- Periodicals
- Personal communications
- Multimedia and Internet sources

The examples that follow will illustrate the most common list entries for these documents. Consult an APA or MLA handbook to find detailed instructions for the many varieties of each category.

Online books, journals, newspapers, e-mail, and Web sites will be covered in the same category as their printed version.

# Books and Book Parts

The information required about a book includes the author's name, the book title, the location of publication, the publisher, and the date. If different authors wrote or compiled specific parts of the book, then the entry must also include the chapter author, chapter title, and page numbers. If the book appears online, the URL and date of access are added.

## ENTRIES FOR BOOKS AND BOOK PARTS

### Authored Book

MLA Works Cited     Ehrlich, Paul R., and Anne Ehrlich. <u>Extinction: The Causes and Consequences of the Disappearance of Species</u>. New York: Random House, 1981.

APA References     Ehrlich, P.R., & Ehrlich, A. (1981). *Extinction: The causes and consequences of the disappearance of species*. New York: Random House.

### Chapter in an Anthology or Collection

MLA Works Cited     Scraton, Phil and Deena Haydon. "Challenging the Criminalization to Children and Young People." <u>Youth Justice: Critical Readings</u>. Eds. John Muncie, Gordon Hughes, and Eugene McLaughlin. London: Sage, 2002. 311–28.

APA References     Scraton, P., & Haydon, D. (2002). Challenging the criminalization to children and young people. In J. Muncie, G. Hughes, & E. McLaughlin (Eds.), *Youth justice: Critical readings*. (pp. 311–328). London: Sage.

### Article in an Encyclopedia or Dictionary

MLA Works Cited     "Yosemite National Park." <u>Columbia Encyclopedia</u>. Sixth Edition, 2002. New York: Bartleby <www.bartleby.com/65/yo/Yosemite.html> (14 Oct. 2003).

APA References     Yosemite national park. (2002). *Columbia encyclopedia* (6th ed.). New York: Bartleby. Retrieved October 2003, from www.bartleby.com/65/yo/Yosemite.html

### Government Publication (online)

MLA Works Cited     U.S. Environmental Protection Agency. Office of Water. <u>President Clinton's Clean Water Initiative.</u> EPA 800-R-94-001.

APA References    U.S. Environmental Protection Agency. Office of Water. (1994, February). *President Clinton's clean water initiative.* Feb. 1994. epa.gov (14 Oct. 2003). *Initiative.* EPA 800-R-94-001. Retrieved October 14, 2003, from http://epa.gov

# Periodicals

Periodicals are publications that come out on a regular basis (or periodically) (Chapter 3). They include newspapers with daily issues, magazines with weekly issues, scholarly journals with quarterly issues, and trade journals that appear monthly. Because there are so many issues, a periodical is usually identified by a volume number (that goes up by one each year) and an issue number (that depends on how many times the periodical appears each year). This information appears in a source list entry along with the article's author(s), the article title, the date, and the pages on which the article appears. If the article appears online, the URL and date of access are added.

## ENTRIES FOR ARTICLES IN PERIODICALS

### Journal Article (Online Journal Web site)

MLA Works Cited    Meares, Tracy L. and Dan M. Kahan. "When Rights are Wrong: Chicago's Paradox of Unwanted Rights." <u>Boston Review</u> 24.2 (April/May 1999). 17 Sept. 2002 <bostonreview.mit.edu/ br24.2/meares.html>.

APA References    Meares, T.L. & Kahan, D.M. (1999). When rights are wrong: Chicago's paradox of unwanted rights. *Boston Review,* 24(2). Retrieved September 17, 2000, from bostonreview.mit.edu/br24.2/meares.html

### Newspaper Article (Online, Author Unknown)

MLA Works Cited    "Sniper Trial Jury Pool Mulls Va. Death Penalty." <u>New York Times</u> 15 Oct. 2003. 10 Apr. 2004 <www.nytimes.com/reuters/news/ news-crime-sniper.html>.

APA References    Sniper trial jury pool mulls Va. death penalty. *New York Times,* (2003, 15 October). Retrieved April 10, 2004, from www.nytimes.com/reuters/news/news-crime-sniper.html

### Letter to the Editor

MLA Works Cited    Murkowski, Frank H. "Oil vs. Wilderness." Letter. <u>New York Times</u> 30 Mar. 1999, sec. A: 22.

APA References    Murkowski, F.H. (1999, March 30). Oil vs. wilderness. [Letter to the editor]. *New York Times,* p. A22.

### Article Found on Library Database

MLA Works Cited     Shiflett, Dave. "Parks and Wreck: Against Jet Skiers, Snowmobilers, and Other Louts." <u>National Review</u> 53.5 (19 Mar. 2001). <u>Expanded Academic ASAP</u>. 10 April 2004 <www.galegroup.com>.

APA References     Shiflett, D. (2001). Parks and wreck: Against jet skiers, snowmobilers, and other louts. *National Review, 53*(5). Expanded Academic ASAP database. Retrieved April 10, 2004, from www.galegroup.com

## Personal Communications

Personal communications include phone calls, interviews, personal letters, memos, e-mails, and messages posted to electronic discussion groups or bulletin boards. These documents are hard for readers to see for themselves, so it is important to provide information about the author, the type of communication, and the date on which it occurred. In the social sciences, these documents are cited far less often than in the humanities. The APA entries used here follow the usual template as much as possible.

### ENTRIES FOR MEMOS, LETTERS, E-MAIL AND ONLINE POSTS

MLA Works Cited     Barr, Graham. "Re: Crime Statistics." E-mail to the author. 20 Sept. 2003.

Lasky, Kristen. Letter to the author. 27 Oct. 2003.

Lewis, Ray. "Re: National Crime Survey Discussion." 3 March 1998. Online posting. National Crime Survey. 6 Oct. 2003 <Listserv. legalminds.lp.findlaw.com/list/ncs-l/msg00007.html>.

Miller, Evelyn. "Proposal to Purchase Area Wetlands." Memo to the Conservation Committee, Goffstown, New Hampshire. 13 Oct. 2003.

APA References     Barr, G. (2003, 20 September). Re: Crime statistics. E-mail to the author.

Lasky, K. (2003, 27 October). Letter to the author.

Lewis, R. (1998, Mar. 3). National crime survey discussion. Message posted to National Crime Survey Retrieved Oct. 6, 2003, from legalminds.lp.findlaw.com/list/ncs-l/msg00007.html

Miller, E. (2003, 13 October). Proposal to purchase area wetlands. Memo to the Conservation Committee, Goffstown, New Hampshire.

## Multimedia and Internet Sources

Multimedia sources include films, TV shows, and radio programs as well as personal or organizational Web sites that change at unpredictable times. Unlike personal communications, these sources are aimed at a large audience rather than a specific recipient. So their contents are easier for readers to check than personal communications, but more difficult than periodicals, which are constantly tracked and indexed. It is difficult to refer to a specific scene or turn in a conversation.

The source list entries for this kind of information should include as much specific detail as possible about an author, a sponsoring or production group, a date of transmission or posting, the title of the entire work, and the title of the specific segment being cited.

## ENTRIES FOR INTERNET AND MULTIMEDIA SOURCES

### Film, TV, and Radio

MLA Works Cited

United States Department of Justice, Office for Victims of Crime. The News Media's Coverage of Crime and Victimization. 2000. Film clip. 17 Oct. 2003 <www.ojp.usdoj.gov/ovc/videos/mov/newsmedia.html>.

Keith, Tamara. "Debate Revived Over Yosemite Land Use." Morning Edition. National Public Radio, Washington, D.C. 18 September, 2003. Radio broadcast. 8 Feb. 2003 <www.npr.org/templates/story/story.php?storyId=1435041>.

APA References

United States Department of Justice, Office for Victims of Crime. (2000). *The news media's coverage of crime and victimization.* Film clip. Retrieved October 17, 2003, from www.ojp.usdoj.gov/ovc/videos/mov/newsmedia.html

Keith, T. (2003, 18 September). Debate revived over Yosemite land use. Radio broadcast. Morning Edition. Washington, D.C.: National Public Radio. Retrieved February 8, 2003, from www.npr.org/templates/story/story.php?storyId=1435041

### Web sites

MLA Works Cited

"Stats and Resources." *MADD Online.* 29 Apr 2002. 1 May 2004 <http://www.madd.org/stats/>.

APA References

Stats and resources. (2002, 29 April). *MADD Online.* Retrieved May 1, 2004, from http://www.madd.org/stats/

# Glossary

**A BUT B problem statement** A technique for exploring the crux of a problem. The A Statement describes a goal or value that the writer or readers care about such as lives, ethics, or beauty. Statement B describes a clashing goal or an obstacle in cases of the problem that directly jeopardizes the goals in Statement A. *See* Exigence.

**Action** A stasis where readers are urged to take specific steps. Action or proposal claims concern who should take action, what steps to take, when to take them, and how to carry them out.

**Affect** *See* Effect.

**Agent** A person who intentionally takes action. Can also refer to an inanimate factor: "Bleach is a cleaning agent."

**Appeals** Reasons and evidence that support a claim that come from observation and common sense (logos), the credibility of a witness or expert (ethos), or the emotions and senses (pathos).

**Argument** One or more claims combined with support. The five types (stases) of claims can be developed with additional claims. The claims in an extended argument are supported with reasons and evidence (appeals).

**Association** *See* Correlation.

**Author** A writer who constructs a line of argument on an issue that contributes to the current discussion. An author develops and supports claims that she thinks are true and important and expresses them in her own words.

**Authorities** The person or people in a specific situation who have the power to carry out an action and who are held responsible for its success or failure. Authorities often oversee the budget and schedule of a plan.

**Bandwagon** A solution that is considered more for its popularity than for its merits. Bandwagon solutions oversimplify the problem and propose broad, easy-sounding steps.

**Case** An object, event, or subcategory that can be considered for membership in a more general category. A typical case has the most common characteristics of other members. A borderline case has just enough similar characteristics to belong. An outsider is a similar case that has one or more key differences that disqualify it from membership.

**Category** A group of objects or events or subcategories that share enough characteristics that they should be treated in the same way. Some categories have strict criteria for membership.

**Cause** A stasis where events and changes are explained. In a Problem span, cause claims lay out the effects of the problem on stakeholders. Cause passages also concern the factors and events that produced the problem and obstacles that prevent simple solutions. In a Solution span, cause passages concern what will happen if a particular action is taken.

**Chronological arrangement** An arrangement that organizes past or future events in a time sequence. *See* Merit-based arrangement.

**Claim**  A debatable statement about objects, events, or categories. The five types (stases) of claims are existence, definition, value, cause, and action. Claims at each stasis can be extended with specific types of additional claims.

**Clash**  *See* Tension.

**Commonplaces**  Phrases that sum up or epitomize a common sense viewpoint, such as "That dog won't hunt." During planning, they can remind you of aspects of your argument to develop. For example, a plan that has failed in the past is like a dog that won't hunt.

**Contribution**  A contribution is an argument that advances understanding of an issue for some conversational group.

**Controversy-last arrangement**  An arrangement that begins with approaches that readers tend to prefer most, with the writer pointing out their strengths and weaknesses, and then ending with an approach that the writer feels is best that readers may have been reluctant to consider. *See* Merit-based arrangement.

**Correlation**  A comparison of the intensities on two scales. Two qualities are correlated if the values on both scales increase together. For example, young children get heavier as they get taller, so height is correlated with weight. Two qualities are negatively correlated if one goes up when the other goes down. For example, because fire consumes oxygen, the amount of oxygen in a closed room is negatively correlated with the length of time a fire is burning.

**Criterion (sing.; pl., criteria)**  Standard by which an item is judged. A criterion usually refers both to a feature and a value. For example, the legal criterion for being drunk in many U.S. states is to have a blood alcohol concentration higher than 0.08.

**Definition**  A stasis where something is analyzed to see if it can be treated like other similar things. Definition claims concern whether an object, event, or phenomenon is a member of a known category, according to a set of membership criteria.

**Demagogue**  Someone who will say anything to help his or her side win and make opponents look bad; someone who is willing to gain popularity by exaggerating, spreading false claims, or playing on popular prejudices.

**Devil's advocate**  A friend who has adopted the role of a challenger to help you find points in your argument that need to be added or strengthened.

**Dogmatist**  Someone whose mind is so completely made up about the absolute truth of his position that he won't admit that it has any weaknesses and won't treat any other views as reasonable.

**Effect**  An outcome or change in a phenomenon described in a causal argument. Factors have effects on a phenomenon. Effect is the noun form for an outcome, as in "Banning hunting had a long-term effect on tourism." The verb form is to *affect*, as in "Banning hunting affected tourism over the long term."

**Emcee**  Someone who keeps a ceremony or entertainment program moving along, a "Master of Ceremonies" or MC. Emcees are not really authors because they only introduce the main performers, they do not make their own contributions.

**Ethos**  An appeal based on the reputation or credibility of an expert or witness. An author establishes ethos by referring to personal experience or training, adopting an insider style, and displaying knowledgeability and fairness.

**Event**  A sequence of occurrences that can be described as a narrative with such elements as a setting, agents, motives, actions, victims, witnesses, and/or outcome.

**Exigence**  *See* Tension.

**Existence**  A stasis where the reader's attention is drawn to a topic of discussion. Existence claims are about the possibility that an object exists or that an event happened; about the characteristics of an object, event, or phenomenon; or about the situation in which it was observed.

**Experiment**  An effort to identify necessary and sufficient factors. In a simple experiment, a researcher creates two similar cases under controlled conditions. She adds the test factor to one case and leaves the other case alone. If the factor is necessary, the effect will occur in the first case but not the other.

**Explorer**  Someone who wants to find out something new; someone who has a goal in mind but who is willing to move aside to consider other viewpoints; someone who designs a route that others will want to follow.

**Factor**  An element that could be responsible for causing or preventing some change. A sufficient factor is an element that can trigger or prevent the action all by itself. For example, spotting a single shark is sufficient reason for closing a beach. A necessary factor is an element that must always be present for the change to occur, such as fuel for a fire.

**Grassroots audience**  A large group of readers that includes stakeholders as well as people who care about an issue in principle, out of curiosity or sentiment, or because of membership in a fan club or interest group.

**Hypothetical**  Something that has been hypothesized but has not been observed. If the police have several suspects for a crime, they might construct hypothetical descriptions of how each one could have committed the crime.

**Issue span**  The segment of a policy argument that calls attention to the issue and defines the focus of the argument to come.

**Issue**  Unsettled questions that matter to a lot of different people. Sometimes settled questions turn back into issues when someone detects a problem or opportunity.

**Logos**  An appeal to logical or commonsense reasoning or to observational evidence.

**Main path**  A line of argument made up of spans and stases that the author wants you to follow; opposing claims are sidetracks or crossroads that invite you to turn in a different direction, onto a path that, according to the author, might lead you astray.

**Merit-based arrangement**  An arrangement that organizes items by quality, either increasing or decreasing. Merit-based arrangements include "Save the Best for Last," "Agreement First," and "Extremes-Means" arrangements. *See* Chronological arrangement.

**Motive**  An element of a problem case that describes why an agent took action.

**Necessary factor**  *See* Factor.

**Object**  Material things like chairs and abstract things like democracy.

**Opponent**  An author with a different position. Not to be confused with someone who is hostile, such as an antagonist or adversary.

**Outcome**  An element of a problem case that describes how things were after an agent acted.

**Panacea**  A medical treatment that supposedly cures every possible disease, usually recognized as fraudulent. A public policy solution is like a panacea if it is presented without acknowledgement of limitations or drawbacks.

**Paradigm**  An important example or model that captures the key features of the entire category. A paradigm case is a real world instance of a problem that symbolizes the problem for the author or for the audience.

**Pathos**  An appeal to emotions or senses.

**Phenomenon (sing.; pl., phenomena)** An object or event that might be observed in the world. The reality of a phenomenon is a matter for argument at the stasis of existence.

**Presence** The amount of relevance or the intensity of conscious attention given to something. Also called salience.

**Problem** A sore point in the current situation that an author wants to change because it prevents a goal from being achieved, endangers something valuable, or presents a mystery or puzzle. *See* A BUT B problem statement.

**Problem span** The segment of a policy argument that presents claims about the existence, nature, causes, and significance of the problem.

**Public record** An account of someone's observations that is published in a public newspaper or journal or filed by a public agency.

**Pundit** A critic, often a journalist, who writes opinion pieces for a Web site, a popular magazine or a newspaper, or who appears on news programs.

**Qualifiers** Terms that strengthen or weaken the degree of certainty of a claim, such as all/some, never/rarely, often/always, must/might.

**Record** A symbolic piece of physical evidence such as a receipt or a logbook. *See* Public record.

**Relationship (between factors)** *See* Correlation.

**Rogerian argument** A strategy for encouraging fair and productive exchanges among strong opponents. After Speaker A states a position, Speaker B must paraphrase it accurately—as judged by Speaker A—before he or she can respond.

**Salience** *See* Presence.

**Solution** A plan of action intended to change a problematic situation by eliminating a problem, reducing its significance, or transforming it into something acceptable.

**Solution span** The segment of a policy argument that presents claims about the existence, nature, effects, costs and benefits, and implementation of a solution.

**Spans** Three segments of a policy argument: the issue, the problem, and the solution. A policy argument might not contain all three.

**Stakeholder** Any person who is directly affected by a problem or by a proposed plan of action, including those who are experiencing a problem, those whose actions or values are seen as the cause of a problem, and authorities who choose or implement a solution.

**Stakes** Things of value, such as principles, plans, personal or material interests, that could be at risk if one proposal is adopted instead of another.

**Stasis (sing.; pl., stases)** Five types of claims (existence, definition, value, cause, action) that move an argument from one span to another. A single stasis is a standpoint where an author may spend time providing a set of claims, supporting evidence (appeals), and responding to arguments from people who might disagree.

**Stipulate** To agree with an opponent to accept a claim as true without requiring either side to produce supporting evidence.

**Strawman** A weak hypothetical opponent. Knocking down a strawman is not an impressive feat, so refuting a strawman's argument does not help an author come across as fair and open to challenge.

**Sufficient factor** *See* Factor.

**Support** Reasons or evidence used to back up a claim. Supporting claims appeal to logos, pathos, or ethos.

**Synthesis tree** A diagram that represents the positions of authors on an issue. A major branching in the tree separates groups with serious disagreements. Authors within a group of allies branch off into subgroups on points where they disagree.

**Tension** A sense of unquiet, a felt difficulty. A strong pull between what is desired and what is real. Also called clash, exigence, urgency.

**Testimony** Verbal or written statements describing what a person has observed. Testimony is used to appeal to logos. The credibility of the person giving the testimony is described in an appeal to ethos.

**Tourist** Someone who wants to see the attractions without putting in the effort to create a new path; someone who chooses from routes designed by others; someone who is visiting the area temporarily, who does not have a stake in the issue.

**Urgency** *See* Tension.

**Value** A stasis where cases within a category are rated on evaluative scales, such as better/worse or newer/older. Evaluation passages concern whether a specific object, event, or phenomenon ranks high or low relative to the rest.

# Bibliography

Abbey, Edward. *Beyond the Wall.* New York: Henry Holt, 1984.

ACLU. "Chicago City Council Adopts New Gang Loitering Ordinance." *Criminal Justice.* 16 Feb 2000 <www.aclu.org/CriminalJustice/CriminalJustice.cfm?ID=7832&c=46>.

Arndt, John. "Letter to the Editor" in *Mother Jones* July/Aug 1995 (appearing in response to Castleman's "Opportunity Knocks." in *Mother Jones* May/June 1995).

Baroody, Michael. "Letter to the Editor" in the *New York Times* (appearing in response to Kristof's "In Praise of Snowmobiles" in the *New York Times*, 12/24/02).

Blair, Jackson, "How to Sustain Southern Bluefin Tuna." Essay written for RHE 309, University of Texas at Austin, Spring 2003.

Brooks, George. "Let's Not Gang Up on our Kids." *U.S. Catholic* 62.3 (Mar 1997): 18–20.

Brower, David. "A Return to the Peaks." *Sierra* 77.3 (May-June 1992): 90–96.

Burnside, Joseph. "National Park Overflights: Reader Comments." *AV Web* 30 Jun 2003 <www.avweb.com/qotw/qotwform.cgi?0010CON:>.

Burger, Joanna, and Michael Gochfeld. "The Tragedy of the Commons." *Environment* 40.10 (Dec 1998): 4.

Canedy, Dana. "Land Advocates and Drivers Reach Fork in the Off-Road" *New York Times* (24 March, 2002).

Carlson, Tucker. "Letter to the Editor" in *Mother Jones* July/Aug 1995 (appearing in response to Castleman's "Opportunity Knocks." in *Mother Jones* May/June 1995).

Carroll, Michael. "Do Mountain Bikes Belong in the Wilderness? NO: We Can Prevent Trail Degradation." *Denver Post* (12 Jan 2003): E4.

Castleman, Michael. "Opportunity Knocks." *Mother Jones* 20 (May/June 1995) <http://www.motherjones.com/commentary/columns/1995/05/castleman.htmlCON:>.

Choat, Michael. "The Debate on Technology in the Wilderness." Essay written for RHE 309, University of Texas at Austin, Spring 2003.

Chivers, C. J. "Scraping Bottom." *Wildlife Conservation* 103 (Feb 2000): 46–51.

Cockburn, Alexander. "How to Make a Criminal." *The Nation* 270.10 (13 March 2000): 10.

Colatosi, Tom. "The Two Faces of Face-Recognition Technology." *Access Control & Security Systems Integration* (October 2001).

Corbett, Jeff. "Identifying Underage Drinkers." Essay written for RHE 309, University of Texas at Austin, Spring 2002.

Creighton, Allan. "Letter to the Editor" in *Mother Jones* July/Aug 1995 (appearing in response to Castleman's "Opportunity Knocks." in *Mother Jones* May/June 1995).

DiIulio, John J., Jr. "Broken Bottles." *The Brookings Review* 14.2 (Spring 1996): 14+.

DiIulio, John J., Jr. "Unlock 'Em Up." *Slate* (20 Dec 1996).

Downey, Lauren. "Blue Crime." Essay written for RHE 309, University of Texas at Austin, Spring 2002.

Dudzik, Eileen. "The Rainforest is in Houston's Backyard." Essay written for RHE 309, University of Texas at Austin, Spring 2003.

Dumaine, Brian. "Beating Bolder Corporate Crooks." *Fortune* 117.9 (1988): 193+.

Easterbrook, Gregg. "They Stopped the Sky from Falling." *Washington Monthly* 27.5 (May 1995): 34–42.

Ehrlich, Paul R., and Anne Ehrlich. *Extinction: The Causes and Consequences of the Disappearance of Species*. New York: Random House, 1981.

Fallows, James. "Saving Salmon, or Seattle?" *The Atlantic Monthly* (October 2000).

Garvey, Megan and Richard Winton. "Tracking of Gang-Related Crime Falls Short." *Los Angeles Times* (24 Jan 2003): Part 1, page 1.

Gilmore, Shay. "Solutions to Corporate Crime." Essay written for RHE 309, University of Texas at Austin, Spring 2002.

Glaberson, William. "Justice, Safety, and the System: A Witness Is Slain in Brooklyn." *New York Times* (6 Jul 2003).

Glanz, James. "Robotic Telescope Affirms Assumption on Universe's Birth." *New York Times* (7 June 2000): A1.

Gómez-Pompa, Arturo, and Andrea Kaus. "Taming the Wilderness Myth." *Bioscience* 42.4 (Apr 1992): 271–280.

Hardner, Jared, and Richard Rice. "Rethinking Green Consumerism: Buying Green Products Won't Be Enough to Save Biodiversity in the Tropics." *Scientific American* 286 (May 2002): 88+.

Herman, Ken. "Godless Group Gets Religious Exemption." *Austin American Statesman* (26 June 1997): B1.

Jones, Laura, and Liv Fredericksen. "Crying Wolf? Public Policy on Endangered Species." *Critical Issues Bulletin*, Fraser Institute, October 1999 <www.fraserinstitute.ca/shared/readmore.asp?sNav=pb&id=214>.

Junod, Tom. "One Too Many." *Esquire* 129.6 (June 1998): 126.

Kleck, Gary. "There Are No Lessons to Be Learned from Littleton." *Criminal Justice Ethics*, Summer/Fall 1998, 61–63.

Kollin, Joe. "Why Don't We Name Juveniles." *Quill* 91.3 (April 2003): 12–13.

Kristof, Nicholas D. "In Praise of Snowmobiles." *New York Times* Op-Ed (24 Dec 2002).

Kristof, Nicholas D. "Lock and Load." *New York Times* Op-Ed (13 Nov 2004).

Kucera, Katie. "Loved to Death: A Response to C. J. Chivers." Essay written for RHE 309, University of Texas at Austin, Spring 2003.

Laurance, William F., Mark A. Cochrane, Scott Bergen, Philip M. Fearnside, Patricia Delamonica, Christopher Barber, Sammya D'Angelo, and Tito Fernandes. "The Future of the Brazilian Amazon." *Science* 291 (19 Jan 2001): 438-439.

Limbaugh, Rush. "Blame the Bombers Only." *Newsweek* 125 (8 May 1995): 19+.

Loomis, Andrew. "Who Is Responsible for Crime?" Essay written for RHE 309, University of Texas at Austin, Spring 2002.

Manning, Terry. "Letter to the Editor" in the *New York Times* (appearing in response to Kristof's "In Praise of Snowmobiles" in the *New York Times*, 12/24/02).

Markarian, Michael. "Letter to the Editor" in the *New York Times* (appearing in response to Kristof's "In Praise of Snowmobiles" in the *New York Times*, 12/24/02).

Margolis, Jon. "Park Wars: It's the Snowmobilers (and the Recreation Industry) against the High-Country Hikers (and the Environmentalists) in the Battle for the Future of America's Parkland." *The American Prospect* 13.16 (9 Sep 2002): 29–33.

Maxwell, Monica. "Shiflett's Show." Essay written for RHE 306, University of Texas at Austin, Fall 2001.

McGaha, Anna. "Prostitution is a Feminist Cause." Essay written for RHE 309, University of Texas at Austin, Spring 2002.

Meares, Tracey L., and Dan M. Kahan. "When Rights are Wrong: Chicago's Paradox of Unwanted Rights." *Boston Review* 24.2 (April–May 1999) <bostonreview.mit.edu/br24.2/meares.html>. (17 Sept. 2000).

Meehan, Albert J. "The Organizational Career of Gang Statistics: The Politics of Policing Gangs." *The Sociological Quarterly* 41 (Summer 2000): 37+.

Morrison, Adrian R. "Perverting Medical History in the Service of 'Animal Rights.'" *Perspectives in Biology and Medicine* 45.4 (Autumn 2002): 606–620.

Moustakis, Philip. "Letter to the Editor" in the *New York Times* (appearing in response to Kristof's "In Praise of Snowmobiles" in the *New York Times*, 12/24/02).

Myers, Jim. "Notes on the Murder of Thirty of My Neighbors." *The Atlantic Monthly* 285 (March 2000): 72–86 <www.theatlantic.com/issues/2000/03/myers.htm>.

Nader, Ralph. "Corporate Unpatriotic Behavior." *In the Public Interest* (2 July 2004). The Nader Page. www.nader.org/interest/070204.html

Naylor, R.T. "License to Loot? A Critique of Follow-the-Money Methods in Crime Control Policy." *Social Justice* 28.3 (Fall 2001): 121+.

Nealson, Christina. "In Wilderness, Don't Phone Home." *High Country News* 30.15 (17 Aug 1998) <www.hcn.org/servlets/hcn.Article?article_id=4399>.

New Jersey Fishing. "Fishermen, Scientists, Environmentalists Respond to Most Recent Assault on Traditional Fishing Gear." FishNet USA News Release, 13 Dec 1998.

Nie, Martin A. "In Wilderness Is Dissension: The Contentious Battle over Utah's Wilderness Is Marked by a Cultural Clash." *Forum for Applied Research and Public Policy* 14.2 (Summer 1999): 77.

Pataki, George E. "The Death Penalty Is a Deterrent." *USA Today Magazine* 125.2622 (March 1997): 52.

Power, Thomas Michael. "Wilderness Economics Must Look Through the Windshield, Not the Rearview Mirror." *International Journal of Wilderness* 2 (May 1996).

"Public Concerns from the Draft Merced Wild and Scenic River Plan/EIS Process and Responses Relating to Yosemite Valley Planning." Final Yosemite Valley Plan Supplemental Environmental Impact Statement (22 Jan 2001) <www.nps.gov/yose/planning/yvp/seis/vol_III/chap5_3.html>.

Public Use Statistics Office, National Park Service (www2.nature.nps.gov/stats/). Listing of Acreages by Park 2001, National Park Service <http://www2.nature.nps.gov/stats/acrebypark01cy.pdf>.

Pugh, Donald. Disabled Equestrians Organization. [Letter to Department of Justice.] July 11, 2000 <www.disabledequestrians.org/PubFiles/Justice_Dept_Advice.htm>.

Robinson, John G. "The Responsibility to Conserve Wild Species." *Social Research* 62.3 (Fall 1995): 816–822.

Russell, Dick. "Hitting Bottom: As Trawling Goes into High Gear, Undersea Coastal Habitat Is Being Razed." *The Amicus Journal* 18 (1997): 21.

Safina, Carl. "Scorched-Earth Fishing." *Issues in Science and Technology* 14 (1998): 33.

Scales, Peter C. "The Public Image of Adolescents." *Society* 38.4 (May 2001): 64

Scraton, Phil, and Deena Haydon. "Challenging the Criminalization of Children and Young People." *Youth Justice: Critical Readings*. Eds. John Muncie, Gordon Hughes, and Eugene McLaughlin. London: Sage, 2002. 311–28.

Shapiro, Bruce. "One Violent Crime." *The Nation* 260.13 (3 Apr 1995): 437(8).

Shiflett, Dave. "Parks and Wreck: Against Jet Skiers, Snowmobilers, and Other Louts." *National Review* 53.5 (19 Mar 2001).

Stevens, William K. "Conservationists Win Battles but Fear War Is Lost" *New York Times* (11 Jan 2000).

vande Kopple, Willem. Personal communication.

Whitmore, George. "Scoping Comments, Yosemite Falls Restroom Relocation." Sierra Club, Yosemite Committee. 20 August 2001 <california.sierraclub.org/yosemite/comments_falls_restroom.html>.

# Index

Note: Information presented in tables and figures is denoted by *t* or *f*.

arrangement, (*continued*)
    top-down, 320
arrogance, certainty and, 72
aspects, variation in, with hypotheticals, 268–69
attitudes
    problem cases and, 268
    value claims and, 45
attribution
    to author, 333
    verbs of, 103, 104*t*, 105, 119
audience
    action claims and, 60–61
    addressing, 420–21
    insiders *vs.* outsiders, 419
    for narration of cases, 238
    planning for, 318–19
    for problem-based papers, 365–66
    relating to, 418–20
    of response essays, 330, 334
    for solution-based papers, 382–83
    for state of debate papers, 347–48
authenticity, 7, 199–200
authority
    adopting role of, 418
    in appeals to ethos, 75
authors
    attributions to, 333
    grouping of, 298–300
    information about, 396
    relationships among, 290–91
    relevance of, 292–93
    responding to, 241–53
    role of, 313
    as topic of sentence, 321, 333
    understanding, for critical reading, 396

## B

balance, in synthesis trees, 307
beliefs, influence of, 268
Blair, Jackson, 374–77
books
    as sources, 229
    in works cited list, 435
brainstorming, with storyboard, 410*f*
Brooks, George, 180–82

## C

cases
    collection of, 267–68
    comparison of, 268
    elements of, 266–67
    as entry point, 200–204
    grouping of, 267–68
    hypothetical, 203–4, 267, 268–69
    ideal, 202–3
    narration of, 238–41
    paradigm, 16, 271
    problem, 201–2
        analysis of, 265–71
        predicting effects on, 285–86

    testing synthesis trees with, 306–7
    for problem description, 266
    testing solutions with, 285–87
    types of, 40, 200
Castleman, Michael, 159–65
categories
    consequences of, 38
    definition of, 35
    establishment of, 35–36
    in existence claims, 34
    membership criteria for, 40
cause claims
    action claims and, 59
    agent in, 54
    assessment of, 246
    assumptions in, 51
    comparison in, 54
    correlation in, 55–56
    definition of, 51
    development of, 53–58
    experimentation in, 57–58
    factors in, 51
    necessity in, 57
    outcomes in, 54
    persistence of problem and, 52
    prediction in, 52
    purpose of, 52–53
    spotting, 58
    sufficiency in, 56
    words in, 58–59
cause factors
    in cause claims, 54
    definition of, 51
    devil's advocate position and, 250
    exploration of, 263
    identifying, 263
    synthesis tree of, 294*f*, 296*f*
    validity of, 55
certainty
    absolute, 72
    in academic style, 115
    in appeals to logos, 72–74
    challenging, 99
    in journalistic style, 113
    in popular opinion style, 111
    of scholars, 205–6
    of stakeholders, 207
challenging
    of appeals, 249
    choosing points for, 331
    of claims, 98–99
    devil's advocate method for, 249–51
    returning to main path after, 101
    of supports, 99–100
charitable reading, of provocative style, 120
Chivers, C. J., 129–34
Choate, Michael, 339–43
citations, 430–38
claims
    action